ROBERT DE VERE, EARL OF OXFORD AND DUKE OF IRELAND (1362–1392)

Robert de Vere, Earl of Oxford and Duke of Ireland (1362–1392)

The Rise and Fall of a Royal Favourite

James Ross

THE BOYDELL PRESS

© James Ross 2024

All Rights Reserved. Except as permitted under current legislation no part of this work may be photocopied, stored in a retrieval system, published, performed in public, adapted, broadcast, transmitted, recorded or reproduced in any form or by any means, without the prior permission of the copyright owner

The right of James Ross to be identified as the author of this work has been asserted in accordance with sections 77 and 78 of the Copyright, Designs and Patents Act 1988

First published 2024
The Boydell Press, Woodbridge

ISBN 978 1 83765 194 8

The Boydell Press is an imprint of Boydell & Brewer Ltd
PO Box 9, Woodbridge, Suffolk IP12 3DF, UK
and of Boydell & Brewer Inc.
668 Mt Hope Avenue, Rochester, NY 14620–2731, USA
website: www.boydellandbrewer.com

A CIP catalogue record for this book is available
from the British Library

The publisher has no responsibility for the continued existence or accuracy of URLs for external or third-party internet websites referred to in this book, and does not guarantee that any content on such websites is, or will remain, accurate or appropriate

For Chloe Elizabeth Ross

Contents

	List of Illustrations	ix
	Acknowledgements	xi
	List of Abbreviations	xiii
	Introduction	1
1	Royal Favourites and their Opponents in the Later Middle Ages	13
2	Family Background and Early Career	45
	Minority	45
	Landed Inheritance	54
	Aubrey de Vere	60
3	Politics, Court and Patronage, 1381–5	75
	Robert and Richard	78
	Patronage	86
	Politics	96
	Royal Court and Household	107
4	Ireland, 1385–7	117
	The Grant of Ireland	117
	Resources	127
	The Duchy of Ireland: Military Forces and Administration	135
5	Downfall, Exile and Death, 1386–92	149
	The 'Wonderful' Parliament of 1386 to Summer 1387	149
	The Divorce	158
	Chester and the Autumn of 1387	166
	The Battle of Radcot Bridge	174
	Exile	185
	Death and Funeral	195
6	Affinity, Regional Influence and Lifestyle	201
	Local Influence in East Anglia, Officials and Associates	201
	Lifestyle	225
	Conclusion	237
	Appendix: Known Locations of Robert de Vere, 1385–7	243
	Bibliography	247
	Index	273

Illustrations

Figure 1	Robert de Vere, duke of Ireland, and his family	xv
Map 1	Estates of Robert de Vere in eastern England	xvi
Map 2	Estates of Robert de Vere in western and northern England	xvii
Table 1	Estates of de Vere family, 1383	71
Plate 1	Arms of de Vere, Ireland and de Coucy, Lavenham Church, Suffolk. Photograph author's own	233

The author and publisher are grateful to all the institutions and individuals listed for permission to reproduce the materials in which they hold copyright. Every effort has been made to trace the copyright holders; apologies are offered for any omission, and the publisher will be pleased to add any necessary acknowledgement in subsequent editions.

Acknowledgements

This book has had a very long gestation. When I started my doctoral research in 1999, my plan was to study the de Vere earls of Oxford from 1371 to 1513, from Robert, ninth earl of Oxford, the subject of this book, to John, thirteenth earl of Oxford, and research to this end occurred over the next three years. During this time, I delivered a paper on Robert de Vere to the Late Medieval Seminar at the Institute of Historical Research, which has been an important part of my academic milieu ever since. However, when the first full draft of the thesis was put together in 2002, it was considerably longer than the maximum allowed by the University of Oxford. My doctoral supervisor, Dr Rowena E. Archer, and I agreed that rather than trying to undertake the near-impossible task of cutting so many words from existing chapters, the two chapters covering Robert de Vere and his successor Aubrey, the tenth earl, should be left out. While I always intended to return to the research I had done on Robert de Vere, my initial focus, on top of a full-time job at the National Archives, was to complete a monograph on the thirteenth earl, which appeared in 2011. Subsequently other publications, research and teaching at the University of Winchester prevented me from returning to work on Robert de Vere in any meaningful way, though I continued to collect references to him when I came across them.

It was only in 2021 that I found myself with the time to revisit what I had written on Robert. I quickly realised that the chapter on him could and should be turn into a fuller study; it has quintupled in length since then, for good reasons. Much has been written on the reign of Richard II in the last two decades, while I located much more by the way of sources than I did twenty years earlier, and indeed I needed to reread and revisit almost everything I had looked at in my doctoral research. My opinions on Robert de Vere have changed substantially as I have changed as a historian. As a result, essentially this book is a product of the last two years of work.

Support from family and friends within and without the historical community was essential and never taken for granted. References, advice and discussion on a wide variety of points have come from many historians since 2021, including Profs Peter Clarke, Maria Hayward and Jenny Stratford, Drs Sophie Ambler, Andrew Breeze, Hannes Kleineke, Stephen O'Connor, Simon Payling and Euan Roger, to all of whom I am very grateful. Professor Michael Bennett generously shared forthcoming material on Agnes Lancecrone with me and sent me a number of references. Dr Aline Douma undertook, on my behalf and as a result of a grant by the University of Winchester, the thankless task of trawling through archival collections in Belgium looking for material on Robert de Vere, and she went above and beyond what was required in her efforts. On many occasions while we were doctoral students together, as well as subsequently, Dr Chris Fletcher and I discussed Richard II and Robert de Vere; his book on Richard beat mine on Robert into print by sixteen years. Dr Laura Tompkins read Chapter 1 and I am very grateful for her comments and advice. Dr Peter Crooks, who read Chapter 4, was generous with his time and expertise, improved the chapter in a number of places, and forced me to reassess the sheer novelty of what Richard II granted Robert de Vere in 1385. The anonymous reader of the first draft of this book for Boydell and Brewer made a number of excellent suggestions, comments and criticisms.

A huge debt is owed to Dr Rowena E. Archer, whose advice shaped the genesis of the research underpinning the book as well as my early development as a historian. Lastly, Professor Chris Given-Wilson read this study in draft, and his insightful comments, references and advice have immensely improved the book.

All errors, of course, remain my own.

Abbreviations

BL	British Library
BIHR	*Bulletin of the Institute of Historical Research*
BJRL	*Bulletin of the John Rylands Library*
CA	Cambridgeshire Archives, Ely
CCR	*Calendar of Close Rolls*
CChR	*Calendar of Charter Rolls*
CFR	*Calendar of Fine Rolls*
CIM	*Calendar of Inquisitions Miscellaneous*
CIPM	*Calendar of Inquisitions Post Mortem*
CP	*The Complete Peerage*, ed. G.E. Cokayne, rev. and ed. V. Gibbs (14 vols in 15, London, 1910–98)
CPR	*Calendar of Patent Rolls*
EAH	*Essex Archaeology and History* (until 1972 *Transactions of the Essex Archaeological Society*)
EETS	Early English Text Society
EHR	*English Historical Review*
Froissart, ed. Johnes	J. Froissart, *Chronicles of England, France, Spain and the Adjoining Countries*, ed. T. Johnes (2 vols, London, 1839)
Froissart, ed. Lettenhove	J. Froissart, *Oeuvres*, ed. K. de Lettenhove (Brussels, 26 vols, 1867–77)
HoC	J.S. Roskell, L. Clark and C. Rawcliffe, *History of Parliament: The Commons 1386–1421* (4 vols, Stroud, 1992)
KC	*Knighton's Chronicle, 1337–96*, ed. G.H. Martin (Oxford, 1995)
ODNB	*Oxford Dictionary of National Biography*, www.oxforddnb.com/
PPC	*Proceedings and Ordinances of the Privy Council*, ed. N.H. Nicolas (7 vols, London, 1834–7)

PROME	*Parliament Rolls of Medieval England*, ed. C. Given-Wilson, P. Brand, S. Phillips, M. Ormrod, G. Martin, A. Curry and R. Horrox (17 vols, Woodbridge, 2005)
RPC	*Rotulorum Patentium et Clausorum Cancellarie Hibernie Calendarium*, ed. E. Tresham (Irish Record Commission, 1828), now calendared online at https://chancery.tcd.ie/content/welcome-circle
RS	Rolls Series
SAC	*The St Albans Chronicle. The Chronica Maiora of Thomas Walsingham*, eds J. Taylor, W.R. Childs and L. Watkiss (2 vols, Oxford, 2003–11)
TNA	The National Archives
WC	*The Westminster Chronicle, 1381–94*, eds L.C. Hector and B.F. Harvey (Oxford, 1982)

Note: All manuscript references are to the National Archives unless otherwise stated.

Robert de Vere, Duke of Ireland and His Family

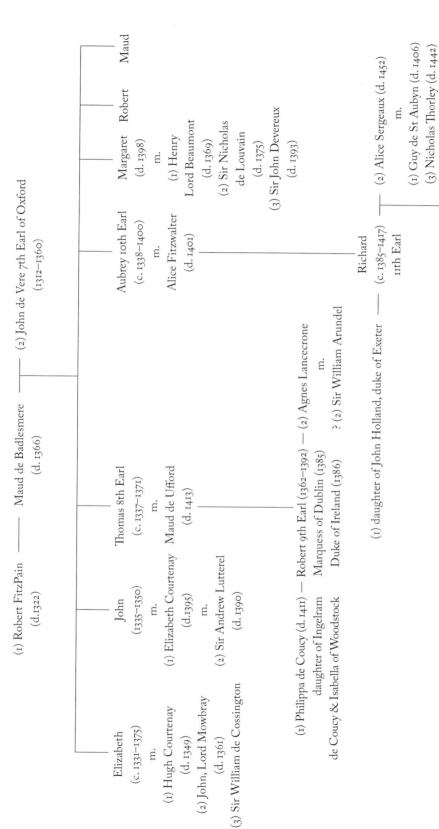

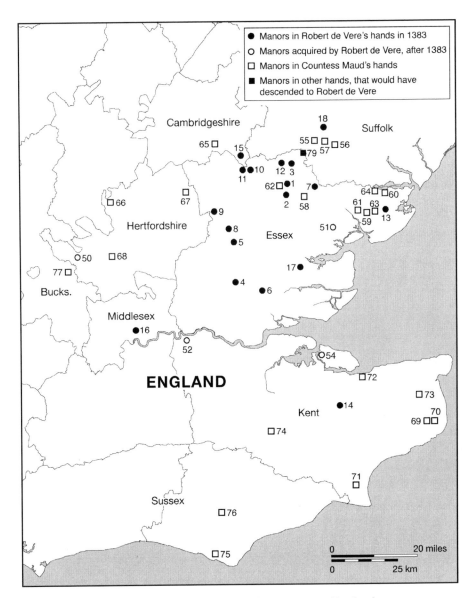

Map 1. Estates of Robert de Vere in eastern England.

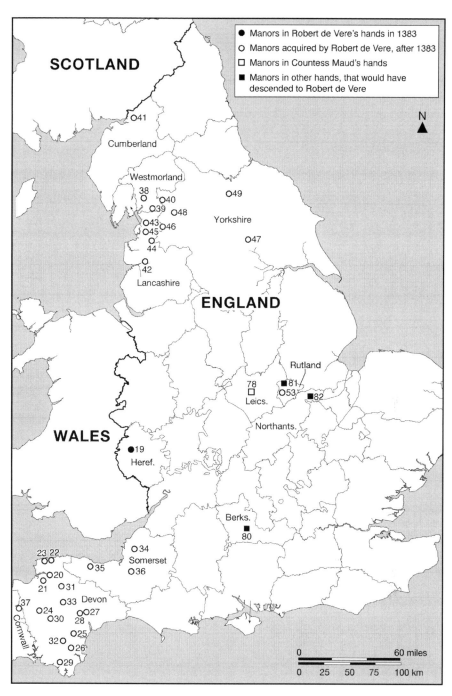

Map 2. Estates of Robert de Vere in western and northern England.

Key to Maps 1 and 2

● Ancestral Manors in Robert's Hands in 1383

1. Castle Hedingham
2. Sible Hedingham and Bourehall
3. Little Yeldham
4. Doddinghurst
5. Fingrith
6. Downham
7. Bures Giffard
8. Great Canfield
9. Stansted Mountfitchet
10. Steeple Bumpstead
11. Helions Bumpstead
12. Tilbury
13. Beaumont
14. Badlesmere
15. Castle Camps
16. Kensington
17. West Whetenham
18. Cockfield
19. Lyonshall

Manors acquired by Robert de Vere, after 1383

A: Audley estates

20. Barnstaple
21. Fremington
22. Combe Martin
23. Ilfracombe
24. Holsworthy
25. Bovey Tracy
26. Dartington
27. Langacre
28. Upex (Uppexe, Rewe, Exeter)
29. Kingston (Ermington Hundred)
30. Norleigh
31. South Molton
32. Holne
33. Nymet Tracy
34. Blagdon
35. Staunton
36. Lydford, West Lydford
37. Tackbeare

B: De Coucy

38. Kendal
39. Holme
40. Casterton
41. Lyneside
42. Ashton
43. Warton and Carnforth
44. Wyresdale
45. Scotforth
46. Whittington
47. Coghill
48. Thornton (Lonsdale)
49. Middleton Tyas, Kneeton

C: Other (including castles and residences)

50. Berkhamsted
51. Colchester
52. Kennington
53. Oakham
54. Queenborough

□ Manors in Countess Maud's Hands

55. Lavenham, 'Overhall' and 'Netherhall'
56. Aldham, with Hellond
57. Preston
58. Earls Colne
59. Great Bentley
60. Ramsey
61. Frating
62. Hedingham Vaux
63. Cruswiche
64. Wrabness
65. Great Abington
66. Welles
67. Great Hormead
68. Westwick
69. Ringwold, Charlton
70. Old Romney/Langport
71. Kingsdown
72. Whitstable
73. Fleet
74. Bockingfield
75. West Dean
76. Laughton
77. Chesham
78. Wigston Magna

■ Manors in other hands which would have descended to Robert

79. Easton Hall
80. Langley and Bradley
81. Market Overton
82. Milton and Paston

Introduction

> This Duc of Yrland, of England Chaumburleyn.
> Which in plesaunce so he ledde his lyf,
> Tyl fortune of his welth hade disdeyn,
> That causeles he parted was frome his wyf,
> Which grounde was of gret debate and stryf,
> And his destruccion, if I shal not lye,
> For banned he was, and did in meschef dye.
>
> (John Lydgate, 'Of the Sudden Fall of Certain Princes of England and France, now late in our day', perhaps early 1430s)[1]

On Thursday 13 February 1388, Robert de Vere, ninth earl of Oxford, first and only duke of Ireland, was found guilty of treason by Parliament and condemned to death. De Vere was not present to defend himself before the Lords and Commons, as, defeated in the skirmish known as the battle of Radcot Bridge in December 1387, he had fled abroad, to Brabant, in modern-day Belgium, where he died in 1392, aged just thirty. It was a dramatic fall for a man who had enjoyed the exceptional favour of the teenaged Richard II for most of the 1380s. Indeed, what happened in 1388 was not about de Vere alone, though he was the highest profile of the men condemned in the Merciless Parliament of 1388; it was an indictment of a group or faction around the king by a number of alienated aristocrats, the Lords Appellant, with considerable support amongst the political community. It was also an attack on Richard II's kingship, and his deposition was almost certainly temporarily enacted for three days in the febrile atmosphere of late December 1387 before being reconsidered.[2]

The rolls of the Merciless Parliament of 1388 are fulsome in their record of the appeal of treason of de Vere and his fellow Appellees, Michael de la Pole, earl of Suffolk, Alexander Neville, archbishop of York, Robert Tresilian, chief justice of the King's Bench, and Nicholas Brembre, former mayor of London.

---

[1] *The Minor Poems of John Lydgate. II: Secular Poems*, ed. H.M. McCracken (EETS, Original Series, 192, 1934), 660–1.

[2] C. Given-Wilson, *Henry IV* (London, 2016), 50–1.

The accusations run to thirty-nine articles, which took the clerk of the parliament two hours to read out to the assembly.[3] Only fourteen of the charges were in fact deemed to be treasonable, but that was more than sufficient for guilt to be established and a death sentence imposed. Yet, de Vere was not guilty of treason in its key components as set out in the great treason statute of 1352. That defined that crime rather narrowly, essentially restricting the crime to plotting to kill the king, levying open war against him, or conspiring with a domestic or foreign enemy, and all would have known that the accusations that he had done so levelled by the Appellants were concocted.[4] The more believable accusations against the defendants focused on impeding access to the king, enriching themselves in a variety of ways, and of accroaching – usurping – the royal power. These actions, however, were not legally treasonous; accroaching had been deliberately omitted from what was defined as treason in the statute of 1352. However, they reflect a definition of treason not enshrined in law but circulating in the political culture of the time, that treason could be committed against the kingdom, particularly by causing a division between the king and his realm.[5] Nonetheless, the awkward nature of the process and of the accusations reflect the fact there was almost no other way to remove a man high in royal favour, a favourite, than by accusing him of treason, if the favourite could not be apprehended and eliminated, as had happened to an earlier royal intimate, Piers Gaveston, in 1312. Thus, even a partisan parliament in 1388 could find only fourteen of the thirty-nine articles against the Appellees treasonable.[6] It was a legal attempt to solve a political problem and was almost certainly understood as such rather than most of the accusations of treason being taken at face value by the politically literate audience in parliament. How far the treasonable charges were believed by the wider court of public opinion is harder to say. There was a further layer of difficulty in taking such public action against the king's friends and ministers. Much of the blame lay with the king, but it was not politic to say so in public, and all that had gone wrong in the polity had to be framed as the fault of the favourites, the wicked and greedy advisors of the king, in order to protect the basis of public authority, the monarchy, in the longer

---

[3] *PROME*, vii, 58, 83–98.

[4] *PROME*, vi, 44–5; J.G. Bellamy, *The Law of Treason in the Later Middle Ages* (Cambridge, 1970), ch. 4. It has been calculated that perhaps only nine of the thirty-nine articles fell within the compass of the 1352 statute: A. Rogers, 'Parliamentary Appeals of Treason in the Reign of Richard II', *American Journal of Legal History*, 8 (1964), 110–11.

[5] Bellamy, *Law of Treason*, 209–10.

[6] *PROME*, vii, 102.

term.[7] Only when a king was deposed – which Richard II was ultimately not in 1387–8 – could direct criticism of the monarch be levelled publicly.

So, if de Vere was not guilty of treason in any meaningful sense, why were he, and to a slightly lesser extent his colleagues, so objectionable to the political nation? In the most general terms, he was perceived as a courtier. Courtiers were always resented by those outside the court and the subject of a long tradition of critical literature. The role of courtiers in the 1380s was particularly sensitive after the criticism on the 'court covine' had culminated in the attack on Edward III's inner circle in the Good Parliament of 1376, just a few years before de Vere came of age.[8] It should be noted, however, that the most vociferous critics in the 1380s – the Lords Appellant – were also, as great nobles, courtiers, even if slightly less frequently present there than some of the accused. De Vere was also – in the broadest sense of the term – a royal favourite, another objectionable category as far as the public were concerned. Indeed, one modern writer has described him as the only one of the five Appellees who truly fitted that description, though quite how a royal favourite should be defined will be investigated in Chapter 1.[9] Certainly he was perceived as having received a disproportionate amount of royal patronage during the 1380s, which was always a matter of great sensitivity for the political elites. He had been promoted to novel and unprecedented heights in the peerage for someone not directly a member of the royal family. He had been entrusted with the lordship and rule over a major part of the Plantagenet empire, Ireland, when others would have thought themselves better qualified for the role. More indefinably, to those outside the king's inner circle he seemed

---

[7] For a discussion, see J.T. Rosenthal, 'The King's "Wicked Advisors" and Medieval Baronial Rebellions', *Political Science Quarterly*, 82 (1967), 595–618, esp. 596–7.

[8] For discussion, see R. Horrox, 'Caterpillars of the Commonwealth? Courtiers in Late Medieval England', in R.E. Archer and S. Walker, eds, *Rulers and Ruled in Late Medieval England. Essays Presented to Gerald Harriss* (London, 1995), 1–16, esp. 4–5 where she notes that much of the criticism of courtliness came from clerical pens; M.A. Vale, 'Courts', in C. Fletcher, J.P. Genet and J.L. Watts, eds, *Government and Political Life in England and France, c. 1300–c.1500* (Cambridge, 2015), 24–40; C. Fletcher, 'Corruption at Court? Crisis and the Theme of *luxuria* in England and France, c. 1340–1422', in S.J. Gunn and A. Janse, eds, *The Court as a Stage. England and the Low Countries in the Later Middle Ages* (Woodbridge, 2006), 28–38; L. Patterson, 'Court Politics and the Invention of Literature: The Case of Sir John Clanvowe', in D. Aers, ed., *Culture and History 1350–1600. Essays on English Communities, Identities and Writing* (Hemel Hempstead, 1992), 7–41; J. Coleman, *English Literature in History, 1350–1400. Medieval Readers and their Writers* (London, 1981), 95–113. For the most recent discussion of the court and the Good Parliament, see W.M. Ormrod, *Edward III* (London, 2011), chapters 19 and 20, esp. 529–37, 551–62.

[9] C. Oliver, *Parliament and Political Pamphleteering in Fourteenth-Century England* (York, 2010), 143.

to dominate the king in a way that no subject should: the Appellants accused de Vere and his fellow Appellees of 'enslaving' the king.[10] De Vere's political methods may have been unsavoury at best and lethal at worse: he was possibly the instigator of, and was probably a participant in, a conspiracy to kill the king's uncle, John of Gaunt; less convincingly he was accused of plotting the death of another, Thomas of Woodstock. He was then, in some respects, a typical royal favourite in a century that had a number of outstanding examples of the genre in Piers Gaveston, Hugh Despenser the Younger, and, in a different way, Alice Perrers, mistress of Edward III.

That the victors write history is a truism but entirely accurate in the case of Robert de Vere. Almost all the major contemporary writers on Richard II composed their narratives after the events of 1388 and many wrote or revised their accounts after Richard II's deposition in 1399.[11] They are uniformly hostile to Robert de Vere. The most prolific chronicler, the Monk of St Albans, Thomas Walsingham, provided the most enduring and influential picture of de Vere, as a 'mediocre' man, who was 'seducing the infatuated king'; the homosexual overtones of the latter quote were entirely deliberate on Walsingham's part.[12] The great chronicler of chivalry, Jean Froissart, captured the critical view of the relationship between de Vere and the king perfectly, saying that Richard was so blinded by the duke of Ireland that if the latter had said 'black was white, the king would not have said to the contrary'.[13]

Historians have generally followed the source material, most by no means uncritically, though occasionally verdicts on de Vere are extreme. Anthony Steel's description of him as 'a handsome, frivolous young man of more than ordinary incompetence, both as a soldier and administrator' could be challenged on most levels, either through lack of evidence – there is no description of his appearance, his personality opaque at best – or through close reading where evidence survives.[14] For T.F. Tout, while dismissing the charges of gross immorality as the common lot of royal favourites, 'the impression left of him is primarily not so much of vice as of incompetence and folly', and that any ideas underlying the royal policy should be ascribed to Michael de la Pole or Simon Burley or the king himself: de Vere was 'never more than a favourite'.[15] Edouard Perroy describes de Vere and others as

[10] *PROME*, vii, 85.

[11] For discussion, see below, pp. 6–8.

[12] *The Chronica Maiora of Thomas Walsingham, 1376–1422*, trans. D. Preest and ed. J.G. Clark (Woodbridge, 2005), 242, 244.

[13] Froissart, ed. Johnes, ii, 264.

[14] A. Steel, *Richard II* (Cambridge, 1941), 112.

[15] T.F. Tout, *Chapters in the Administrative History of Medieval England* (7 vols, Manchester, 1930), iii, 407.

Richard's 'companions in his sports and spongers on his treasury'.[16] Thomas Costain states that he seems to have been 'lacking in that quality [charm], a rather plain stripling, without any particular degree of talent, ambitious without the qualities or energy to warrant his pretensions, selfish, unreliable, and grasping'.[17] Joel Rosenthal has described the 'coterie of young and *nouveau riche* nobles surrounding Richard II – Oxford, de la Pole, and the like'.[18] Oxford was in his twenties but he cannot be described as *nouveau riche*, while de la Pole was not young and was second-generation wealth, if first-generation noble. Anthony Tuck states that 'de Vere above all was disliked' and that he 'seemed to epitomize in his person all that was objectionable about Richard's court'.[19] Anthony Goodman characterises de Vere as 'a lightweight youth, pleasure-seeking, acquisitive and commendable only in his devotion to the king'.[20] Laura Ashe, in a recent popular study of Richard's reign, paraphrases Walsingham on Robert de Vere – his promotions 'had evidently arisen from no particular virtue the man possessed, but solely from the king's affection for a friend from boyhood' – and insists on putting de Vere's title as duke of Ireland in inverted commas.[21] Michael Bennett took a more balanced stance on de Vere and Richard's other favourites, noting the earl of Suffolk and Burley 'may have been arrogant and grasping, but they were men of experience and ability. De Vere was clearly no fop; he was of distinguished lineage and showed some vigour in arms and tournaments.'[22] Yet there has been little study of de Vere's career, beyond a relatively brief article by Robert Halliday in 1993 that did not go beyond printed source material, Tuck's entry in the *Oxford Dictionary of National Biography* and a short, popular study by Jane Greatorex.[23]

This study is designed to be a reappraisal of Robert de Vere. By approaching him in more depth than previously and in his context as a member of the titled nobility rather than just as a courtier and favourite, aspects of his career become

[16] E. Perroy, *The Hundred Years War*, trans. W.B. Wells (London, 1951), 184.
[17] T. Costain, *The Last Plantagenets* (New York, 1962), 115.
[18] Rosenthal, 'Baronial Rebellions', 615.
[19] A. Tuck, *Richard II and the English Nobility* (London, 1973), 114, 115.
[20] A. Goodman, *John of Gaunt. The Exercise of Princely Power in Fourteenth Century Europe* (London, 1992), 102.
[21] L. Ashe, *Richard II. A Brittle Glory* (London, 2016), 15, 49 (quote), 50, 66.
[22] M.J. Bennett, *Richard II and the Revolution of 1399* (Stroud, 1999), 25.
[23] R. Halliday, 'Robert de Vere, Ninth Earl of Oxford', *Medieval History*, 3 (1993), 71–85; A. Tuck, 'Vere, Robert de, Ninth Earl of Oxford, Marquess of Dublin, and Duke of Ireland (1362–1392)', *ODNB*. The popular study by Greatorex within its fifty-eight pages covers not only Robert's life (pp. 1–19) but also his uncle Aubrey (20–1), Richard II (22–30) and Robert's mother (32–43): *Robert de Vere, 1362–ca. 1392, 9th Earl Oxenforde, & King Richard II* (Lavenham, 2018).

more understandable. A close study of what evidence survives enables some accusations made by contemporary chroniclers, by the Appellants themselves, and by certain modern historians, to be proven inaccurate or false. It is not, however, designed to be a whitewash. Clearly, many contemporaries found Robert de Vere objectionable, certainly politically, probably personally, and they had grounds to do so. If some of de Vere's actions are understandable and excusable by the standards of the time, others – perhaps most notably plots to kill the king's uncle, John of Gaunt (if the chronicles are accurate on this) and his abandonment and divorce of his wife – are rather less so. Furthermore, de Vere was a failure. He died in exile, stripped of his titles and estates. He had no children to pass on his claims to and he left the future of the earldom of Oxford he inherited in real jeopardy. These were serious matters for the late medieval nobility for whom the preservation of title and estates and the transmission of these undiminished to the next generation without any stain on the family honour were essential. While the earldom was restored to de Vere's uncle Aubrey after his death, the family lost many estates as a result of de Vere's forfeiture and seventy-five years later, de Vere's distant cousin, John, thirteenth earl of Oxford, was seeking a reversal of Robert de Vere's forfeiture. This was not so much for material benefits – which were not really forthcoming – but to remove the damage to the reputation of the family.[24] No study of Robert de Vere can therefore ignore his shortcomings, but it can and should treat critically the hostile contemporary material which frequently overemphasises them.

The source material for Robert de Vere's career is problematic, however. There are a number of fine contemporary histories and chronicles covering the late fourteenth century, and it is from them that historians have gained the greatest understanding of events and players during that time.[25] Yet, as already mentioned, the English chroniclers are almost uniformly hostile to Richard II and his intimates, notably de Vere, for a variety of reasons, such as Appellant patrons, political circumspection after 1388 or 1399, or from genuine personal opinion.[26] Chris Given-Wilson has also noted how the three major chroniclers of the crisis of 1386–8, Henry Knighton, the anonymous Westminster chronicler and Thomas Walsingham were influenced by pro-Appellant propaganda, the first two copying

---

[24] *PROME*, xiii, 204–7.

[25] For an authoritative overview, see A. Gransden, *Historical Writing in England c.1307– early Sixteenth Century* (London, 1982), ch. 6. For a positive take on the use of chronicles for Richard II's reign, see G.B. Stow, 'Chronicles Versus Records: the Character of Richard II', in J.S. Hamilton and P.J. Bradley, eds, *Documenting the Past. Essays in Medieval History Presented to George Peddy Cuttino* (Woodbridge, 1989), 155–76.

[26] For the reliability and political outlook of the key chronicles, see Gransden, *Historical Writing*, 177–87.

newsletters and official documents into their texts.[27] Dissenting voices to the Appellant narrative are hard to find, though the Dieulacres chronicle, written by a pro-Ricardian and pro-Cestrian author, is a rare example.[28] Two sources are focussed on the proceedings of the Merciless Parliament of 1388 that condemned de Vere and his fellows, and certainly the better-known of the two by Thomas Favent is thoroughly supportive of its actions.[29] Such criticism could take different forms and stem from different attitudes: Given-Wilson has suggested that 'whereas Walsingham can almost be pictured rubbing his hands with glee at the king's every foible, the Westminster Chronicle conveys more of a sense of sadness at his lack of statesmanship'.[30] Courtiers were also always targets of criticism by chroniclers throughout the Middle Ages, with the besetting sins of pride, avarice and lust ascribed to them consistently – and de Vere of course was closely associated with the court.[31]

The hostility of the chroniclers to Richard and his court is most clearly demonstrated in the works of Thomas Walsingham. Walsingham's homiletic tone led him to criticise severely the moral failings of great men, notably John of Gaunt, Edward III (in his later years) and others.[32] De Vere's scandalous divorce, amongst other perceived failings, made him a target for Walsingham's deep disapproval. He was the most prolific and influential writer on Richard II's reign, composing, amongst other works, a history of England, which he subsequently revised in a number of versions.[33] The manuscript history of Walsingham's work is tortuous

---

[27] C. Given-Wilson, *Chronicles. The Writing of History in Medieval England* (London, 2004), 205.

[28] The chronicle of Dieulacres Abbey, 1381–1403, is printed with discussion in M.V. Clarke and V.H. Galbraith, 'The Deposition of Richard II', *BJRL*, 14 (1930), 164–81. Another independent chronicle is that of the abbey of Louth Park, Lincolnshire, which, under the entry for 1377 describes Richard II immediately despising the counsel of the wise and attending to the suggestions of the young, like the biblical king Rehobam. However, it also takes a critical line on the Appellants 'conspiring against their King', and inhumanly putting to death some of Richard's circle: *The Chronicle of Louth Park Abbey*, ed. E. Venables (Lincoln Record Society, i, 1889), 41–2.

[29] Given-Wilson, *Chronicles*, 176–7; Gransden, *Historical Writing*, 185–6. For discussion of Favent's work and his motives for writing, see Oliver, *Parliament and Political Pamphleteering* and the critique by G. Dodd, 'Was Thomas Favent a Political Pamphleteer? Faction and Politics in Later Fourteenth-Century London', *Journal of Medieval History*, 37 (2011), 397–418.

[30] Given-Wilson, *Chronicles*, 155.

[31] Given-Wilson, *Chronicles*, 156–7.

[32] Gransden, *Historical Writing*, 129–30.

[33] For a good summary of Walsingham's work and influence, see Gransden, *Historical Writing*, ch. 5.

and modern historians have created further difficulties by the various overlapping editions that have been printed. For the purposes of this work, the key texts are the earliest version of Walsingham's history – printed as the *Chronicon Angliae* in 1874 – which covered the period up to 1388 and was probably completed shortly after that date and certainly by 1394. Later versions of Walsingham's *Chronica Maiora* revised and expanded this section significantly, while continuing the chronicle on to 1422. This was originally printed as the *Historia Anglicana* in 1863–4, though more complete modern editions and translations have been published.[34] The most authoritative is that edited by Taylor, Childs and Watkiss and published in two volumes as *The St Albans Chronicle*, containing a composite text from the most contemporary manuscripts, amongst which MS Royal 13 E. IX, composed in the 1390s, is the most important to cover the 1380s.[35] Nonetheless, care must be taken with the various revisions of Walsingham's manuscripts, as is discussed below regarding the well-known but problematic description of Richard II at de Vere's funeral.[36]

None of this is to dismiss Walsingham in particular or the chronicles in general. Much can be gleaned from them in regards to reconstructing de Vere's career and the politics of the 1380s. The Westminster Chronicle in particular maintains some objectivity and is more detailed and reliable than others. Froissart, meanwhile, has a surprising level of detail on de Vere in exile after 1388, perhaps because of his time at the French royal court, and is essentially the only narrative source for the last four years of his life. All chronicles can give some insight into perceptions of de Vere after his fall. Yet, while the chronicles covering the 1380s are essential in building an understanding of de Vere's career, their hostility is also problematic. Their explicit judgements on him and the implicit picture they create through inclusions, omissions, and even the order of factual statements, as well as the subtle choice of vocabulary means they must be treated with real caution as sources for de Vere's career. The chroniclers were not eyewitnesses to most events they described, none were present in the royal council chamber or the royal bedchamber, and they relied on sources, written and oral, that were not sympathetic to de Vere, the king or the men around him.

As with most late medieval public figures, royal administrative documents need to be used alongside the chronicles to establish any nuanced understanding.

---

[34] *Chronicon Angliae, 1328–88*, ed. E.M. Thompson (RS, 1874); *Historia Anglicana, 1272–1422*, ed. H.T. Riley (2 vols, RS, 1863–4); *Chronica Maiora*, trans. Preest and ed. Clark.

[35] *The St Albans Chronicle. The Chronica Maiora of Thomas Walsingham*, eds J. Taylor, W.R. Childs and L. Watkiss (2 vols, Oxford, 2003–11). For the manuscript history, see ibid., xxvii–lxvii. For the dating, see also G. B. Stow, 'Richard II in Thomas Walsingham's Chronicles', *Speculum*, 59 (1984), 68–102.

[36] See below, p. 199.

English administrative sources cast light on the patronage de Vere received, the accusations made against him after his fall, and – patchily – his presence at court. These sources are skewed, however, as there is considerably more material amongst the archives of the crown on de Vere in the year or so after his forfeiture than in the previous half dozen of his ascendency. However, while by no means complete, these sources from 1388 onwards do allow some discussion of his estates and the material goods he purchased and acquired, and which were seized after his fall. While most of the records of the medieval Anglo-Irish administration in Dublin do not survive, what was copied in late nineteenth-century editions, however unsatisfactory, does shed some light on de Vere's administration in Ireland; recent scholarship has made these more accessible and understandable.[37] One further subset of the records of the crown is less informative than might be expected. Whereas the records of the royal law courts are widely acknowledged as a key source for the study of late medieval noblemen and their localities in general, they are extremely uninformative for Robert de Vere. He was very rarely a plaintiff or defendant in cases. Perhaps because his career was so centred around the royal court, common law records do not show much of his influence in the regions where he held land and little about his local following or his estate management.

Perhaps the most important loss is the records of Robert de Vere's own administration. The survival rate of records of noble families that came into the crown hands is extremely patchy – those of the House of Lancaster in 1399 have survived very well, those of the House of York after 1461 very poorly – and regrettably those of de Vere, which were presumably seized in Castle Hedingham, Chester and London around Christmas 1387, are no longer extant. Indeed, no household or estate records for de Vere survive at all. This is a major loss; much can be discovered from such ostensibly dry records as estate accounts, which can illuminate parts of a lord's affinity and the financial position of the landowner in question, while household accounts can shed light on lordly lifestyle, itinerary, expenditure and servants. Some scraps can be gleaned on these topics from royal records from 1388 and after, while tangential light is shed on de Vere's lands and local connections through an estate account and a household account of Maud, Countess of Oxford, de Vere's mother, from the period around his fall. However, there are enormous lacunae in what we know about de Vere, particularly in his capacity as a great magnate.

Lastly, this study cannot be a biography of Robert de Vere in any modern sense. There is very little evidence that might show what he was thinking,

---

[37] Notably, the *Circle* project, an online calendar of Irish chancery letters, c. 1244–1509, https://chancery.tcd.ie/content/welcome-circle, and the developing *Virtual Record Treasury of Ireland*: https://virtualtreasury.ie/ both led by Dr Peter Crooks of Trinity College Dublin.

his motivations or his emotions: we have no private letters, no will and testament, no confession like that of Edmund Dudley, Henry VII's minister, nor a reflection on his life and career like Henry of Grosmont's *Livres des seynts medecines*.[38] We cannot infer motive and personality from his childhood experiences as his early years are almost as complete a blank as his last four years in exile. The historian can only try and piece together motive, personality and emotion from political actions, usually reported second-hand.

Nonetheless, while acknowledging the issues with the evidence, much can be said on Robert de Vere. The purposes of this study are threefold. It aims to reconstruct his political career, as far as is possible, during the six and a half years between the Peasants' Revolt of the summer of 1381 and the Merciless Parliament of 1388. This can only be done in the context of an extended discussion of the troubled politics of Richard II's minority, the unsuccessful phase (for the English) of the Hundred Years' War during the 1380s, and the problematic position of the English lordship in Ireland, with which de Vere became closely involved. There has been an immense amount of scholarship on the reign of Richard II in the last forty years, both studies of the king himself, of the Lords Appellant, of the royal court and household, and this study will place de Vere and his career within this historiography.[39] It is worth noting, however, the emphasis within this body of research, picked up in an article written all of fifty years ago: 'each succeeding study [of the political crisis of the mid-1380s] has demonstrated how complex and diverse were the implications of the actions… of those magnates most fervently opposed at that time to Richard II, his court and his ministers'.[40] The focus has traditionally been on the Appellants and the opposition to the king, not on those

---

[38] For Edmund Dudley's confessional petition and separately his reflections from prison on politics and political life, see C.J. Harrison, 'The Petition of Edmund Dudley', *EHR*, 87 (1972), 82–99 and Edmund Dudley, *The Tree of Commonwealth*, ed. D.M. Brodie (Cambridge, 1948). For Henry, duke of Lancaster's work, see *Le Livre des seyntz medicines / The Book of Holy Medicines*, ed. C. Batt (Medieval and Renaissance Texts and Studies, 419, 2015).

[39] Among other works, key studies are N. Saul, *Richard II* (New York and London, 1997); C. Fletcher, *Richard II. Manhood, Youth and Politics, 1377–99* (Oxford, 2008); C. Given-Wilson, *The Royal Household and the King's Affinity* (New Haven, CT and London, 1986). Saul's fine study remains the standard work on the reign, and while this book disagrees with it on points of detail, it owes a great deal to Saul's scholarship. Older but still useful works include Tuck, *Richard II*; A. Goodman, *The Loyal Conspiracy. The Lords Appellant under Richard II* (London, 1971); G. Mathew, *The Court of Richard II* (London, 1968). See also the study of the Appellant Lord, the earl of Warwick: A.K. Gundy, *Richard II and the Rebel Earl* (Cambridge, 2013).

[40] R.G. Davies, 'The Episcopate and the Political Crisis in England of 1386–1388', *Speculum*, 51 (1976), 659.

around Richard, while studies of the king himself have much broader remits. There has been little study on de Vere, but there are also no full-length studies of Michael de la Pole, Simon Burley, Alexander Neville or Nicholas Brembre either, nor a collective study on the Appellees to match that by Goodman on the Appellants.[41] This work on Robert de Vere has to break new ground in places in its focus on the court circle. But doing so allows a greater understanding and a more balanced assessment of de Vere's career and its context.

Secondly, de Vere is put within his family context, as the scion of an ancient lineage amongst the English higher nobility, one whose lands and wealth have been underestimated, and whose grandfather and father had successful comital careers, both in royal service and in terms of advancing the familial interests. The great late medieval historian K.B. McFarlane noted the need to assess the nobility through their own records and on their own terms, rather than through the eyes of King's Friends.[42] While this has a double meaning when discussing a royal favourite, looking at de Vere on his own terms as a member of the nobility and within the context of his family background brings new insight into his role at the centre of politics. As a member of the higher nobility there was nothing at all illegitimate about de Vere being at the centre of the court, giving advice and counsel to the king, and as hereditary great chamberlain of England, he had a

---

[41] For de la Pole, A. Tuck, 'Pole, Michael de la, First Earl of Suffolk', *ODNB* is the only account of his career. While much has been written about his impeachment in 1386, the focus has been on the constitutional importance of the event, although consideration has also been given to the veracity of the charges: J.S. Roskell, *The Impeachment of Michael de la Pole, Earl of Suffolk in 1386 in the Context of the Reign of Richard II* (Manchester 1984); J.J.N. Palmer, 'The Impeachment of Michael de la Pole in 1386', *BIHR*, 42 (1969), 96–101; J. Sherborne, 'The Defence of the Realm and the Impeachment of Michael de la Pole in 1386', in J. Taylor and W. Childs, eds, *Politics and Crisis in Fourteenth Century England* (Gloucester, 1990), 97–116. For Neville, see R.G. Davies, 'Alexander Neville, Archbishop of York 1374–1388', *Yorkshire Archaeological Journal*, 47 (1975), 87–101; R.B. Dobson, 'The Authority of the Bishop in Late Medieval England: the Case of Archbishop Alexander Neville of York, 1374–1388', in B. Vogler, ed., *Miscellanea Historiae Ecclesiasticae*, 8 (Louvain, 1987), 181–91. For Burley, see J.L. Leland, 'Burley, Sir Simon (1336? –1388)', *ODNB*. See also L.A. Hibbard, 'The Books of Sir Simon Burley, 1387', *Modern Language Notes*, 30 (1915), 169–71; V.J. Scattergood, 'Two Medieval Book Lists', *The Library*, 5th series, 23 (1968), 236–9. For Brembre: A. Prescott, 'Brembre, Sir Nicholas (d. 1388)', *ODNB*.

[42] K.B. McFarlane, *The Nobility of Later Medieval England* (Oxford, 1973), 2. For other key studies of the fourteenth-century nobility, see R.R. Davies, *Lords and Lordship in the British Isles in the Late Middle Ages*, ed. B. Smith (Oxford, 2009) and C. Given-Wilson, *The English Nobility in the Late Middle Ages. The Fourteenth Century Political Community* (London, 1987). A. Dunn, *The Politics of Magnate Power. England and Wales 1389–1413* (Oxford, 2003) covers the period immediately after Robert de Vere's fall.

more than ceremonial role at court and in the royal household that was significant. Conversely, as Richard II's patronage extended de Vere's political, landed and administrative interests to the West Country, Chester and Ireland, he lost the connection to his ancestral heartland in Essex and Suffolk that would have allowed him to challenge his local (as well as national) rival, Thomas, duke of Gloucester, there. The increasing disconnect between his family background and traditional roots in eastern England and the trajectory of his career is a theme throughout this study. The role of the nobility in the reign of Richard II has been of considerable interest to historians for many years, and there is certainly a historiographical consensus regarding the full engagement of the peerage in royal government, in council and in military service, notably during the king's minority when they were largely responsible for keeping the show upon the road.[43] Thereafter, particular in regard to the 1380s, the consensus breaks down, and there has been a tendency in some writing to regard that period as being dominated by conflict between the nobility on the one side and the royal court and household on the other.[44] Yet of course, the court and household were run by members of the titled nobility and their kin – exemplified by the great chamberlain, Robert, earl of Oxford - and the picture of conflict between court and nobility will be reassessed.

Finally, this study will open with an assessment of the royal favourite in late medieval English history. Since de Vere is usually seen as a royal favourite, with all the often ill-defined baggage that term is associated with, several questions must be addressed. Firstly, how did contemporaries and how do modern historians define a royal favourite and why were they apparently so problematic to the late medieval English polity? Who opposed royal favourites and why? Can a checklist of accusations against royal favourites be drawn up from the careers of men like Piers Gaveston, Hugh Despenser, William, duke of Suffolk and others in later medieval England? How far can Robert de Vere be compared to such men and how many boxes on such a favourite's checklist does he tick?

---

[43] Doctoral theses studying aspects of the nobility, with considerable emphasis on the engagement with, and importance of, groups of nobles in royal government during the period include C.C. Featherstonhaugh, 'Earls and the Crown in England, 1360–1385' (unpublished PhD, University of Cambridge, 2014) and K.E. Fildes, 'The Baronage in the Reign of Richard II, 1377–1399' (unpublished PhD, University of Sheffield, 2009), esp. chs 3–5. Other studies covering the nobility and Richard's reign include Tuck, *Richard II*; C. Given-Wilson, 'Richard II and the Higher Nobility', in A. Goodman and J.L. Gillespie, eds, *Richard II. The Art of Kingship* (Oxford, 1999), 107–28.

[44] This is especially true of Tuck, *Richard II*, whose chapter titles 'The Retreat of Aristocratic Influence 1382–6' and 'The Growth of Aristocratic Hostility, 1382–8' rather presuppose polar opposites, as does his language at times, e.g. 'the first hint of friction between the court and nobility…' (87).

1

Royal Favourites and their Opponents in the Later Middle Ages

> More… knights of Venus rather than of Mars, showing more prowess in the bedroom than on the field of battle, defending themselves more with their tongue than with their lance, being alert with their tongues but asleep when martial deeds were required.
>
> (Thomas Walsingham, *The St Albans Chronicle*, on Richard II's companions)[1]

During the reign of every medieval king, some men always enjoyed the trust of the monarch and were rewarded either for the service that they had done or were expected to do. However, from Henry III's Poitevins, and Edward II's favourites, to William de la Pole, duke of Suffolk (d. 1450) and Edmund Beaufort, duke of Somerset (d. 1455), under that nadir of English kingship, Henry VI, some men were perceived as having too much of the royal favour, of having been rewarded beyond their services and were thought to be illegitimately dominating royal government. These men usually had spectacular falls from their seemingly undeserved political heights and often deeply unpleasant and violent deaths. The fourteenth century has the most notorious examples of any medieval period: Piers Gaveston (d. 1312) and Hugh Despenser the Younger (d. 1326), to whom Edward II was passionately attached, loom large in any discussion of medieval favourites. Does Robert de Vere deserve inclusion in this disreputable company? There is certainly more than an echo of Gaveston and Despenser in discussions in both contemporary sources and in modern historiography on Robert de Vere, and far more so for him than any of Richard II's other favourites and ministers who fell in 1387–8.

To answer the question, the problem of what a royal favourite was needs to be addressed. There is no particular agreement amongst historians, and English medieval historians in particular have not looked at the term 'favourite' in

---

[1] *SAC*, i, 814–15.

much detail or approached them collectively or categorically.[2] Klaus Oschema has cited a definition of a favourite as a courtier 'whose position of power is exclusively founded on the ruler's personal affection and a dominant position at court', and added that the position 'is directly related to his privileged individual bond with the ruler' not 'legitimized either by traditional claims deduced from his parental background, nor by his professional expertise'.[3] Such a definition is thoroughly awkward in a medieval English context. Many of the most notorious English favourites – Despenser, both Michael and William de la Pole, Edmund Beaufort and de Vere himself, as well as two of the primary targets of the Good Parliament of 1376, William, fourth Lord Latimer and John, third Lord Neville – were members of the English peerage before acquiring favour. They, therefore, had every right to be present at court and attempt to exercise influence and offer advice while there as a result of their noble birth, however much they then built on that privileged access to court and monarch to try and dominate patronage and favour. Arguably only Piers Gaveston really fits the definition of a favourite cited by Oschema until Thomas Cromwell in the 1530s, although even the latter proved his expertise in governmental affairs.

An alternative, if simpler, definition, that an English medieval favourite was simply someone who, regardless of their parental background, received an undue or illegitimate proportion of royal favour and exploited that to his or her benefit, runs into problems as well. How can we judge what was excessive royal favour? In particular, how far can we rely on contemporary verdicts on this to identify favourites? Richard II and those around him would not have judged royal favour to Robert de Vere in the 1380s as excessive, while the Lords Appellant and their allies reached the opposite conclusion. Almost all the men mentioned in the preceding paragraph fell from power and died violently or in exile and could therefore be criticised or excoriated by contemporaries. Arguably, a clearer royal 'favourite' was Reginald Bray, Henry VII's low-born, hard-nosed, and thoroughly influential advisor. Yet, because he predeceased his royal master and Perkin Warbeck's rebellion – which vilified him and

---

[2] There is some French and German historical literature on the topic: see K. Oschema, 'The Cruel End of the Favourite. Clandestine Death and Public Retaliation at Late Medieval Courts in England and France', in K-H. Spiess and I. Warntjes, eds, *Death at Court* (Wiesbaden, 2012), 175–6 and the references therein. The term commands more widespread use in early modern English historiography: see for example, L.W.B. Brockliss, ed., *The World of the Favourite* (New Haven, CT, 1999).

[3] Oschema, 'Cruel End of the Favourite', 176, translating and citing the definition by R.G. Asch in W. Paravicini, J. Hirschbiegel and J. Wefflaufer, eds, *Höfe und Residenzen in spämittelalterlichen Reich. Bilder und Begriffe* (2 vols, Ostfildern, 2005), i, 64.

others as 'caitiffs and villeins' – failed to unseat Henry VII, that label is very rarely applied to Bray.[4] A definition that relies so much on the judgement call of the historian, assessing the posthumous verdicts of contemporaries, is clearly problematic.

Oschema picks up on a further awkward aspect of trying to define a favourite and that is the distinction, if any, to be made, between a favourite and a minister (not a widely used contemporary term) or senior royal officer, and the extent to which a minister can be separated from more contemporary terms with similar meanings such as advisor and counsellor. The minister-favourite of the early modern period, such as Cardinal Richelieu, is less a phenomenon of the later Middle Ages, though the case has been made that the Younger Despenser perhaps came closest.[5] In the fourteenth and fifteenth centuries, the term minister could be restricted to the 'five principal officers' as defined by the Parliament of 1380: the chancellor, treasurer, keeper of the privy seal, and the two most senior officers of the royal household, the steward and the chamberlain.[6] However, all of these terms – minister, advisor, counsellor – could be prefixed in contemporary political criticism with the word 'wicked', 'evil', 'false' or particularly in fifteenth-century England 'covetous', and thus potentially overlap with the favourite, in the caricature of the latter as personally greedy and exercising malign influence.[7] Yet, all also imply input into, or control over, royal policy; the term 'favourite' does not automatically contain such a connotation.

Perhaps the easiest distinction to be made is between a favourite and a chief minister. There were few men who could genuinely be described as chief ministers, whose name could be applied to a regime – perhaps Hubert de Burgh and briefly Peter des Roches during the early years of Henry III's adult rule, the dukes of Suffolk and Somerset under Henry VI, and Thomas Wolsey and Thomas Cromwell under Henry VIII.[8] William of Wykeham, bishop of Winchester and chancellor of England from 1367 to 1371, was described by

---

[4] M.M. Condon, 'From Caitiff and Villein to *Pater Patriae*: Reynold Bray and the Profits of Office', in M.A. Hicks, ed., *Profit, Piety and the Professions in Late Medieval England* (Gloucester, 1990), 137–68.

[5] M.J. Lawrence, 'Power, Ambition and Political Rehabilitation: the Despensers, c. 1281–1400' (unpublished DPhil., University of York, 2005), 194–5.

[6] *PROME*, vi, 149.

[7] For a discussion of the problem of 'covetous counsel', see J.L. Watts, *Henry VI and the Politics of Kingship* (Cambridge, 1996), 40–1.

[8] D. Carpenter, *Henry III: the Rise to Power and Personal Rule, 1207–1258* (London, 2020), chs 2 and 3. For Suffolk and Somerset, see Watts, *Henry VI*, chs 5, 6 and 7. For the most recent studies of Henry VIII's chief ministers, see G. Richardson,

Mark Ormrod as a chief minister, and Froissart said that 'everything was done by him, and nothing was done without him'.[9] Yet, with a still active king, adult princes of the blood and others with influence, Wykeham did not dominate the entire regime. Clearly there had to be significant overlap between the categories of leading minister and favourite: no chief minister could be such without being the most influential man around the king, without some control, either directly or through allies, of access to the king, and no such minister failed to take opportunities to enrich themselves or enhance their rank. All these were, as will be discussed shortly, also hallmarks of the favourite. Yet, historians have tended to be less critical of those who might be described as a chief minister, in control of the direction of royal policy, and approach them in different ways to favourites. Serious efforts, for example, have been made to rehabilitate William, de la Pole, duke of Suffolk, as a statesman doing the best he could during the 1440s in the nearly impossible circumstances of the vacuum of effective leadership from his king, Henry VI, and in his rule of East Anglia.[10] In some respects, his grandfather, Michael de la Pole, first earl of Suffolk, chancellor of England until his impeachment in 1386 and clearly a man of some experience and ability, has been treated differently to de Vere – he has had a reasonable press from modern historians while de Vere has not.[11] This historiographical trend contrasts with contemporary attitudes as clear association with unpopular or failed royal policy could make attacks on a leading minister even more vitriolic than a 'mere' favourite. The duke of Suffolk was hounded by parliament and not 'merely' an aristocratic faction in 1450, and even after his death his association with defeat in foreign war and corruption at home was one cause of a major popular revolt. Likewise, Michael de la Pole, the target of impeachment in the Wonderful Parliament of 1386, received an extraordinary denunciation by Walsingham when his death was recorded in 1389: 'that summer the instigator of treachery, the cesspool of avarice, the charioteer of treason, the receptacle for malice, the disseminator of hatred, the fabricator of lies, that evil tell-tale, notorious for his deception, an artful-back-biter, and a traitor to his country – I mean Michael de la Pole – breathed his last in Paris'. It is telling that Walsingham then goes on to call

---

Wolsey (Basingstoke, 2014); D. MacCulloch, *Thomas Cromwell: A Life* (London, 2019).

[9] Ormrod, *Edward III*, 490–2; Froissart, ed. Lettenhove, vii, 101.

[10] Watts, *Henry VI*, 205–60; H.R. Castor, *The King, the Crown and the Duchy of Lancaster. Public Authority and Private Power, 1399–1461* (Oxford, 2000), ch. 4.

[11] Roskell, *Impeachment of Michael de la Pole*, 3–6, surveys the dismissal of most of the charges against him by nineteenth- and twentieth-century historians.

him an 'evil counsellor' rather than a favourite or a courtier.[12] No such vitriolic condemnation was made against de Vere when his death was recorded by the St Albans chronicler.

Part of the distinction between favourite and minister is about age: both William and Michael de la Pole, in their mid-fifties at their respective falls, were far older than de Vere (twenty-six in 1388), Gaveston (twenty-eight at his death) and the younger Despenser (forty at his death, though of an age with his king). Likewise, Thomas Wolsey was over forty by the time he became obviously the leading man around Henry VIII in or around 1513 while Thomas Cromwell was approaching fifty in the early 1530s when he rose to singular prominence under the same king. One exception might be Hugh Despenser the elder, often labelled a favourite and sixty-five at his execution in 1326.[13] Perhaps connected to age is another distinction that can be drawn between the favourite and the chief minister. Generally, the latter were not accused of the sexual disorder which the former were frequently alleged to be committing, particularly in terms of a relationship with the king. Their role at the centre of government was based on their talents or their unscrupulous manipulation of power, depending on the eye of the beholder. However, one or two chief ministers were accused of using sorcery to maintain their hold over the king, another allegation levelled at some male and female favourites.[14] Yet, while age plays a role, a distinction between minister and favourite is also about perceptions by historians. For all de Vere's influence with Richard II, he is never credited with the direction of overall royal policy, nor is Gaveston with Edward II. Hamilton has said of Gaveston that 'Such ostentation and arrogance, rather than any political ambition or agenda, was ultimately to be his undoing.'[15] In contrast, however, the dukes of Suffolk and Somerset from the later 1430s to 1455 under Henry VI are perceived as chief ministers by historians and not just, or even primarily, favourites.

Moving from chief minister to ministers, advisors and counsellors, which all kings had, adds a layer of complexity. All three of these terms are subtly different to – and less pejorative than – that of favourite in modern eyes. Yet, it is not clear how far contemporaries made such distinctions: the terminology used to

---

[12] *SAC*, i, 878–9.

[13] M. Lawrence, 'Rise of a Royal Favourite: the Early Career of Hugh Despenser the Elder', in G. Dodd and A. Musson, eds, *The Reign of Edward II: New Perspectives* (York, 2006), 205–19.

[14] This was true of Hubert de Burgh and of Cardinal Wolsey: W.R. Jones, 'Political Uses of Sorcery in Medieval Europe', *The Historian*, 34 (1971–2), 675–6.

[15] J.S. Hamilton, 'Gaveston, Piers, Earl of Cornwall', *ODNB*.

denigrate Edward III's unpopular intimates in Thomas Brinton's famous sermon during the Good Parliament of 1376 was 'counsellors' ('consiliarii'), not favourites.[16] Indeed a case study – thoroughly relevant to the subject of this study – makes that clear. There was a wide variety of terminology and language used to describe Robert de Vere and his fellow Appellees by the three major chroniclers of the 1380s, Henry Knighton, Thomas Walsingham and the Monk of Westminster. There are three occasions when the Westminster Chronicle applied epithets to those around Richard II in the mid-1380s (excluding reported speech or copied documents). In chronological order in the narrative, they are 'intimates' ('familiares'), 'persistent supporters' ('jugiter adherebant'), and 'incompetent advisors' ('per minus sufficientes homines fuit rex actenus gubernatus').[17] The chronicler thus mixed advisors and favourites but shows a clear development from more neutral to more derogatory language. Knighton was considerably more consistent both in his derogatory language and the emphasis on favourites rather than advisors. On the first two occasions when he described Richard's inner circle he employed the same phrase, 'seducers of the king' ('seductores regis') and it is used again later in the narrative.[18] The next four are translated as 'favourites' by the editor, though two Latin words are used – 'auriculares' and 'fautores' – the first being prefaced by 'false' ('reprobis').[19] The last two terms, each employed twice, are 'traitors' ('proditores'), and 'predators' ('predones').[20] Walsingham, however, largely eschews the terms for favourites. Instead, there are single examples of 'fellow-plotters' and 'evil councillors' ('traditatores' and 'nequam consiliari'), but he preferred to focus on describing the Appellees as 'traitors', using this four times, and 'enemies of the country' ('hostibus regni') on a further occasion.[21] While the choice of vocabulary made by each chronicler varied and was to some extent driven by the narrative context, the usage suggests contemporaries did not always draw sharp distinctions between 'favourites' and

---

[16] *Preaching in the Age of Chaucer. Selected Sermons in Translation*, ed. S. Wenzel (Washington, DC, 2008), 252–3; Thomas Brinton, *The Sermons of Thomas Brinton, Bishop of Rochester (1373–89)*, ed. M.A. Devlin (2 vols, Camden Society, 3rd ser., 85–6, 1954), ii, 320.

[17] *WC*, 114, 202, 206.

[18] *KC*, 392 (bis), 394, 404, 412.

[19] Ibid., 400, 402tres, 404.

[20] Ibid., 414bis, 416bis. The editor translates both as 'betrayers', though 'proditores' in particular is surely a more specific reference to their treason, especially as Knighton was writing after they were condemned for that crime in 1388. For Knighton's use of 'seducers' and his likely reliance on another narrative source, which used that language, see ibid., xlvii.

[21] *SAC*, i, 824, 828tres, 836bis, 842.

'counsellors'. Indeed, more than one contemporary chronicle mixes the two types of accusation. The *Continuatio Eulogii* describes the king seeking advice from de Vere, de la Pole, Burley and other 'sycophants' ('adulators') while Thomas Favent names the five men as 'governors and close councillors of the king' but the same sentence continues that they were 'concerned neither with the king's nor the kingdom's business but embracing the mammon of iniquity for themselves'.[22] Two of these men – Michael de la Pole and Simon Burley – were also among the five principal ministers of the crown in the mid-1380s, being chancellor and chamberlain of the household, respectively. Another writer who mixed both types of terms, and also picked up the theme of age, was John Gower in his *Cronica Tripertita* who focused on the advice the king received: 'Unsound advice from foolish youth he took as guide' and 'By young men's counsel he breathed out a deadly breath', but added 'Thus he became their friend as bad with bad combined' and 'Such young men stood beside that he called "special friends"' ('speciales').[23] Thus a favourite, in contemporary views, was not merely one much in the king's presence; he could and did advise and counsel the king. The emphasis, instead, was on the poor quality of the advice and the covetousness (and at the extreme end treasonous) motives that lay behind the counsel. Conversely, being a minister of the crown, in the eyes of their critics, gave ministers greater opportunity to enrich themselves, and it was several office holders who came in for the harshest criticism in the Good Parliament of 1376, notably William Latimer, the chamberlain, and John Neville, the steward of the household.[24]

Notorious favourites were rarely women. The only real example in England in the later Middle Ages was Alice Perrers, mistress of Edward III in his last years.[25] Perrers was certainly perceived as having considerable influence

---

[22] *Continuatio Eulogii. The Continuation of the Eulogium Historiarum, 1364–1413*, ed. C. Given-Wilson (Oxford, 2019), 50–1; Thomas Favent, 'History or Narration Concerning the Manner and Form of the Miraculous Parliament at Westminster in the Year 1386, in the Tenth Year of the Reign of King Richard the Second after the Conquest, Declared by Thomas Favent, Clerk', trans. A. Galloway, in E. Steiner and C. Barrington, eds, *The Letter of the Law: Legal Practice and Literary Production in Medieval England* (Ithaca, NY, 2002), 232.

[23] John Gower, *Poems on Contemporary Events*, ed. D. Carlson and trans. A.G. Rigg (Toronto, 2011), 251–3.

[24] G. Holmes, *The Good Parliament* (Oxford, 1975), 65–8.

[25] C. Given-Wilson, 'Perrers [*other married name* Windsor], Alice (*d.* 1401/02)', *ODNB*. Laura Tompkins's forthcoming monograph on Alice Perrers will be important in understanding Alice herself, the role of the female favourite and the politics of the last years of Edward III. See also, eadem, 'Alice Perrers and the Goldsmiths' Mistery: New Evidence Concerning the Identity of the Mistress of Edward III',

over the king and of having enriched herself at the expense of others and to the detriment of the realm; when added to the category of perceived sexual domination of the king, she did thus tick some of the boxes of the favourite which will be discussed shortly. Other kings had mistresses but were not perceived by contemporaries as being dominated by them or the mistresses were not thought to have abused their position. Elizabeth (Jane) Shore was said by Thomas More to have had some influence with her lover, Edward IV, but was not showered with rewards by the king nor, in More's words, did she misuse her influence: Edward's 'favour to say truth… she never abused to any man's hurt… either for that she delighted to be sued unto and show what she was able to do with the king, or for that wanton women and wealthy be not always covetous'.[26] Queens could and did exercise considerable influence over their husbands, but their position within the polity and the joint-stock nature of monarchy meant they were rarely criticised for doing so. Perhaps only hostile comment on Margaret of Anjou, queen to Henry VI, in the late 1450s amidst a civil war, came close to the type of vitriol aimed at favourites: 'the quene with such as were of her affynyte rewled the reame as her liked, gaderyng ryches unnumerable' claimed the incorrigibly Yorkist *English Chronicle*.[27] Beyond wives and mistresses, women were rarely perceived as favourites. Interestingly, Richard II was accused of being influenced by women. In the first parliament of the reign of Richard's nemesis, Henry IV, the chancellor, Archbishop Arundel described Richard's England as being 'led, ruled and governed by children, and by the advice of widows'.[28] Richard certainly seems to have enjoyed the company of women, and recent work is showing that there were more women at court during his reign than was normally the case.[29] Three women were

---

EHR, 130 (2015), 1361–91; eadem, '"Said the Mistress to the Bishop": Alice Perrers, William Wykeham and Court Networks in Fourteenth-Century England', in R. Ambühl, J. Bothwell and L. Tompkins, eds, *Ruling Fourteenth-Century England. Essays in Honour of Christopher Given-Wilson* (Woodbridge, 2019), 205–26.

[26] Sir Thomas More, *The History of King Richard III*, ed. R.S. Sylvester (New Haven, CT, 1963), 55–6.

[27] *An English Chronicle, 1377–1461*, ed. W. Marx (Woodbridge, 2003), 78. Margaret was also believed by one foreign correspondent to have poisoned Henry VI: H. Maurer, *Margaret of Anjou. Queenship and Power in Late Medieval England* (Woodbridge, 2003), 201. For discussion of Margaret's power and influence between 1456 and 1460 during which language often applied to a favourite was directed against her, see M. Hicks, *The Wars of the Roses* (New Haven, CT and London, 2010), 122–30; R.A. Griffiths, *The Reign of King Henry VI* (London, 1981), 775–7.

[28] *PROME*, viii, 9.

[29] Notably, C. McKenzie, 'Ladies and Robes of the Garter: Kingship, Patronage, and Female Political Agency in Late Medieval England, c.1348–1445' (unpublished

expelled from the court in 1388 – named by the Westminster Chronicle as Ladies Poynings, Mohun and Moleyns – but few were clearly and obviously influential with the king and the hostile nature of the accusations in 1388 and 1399 means care must be taken with such allegations.[30]

Many of the attacks against notorious favourites from the reign of Henry III to that of Henry VI royal favourites were during periods when foreign wars in Scotland and France were going badly for the English; this, of course, was not coincidence. Indeed, most of the favourites were held responsible for military failures. This might be either directly in terms of military defeats and active treason – these were the accusations made against the dukes of Suffolk and Somerset in 1450 – or indirectly through appropriation of revenue that should have been used for war. The Commons in the Good Parliament, having noted Alice Perrers had several thousand pounds annually from the treasury, said she should be removed from the king 'both as a matter of conscience and of the ill prosecution of the war'.[31] Such matters of military honour meant much to the nobility, sections of which were usually, though not invariably, the prime movers against royal favourites. However, making scapegoats of men close to the king seems to have been of greater attraction than analysing more deeply rooted reasons for English failure in war amongst most sections of the political community. The paramount importance of the defence of the realm and taxation granted for it – particularly if such taxation was thought to be misspent – in the public consciousness, both in parliament itself and by parliamentary voters and taxpayers in towns and shires, meant that it was not just the nobility to whom the issue was of the greatest sensitivity. John Watts has described such periods as these as bringing 'systemic' pressure on the political system.[32] Many of the attacks on courtiers and favourites in parliament were framed in financial terms, notably the impeachment of Michael de la Pole in 1386 and during the Good Parliament of 1376.[33] Conversely, when the realm was successful in foreign war, or during periods of peace, men high in royal favour, recipients of considerable patronage, such as William Montagu,

---

PhD Thesis, University of Southampton, 2019).

[30] *WC*, 230–1. Knighton is less accurate: *KC*, 428–9.

[31] *The Anonimalle Chronicle, 1333 to 1381*, ed. V. H. Galbraith (Manchester, 1927), 87; J. Taylor, *English Historical Literature in the Fourteenth Century* (Oxford, 1987), 308.

[32] J.L. Watts, 'The Problem of the Personal: Tackling Corruption in Late Medieval England, 1250–1550', in R. Kroeze, V. André and G. Geltner, eds, *Anti-Corruption in History: From Antiquity to the Modern Era* (Oxford, 2017), 97.

[33] On the latter, see Holmes, *Good Parliament*, 63–9, 108–26. It was only towards the end of the attack on the court that the emphasis in the charges turned towards treason: ibid., 105–6, 126–34.

promoted to first earl of Salisbury, under Edward III or William, Lord Hastings, the king's chamberlain, under Edward IV have not usually received the label 'favourite' from historians nor attracted such disapprobation from contemporaries.[34] Montagu and Hastings are, rightly, described as the king's friends by historians, yet Gaveston and de Vere were surely also the friends of Edward II and Richard II, but are rarely described as such in modern writing. The political context is thus important. Close friendship between monarch and subject was acceptable in the right circumstances, with the right man or men, and in the right way. Mark Ormrod summed this up when discussing a particular example: 'since Edward III's friendship with William Montagu never threatened to destabilize domestic politics or foreign policy, his subjects quite simply never needed to turn it into a scandal, sexual or otherwise'.[35] Edward IV's friendship with Hastings was criticized subsequently by Richard III in an attempt to blacken his brother's regime, and a generation later Thomas More reported that the queen hated Hastings partly because she suspected that he was 'secretly familiar with the king in wanton company', but then so were her sons and one of her brothers.[36] Yet during Hastings's lifetime there was little criticism despite his power and influence. In 1472, when a correspondent of the Paston family said of Hastings 'what my seyd lord Chamberleyn may do wyth the Kyng and wyth all the lordys of Inglond I trowe it be not unknowyn to yow, most of eny on man alyve', this was not a criticism. Rosemary Horrox has noted that 'Unusually for a royal favourite, Hastings seems to have been not only successful, but well liked too.'[37]

The correspondence of unsuccessful foreign policy and attacks on favourites points to the crux of the matter. Unpopular favourites were, or could be, a symptom of the underlying malaise of unsuccessful kingship. The articles of deposition against Edward II in 1327 accused him of being personally incapable of governing, of allowing himself to be led and governed by others who advised him badly, and of refusing to remedy these defects when asked to do so by the

---

[34] W.M. Ormrod, 'Montagu, William [William de Montacute], first earl of Salisbury (1301–1344)', *ODNB*; R. Horrox, 'Hastings, William, first Baron Hastings (c. 1430–1483)', *ODNB*.

[35] Ormrod, *Edward III*, 137 (and more generally 134–7). Ormrod makes the contrast explicit 'Far from emerging as a new Piers Gaveston or Hugh Despenser... the earl of Salisbury was seen as deserving of his rewards' (137).

[36] More, *Richard III*, ed. Sylvester, 10–11; C.D. Ross, *Edward IV* (London, 1974), 316–17.

[37] *Paston Letters and Papers of the Fifteenth Century*, ed. N. Davis, 1 (EETS, Supplementary Series, 20, 2004), 581; Horrox, 'Hastings, William', *ODNB*.

great and wise men of the kingdom.[38] Yet, frequently it was favourites rather than the monarchs who were targeted. Rosenthal has described attacks on royal favourites and their justifications as 'either a transparent bit of propaganda, fooling no one and therefore convincing no one, or else a tortuous legal fiction, devised to expiate the rebel's guilt and to placate hostile public opinion'.[39] In some cases he is right, and clearly no king whose closest advisors or intimates were highly unpopular was quite getting the balance right. Yet virtually every king – successful or not – was criticised at some point for their advisors. Henry VII's new men were a target for Perkin Warbeck in his manifesto of 1496: 'he hath none in favour in trust about his person', Warbeck claimed, except for a list of men who were 'caitiffs and villeins of simple birth'.[40] During the political crisis of 1341, the Archbishop of Canterbury pointedly reminded Edward III of the example of the Old Testament king Rehoboam, who followed 'the counsel of young men who wished to please him and knew little; whereby he lost all the land of Israel'.[41]

Care, therefore, must be taken not to generalise too far. While on occasion clearly the king was the real target of attacks of favourites, on others occasions the weight of blame was perhaps more clearly with the favourite or the king could be excused for one or more reasons. The attacks on Gaveston in 1308–12 were designed to remove him from Edward II by one method or another; it was then hoped Edward, freed from his dependence on him, could rule in a different style. The attack in the parliament of 1321 on the Despensers had similar aims, though perhaps patience with Edward II was wearing very thin by then.[42] The actions against Henry VI's ministers (or were they favourites?) in 1450 and 1455 are a case in point. It would have been obvious to all in the political elites by the 1440s that Henry VI was an inadequate and unsuccessful king, but those were not grounds for deposition as he was not tyrannical or flouting the laws or most of the political conventions of the time. Instead, bringing down the duke of Somerset was the end goal for the duke of York in 1455, as York sought to replace Somerset as chief minister, not replace Henry

---

[38] J.R.S. Philips, *Edward II* (London, 2010), 529–30.

[39] Rosenthal, 'King's "Wicked Advisors"', 595. He goes on to say that these 'interpretations are accurate but inadequate as explanations of the phenomena to which they apply'. Nonetheless, the thrust of the article is that attacks on wicked advisors and favourites were generally tactics of expediency rather than being genuine.

[40] R. Henry, *A History of Great Britain*, vol. 6 (Dublin 1794), 321.

[41] *English Historical Documents, 1327–1485*, ed. A.R. Myers (London, 1969), 72. For the context, see Ormrod, *Edward III*, 230–9.

[42] *PROME*, iii, 426–32.

VI as king, while the removal of Suffolk in 1450 would allow a better minister or ministers to rule under Henry VI in the eyes of the MPs pushing for his impeachment. Equally, the aged and failing Edward III in 1376 was not the real target of action taken against Alice Perrers and the courtly regime.[43] Arguably the crisis of 1386–8, which saw a sustained and targeted attack on Richard II's favourites and advisors was another occasion when the favourites were genuinely as much the target as the king. Richard was, as a result of his own actions in precipitating military action, vulnerable to deposition in December 1387 and it was certainly discussed and probably temporarily enacted. However, his youth – he was still only twenty – and the fact that he could be expected to mature and improve as a king, as well as the vexed question of who could replace him, meant that the target of the opposition was genuinely also the men around him who were so objectionable to many amongst the political elites. The Appellants, of course, completed a clean sweep in the removal of Richard's intimates. In other words, care must be taken not to ignore the explicit statements of various opponents of particular regimes in regards to favourites, while also being open to other, implicit, motives.

Bringing down a monarchical favourite or favourites was a difficult task. The fact that such men clearly enjoyed royal approval and the king could be expected to support them meant that actions against royal favourites were often directly or indirectly actions against the king and were certainly interpreted as such by the kings themselves. While even violent action could be parsed by the perpetrators as for the good of the king and kingdom, yet it left them vulnerable in the longer term to reprisals. Perhaps the most extreme example was in 1455 when the duke of York and the earls of Warwick and Salisbury knelt before a bleeding Henry VI (wounded in the neck by a Yorkist arrow), having killed his favourite and chief minister, the duke of Somerset, two other peers and dozens of men in the royal entourage, and proclaimed their 'humble obedience' to him in the aftermath of the battle of first St Albans.[44] Although, in charge of the government, these lords were able to ensure they were pardoned in parliament later that year, what one parliament did, another could undo, and their actions at St Albans formed one major justification for their

---

[43] Ormrod, *Edward III*, 531–7, 552–62.

[44] *John Benet's Chronicle, 1399–1462: an English Translation with New Introduction*, ed. A Hanham (Basingstoke, 2015), 38; *The Paston Letters*, ed. J Gairdner (6 vols, London, 1904), iii, 28–9; C.A.J. Armstrong, 'Politics and the First Battle of St. Albans'. in idem, *England, France and Burgundy in the Fifteenth Century* (London, 1983), 63–5.

attainder at the Parliament of Devils in 1459.[45] Although Edward II pardoned those responsible for the death of Piers Gaveston in 1312, as late as 1320 at the siege of Berwick he was said to have muttered 'When this wretched business is over, we will turn our hands to other matters. For I have not yet forgotten the wrong that was once done to my brother Piers.'[46] This was the problem for opponents: unless the attack on royal favourites was also to lead to a change in monarch, the king and/or a royalist faction could be expected to seek revenge at a later date. Such royalist revanches occurred during the Barons War, as well as in 1322 and 1459, and most pertinently for this study in 1397. Then, Richard II, deciding his dish of revenge was cold enough, took action against the men he held most responsible for the downfall of Robert de Vere and his fellow Appellees, as well as his own humiliation, nine years earlier.

Nonetheless, opponents of royal favourites and the royalist regime sought what might be termed constitutional cover for their actions, often preceding violent action. In 1258, Simon de Montfort and his allies imposed a conciliar government of twenty-four magnates and ecclesiastics on Henry III; such government was, in part, to end the depredations of Henry's Lusignan relatives.[47] In 1308, opponents of Edward II and Gaveston introduced three articles against him in parliament, leading to the latter's exile. In 1310, more famous grievances, drawn up by the Lords Ordainers and totalling forty-one articles, were made against Edward II's regime in parliament, in order to reform the realm.[48] In 1327, the deposition of Edward II was effected while parliament was sitting, though a number of the key events took place outside it, including the rather confused procedure used to 'try' the younger Despenser for his crimes.[49] In 1450, the duke of Suffolk was even allowed the right of reply to the accusations of treason and corruption made against him, with his response and his protestation of loyalty being enrolled on the parliament roll.[50] As will be seen in 1386–7, Richard II was effectively deprived of access to the

---

[45] *PROME*, xii, 456–7; Griffiths, *Henry VI*, 746–8, 824; Watts, *Henry VI*, 315–21, 352–4; Hicks, *Wars of the Roses*, 112–14.

[46] *Vita Edward Secundi. The Life of Edward the Second*, ed. W.R Childs (Oxford, 2005), 176–9, and for other instances when the *Vita* states Edward swore or desired revenge, see 52–3, 130–1.

[47] S.T. Ambler, *The Song of Simon de Montfort* (London, 2019), ch. 8.

[48] *PROME*, iii, 12, 18–24; J.S. Hamilton, *Piers Gaveston, Earl of Cornwall, 1307–1312* (Detroit, MI, 1988), 48–51, 78–89.

[49] C. Valente, 'The Deposition and Abdication of Edward II', *EHR*, 113 (1998), 862–8; *PROME*, iv, 8; G.A. Holmes, 'Judgement against the Younger Despenser', *EHR*, 70 (1955), 261–7.

[50] *PROME*, xii, 92–3.

machinery of royal government, which was to be exercised by a commission for a year.[51] The extreme difficulty of stripping the king of power for any period beyond the short term, however, made most of these efforts failures, and in almost every case war or violence followed. Yet, as discussed, in a number of examples the king was not the ostensible target and Henry III, Edward II, Richard II and Henry VI were all left on the throne, if temporarily stripped of power, after military actions against their favourites and their regimes in 1264, 1311, 1387 and 1455 and it was thought necessary to condemn the favourites in the most complete and often extravagant terms. The only possible mechanism for opponents of the regime to justify their actions was through parliamentary acts, as parliament was the sole body with sufficient constitutional power to offer post-factum authorisation.[52] Another constitutional keystone, Magna Carta, was, as Nigel Saul has pointed out, little use as it had little to say on the king's prerogative to choose his own counsellors or dispense patronage.[53] When the king was not deposed, such justifications had to focus on the favourite(s) as the reason for the actions taken, and that his or their removal would lead to the restoration of good government, rather than on the failings of the king himself. On occasion, there were attempts at reform of the realm and limitation of the king's power in the longer term through council and parliament as well – notably with the Provisions of Oxford of 1258 and Richard of York's second protectorate in 1455.[54]

When monarchical or dynastic change was sought, in 1327, 1399 and 1461, detailed articles of deposition were drawn up, and favourites were highlighted and foregrounded within these.[55] It is perhaps noteworthy that of the six articles of deposition drawn up against Edward II in 1327, the first focussed on Edward's incapacity to govern and that he had allowed himself to be led and governed by 'other who give him evil counsel' to his dishonour, the destruction of the church and the destruction of the realm.[56] Likewise, the first article concerning the deposition of Richard II highlighted the king's evil

---

[51] *PROME*, vii, 46–7.

[52] For discussion, see Rogers, 'Parliamentary Appeals of Treason in the Reign of Richard II', 95–124.

[53] N. Saul, 'Magna Carta in the Late Middle Ages, c. 1320–c.1520', in L. Clark, ed., *The Fifteenth Century XIX: Enmity and Amity* (Woodbridge, 2022), 130.

[54] For discussion, see Ambler, *Song of Simon de Montfort*, ch. 9; Griffiths, *Henry VI*, 746–57; P.A. Johnson, *Duke Richard of York, 1411–1460* (Oxford, 1988), 169–73.

[55] *PROME*, viii, 11–25; xiii, 13–21, 42–6. Those of 1327 do not survive on the parliament roll: see Valente, 'Deposition and Abdication of Edward II'.

[56] Valente, 'Deposition and Abdication of Edward II', 880.

rule, 'namely... in giving his goods and possessions pertaining to the crown to unworthy persons' and described the king's accomplices acting with him.[57]

The distinction between what happened to favourites who were brought down and their kings who suffered the same political catastrophe has been elegantly explored by Klaus Oschema.[58] The contrast between the 'public' and 'cruel' ends of favourites – the grotesque end of Hugh Despenser the younger is the best known but Gaveston and Suffolk were publicly beheaded – and the 'clandestine' and to some extent mysterious deaths of Edward II, Richard II and Henry VI is a vivid one, even if care must be taken with the concepts involved in the use of public, private and cruelty in such discussions.

Who were the opponents to royal favourites? Historians have traditionally answered that it was the nobility. An example can be found in the view expressed by Natalie Fryde, discussing the reign of Edward II in particular, and late medieval society in general, who had this to say about the relationship between the nobles and royal favourites:

> The nobility mostly justified their opposition to royal government by claiming that they were attacking not the king's proper authority, but one perverted by the counsel of evil favourites. Favourites were in any case a considerable threat to the magnates' possibilities of bettering themselves, or even of surviving. Those magnates rich and important enough to frequent the court were always haunted by the fear that their power, based on a quasi-monopoly of royal favour and patronage, might be eroded by the arrival of newcomers or monopolised by one or two individuals.[59]

However, there are problems here. The first is that 'the nobility' will not do as a description of opponents of the court, particularly with the implication of perpetual or constant opposition – although just occasionally this reflects contemporary language.[60] Much more accurate on every occasion would be a 'group of nobles' or 'a faction amongst the nobility'. The nobility was not a monolithic group, permanently in opposition to royal power and government;

---

[57] *PROME*, viii, 15.
[58] Oschema, 'Cruel End of the Favourite', 171–95.
[59] N. Fryde, *The Tyranny and Fall of Edward II, 1321–6* (Cambridge, 1979), 13.
[60] Brinton's 1376 sermon has the nobles and prelates failing to receive an audience from the king, concluding that 'the noblemen of England cannot get their rights, though they ask for them with all their power': *Preaching in Age of Chaucer*, ed. Wenzel, 252–3.

this was one of K.B. McFarlane's most important insights.[61] At almost every point of political crisis, there were senior nobles amongst the favourites and the king's supporters. Other nobles, for a wide variety of reasons, steered clear of conflict. One of these reasons was undoubtedly that to act against a royal regime carried a significant risk of political disaster and indeed violent death – earls and barons died even in 1321–6 and 1455–60 when, arguably, the rebellions were about good government and royal favourites rather than the removal of the king. More died in 1327, 1399–1403, and during the Wars of the Roses when the deposition of a king and/or dynastic change was also on the agenda.

Fryde's emphasis on patronage as the primary motivator is also problematic. While of high political sensitivity, few magnates depended on patronage for their financial well-being and nor did most noble affinities require access to royal patronage for their continuing existence.[62] Instead, a mixture of motives influenced decisions to oppose courtly regimes. Unequal distribution of patronage was certainly part of the cocktail and could be guaranteed to cause resentment – and this is demonstrated in the criticism by commentators at the time – as the contemporary diagnosis was that royal patronage to those ill-deserving of it was wasted funds that should have been spent on the royal household or foreign warfare. However, also part of the mix was a desire for good governance when things were going badly, a factor that should not be underestimated, and anger or embarrassment at foreign policy reverses, often alongside noble frustration that their advice was being ignored. Harder to identify and measure is so-called 'aristocratic constitutionalism', though scholars have stressed the limited and flawed nature of any basis for opposition to the crown. For some individuals a familial memory of opposition to royal misgovernance (notably in the Lancastrian family) might also be present.[63] One

---

[61] McFarlane, *Nobility*, 2–3; idem, *England in the Fifteenth Century* (London, 1981), 232–3.

[62] For studies downplaying the importance of patronage as a motivating force in fifteenth-century political society and for historians' understanding of it, see C. Richmond, 'After McFarlane', *History*, 68 (1983), 46–60; E. Powell, 'After "After McFarlane": The Poverty of Patronage and the Case for Constitutional History', in D.J. Clayton, R.G. Davies and P. McNiven, eds, *Trade, Devotion and Governance: Papers in Later Medieval History* (Stroud, 1994), 1–16; C. Carpenter, 'Political and Constitutional History: Before and After McFarlane', in R.H. Britnell and A.J. Pollard, eds, *The McFarlane Legacy: Studies in Late Medieval Politics and Society* (Stroud, 1995), 175–206. For the application of the arguments of Powell and Carpenter to the late fourteenth century, see Gundy, *Richard II and the Rebel Earl*, 13–17.

[63] For theories of resistance against the king, primarily in stressing the primacy of law in the state above the king, and the role of the aristocracy in asserting this, see Rosenthal, 'Wicked Advisors', 604–9. See also Watts, *Henry VI*, 76–7.

should also not, in attributing idealistic motives to members of the nobility, underestimate less high-minded motives – ambition may have galvanised some while sheer personal dislike of favourites was quite clearly identified by contemporaries on occasions as a driving factor for others.

It was, of course, not just some groups amongst the nobility who acted against royal favourites, courtly regimes and the king. There has been important work in the last two decades on public opinion and popular politics, a lot focussing on the fifteenth century, but also on 1376 and 1381, where there is clear evidence of wider public opinion.[64] For obvious reasons much of this has focused on parliament, and parliament reflected, in large part, the views of the nobility, both secular and ecclesiastical, in the Lords, and the gentry who formed the majority of the MPs, and whose views as members of the same landowning elite as the nobility were usually not hugely different. In 1450 it was the Commons who led the attack on the duke of Suffolk and the impeachment of Michael de la Pole in 1386 was an alliance of a faction amongst the lords and the commons. However, there was clearly a wider body of public and popular opinion beyond parliament. The ordinary people must have formed opinions on political matters – they were taxpayers, soldiers, users of the legal system(s) and, as jurors, church wardens, bailiffs and other local

---

Given-Wilson, *Henry IV*, 22, suggests a Lancastrian identity amongst the family and its affinity (and in wider political consciousness), based on the widely circulated idea of Earl Thomas's 'martyrdom' at the hands of a despotic king in 1322.

[64] See in particular J.L. Watts, 'The Pressure of the Public on Later Medieval Politics', in L. Clark and C. Carpenter, eds, *The Fifteenth Century IV: Political Culture in Late Medieval Britain* (Woodbridge, 2004), 159–80; J.L. Watts, 'Public or Plebs: the Changing Meaning of "the Commons", 1381–1549' in H. Pryce and J.L. Watts, eds, *Power and Identity in the Middle Ages: Essays in Memory of Rees Davies* (Oxford, 2007), 242–60; V. Challet and I. Forrest, 'The Masses', in Fletcher, Genet and Watts, eds, *Government and Political Life*, 279–316; S.J. Walker, 'Rumour, Sedition and Popular Protest in the Reign of Henry IV', *Past & Present*, 166 (2000), 31–65; G.L. Harriss, 'The Dimensions of Politics', in Britnell and Pollard, eds, *The McFarlane Legacy*, 1–20; I.M.W. Harvey, 'Was there Popular Politics in Fifteenth-Century England?', in Britnell and Pollard, eds, *The McFarlane Legacy*, 155–74; A.J. Pollard, 'The People and Parliament in Fifteenth Century England', in H.W. Kleineke, ed., *The Fifteenth Century X: Parliament, Personalities and Power: Papers Presented to Linda S. Clark* (Woodbridge, 2011), 1–16; A.J. Pollard, 'The People, Politics and the Constitution in the Fifteenth Century', in R.W. Kaeuper, ed., *Law, Justice and Governance: New Views on Medieval Constitutionalism* (Leiden, 2013), 311–29; C.D. Liddy and J. Haemers, 'Popular Politics in the Late Medieval City: York and Bruges', *EHR*, 128 (2013), 771–805; S. Justice, *Writing and Rebellion. England in 1381* (Berkeley, CA, 1994); S.K. Cohn, Jr, *Popular Protest in Late Medieval English Towns* (Cambridge, 2013).

private and public officeholders, small cogs in the administrative machines that ran the localities – and they would have exchanged those opinions and acted upon them on occasion.[65] The frequency with which the topos of the 'evil councillors', greedy and traitorous, occurs throughout late medieval literature, manifestos and other popular sources is, as Watts has noted, a reminder of the diffusion of political ideas at all levels.[66] The Peasants' Revolt of 1381 was a very recent reminder to the political elites in the mid-1380s that popular opinion mattered.

When favourites were attacked, what were the usual accusations made? A recent comparative study of accusations against favourites in late medieval Europe came up with the following charge sheet: sodomy; unrestrained love of the favourite by the king; the exclusion of all others, both in terms of advice and counsel but also physical access to the king; receipt of excessive generosity by the favourite from the king; and difference in rank, which could be glossed as promotion in social rank, sometimes from a position of low birth.[67] In a solely English context, manipulation of the common law to the advantage of the favourite should be added. More seriously, albeit again in an English context, what the charge sheet noted above does not discuss is the way treason was included in accusations against royal favourites in parliamentary proceedings in 1308, 1311, 1327, 1388, and 1450.[68] These were the most serious and least believable of accusations, but crucially treason was the only crime for which the punishment was death. Sodomy was an accusation for the church courts, financial corruption could see dismissal from office or a fine but not execution, while social promotion, control of access and the paramountcy of a favourite's advice over others were politically objectionable but were not easily classed as criminal, despite the charges of accroaching royal power sometimes seen. Treason was a capital crime, and the death of the favourite was clearly the best result for the group in arms against the regime. This, of course, heightened the importance of defeat or stalemate in foreign war as this was a fruitful context to develop treasonable accusations. Yet, it could occur in other contexts too. Henry VII's ministers, Richard

---

[65] J.L. Watts, 'Popular Voices in England's Wars of the Roses, c. 1445–c. 1485', in J. Dumolyn et al., eds, *The Voices of the People in Late Medieval Europe: Communication and Popular Politics* (Turnhout, 2014), 107–22, esp. 108–9.

[66] Watts, 'Pressure of the Public', 168–9.

[67] H. Bagerius and C. Ekholst, 'Kings and favourites: Politics and Sexuality in Late Medieval Europe', *Journal of Medieval History*, 43 (2017), 298–319.

[68] *PROME*, iv, 11; xii, 94–105. Oddly, it was not done in 1455, where, although the blame for St Albans was placed upon the duke of Somerset and one or two others, they were not described as traitors on the parliament roll directly; ibid., xii, 338–44.

Empson and Edmund Dudley, were brought down just after his death for their leading and unpopular role in his harsh financial policies, but the way they were accused of, and tried for, treason, in Steve Gunn's words, 'strained both the contemporary construction of the statute of treason and the credulity of subsequent commentators'.[69] More generally, parliamentary impeachment – in 1386 and 1450 – and the bill of attainder were developed and used as tools to bring down favourites, though the latter was, of course, used as frequently against opponents of a regime by the king.

It is worth exploring the charge sheet of accusations made against favourites in late medieval Europe in a little more detail, focussing primarily on English examples, in order to explore the context in which the accusations against Robert de Vere were made. He was accused of every one of the crimes, misdemeanours and breaches of the political code just listed in the written sources of parliament and chronicles. The first two accusations – homosexuality and unrestrained (non-physical) love for the favourite by the king – can be linked as relating to the personal relationship between two men. Direct accusations or indirect insinuations of homosexuality were highly damaging within a society whose social, moral and religious code condemned it. Homosexuality generally and sodomy in particular were seen as a sin against nature and an inversion of the natural order.[70] In political terms such derogation was easy to make but difficult to disprove and thus such allegations had real utility to their users. It has been noted that while accusations of homosexuality were made against Richard II in Lancastrian propaganda and pro-Lancastrian chronicles after 1399 – most famously by Adam of Usk who refers to Richard's 'sodomies' – during Richard's reign itself, only a few hints were made.[71] Some commentators on Edward II's reign were less reticent, but again more accusations were made in its aftermath than during it. Care must of course be taken here, particularly with terminology. If Edward II had homosexual relationships with Gaveston and Despenser, then all three of these men were bisexual, as all of them were married and had children. It is not possible to say with certainty that there was a physical relationship between Edward II and his favourites, likely though that was, but

---

[69] S.J. Gunn, 'The Accession of Henry VIII', *Historical Research*, 64 (1991), 285.

[70] Bagerius and Ekholst, 'Kings and Favourites', 301–2.

[71] *The Chronicle of Adam of Usk, 1377–1421*, ed. C. Given-Wilson (Oxford, 1997), 63; S. Federico, 'Queer Times: Richard II in the Poems and Chronicles of Late Fourteenth-Century England', *Medium Aevum*, 79 (2010), 25–46, at 26.

there was undoubtedly an emotional one.[72] As Mark Ormrod has noted, the lack of certainty about Edward's private life does not matter; that his public reputation was stained with allegations or references to his sexuality did.[73] It is fair to say that Edward had a reputation for degeneracy and of conduct and habits unfitting for a king, of which allegations of sodomy formed an important plank; Richard II, however, did not, although his actual youth in the 1380s and his alleged youth in the 1390s may have adversely affected his reputation.[74]

One other angle was used on occasion by contemporary writers to explain the unnatural domination, as they saw it, of the king by a favourite and that was sorcery and black magic.[75] The *Vita Edward Secundi* states that Gaveston was regarded as a sorcerer because Edward forgot himself when he was with him.[76] Such an accusation of sorcery was made against Robert de Vere with Richard II as well, though more in passing than as a sustained case.[77] It was, however, an accusation that was aimed more often at women rather than men: Alice Perrers, Isabeau of Bavaria, queen of France, and Jacquetta of Luxembourg were victims of this slur as a way of explaining their dominance over the king, or in the latter case, his surprising decision to marry her daughter.[78] Thomas Walsingham called Perrers an 'evil enchantress' as part of his explanation for her relationship with the king, explaining that she employed a Dominican Friar to use magical devices to get whatever she wanted from the king.[79]

There was a side effect of such intense personal male–male relationships as well. When the king was under the domination of a favourite, sexual misconduct might arise in a different way. While Queen Isabella famously

---

[72] For discussion, see K. Warner, *Hugh Despenser the Younger and Edward II: Downfall of a King's Favourite* (Barnsley, 2018), 66–7.

[73] W.M. Ormrod, 'The Sexualities of Edward II', in Dodd and Musson, eds, *Reign of Edward II*, 22. For a different perspective, see I. Mortimer, 'Sermons of Sodomy: A Reconsideration of Edward II's Sodomitical Reputation', in Dodd and Musson, eds, *Reign of Edward II*, 48–60.

[74] For Edward's reputation, see Ormrod, 'Sexualities of Edward II', 28–35. For Richard's youth, see Fletcher, *Richard II*.

[75] For discussion, see Jones, 'Political Uses of Sorcery in Medieval Europe'.

[76] *Vita Edwardi Secundi*, ed. Childs, 29.

[77] See below, p. 78.

[78] For Jacquetta, see C.L. Scofield, *The Life and Reign of Edward IV* (2 vols, reissued Stroud, 2016), i, 498.

[79] *SAC*, i, 46–9, 56–7.

complained in October 1325 that 'someone has come between my husband and myself and is trying to break that bond [of matrimony]', referring to Despenser, she probably took Roger Mortimer as a lover in France around this time, if not earlier, to the scandal of her natal family.[80] Accusations were made in the late 1450s that the duke of Somerset was the father of Edward of Lancaster, the only child of Margaret of Anjou, rather than her husband, Henry VI.[81] Clearly, in contemporary eyes, the unmanly subordination of a king by his favourite might lead to the queen seeking a more manly paramour elsewhere. This was particularly damaging in Margaret's case as Prince Edward was the heir to the throne, with all the dynastic ramifications that potential illegitimacy might bring. Interestingly, no such accusation of infidelity was ever made against Anne of Bohemia, Richard II's queen from 1382 to 1394. Yet, favourites could be perceived as upsetting the balance of kingship and queenship, not least as the king's unmanliness led to accusations of the queen taking on roles not appropriate to contemporary gender norms.[82]

Whether or not there were sexual relationships between Edward II and his favourites, what is clear is that the king had lost appropriate restraint in his affection for them. Chroniclers noted that when Edward II returned from France with Isabella in February 1308, the great men of the realm gathered to meet them. The king, unable to restrain himself, ran to Piers, who was among them, 'giving him kisses and repeated embraces'.[83] As this scene demonstrates, the absence of dignity, the loss of personal control and the impropriety were all part of the problem with such relationships. The Anonimalle Chronicler said that 'the king loved [Hugh Despenser] dearly, with all his heart and mind, above all others', while another chronicler called them 'the king and his husband', which, while also invoking the idea of sodomy, captures perfectly the reversal of normal relations as contemporaries understood them.[84] Pierre Chaplais has suggested a different interpretation of the relationship between Edward II and Piers Gaveston, that of a formal compact of brotherhood, the language

---

[80] *Vita Edward Secundi*, ed. Childs, 242–3; Philips, *Edward II*, 484–5, 488–91; Ormrod, 'Sexualities of Edward II', 40–6.

[81] For a discussion of the rumours circulating from 1460 onwards regarding the parentage of Prince Edward, see Maurer, *Margaret of Anjou*, 176–8.

[82] See in particular for Margaret of Anjou, K.J. Lewis, *Kingship and Masculinity in Late Medieval England* (Abingdon, 2013), esp. ch. 12.

[83] *Chronica monasterii S. Albani: Johannis de Trokelowe et Henrici de Blaneforde*, ed. H.T. Riley (RS, 28, 1866), 65.

[84] *The Anonimalle Chronicle, 1307 to 1334*, eds W.R. Childs and J. Taylor (Leeds, 1991), 92–3; Phillips, *Edward II*, 98.

of which was used by the more reliable chronicles of the reign.[85] Nonetheless, even such an agreement of brotherhood, by raising a subject outside the blood royal to such a height, was unprecedented and deeply problematic for the polity. For the king 'to tie himself to him [Piers], against all mortals, in an unbreakable bond of affection' lost him the position of judge and arbiter above all others that he ought to have occupied as king.[86] Richard II, rather more conscious of his dignity except when moved to anger, was more restrained in public, but was clearly emotionally close to several of the men around him.[87] Of Edward, earl of Rutland and duke of Aumale, it was said that 'there was no man in the world whom Richard loved better', and one contemporary source said Richard even considered abdicating the throne in his favour, though this may be doubted.[88] All in all, in these types of accusations against favourites, there was a sense of the inversion of the right pattern, a subordination of the king to one or more of his subjects. Two chronicles described Gaveston as a king: the *Vita Edwardi Secundi* called him 'a second king' while the St Paul's Annalist said there were 'two kings reigning in one kingdom, one in name and the other in deed'.[89] A Latin song celebrating Gaveston's death stated that he had reigned much too long.[90] In 1464, one witty foreign observer, not quite grasping the strength of the young Edward IV and assuming the paramountcy of the powerful and famous Kingmaker, stated that in England 'they have but two rulers, M. de Warwick, and another, whose name I have forgotten'.[91]

It is worth noting also that sexual misbehaviour was attributed to favourites and courtiers far more generally in the later Middle Ages, in courts across Europe, and did not relate simply to the relationship between the favourite and the king. This was, of course, true for Robert de Vere regarding his divorce of his royal wife, Philippa de Coucy, in order to marry the queen's lady-in-waiting Agnes Lancecrone. However, there were other notable examples, including Joan of Kent's turbulent marital history, simultaneously married

---

[85] Chaplais, *Piers Gaveston*, 10–13.

[86] BL, MS Cotton Cleopatra D ix, fol. 86r, cited in Chaplais, *Piers Gaveston*, 12–13.

[87] C. Given-Wilson, 'The Earl of Arundel, the War with France and the Anger of King Richard II', in R.F. Yeager, T. Takamiya, and T. Jones, eds, *The Medieval Python: the Purposive and Provocative Work of Terry Jones* (Basingstoke, 2012), 27–38.

[88] 'A Metrical History of the Deposition of Richard II attributed to Jean Creton', ed. J. Webb, *Archaeologia*, 20 (London, 1814), 309.

[89] Cited in Philips, *Edward II*, 135–6.

[90] *The Political Songs of England from the Reign of John to that of Edward II*, ed. T. Wright (Camden Society, first series, 6, 1839), 259.

[91] Cited in Ross, *Edward IV*, 63n.

to William Montagu and Thomas Holland, or Jane Shore's possible liaisons with Thomas Grey, marquess of Dorset and William, Lord Hastings, as well as Edward IV, about which Richard III tried to make political and moral capital.[92] The issue moved beyond gossip and scandal as contemporaries linked moral misbehaviour and *luxuria* with political negligence, military failure and covetous appropriation of the king's resources, as Chris Fletcher has shown.[93]

Exclusion or attempted exclusion of all others from access to the king, or at least control over such access, was also a major factor; for the early modern period, where it has had considerable study, this has been described as the 'politics of access'.[94] Contemporaries were sensitive to the importance of access to the king: the Anonimalle Chronicle, for example, noted that during the regime of Queen Isabella and Roger Mortimer in 1329 the earl of Lancaster, 'who by common assent of the realm at the king's coronation was made his chief guardian, could not come near to him to advise or protect [the young Edward III]'.[95] Access as a source of tension, and thus a potential source of allegations against favourites, stemmed from two issues. One was the perceived right of the nobility to give counsel to the king and for the king to listen to it, and for the king to be accessible to listen to all types of complaints and administer justice. The second was that if a monopoly of advice and control over access was achieved, the favourite could enrich himself or herself by persuading the king to grant the most advantageous items available from the pool of patronage as well as selling access to the king or promising to bend the king's ear on behalf of another, for a price. In reality, care must be taken over too easy a link between access and power as a great deal depended on the personality of the monarch but again this was as much about external perception as the actuality of the relationship. Control over access to the king's person was immeasurably helped by occupation of the office of chamberlain, either that of the royal household – normally seen as the key position – or of the Great Chamberlainship of England, whose deputy the chamberlain of the household was. The Great Chamberlainship was hereditary in the de Vere

---

[92] R. Barber, 'Joan, suo jure countess of Kent, and princess of Wales and of Aquitaine [called the Fair Maid of Kent], c. 1328–1385', *ODNB*; R. Horrox, 'Shore [*née* Lambert], Elizabeth [Jane] (d. 1526/7?)', *ODNB*.

[93] Fletcher, 'Corruption at Court?', 28–38.

[94] The classic study in an English context is D. Starkey et al., *The English Court from the Wars of the Roses to the Civil War* (London, 1987). A recent edited collection shows the fruitful application of the concept across a wide range of early modern European courts: D. Raeymakers and S. Derks, eds, *The Key to Power? The Culture of Access in Princely Courts, 1400–1750* (Leiden, 2016).

[95] *Anonimalle Chronicle 1307–1334*, ed. Childs and Taylor, 141.

family, through a grant of unimpeachable antiquity by Henry I in c. 1115, albeit they lost the office between 1265 and c. 1345 after supporting the wrong side during the Barons War.[96] The chamberlainship of the household was a post in the king's gift, albeit parliament might, on occasion, seek to influence who was appointed.[97] The role of the chamberlain(s) was to control access to the king's chamber, and was therefore of significant political importance in England and in France. Malcom Vale has noted the growth of the importance of the royal chamber in England and France during the thirteenth and fourteenth centuries and particularly emphasised the key role of chamberlains in the reign of Charles VII of France: 'it was through them that that influence might be exerted and favours obtained'.[98] Almost contemporaneous with Robert de Vere and Simon Burley was the rise of the 'Marmousets' in France in 1388, a group of men of the king's chamber who, it was alleged, dominated patronage and government under the young Charles VI until their fall in 1392 after the king's protection for them was removed.[99] In England from the 1360s onwards, a small group of chamber knights became differentiated from a larger group of king's knights who were not, by and large, associated with the royal household or had duties there. By contrast the chamber knights served regularly in attendance on the king, probably on a rotational basis, and thus were much in the king's presence.[100]

Control over access to the king by a chamberlain had already become a sensitive issue by the time of the Good Parliament in 1376. Two of the key officers of the royal household, William, Lord Latimer, the chamberlain, and John, Lord Neville, the steward, were the primary targets of the righteous wrath of the Commons, both for peculation and for their influence over the king. In Latimer's case, a revealing anecdote shows the problems that might emerge with restriction of access to the king. When the earl of Pembroke, furious with Lord Grey of Ruthin, sought to gain access to the king at Marlborough in 1371,

---

[96] See *CP*, x, app. F, 54–63; *CPR, 1381–5*, 65.

[97] For discussion of the office, see Given-Wilson, *Royal Household*, 71–3.

[98] Vale, 'Courts', in Fletcher, Genet and Watts, eds, *Government and Political Life*, 25–6; idem, *The Princely Court. Medieval Courts and Culture in North-West Europe 1270–1380* (Oxford, 2001), 59–61; idem, *Charles VII* (London, 1974), 90 (quote).

[99] D. Potter, 'The King and his Government under the Valois, 1328–1498', in idem, ed., *France in the Later Middle Ages* (Oxford, 2002), 162–3.

[100] Given-Wilson, *Royal Household*, 207–11; M. Hefferan, 'Household Knights, Chamber Knights and King's Knights: the Development of the Royal Knight in Fourteenth-Century England', *Journal of Medieval History*, 45 (2019), 80–99. More generally, see M. Hefferan, *The Household Knights of Edward III: Warfare, Politics and Kingship in Fourteenth-Century England* (Woodbridge, 2021).

he was told that the king was ill and that he would have to present his case through Latimer as chamberlain. As Ormrod has remarked, while Latimer did have the authority to determine who could access the king's private apartments and speak with him, 'to refuse so distinguished a supplicant... was, however, an outrageous abuse of power and a major affront to the nobility's trust in the politics of access'.[101] Another example is equally revealing. The chamberlain who replaced Latimer between 1376 and 1377, Roger Beauchamp, refused to pass a bill for a pardon from Alice Perrers, the king's mistress, to the king.[102] For Beauchamp to refuse so influential a petitioner was brave, if futile, as Alice was able to gain access to the king by the next day. Perceptions of control of access by a chamberlain was not just an English problem, as the downfall of Enguerrand de Marigny, chief chamberlain of France, in 1315 shows, though here the chamberlain was the leading minister of Philip IV as well, and it was a reaction against policy as well as against the favourite that led to his downfall and hanging under Louis X.

How successful any one favourite could be in terms of controlling access has been questioned. Rosemary Horrox has argued that 'in reality no individual (however powerful) *could* literally control access', but that they might benefit financially from allowing access and might dominate the advice channels.[103] Yet the chamberlain(s) did play a major role in who was admitted to see the king and if they could not completely control access, they might partially do so; therein lay part of their power. To be close physically to the king was to have the potential of influence. English magnates also assumed a right to offer counsel to the king. If access was denied, restricted or minimised, then offence was given, as the case of the earl of Pembroke demonstrates.[104] This is what was alleged against favourites. The accusations against the Despensers in the parliament of 1321 stated that 'by their wicked greed, and by their usurpation of royal power, they did not allow our lord the king to hear, nor do right to, the great men of the land' nor could anyone approach the king nor speak with him until they had paid a fine to the Younger Hugh.[105]

Most of the notorious English favourites held either the chamberlainship of the household or the Great Chamberlainship. There is some disagreement as to whether Gaveston occupied the office of chamberlain: he is described as

---

[101] Ormrod, *Edward III*, 534; Given-Wilson, *Royal Household*, 71; R.I. Jack, 'Entail and Descent: the Hastings Inheritance 1370–1436', *BIHR*, 38 (1965), 6.

[102] *PROME*, vi, 27–30; Given-Wilson, *Royal Household*, 72–3.

[103] Horrox, 'Caterpillars of the Commonwealth', 9.

[104] Bagerius and Ekholt, 'Kings and Favourites', 308–11.

[105] *PROME*, iii, 429; Fryde, *Edward II*, 47.

such by the *Vita Edwardi Secundi*, but perhaps in a non-technical way, and the St Paul's Annalist. Both Pierre Chaplais and Seymour Philips have suggested that he was chamberlain, while T.F. Tout and Jeffrey Hamilton have argued that he was not, with the latter stating that Gaveston did control access to both the king and his patronage but 'that he neither required nor desired any official capacity to do so'.[106] The younger Despenser was, however, chamberlain of the household, and this was clearly of significance to his career – his appointment in 1318 marked the beginning of his close relationship with the king, and he clearly used and abused his position to enrich himself and enhance his power.[107] William de la Pole, duke of Suffolk, acquired the office of great chamberlain of England as soon as it became available after the death of Humphrey, duke of Gloucester, in 1447, seeing it as preferable to steward of the household, which office he resigned just a few weeks beforehand (though keeping his role as steward of England) and presumably in the full foreknowledge of Gloucester's forthcoming downfall. It would be hard not to see this as an attempt to complete his control over the royal household by allowing him to appoint a trusted ally to replace him as steward to control the day-to-day running of the lower household while taking overall responsibility for the king's chamber in its upper echelons.[108]

Enrichment of the favourite was certainly a major issue and had a number of strands, including financial, social – in terms of promotion in rank – and in manipulation of the law for their own ends. Excessive social promotion was linked to the idea of the illegitimacy of the king being surrounded by low born men, who were not the king's natural counsellors and might be expected to enrich themselves rather than having been born to wealth. While this idea perhaps reached its highest currency in the second half of the fifteenth century, the idea of 'men raised from dust' had a long history, and the social construction of courtier identity has been contrasted with that of the natural or hereditary aristocratic one.[109] Piers Gaveston, the son of a Gascon knight, became earl of Cornwall – the first promotion to an earldom of a man outside

---

[106] J.S. Hamilton, 'Tout and the Royal Favourites of Edward II', in C.M. Barron and J.T. Rosenthal, eds, *Thomas Frederick Tout (1855–1929): Refashioning History for the Twentieth Century* (London, 2019), 127–8. For the view that he was, see Chaplais, *Piers Gaveston*, 101–4; Philips, *Edward II*, 137–8.

[107] For discussion, see Warner, *Hugh Despenser*, 60–2.

[108] J.L. Watts, 'Pole, William de la, first duke of Suffolk (1396–1450)', *ODNB*.

[109] For discussion, see S.L. Peverley, 'Political Consciousness and the Literary Mind in Late Medieval England: Men "Brought up of Nought" in Vale, Hardyng, Mankind and Malory', *Studies in Philology*, 105 (2008), 1–29; Patterson, 'Court Politics and the Invention of Literature', 20–1.

the royal family for almost a century, as well as to a title closely associated with the royal family. While Hugh Despenser the Younger did not receive an earldom, he seems to have been working on acquiring the title (and estates) of the earldom of Gloucester as one of the co-heirs in right of his wife; he would also, in the normal course of events, have inherited the title of earl of Winchester, to which rank his father had been raised in 1322.[110] Richard II's promotions of four men to the rank of duke in 1397 earned them the derisive nickname of 'duketti'[111] while William de la Pole, already earl of Suffolk, became a marquess in 1444 and then a duke in 1448.

Manipulation of the machinery of the law through influence over the king occurs in complaints against English favourites. The Despensers' control over the machinery of the law, exploited for their own ends, has been explored by a number of authors, including Richard Kaeuper, who argues that 'The two Despensers were probably the masters in malicious prosecution through Oyer and Terminer'; this was also one of the charges against them in 1321.[112] Fryde has said of the Younger Despenser that 'no other favourite in English history was ever able to take such liberties with the properties of the king's subjects and with the law of the realm.'[113] It was said of Alice Perrers in 1374 that 'she had such power and eminence in those days that no-one dared to prosecute a claim against her'.[114] The parliamentary indictment of Suffolk in 1450 claimed that 'they who would not be of his affinity in their areas were oppressed, every mater true or false that he favoured was furthered and expedited, and true maters of such persons as had not his favour were hindered and delayed'.[115] Specific allegations of fraudulent pardons acquired by Suffolk followed the generalised accusation, focussing on William Tailboys, esquire, a fellow member of the royal household but a notoriously violent criminal.[116]

---

[110] M. Lawrence, 'Edward II and the Earldom of Winchester', *Historical Research*, 81 (2008), 732–40.

[111] Thomas Walsingham, 'Annales Ricardi Secundi et Henrici Quarti', in *Chronica monasterii S. Albani: Johannis de Trokelowe et Henrici de Blaneforde*, ed. Riley, 223.

[112] R.W. Kaeuper, 'Law and Order in Fourteenth-Century England: the Evidence of Special Commissions of Oyer and Terminer', *Speculum*, 54 (1979), 778; N. Saul, 'The Despensers and the Downfall of Edward II', *EHR*, 99 (1984), 1–33, esp. 22–6.

[113] Fryde, *Edward II*, 106–7.

[114] *Gesta abbatum monasterii Sancti Albani, a Thoma Walsingham*, ed. H.T. Riley (3 vols, RS, 28:4, 1867–9), iii, 228.

[115] *PROME*, xii, 103.

[116] *PROME*, xii, 103; R. Virgoe, 'Tailboys, Sir William', *ODNB*.

The Paston experience of Suffolk and his affinity in their locality in Norfolk would bear out the broader allegation, though how typical they were and how common their experience was is a matter of some debate. Yet it is, of course, strictly contemporary evidence of a view of Suffolk when Margaret Paston wrote to her husband in 1448 saying 'there shall no man be so hardy to do nor say against my Lord of Suffolk nor none that belong to him; and all that have done and said against him, they will sore repent them'.[117]

The excessive distribution of royal patronage to the accused was the most frequent and in some ways the most bitter complaint against royal favourites. There may well have been truth in many of these allegations: Gaveston was granted land worth 6,000 marks a year on one day in 1308, and between them the Despensers had lands worth over £10,000 per annum in 1326, and goods and cash totalling nearly £12,000, though some of this was acquired through their own actions rather than directly through royal patronage.[118] Alice Perrers had lands in twenty-eight counties and London by the time of her fall, and while the accusation that she had passed jewels worth £20,000 to her ally William Windsor is highly likely to be an exaggeration, jewels worth £3,000 were recovered from her after her arrest.[119] Again, not all of this was direct royal patronage and her own actions as a businesswoman expanded her landed portfolio.[120] Alongside the four articles brought against Michael de la Pole in 1386 that touched on his negligence in his office as chancellor, he was accused and found guilty of three charges of peculation, including regarding his excessive endowment with land when he was promoted to earl of Suffolk.[121] His grandson, the duke of Suffolk, was accused of enriching himself and his friends at the crown's expense to the tune of £60,000 by 1450, alongside acquiring the earldom of Pembroke, the reversion of the lordship of Haverfordwest and the valuable wardship of Margaret Beaufort.[122]

---

[117] *Paston Letters and Papers*, ed. Davis, i, 222. Author's modernisation of Middle English.

[118] Warner, *Hugh Despenser*, 104–5; Philips, *Edward II*, 417–18; Fryde, *Edward II*, 107–8.

[119] Given-Wilson, 'Alice Perrers', ODNB.

[120] L. Tompkins, '"Edward III's Gold-Digging Mistress": Alice Perrers, Gender and Financial Power at the English Royal Court, 1360–1377', in C. Sarti, ed., *Women and Economic Power in Premodern Royal Courts* (Pittsburgh, PA, 2020), 59–71; J. Bothwell, 'The Management of Position: Alice Perrers, Edward III and the Creation of a Landed Estate, 1362–1377', *Journal of Medieval History*, 24 (1998), 31–51.

[121] Roskell, *Impeachment of Michael de la Pole*, 111–84, for the charges of peculation.

[122] *PROME*, xii, 99–102. A second set of allegations set out a schedule of the grants made to him (ibid., 107–8).

All men who had access to the king's ear could be accused of such crimes or just of having undue influence with the king. Even the royal confessor was not exempt, as Chris Given-Wilson has shown. Richard's first confessor, Thomas Rushook, was unpopular from as early as 1381 when parliament asked for his removal, although characteristically Richard maintained him in his role despite criticism and raised him to the episcopate.[123] Rushook was finally brought down in the parliament of 1388. More direct action was taken against Bishop Aiscough of Salisbury, Henry VI's confessor, when he was killed by a mob in 1450. Amongst the accusations levelled at Aiscough were that he, along with Suffolk and others, 'forbade all access whatever to all such as attempted to gain the king's favour or to appear in his presence without their own connivance' as well as being 'inflamed with the inextinguishable ardour of cupidity'.[124] Both Aiscough's successor as confessor, Bishop John Stanbury of Bangor and the queen's confessor, Bishop Walter Lyhert of Norwich, also attracted popular criticism the same year.[125]

Such enrichment was seen to be part of the depletion of the financial resources of the crown, to the detriment of the political community more generally, and the inability of the king to fulfil his perpetual commitments of enforcing justice and the defence of the realm. They tended to lead, in the eyes of many of the political community, to an excessive reliance on taxation for the ordinary expenses of the crown. This, of course, ties in with the lack of success in foreign warfare; if there was insufficient money to prosecute war successfully, the more popular constituency in politics, represented by the House of Commons, tended to blame the royal household and the favourites around the king of enriching themselves rather than the instinctive reluctance of the Commons to grant taxation. John Watts has noted how all but three accusations against William, duke of Suffolk, in 1450 were explicitly fiscal in nature, and that his 'covetise' was seen as being his primary motive for the treasons he was accused of.[126] Part of the problem was also that the crown

---

[123] C. Given-Wilson, 'The King's Confessors and the Royal Conscience', in J. Bothwell and J.S. Hamilton, eds, *Fourteenth Century England XII* (Woodbridge, 2022), 1–28, esp. 12–13.

[124] *Ingulph's Chronicle of the Abbey of Croyland with the Continuations by Peter of Blois and Anonymous Writers*, ed. H.T. Riley (RS, 1854), 410. For a recent, sympathetic, assessment of his career, see S. Lane, 'The Political Career of William Ayscough, Bishop of Salisbury, 1438–50', in L. Clark, ed., *The Fifteenth Century XVI: Examining Identity* (Woodbridge, 2018), 63–82.

[125] Lane, 'Political Career of William Ayscough', 80.

[126] Watts, *Henry VI and the Politics of Kingship*, 248–9, esp. n. 195, and on 'covetise' in the political thought of late medieval England, 40–2.

domain had long been seen as inalienable, being often described as 'the ancient demesne of the crown'.[127] This latter would cover overseas dominions of the crown, as will be seen in the grant of Ireland to Robert de Vere, while the grant of the earldom of Cornwall to Piers Gaveston in 1307 was criticised by several chronicles on those grounds, not least as it had been apparently intended for Edward I's second son by Margaret of France, Edmund.[128] Any alienation of such estates or regions was thus objectionable on customary and legal grounds as well as for fiscal reasons.

Finally, treason was the ultimate accusation against royal favourites. Almost all the men discussed were seen and described as traitors by their political opponents. Gaveston was a 'robber of the people and a traitor to his liege lord and his realm' in 1308 and 'an evident enemy of the king and his people' in 1311.[129] The elder Despenser at his 'trial' in 1326 was accused of treacherously advising the king to act against the prelates of the church and of accroaching royal power through putting Thomas of Lancaster to death.[130] His son was accused of a broader set of treasons, including the death of Thomas of Lancaster, of accroaching royal power and inducing the king to fight in Scotland with the loss of twenty thousand men, of usurping royal power by imprisoning men who were not prepared to swear oaths to support him, and on other counts.[131] The allegations against the duke of Suffolk in 1450 are the most detailed as far as treason is concerned and focus on treason in the purest sense – that of betraying the country and seeking to depose the king – rather than accroaching royal power or alienating the king from his subjects. Specific allegations were made against Suffolk: of plotting with French hostages for the French to invade the realm to depose the king and to place Suffolk's son, who was to be married to Margaret Beaufort, on the throne; of promising to deliver Maine and Anjou to the French, 'the greatest cause of the loss of your said duchy of Normandy'; and the disclosing of the

---

[127] G.L. Harriss, *King, Parliament and Public Finance in Medieval England to 1369* (Oxford, 1975), ch. 6.

[128] For discussion, see L. Benz, 'Conspiracy and Alienation: Queen Margaret of France and Piers Gaveston, the King's Favorite', in Z.E. Rohr and L. Benz, eds, *Queenship, Gender, and Reputation in the Medieval and Early Modern West, 1060–1600* (Cham, 2016), 122–3.

[129] *PROME*, iii, 7, 23.

[130] Philip, *Edward II*, 513.

[131] The original text is in Holmes, 'Judgement against the Younger Despenser', 264–7, which is summarised in Philips, *Edward II*, 517.

king's counsel and the defensive arrangements of Normandy to the French.[132] To modern eyes, the treasonable allegations look ridiculous, and perhaps to many contemporaries they were as well. A second set of allegations submitted a few days later gave an implicit motive as well, perhaps to make them more believable. Suffolk had been captured by the French in 1429 and a high ransom set for his release; the accusations said it was never paid, and it was implied he worked off the debt through treason. Certainly, he seems to have made a compromising arrangement to try to release the duke of Orléans, a long-term prisoner in England.[133] However, it is also worth remembering that far more than in 1308–12, 1321–6 or 1387–8, when sterile campaigns and minor reverses marked an ebb tide of war, in 1450 England was in the midst of a catastrophic military defeat. Most of Normandy, conquered by the popularly revered Henry V, had been lost quickly and in a string of humiliating capitulations rather than a brave battlefield defeat. Perhaps, in the atmosphere of shock and anger, and the need to find alternative explanations to the unpalatable idea of French military superiority, more Englishmen believed the treasonable accusations than might have done at other times. Certainly, those who wrote such claims of treason, alongside more plausible accusations of corruption and incompetence, must have thought there was an audience that would believe them or at least not dismiss them outright. Accusations of treason against the realm were, as Bellamy puts it, 'never the sole basis of an accusation of treason' and were used 'to aggravate charges of treason which were acceptable at common law'.[134] They were thus propaganda and a political appeal rather than a legal ploy; the reception, and the extent to which they were believable, was therefore thoroughly variable.

How do all of these allegations against favourites and councillors relate to Robert de Vere? The issue of the unnatural domination of a king by a royal favourite or favourites was one that cannot have been far from the minds of the political elite in the early 1380s. Political crises in 1307–12, 1321–7 and most recently in 1376–7 had all, in part, been a result of notorious favourites and perceived corruption around the king by a court clique. While the first two were not within living recall, they were recent enough to be within easy familial memory; the grandfathers of two of the Appellants, Warwick and Arundel, were prominent in the opposition to Gaveston, for example. They

---

[132] *PROME*, xii, 95–8 (quote 96).
[133] *PROME*, xii, 154; Watts, 'Pole, William de la', *ODNB*.
[134] Bellamy, *Law of Treason*, 209.

were all also certainly resonant within political culture. The youth of Richard II – aged ten at his accession in 1377 – added a further volatile element to politics. Royal minorities were always periods when the custody, upbringing and friendships of the young king were under particular scrutiny and the fiction of majority rule exercised by a genuine minor from 1377 to (arguably) 1389 made the situation even more difficult.[135] When the extremely difficult circumstances for the English political community in the 1380s are factored in – recently unsuccessful but ongoing war against France, a Scottish threat and limited taxation in the aftermath of the 1381 revolt to deal with these threats – it is unsurprising there was heightened tension around the conduct of government and who influenced the king. To be high in royal favour in late fourteenth-century England was to be on dangerous ground.

Allegations against de Vere by 1388 ticked every one of the boxes discussed in this chapter. His indictment, along with others of the court circle by the Appellants in the Merciless Parliament of 1388, went into considerable detail over his control over the king, exploitation of the king's generosity and his personal enrichment at the expense of the common weal, accroachment of royal power, and treason concerning the campaign of Radcot Bridge in 1387. De Vere was twice promoted to marquess of Dublin and then duke of Ireland, to the apparent chagrin of others amongst the nobility. Modern scholarship, however, has begun to look beyond the contemporary indictments of some of the more notorious of the royal favourites, and assess just how accurate these were. Pierre Chaplais and J.S. Hamilton, both writing on Gaveston in the 1980s, came to more sympathetic conclusions than previous works and John Watts and Helen Castor have begun to rehabilitate William, duke of Suffolk, both as a local lord and as a national statesman.[136] One of the themes of the rest of this study is the extent to which de Vere fits the pattern of royal favourite and it will assess how accurate the contemporary damnation of de Vere was.

---

[135] C. Beem, 'Woe to Thee, O Land! The Introduction', in idem, ed., *The Royal Minorities of Medieval and Early Modern England* (Basingstoke, 2008), 1–16; G. Dodd, 'Richard II and the Fiction of Majority Rule', in Beem, ed., *Royal Minorities*, 103–59.

[136] Chaplais, *Piers Gaveston*; Hamilton, *Piers Gaveston*. Philips's biography of Edward II is balanced and nuanced on Gaveston and Edward: *Edward II*, ch. 4. For Watts and Castor, see above, p. 16, n. 10.

2

Family Background and Early Career

> *Inspeximus* and confirmation, in favour of Robert son and heir of Thomas de Veer, late earl of Oxford, of a charter of Henry [I, *circa* 1115]… granting to Aubrey de Ver and his heirs the chief chamberlainship of England.
>
> (Signet letter of Richard II on 10 January 1382 confirming Robert de Vere in the office of great chamberlain of England.[1])

Minority

The de Veres were the oldest of the comital families by the later fourteenth century, having been based in Essex since 1066 and raised to the rank of earl in 1141, in return for their support for Empress Maud during the civil war. While the family held nineteen manors in East Anglia at Domesday, they struggled to expand their estates significantly over the next two centuries, and it is fair to say that they were neither politically prominent nor particularly wealthy until the fourteenth century. However, John, seventh earl of Oxford, had raised the prestige of his family, by his personal participation in an exceptional number of campaigns, including in Scotland in 1335 and 1343, on the sea in 1339, in Flanders in 1340, in Brittany in 1342 and 1345, at the battle of Crécy and the siege of Calais in 1346–7, at the battle of Poitiers and in Gascony in 1355–7, and at the siege of Rheims in January 1360 where he died.[2] By John's marriage to Maud, sister and co-heir of Giles, Lord Badlesmere, he also significantly increased his landed estates. He was succeeded by Thomas, his eldest surviving son, who had been granted a £40 annuity by Edward III in August 1357 during the lifetime of his father, and who had also fought in France in 1360.[3] Earl Thomas was in France again in September 1369 with a personal retinue of forty men-at-arms and eighty archers, he and the third

---

[1] *CPR, 1381–5*, 65.

[2] *CP*, x, 222–3. His skilful handling of the archers at Poitiers was noted in *Chronicon Galfridi le Baker de Swynebroke*, ed. E.M. Thompson (Oxford, 1881), 143, 148, and see 76 for the Brittany campaign of 1345, 79 for the Crécy campaign, and 124, 127 for his presence in Aquitaine in 1356.

[3] *CPR, 1354–8*, 602; *1358–61*, 435.

earl of March having been sent to reinforce operations 'with a great many ships and a large force of men'.[4]

Despite these distinguished military records, Froissart places a story in the mouth of Thomas, duke of Gloucester, in 1386 about Poitiers three decades earlier, recounting how the earl of Oxford left the Black Prince before the battle, returned to England, and was sent back by the angry king to his son and only then fought at the battle. Aside from the problem of the timing, it is only intended to discredit the duke of Ireland, in connection with whom this story is told. In addition to which he gives the wrong name of the earl (Aubrey) and the wrong relation to Robert de Vere (father, rather than grandfather – Thomas was not present at Poitiers). It may be a malicious or inaccurate reference to an episode during the siege of Calais in 1347 when Oxford and the earl of Pembroke, who had returned to England to purchase horses on the king's orders, were hurriedly recalled when the army was threatened with attack.[5] It does, however, demonstrate the way any tool was used to discredit Robert de Vere after his fall, including besmirching his grandfather's exemplary record of martial service.

Despite, or perhaps because of, his service in France in 1369, by the following year Earl Thomas was in poor health: writs of *diem clausit extremum* ordering an inquisition *post mortem* were erroneously issued in July 1370.[6] It only proved a year premature. Thomas died between 12 and 18 September 1371.[7] His will, dated 1 August 1371 at Great Bentley in Essex, named Simon Sudbury, bishop of London, Maud his wife, Sir William Wingfield, Sir John de Pelham, Sir John de Horsham and John Hawkwood as his executors.[8] Most of his goods

---

[4] *Anonimalle Chronicle*, ed. Galbraith, 61; J. Sherborne, 'Indentured Retinues and English Expeditions to France, 1369–1380', *EHR*, 79 (1964), 722. For his career, see J. Ross, 'Vere, Thomas de, eighth earl of Oxford (1336x8–1371), magnate and soldier', *ODNB*.

[5] Froissart, ed. Lettenhove, xii, 237–8. For the return to England and their recall, see *CP*, x, 223 note g and the sources cited there.

[6] *CFR, 1368–77*, 112.

[7] *CIPM*, xiii, 92–103. Three inquisitions give 12 September, seven 18 September (including the Essex inquisition, taken at Castle Hedingham, which was most likely to be correct) and one 20 September, which is unlikely as writs of *diem clausit extremum* were issued on that latter day and it would be expected that it would take a day or two for information from northern Essex to reach Westminster: *CFR, 1368–77*, 153.

[8] *Registrum Simonis de Sudbiria*, ed. R.C. Fowler and C. Jenkins (2 vols, Canterbury and York Society, 34, 38, 1927, 1938), i, 4–6. Pelham, Horsham and Hawkwood all received bequests of 20 marks in the will. Wingfield, already in possession for life of the de Vere manors of Market Overton, Langley and Bradley, and Milton and Paston, received a bequest of two young horses. Hawkwood – perhaps originally the earl's feudal tenant at Sible Hedingham – was probably on the 1359–60 campaign with Earl John and Thomas. He was in Italy in 1371 and remained there until his

were to go to his only surviving child, Robert de Vere, though gifts of armour were made to Thomas's brother, Aubrey, and to his most prominent gentry associate and executor, Sir William Wingfield.

Earl Thomas had married Maud, daughter of Ralph de Ufford, chief justice of Ireland and brother to Robert de Ufford, earl of Suffolk. She brought the manor of Wrabness in Essex to the family but conveyed no other landed estates to the de Veres. Maud was to have a long and turbulent widowhood, but little survives to say much about her married life, other than she was probably around seventeen when she gave birth to their son and heir.[9] Robert de Vere was born on 16 January 1362, the feast of St Marcellus the Pope, at the priory of Earls Colne in Essex; given the de Vere family had a residence adjacent to the priory, the location might perhaps hint at a difficult birth and the need for monkish prayers or the infirmary there.[10] He was baptised in the parish church of Earls Colne with Sudbury, his maternal great-uncle Robert Ufford, earl of Suffolk, and Alice, widow of Sir Andrew de Bures, lifting him from the font, and acting as godparents. His birth was recorded in a missal in the priory, which was apparently inspected by two witnesses in 1383 for proof as to his being of age. De Vere was an only child, as far as the sources show.

Robert de Vere was nine when his father died. Arrangements for his minority were quickly made. While no formal guardian or ward was appointed, most of his estates were placed in the hands of two Essex landowners, Sir Thomas Tyrell and John James, for a very favourable annual rent of £300.[11] In addition to settling his lands, attention was given to his marriage, and only a month after his father's death, on 16 October 1371, it was granted to Ingelram de Coucy, earl of Bedford, and Isabella his wife, daughter of Edward III, 'in order [for] the contracting of matrimony between the said Robert and Philippa, daughter of the earl and Isabel[la]'.[12] Tyrell was the steward of Isabella's lands, while James

---

death but always seemed keen on a return to England, and other Essex men named him in business capacities, including Sir William Coggeshall in 1384: K. Fowler, 'Hawkwood, Sir John (d. 1394)', *ODNB*; *CPR, 1381–5*, 433.

[9] For her life, see J. Ross, 'Vere, Maud de, [née Maud Ufford], countess of Oxford (1345?–1413)', *ODNB*. For the most dramatic event of her widowhood, idem, 'Seditious Activities: the Conspiracy of Maud de Vere, countess of Oxford, 1403–4', in L. Clark, ed., *The Fifteenth Century III: Authority and Subversion* (Woodbridge, 2003), 25–42.

[10] This and the following two sentences are based on the details in de Vere's damaged proof of age twenty-one years later in 1383; they may therefore be inaccurate in detail or erroneous in part: *CIPM*, xv, no. 889.

[11] *CPR, 1370–4*, 133; *CFR, 1368–77*, 151–2. Occasional other grants were made in relation to his estates during his minority: *CFR, 1369–77*, 162, 209, 216.

[12] *CPR, 1370–4*, 137.

had been the receiver-general of the earl of Bedford (and may have continued in that office for Isabella), so the grant of his marriage confirmed the couple's control of all aspects of de Vere's life.[13] Philippa de Coucy had been born in 1367 and was five years younger than her husband. However, the marriage had taken place by October 1376, probably occurring in the summer of that year, though at just nine years old Philippa was well under the canonical age of marriage.[14]

This was a prestigious marriage for de Vere. He did have some royal blood – his maternal grandmother was the daughter of Henry, earl of Lancaster (d. 1345), grandson of Henry III – but the marriage held out the prospect of their children having much closer familial links to the royal family and a connection to a powerful French family too.[15] There was also the possibility of the inheritance of significant landed estates. The situation was complicated, however. De Coucy had originally come to England as one of the hostages for the payment of the ransom of King John of France under the terms of the treaty of Bretigny in 1360. De Coucy was, according to Froissart, 'in great favour with both French and English', so much so that he married Edward's oldest daughter, Isabella, in 1365 and the following year was created earl of Bedford.[16] Prior to the marriage Edward had granted him lands in four northern English counties to which he had a claim through his grandmother, Catherine de Balliol.[17] However, with the resumption of the Anglo-French war in 1369, he found himself awkwardly placed between his English and French allegiances. Manoeuvring with some skill, he avoided open partisanship with either side until Edward III's death in 1377, when he renounced his English allegiance and served the king of France against the English on several occasions during the 1380s.[18] Isabella did not follow her husband's lead, unsurprisingly for the daughter of King Edward. Husband and wife endured long periods of separation even in the early 1370s, and after 1377 Isabella and Philippa remained in England, while Ingelram and the couple's eldest daughter Mary stayed in France. The intention to split Ingelram's English and French lands between his daughters seems clear even at this stage.[19]

---

[13] For James, see *A Catalogue of the Manuscripts Preserved in the Library of the University of Cambridge*, vol. I (Cambridge, 1855), p. 140, no. 384.

[14] *CPR, 1374–77*, 368; Ormrod, *Edward III*, 562, suggests a possible date of July or August 1376 while Edward was on a modest progress around Kent and Essex.

[15] *CP*, x, 226.

[16] Froissart, ed. Lettenhove, vi, 392.

[17] *CPR, 1361–4*, 427.

[18] For more on his career, see M.H. Keen, 'Coucy, Enguerrand [Ingelram] de, earl of Bedford (c. 1340–1397)', *ODNB*.

[19] It was formally confirmed by the king in 1401: *CPR, 1399–1401*, 528.

Isabella was a prominent figure at court during the 1370s and financially comfortable. Seven men were appointed to receive and pay her the profits from her husband's estates in England for her use in 1377, and she had a substantial landed estate in her own right granted to her by her father during the 1350s and 1360s, in addition to an annuity of 200 marks yearly at the exchequer and a London town house.[20] Although the grant of de Vere's marriage does not explicitly state that Isabella was to have custody of him after the marriage, it is highly likely that this was the case, and certainly an annuity was granted to Isabella from de Vere's estates for Philippa's upkeep, which is also suggestive.[21] It is therefore likely that he grew up in Isabella's household and so in close proximity to the court. The counter-evidence, perhaps suggesting he remained a royal ward, is the fact de Vere was granted robes and items of clothing in November 1375, Easter 1378 and for the hunting season in April 1379 at the king's gift. However, the fact that Henry Bolingbroke, categorically not in wardship at this time, also had robes on one of these occasions, as did Isabella herself and her daughter Philippa, rather suggests a genuine gift and early favour rather than indicating de Vere's formal residence in the royal household.[22] Isabella died in 1382, robbing de Vere of an influential patroness; other possible patrons and allies also disappeared around this time with the extinction of the male line of his maternal relatives, the Ufford earls of Suffolk, in 1382 and the death of his godfather and executor of his father's will, Simon Sudbury, promoted to archbishop of Canterbury in 1375, but murdered by the rebels in 1381.[23] There seems to have been no formal grant of his wardship after Isabella's death in 1382 – not least because, as discussed below, there was no financial profit to be had from it – but he was also only a few months from being formally of age.

De Vere was financially comfortable during his minority. On 14 September 1376, he was granted £100 of the £300 fee farm from his lands for his maintenance,

---

[20] *CPR, 1377–81*, 174–5; B. Wolffe, *The Royal Demesne in English History. The Crown Estate in the Governance of the Realm from the Conquest to 1509* (London, 1971), 243–4; Ormrod, *Edward III*, 317–8.

[21] C66/285, m. 23, confirmed in Edward III's will of 1376: *The Register of Simon Sudbury, Archbishop of Canterbury, 1375–1381*, ed. F.D. Logan (Canterbury and York Society, 110, 2020), 167.

[22] E101/397/20, m. 4 (grant of a 'paltock', a sleeved doublet); E101/400/4, mm. 4, 17; S.M. Mitchell, 'Some Aspects of the Knightly Household of Richard II' (unpublished PhD, University of London, 1998), 229, 300; Given-Wilson, *Henry IV*, 26.

[23] J. Lutkin, 'Isabella de Coucy, Daughter of Edward III: the Exception Who Proves the Rule', in C. Given-Wilson, ed., *Fourteenth Century England VI* (Woodbridge, 2010), 131–48, has redated her death to 1382 (132–3) and notes her influence at court (145–7). See also J.L. Gillespie, 'Isabella, countess of Bedford (1332–1379)', *ODNB*; M.A.E. Green, *Lives of the Princesses of England* (6 vols, London, 1849–55), iii, 163.

and the remaining £200 was granted to his mother-in-law, Isabella, countess of Bedford, for the sustenance of Philippa, de Vere's wife. This last was surrendered on 30 June 1378, when £100 of the fee-farm was granted to William, bishop of London, and Roger de Beauchamp for the use of Philippa.[24] De Vere's own allowance was increased to £200 on 5 February 1380, in consideration of the fact that he was approaching full age, and needed to spend more for his maintenance and estate.[25] Five months later, on 4 July he petitioned the king to discharge the farmers as 'their farm is wholly assigned to him and his wife'. This was duly done, perhaps as he was earning royal and conciliar goodwill by undertaking his first military expedition to France that month under the command of Thomas of Woodstock. Although he was not given formal seisin of his lands until 5 March 1383, the fact that the farmers were discharged in 1380 suggests he may have had effective control over his estates from the latter date.[26] If so, it was either an early mark of favour, or perhaps due to the influence of his uncle Aubrey, who was prominent in the royal household at this time.[27] A further grant was made to him on 26 May 1382 of the knights' fees and advowsons belonging to his lands, which would further suggest practical control over his ancestral lands before his majority, as well as early favour from the king.[28] With the likelihood he was managing his estates and the certainty he was campaigning abroad, he was acting effectively as an adult well before his twenty-first birthday.

De Vere was knighted on St George's Day 1377 by Edward III, along with the future Richard II, Henry of Bolingbroke and Thomas of Woodstock, and he was granted robes for the funerals of Edward the Black Prince in October 1376 and for Edward III in July 1377.[29] His attendance as a minor at these events, and the fact his mother-in-law and probable guardian, Isabella, seems to have been much around court, perhaps in part explain his early close connections with the king and his familiarity with the environs of the court. Certainly Mary Green, in her classic study of English princesses, thought that by his marriage 'this handsome but worthless young nobleman became a frequent resident at court; and an early attachment sprang up between him and his wife's cousin, Prince Richard ... which led to calamities equally disastrous to both'.[30] Thomas Walsingham, in a passage slightly less hostile than usual about de Vere, laid blame for his failings

[24] *CPR, 1374–7*, 368, 377; *1377–81*, 190, 260; *CCR, 1377–81*, 153.
[25] *CPR, 1374–7*, 434; *CCR, 1377–81*, 290.
[26] *CCR, 1377–81*, 402; *CCR, 1381–5*, 254.
[27] *CCR, 1381–5*, 254.
[28] *CPR, 1381–5*, 123.
[29] *Anonimalle Chronicle*, ed. Galbraith, 106; E101/397/20, mm 26, 28, 30. I am indebted to Shelagh Mitchell and Laura Tompkins for the E101 references.
[30] Green, *Lives of the Princesses*, iii, 211.

on his upbringing, though this did enable a diatribe about the decline of morals in his time compared to past ones. Walsingham stated that de Vere 'was indeed a young man who was the ideal person to undertake any task requiring honesty, had he not lacked discipline in his boyhood. But alas, the behaviour of boys at the present time!'[31] While generalising about sons of lords, Walsingham may have been implying something more specific about de Vere's upbringing at the court.

De Vere asked in 1377 to be allowed to execute his hereditary office of great chamberlain at the coronation of King Richard, submitting two petitions, the first concerning the office of chamberlain, the second concerning his right to serve the king with water before and after the meat at the feast, taking the basins and towels as his fee. He claimed both by right of his ancestors time out of mind and submitted sufficient evidence to support his claims that both petitions were 'admitted by the king's consent, notwithstanding the earl's nonage, and the offices performed'.[32] Exercising the office of chamberlain at the coronation came with a financial perk as well, as the traditional fee was the whole contents of the king's bedchamber on the night of the coronation, usually redeemed for a sum of money or a specific gift.[33] The ceremony was also the first of two important occasions during Richard II's formative years where de Vere was present, and may mark the start of the growth of the friendship between the two, especially given that the formal and ancient ceremony may have well had a significant impact on the eleven year old king.[34] De Vere can be seen to have been occasionally with the king at other early dates: he visited St Albans Abbey in December 1377 with the king and Henry Bolingbroke and was admitted to the fraternity of the abbey.[35] Robert de Vere was, at sixteen years old in 1377, one of the closest member of the nobility in age to the king, along with the earls of Nottingham, aged fourteen, and Derby, aged eleven.

De Vere's military experience began early but not too early. There is no evidence he served in the huge and expensive naval expedition to St Malo in 1378, led by John of Gaunt, although his uncle, Aubrey de Vere, served, as did Thomas of Woodstock, earl of Buckingham, with whom de Vere was to serve two years

---

[31] *SAC*, i, 934–5.

[32] *CCR, 1377–81*, 2; and for the petitions, see C54/217, m. 45.

[33] J.H. Round, *The King's Serjeants and Officers of State with their Coronation Services* (London, 1911), 114; a gift of two silver basins worth £28 6s was made to the thirteenth earl of Oxford at Henry VIII's coronation in 1509, while £101 was spent by the crown on the earl's coronation robe in 1485: see J. Ross, *John de Vere, Thirteenth Earl of Oxford, 1442–1513. 'The Foremost Man of the Kingdom'* (Woodbridge, 2011), 116n, 148.

[34] See Saul, *Richard II*, 24–6 for the ceremony and possible impact on Richard.

[35] BL, Cotton Nero D vii, fol. 129v.; Goodman, *Loyal Conspiracy*, 153.

later.[36] It may be that aged sixteen he was deemed a little too young. Instead, his first taste of active service came when he went to France in an army led by Thomas of Woodstock which left England in July 1380, alongside two other Essex peers, Walter, Lord Fitzwalter and John, Lord Bourgchier. All four resident peers of the county were thus present, demonstrating a degree of cooperation between them at the start of the decade, even if this was not to last. De Vere's petition for the discharge of the farmers of his lands noted that the grant of the additional £100 was because he was 'almost of full age and is to sail in this expedition over the sea on the king's service'. Froissart, however, is the only chronicler to mention that he went, making several references to him.[37] As he was under age there are no letters of protection for him nor was he paid directly by the crown but the exchequer issue roll on 21 May records a payment of £18,408 to Buckingham for the wages of his force, comprising himself, two other earls, twelve bannerets, 100 knights, 885 men-at-arms and 1,100 archers, which confirms Froissart's information.[38]

It was not the most auspicious of military debuts for the eighteen-year-old Robert de Vere.[39] The army was intended to support the duke of Brittany, and marched from Calais to Brittany via Vertus, Troyes and Vendôme, burning the countryside as it went. But the French forces were unwilling to offer the battle the English wanted, the countryside was stripped bare of provisions, and the death of Charles V of France on 16 September 1380 changed the diplomatic situation. The duke of Brittany immediately opened negotiations with Paris for a long-term truce and refused to support the English army. Buckingham's army nonetheless besieged Nantes, partly on behalf of the duke, but its strong fortifications, lack of supplies and disease meant that the siege was abandoned on 6 January. The bedraggled army struggled to Brest before sailing home. Goodman commented that 'The failure was due primarily to the diplomatic and military factors handicapping all English offensive operations in France.' However, he might have been more critical of Buckingham's leadership, particularly in his rather naïve dealings with the duke of Brittany, and the expedition was heavily criticised by contemporaries for its lack of any achievements.[40] It did mean that de Vere had first-hand experience of the issues and problems of campaigning in

---

[36] A survey of the muster rolls for Aubrey, the earl of Arundel and other lords, and the particulars of account for Thomas of Woodstock turn up no references: E101/36/31, 32, 39.

[37] *CCR, 1377–81*, 402; Froissart, ed. Lettenhove, 245, 276, 277.

[38] E403/478, m. 21; Fildes, 'Baronage in the Reign of Richard II', 330. The other earl was Devon. See also Halliday, 'Robert de Vere', 73 and Goodman, *Loyal Conspiracy*, 124, 127.

[39] For a detailed account of the campaign, see J. Sumption, *Divided Houses. The Hundred Years War III* (London, 2009), 387–412.

[40] Goodman, *Loyal Conspiracy*, 127.

France; he became closely identified with Richard's increasing desire for peace with France later in the decade. It is tempting to suggest that he may have urged the king to seek alternatives to the expensive and fruitless expeditions launched in the 1370s and the 1380s on the continent as a result of his experience in 1380. However, Richard was more than capable of reaching those conclusions on his own, albeit he did lack the personal experience of a campaign in France.

A further formative event in Richard II's relationship with de Vere was during the Great Revolt of 1381. Essex was one of the centres of the rebellion, and the fact that all four resident peers in Essex were abroad on campaign between July 1380 and May 1381 may indeed have helped the rising to kindle and to spread there, in the absence of the power of the secular peerage to contain and suppress it.[41] Their importance was emphasised in a commission in October when Buckingham, Oxford, Fitzwalter and Bourgchier were the only four named men in a commission issued to deal with insurgents entering Essex from Kent to incite further rebellion.[42] Two important chronicles detail de Vere's presence with the king on three separate occasions during the rebellion, and given the circumstances, he must have been with him throughout the crisis. On Tuesday 11 June, he was one of those who moved with the king to the Tower for security, along with the earls of Arundel, Warwick and Salisbury, and the young Henry Bolingbroke.[43] Two days later Oxford, Warwick, Salisbury and the chancellor took a barge from the Tower with the king to begin parleying with the rebels, although the physical danger to the king from the disordered mass of rebels meant little was achieved. Oxford was also present at the meeting with the rebels at Mile End on the Friday, along with Buckingham, Kent and Warwick, while Aubrey de Vere carried the king's sword.[44] It is noticeable that all of the other men named as being present, with the exception of Bolingbroke, were considerably older than the king. The fact that Richard took de Vere along with him on the barge when few accompanied him (Arundel and Suffolk, for example, seem not to have come with the king) suggests already a certain degree of trust and friendship between the two. It is likely that de Vere was present at the supreme moment of crisis at Smithfield when the rebel leader, Wat Tyler, was killed and Richard showed exceptional courage to defuse the situation. However, none of the contemporary chronicles – and there are at least seven accounts of varying value – note who accompanied Richard on that fateful day, other than the mayor of London and Sir John Newton who played a

---

[41] Buckingham's army landed at Falmouth in Cornwall on 2 May: Sumption, *Divided Houses*, 411.
[42] BL, Add. Ch. 15249; *CPR, 1381–5*, 79.
[43] *Anonimalle Chronicle*, ed. Galbraith, 138; Froissart, ed. Lettenhove, x, 395.
[44] *Anonimalle Chronicle*, ed. Galbraith, 164; Froissart, ed. Lettenhove, x, 398, 403; Saul, *Richard II*, 63–9.

role in Tyler's death.[45] The importance of the event for Richard has been strongly suggested by several historians. His mental state was noted by an eye-witness account when he twice climbed a turret in the Tower to watch the rebels and the fires when they had occupied London, and he watched 'anxious and sad', while his personal courage in the successful denouement to the episode must surely have played a role in the development of his kingship.[46] De Vere's presence and support throughout may, perhaps, have been particularly formative to their friendship.

Landed Inheritance

Much has been made of the supposed poverty of the earls of Oxford in the late fourteenth century. Nigel Saul has commented that the earls, by the late fourteenth century, 'had difficulty in adequately maintaining their rank'. He argues that 'the mainspring of [de Vere's] ambition was necessity – financial necessity'.[47] Halliday also commented that de Vere's estates 'were small for his rank', though Halliday incorrectly estimated the value of the whole earldom at £750.[48] A distinction must be drawn, however, between the estates of the earldom of Oxford as a whole, which were by no means inadequate to sustain a comital rank, and de Vere's position in the early 1380s, at which point a series of life-holdings had substantially reduced the number of estates in his hands. Even then, as will be discussed, the income from his estates when taken together with his wife's lands – which need to be treated as acquired through marriage rather than patronage – meant his income was sufficient to support his earldom.

The earls of Oxford had probably never been as wealthy as they were at the death of Earl Thomas in 1371. The first half of the fourteenth century had seen a significant growth in the estates, partly as a result of the marriage of the seventh earl, John, before 1336, to Maud, sister and co-heiress of Giles, Lord Badlesmere and widow of Robert FitzPain. Maud's estates were scattered but valuable, comprising the castle and manor of Lyonshall in Herefordshire, the

---

[45] For the accounts in translation, see Dobson, *Peasants' Revolt*, 155–209. For recent discussion of the narratives, and particularly that of Froissart, see C. Barron, 'Froissart and the Great Revolt' in J.A. Lutkin and J.S. Hamilton, eds, *Creativity, Contradictions and Commemoration in the Reign of Richard II. Essays in Honour of Nigel Saul* (Woodbridge, 2022), 11–34.

[46] *Anonimalle Chronicle*, ed. Galbraith, 143–4.

[47] Saul, *Richard II*, 121.

[48] Halliday, 'Robert de Vere', 71. He incorrectly states that the income tax of 1436 estimated the earldom at £750, but the then earl was not assessed in that survey, and the estimate comes in fact from H.L. Gray, following tendentious evidence. For the estimate, see H.L. Gray, 'Incomes from Land in 1436', *EHR*, 49 (1934), 617–18; for a dismissal of it, Ross, *John de Vere*, 22–5.

manors of Badlesmere, Bockingfield, Ringwold, Whitstable, Old Romney, Charlton and a small holding in Kingsdown in Kent, Hurdicott in Wiltshire, Laughton, West Dean and the hundred of Shiplake in Sussex, Market Overton in Rutland, Milton and Paston in Northamptonshire, Welles in Hertfordshire and some smaller holdings in Inchiquin and Youghal in Ireland.[49] She also held the hereditary office of the stewardship of the forest of Essex. These estates were worth, not including the Irish lands, a little over £300 annually.[50] During John's career as earl he also acquired the estates of Easton Hall, Frating, Bures Giffard, and the reversion of Crepping, all in Essex.[51] The earl's inquisition *post mortem* estimated that his estates in 1360 were worth annually only £788 15s 2d, though this did not include three manors whose values cannot be ascertained and twelve manors which do not appear in the inquisition.[52] It is possible, however, using later fourteenth-century accounts and inquisitions, to estimate that all Earl

---

[49] The agreement of the division of the English estates between the four coheirs is recorded in *CFR, 1337–47*, 102–4, though not all the estates are mentioned. For the division of the Irish estates, see C47/9/28. The knights' fees were divided among the heirs in 1339: *CCR, 1339–41*, 279–84. The de Vere lands in Ireland were granted to the earl of Ormond in 1367 by Thomas, earl of Oxford: *Calendar of Ormond Deeds*, ed. E. Curtis (6 vols, Dublin, 1932–43), ii, 101–2. The manors of Ringwold, Charlton, Laughton and the hundred of Shiplake were held for life by Giles de Badlesmere's widow, Elizabeth, who later married Hugh le Despenser, and Earl John did not receive seisin until her death in 1359: *CCR, 1354–60*, 582–3. See also G.A. Holmes, *The Estates of the Higher Nobility in Fourteenth Century England* (Cambridge, 1957), 30, for the Badlesmere inheritance.

[50] *CFR, 1337–47*, 103 records extents of Badlesmere, Bockingfield, Whitstable, Milton and Paston, Market Overton, Hurdicott, Lyonshall, a small holding in Cowley, Buckinghamshire, and the bailiwick of the stewardship of the forest of Essex. The other manors can be valued from a receiver-general's account of Maud, countess of Oxford in 1386-7: BL, Harleian Roll N3. Hurdicott was alienated by Maud, widow of the seventh earl, to Henry de Haversham before her death in 1366: C143/372/1.

[51] Bures Giffard: *CIPM*, x, 518; xiii, 94. Crepping: *Feet of Fines for Essex*, eds P.H. Reaney and M. Fitch (4 vols, Colchester, 1899–1964), iii, 113.

[52] C135/153 nos 1–30, printed without valuations in *CIPM*, x, 513–18. No value is given for Chesham in the original, and the manor of Bures and Hedingham Vaux are illegible. The twelve manors missing from this inquisition are Preston and Mendham (Suffolk), Tilbury, Steeple Bumpstead, Beaumont, Downham, Crepping, Ramsey and Easton Hall (Essex), Old Romney in Kent, West Dean in Sussex and Westwick in Hertfordshire. A number had been granted out for life to servants. Tilbury was held in 1342 by a Robert Cheddworth for life, Preston by William la Camber, Downham by William Crouche-man, while Easton Hall was in the hands of Nicholas Pichard and his wife: Bodleian Library, Oxford, Rawlinson B248, fols 20v, 21: *Feet of Fine for Essex*, iii, 64; for Pichard, see below, p. 74.

John's estates were worth together approximately £1,300 p.a.[53] Earl John also held the overlordships of well over one hundred knight's fees in nine counties.[54] There is also evidence of significant cash reserves. By his will of November 1359, the earl left 400 marks for the aid of the Holy Land, 100 marks for the (re)building of the church at Earls Colne, 100 marks for the chapel called 'le newe abbeye' in Castle Hedingham and 1,000 marks for the marriage of his third daughter Maud.[55] His widow, Maud, could bequeath cash gifts totalling just under £300 for charitable purposes and £108 to her servants in addition to unvalued gifts and chattels to her children, relatives, friends and senior servants.[56]

It is also clear Earl Thomas had considerable wealth. In addition to having spent £1,121 just two years before his death buying back the manors of Laughton and Market Overton, after a deathbed enfeoffment for charitable purposes made by his mother in 1366, there were substantial reserves noted in his will. The total value of his goods, excluding all specific bequests to his wife, his son and Lady Joan Wingfield, plus the profits of his lands in the hands of his feoffees and foreign receipts amounted to just over £2,456.[57] While his debts, funeral expenses and payments to his servants swallowed up all but £241 of this sum, he was also still owed 800 marks by the king. Many goods went, unvalued, to his

---

[53] The values of Lavenham, Preston, Aldham, Ramsey, Frating, Colne, Vaux, Chesham, Hormead, Abington, Wigston, Chesham, Westwick, Ringwold, Whitstable, Old Romney, Bockingfield, Fleet, Laughton and West Dean from Countess Maud's receiver-general account of 1386–7, the only near contemporary account from the de Veres' administration: BL, Harleian Roll N3. Lyonshall, Badlesmere, Hurdicott and Milton and Paston values from *CFR*, v, 103 The rest are valued from the generally reliable inquisition *post mortem* of Richard eleventh earl of Oxford in 1417 (though all such sources tend to underestimate landed income): *CIPM*, xx, 201–7, except Whitchurch and Aston Sandford from *CIPM*, xvii, 262–3, and Langley and Bradley from *CIM, 1387–93*, 35.

[54] *CIPM*, x, 518–23. These comprised two in Northamptonshire, eight and a half in Oxfordshire, twelve and a half in Buckinghamshire, seven in Huntingdonshire, just under eighteen in Cambridgeshire, two in Norfolk, four and a quarter and four moieties in Hertfordshire, eight and three-fifths in Suffolk and thirty-eight and twenty moieties in Essex.

[55] Lambeth Palace Library, Reg. Islip, fol. 159v–160r, summarised in *Testamenta Vetusta*, ed. N.H. Nicolas (2 vols, London, 1826), i, 62–3. For the rebuilding of the church at Earls Colne, see A.D. MacKinnon, 'The Arrangements of Monuments and Seating at St Andrew's Church, Earls Colne, during the 17th and Early 18th Centuries', *EAH*, 3rd series, 28 (1997), 170–1.

[56] G.M. Benton, 'Essex Wills at Canterbury', *EAH*, 2nd series, 21 (1934), 263–5.

[57] *Registrum Simonis de Sudbiria*, ed. Fowler, i, 4–6.

wife and child.[58] This was not an impoverished nobleman nor was his son a scion of a noble family with insufficient landed estates.

Instead, what difficulties there were for de Vere sprang from the burden on the estates from 1371 of a long-lived dowager holding much more than the standard dower, as well as two other life holdings, and one permanent alienation.[59] Much the largest burden was that of de Vere's mother, the dowager countess Maud (d. 1413), who was holding not only the traditional third in dower, but also by a series of enfeoffments, a sizeable jointure. The first enfeoffment, by the seventh earl in 1350 at the time of her marriage to his son and heir Thomas, comprised the manors of Chesham, Ramsey and Westwick. The second, by Earl Thomas in September 1369, included the manor of Wigston Magna, and probably also Frating, Hedingham Vaux and Preston, a third in 1370 added the reversion of Market Overton, while a fourth, on 23 April 1371, four months before Thomas's death, comprised the manors of West Dean, Laughton, Bockingfield, Fleet, Whitstable, Old Romney and Welles.[60] Another burden on de Vere's estates was the holdings of Elizabeth Courtenay (d. 1395), widow of his uncle John (d. 1350), who had been enfeoffed to joint tenure with her husband of five manors.[61] The

---

[58] *Registrum Simonis de Sudbiria*, ed. Fowler, i, 4–6. Thomas died owing £628 to the mother of Sir John Pelham. For the enfeoffment see Holmes, *Estates of Higher Nobility*, 31.

[59] For a discussion of the problems of late medieval dowagers for their marital families, see R.E. Archer, 'Rich Old Ladies: the Problems of Late Medieval Dowagers', in A.J. Pollard, ed., *Property and Politics. Essays in Late Medieval English History* (Gloucester, 1984), 15–35.

[60] Bodleian, Rawlinson B248, fols 19r-v, 23; E326/12895; *CPR, 1348–50*, 511; *Feet of Fine for Essex*, iii, 99; *CCR, 1369–74*, 271–2; *Sussex Feet of Fines* (3 vols, Sussex Record Society, 2, 7 and 23, 1903–16), iii, 173; Holmes, *Estates of the Higher Nobility*, 47. The enfeoffment of Wigston is noted in a later legal case (JUST1/477/3), and in Maud's inquisition *post mortem*, which states that she was enfeoffed, presumably during Thomas's lifetime, by a group of feoffees of Wigston to hold for life, with reversion to Robert de Vere, though as this manor is missing from Thomas's inquisition *post mortem*, it is difficult to be certain when: *CIPM*, xix, 378; and see below, p. 73. BL, Harleian Roll, N3, a receiver-general's account for Countess Maud for 1385–8 records the manors of Frating, Hedingham Vaux and Preston in Maud's hands before de Vere's forfeiture but the manors of Preston and Frating are missing from Thomas's inquisition *post mortem*, and no extent is given of Vaux, so it is difficult to know when and on what terms a jointure grant was made of them. For Market Overton, see LR14/562. For the jointure more generally see Goodman, *Loyal Conspiracy*, 35; Holmes, *Estates of the Higher Nobility*, 32, 47.

[61] *CPR, 1340–3*, 254; *CIPM*, xvii, 261–2; *CP*, x, 225. As John died under age in 1350 and held no lands other than the five manors with which he had been enfeoffed with in joint tenure with his wife, she was not entitled to dower. She remarried Sir Andrew Lutterel in 1359, and they were granted a pension of £200 p.a. by Edward III to maintain their estate: *CPR, 1358–61*, 234.

situation was not made easier by the grant by Earl Thomas of several manors for life to his retainer Sir William Wingfield for his service in peace and war.[62] Provision had also been made for de Vere's uncle, Aubrey, in the 1360s, with the grant of several manors and he was to have the reversions of the manors granted to his sister in law, Elizabeth, after her death. Table 1 at the end of this chapter summarises which estates were in whose hands and includes the nearest contemporary value of the estate.[63]

Of the fifty-four manors of his family inheritance which would have descended to him, De Vere was only holding twenty, about 37 per cent, compared to his mother Maud, who was holding twenty-five, a little under half.[64] Her receiver-general's account of 1386–7 records that she had an income of £570, and with some adjustments for the quirks of the account and extraordinary expenses, the optimum income of her estates can be calculated at £649.[65] Without such

[62] William Wingfield (c. 1326–98), ten times MP for Suffolk between 1376 and 1390, had previously been connected with the Black Prince, but moved into Thomas's retinue in the 1360s. His service in peace and war in the grant of Market Overton is referred to in later legal proceedings concerning the manor after his death (C44/22/12). A regular business associate, he made the earl a gift of a coat of mail, which the earl later bequeathed to his brother Aubrey, and the earl, as well as making him an executor, made a number of expensive bequests in his will to Wingfield and his wife: *Registrum Simonis de Sudbiria*, ed. Fowler, 5–6. For a full description of his career, see HoC, iv, 876–9. For the estates, CPR, 1348–50, 511; *Feet of Fine for Essex*, iii, 99; CCR, 1369–74, 271–2; *Sussex Feet of Fines*, iii, 173; Holmes, *Estates of the Higher Nobility*, 47; CIPM, xvii, 262–3; CPR, 1364–7, 62; 1385–9, 549; CIM, 1377–88, 26–7, 209; 1387–93, 34.

[63] There was some inquiry into what estates de Vere held after his death, but this was substantially incomplete: CIM, 1377–88, 206, 226; 1387–93, 3, 11, 34, 35, 41, 53, 89–92, 131, 132; *Calendarium Inquisitionem Post Mortem Sive Escaetarum*, eds J. Caley and J. Bayley (4 vols, London, 1806–28), iii, 165, 173, 180, 210.

[64] See Map 1 in particular, above p. xvi. There is one manor over which there is some doubt. In a case in King's Bench in 1394 (KB27/534, rex rot.2) a case was brought on behalf of the crown alleging that de Vere held the manor of Great Radwinter in Essex on the day he forfeited, as was found by an inquisition before the escheator and others (CIM, 1392–9, 26–7), and that one Robert Henmale had occupied it and enfeoffed others to his use. Henmale claimed de Vere had no estate in the manor, and a jury agreed with him, finding against the crown. The de Vere family had held the overlordship of the manor since the time of Domesday book: J. Ross, 'The de Vere Earls of Oxford, 1400–1513' (Unpublished DPhil., University of Oxford, 2005), 40, 47. De Vere did not hold it directly but it was held of him by a rent of £4 p.a. and it might have been this that misled crown officials (C139/65/15).

[65] BL, Harleian Roll, N3. The account is very unusual in that it is a composite account of receipts from each manor over as many as four regnal years, 9–12 Richard II, but only the tenth year (1386–7) has one or more receipts from each manor. Totalling receipts for that year records £568 7s 2½ d, but in estimating the overall value of the estates of Maud's dower and jointure, adjustments need to be made for pensions and missing

information for de Vere's own estates, estimating his income is extremely difficult, being over-dependant on those notoriously unreliable governmental extents, the inquisitions *post mortem*. De Vere's family lands, from the values given in his successor's inquisition *post mortem* were worth £368, but if his mother, holding only a few manors more had an income of £649, then his lands ought to have been worth closer to £500 p.a. Overall, with another few estates that would revert to the male line, and not including lands worth over £100 annually put aside for Aubrey the estates of the earldom of Oxford can be estimated as being worth about £1,200–£1,300 per annum in the later fourteenth century.

Contemporaries thought that 1,000 marks, or £666, was the minimum required to support the dignity of an earl. Temporarily, de Vere's paternal lands were probably not sufficient to do this (though with his wife's lands he did reach this level of income), but his prospects were much brighter should he outlive his mother. What he had during the 1380s was the rump of the earldom. It did include his ancestral home at Castle Hedingham, but not either of the other two residences which his parents in particular had favoured at Great Bentley and Earls Colne.[66] It is hard to say how comfortable the castle at Hedingham was as a residence at this date. The twelfth century keep was (and is) impressive but was old-fashioned by the 1380s; what other buildings were within the two baileys is unclear, as late-fifteenth-century buildings dominate the archaeological record.[67] It was, however, sufficiently comfortable to host King Richard, most probably

---

receipts. For more details, see J. Ross, 'A Rich Old Lady Getting Poorer. Maud, Countess of Oxford, and the de Vere Estates, 1371–1413', in L. Clark and J. Ross, eds, *The Fifteenth Century XX: Essays Presented to Rowena Archer* (forthcoming, Woodbridge, 2024).

[66] Earls Colne: in the 1540s John Leland recorded that the earls had 'a manor place of theirs, the dikes and plotte wherof yet remayne, and berith the name of the Halle Place': *John Leland's Itinerary. Travels in Tudor England*, ed. J. Chandler (Stroud, 1993), 162. In 1401 the residence was described as a mansion: *CPR, 1399–1401*, 519. See also *The Victoria County History of Essex*, ed. A.H. Doubleday et al. (12 vols, 1903–2020), x, 92–4. More work has been done on Earl's Colne priory nearby: F.H. Fairweather, 'Colne Priory, Essex, and the Burials of the Earls of Oxford', *Archaeologia*, 87 (1937), 275–95. The priory was the subject of a Channel 4 'Time Team' dig in 2012, and the archaeological report can be accessed at: www.wessexarch.co.uk/our-work/colne-priory. Great Bentley: this seems to have been the most favoured residence of Earl Thomas and of his widow. Thomas made his will and died there in 1371; Maud is recorded there on a number of occasions and died there in 1413: Ross, 'Seditious Activities', 31, 32, 34, 35. The parish church had a tower added alongside other substantial alterations in the later fourteenth century, suggesting interest and financial input from the earls: *An Inventory of the Historical Monuments in Essex, Volume 3, North East* (London, 1922), 107–8.

[67] *An Inventory of the Historical Monuments in Essex, Volume 1: North West* (London, 1916), 51–7. A survey of the castle in 1592 is reproduced in L.A. Majendie, 'Notes on Hedingham Castle, and the Family of De Vere, Earls of Oxford', *EAH*, 1st series, 1 (1858), 79.

in 1383, and de Vere was also present there when he issued an undated receipt to the authorities of Colchester for a payment of £25 from the fee farm.[68] The remaining ancestral estates he held were focused on Essex – fifteen of twenty – and there were five more in five other counties. His mother held most of the Suffolk estates of the earldom of Oxford, centred around Lavenham in the liberty of Bury St Edmunds, as well as the Kentish and Sussex estates of the Badlesmere inheritance. A further concentration of estates in Buckinghamshire was entirely out of de Vere's hands and was intended to be permanently alienated from the earldom for the benefit of Aubrey.

Aubrey de Vere

For all the fact that many of his estates were out of his hands, albeit temporarily, de Vere did have a significant advantage in the presence at the heart of Richard II's minority regime of his uncle, Aubrey de Vere. Aubrey was the third son of John, seventh earl of Oxford. The date of Aubrey's birth is unknown, but was certainly after 1337, given that his second brother Thomas was born either in 1336 or 1337.[69] His eldest brother, John, died in 1350, but Thomas succeeded to the earldom, and with the birth of the latter's son, de Vere, in 1362, the prospect of Aubrey's succession to the earldom must have seemed remote. He was, however, adequately provided for, since on the death of his mother, Maud de Badlesmere in 1366, he received the manors of Calverton (Buckinghamshire), Saxton (Cambridgeshire), Crepping and Beaumont Newhall (both Essex), worth together £47 annually, and he also held the reversions of four more manors after the death of his brother's wife, Elizabeth Courtenay, worth about £70 annually, although her longevity meant that he did not acquire these manors until 1395.[70] Overall then, he stood ultimately to have possession of lands worth about £117 p.a. or more from the family estates, which was a respectable income for a younger son. His mother also granted him for life the bailiwick of the forestership of the king's forest of Essex.[71]

Until the death of his sister-in-law, however, he did not have much landed income to maintain the lifestyle of a son of an earl, and therefore needed an alternative source of revenue; a military career was the obvious solution at this

---

[68] See below, p. 81, for Richard's visit. The month and year of the receipt were illegible when the document was transcribed in *The Red Paper Book of Colchester*, ed. W.G. Benham (Colchester, 1902), 152, but must date between autumn 1384 and the end of 1387.

[69] *CP*, x, 227, 233. He must have been about twenty-one or more in 1360 when his mother made a grant of an office to him, *CPR, 1358–61*, 445.

[70] *CIPM*, xii, 61–2; xvii, 262–3; *CPR, 1361–4*, 120. Values from Aubrey's *IPM*, 57–8. For Saxton, see below, p. 74.

[71] See above, p. 55, n. 50.

time, and he found the perfect patron. In November 1367, he was given licence to cross to Gascony with seven yeomen, eight horses and £100 for his expenses, shortly after the Black Prince's campaign in Castile which ended in the victory of Nájera. Within a month of the licence being granted Aubrey was retained to abide for life with the Black Prince, receiving an annuity of 100 marks per annum, half from the Prince's manor of Newport and half from his exchequer at Chester.[72] These were generous terms, given that Aubrey was unlikely to have brought much in the way of men and materiel to the prince's cause for all that he was of noble blood. The Black Prince was, however, famous for his generosity: indeed his funeral oration, given by the bishop of Rochester, noted that he 'was so generous to his servants that he made them rich and himself poor'.[73] Further grants followed: in 1369, when the 50 marks at Chester was replaced by £100 from the stannary of Cornwall; and on 22 July 1375, under the Prince's privy seal, when he was granted the Constableship of Wallingford Castle and the Stewardship of the honours of Wallingford and St Valery, with £40 yearly for his fees, and a day later of an additional £10 annually to pay for his deputy there. This was patronage on a considerable scale, totalling over £173 p.a. For a younger son, this was a very welcome income. He was also knighted at some point after his arrival in Aquitaine and before 16 November 1368.[74] He seems to have returned to England at some point as, along with many others of the Prince's retinue, he mustered at Northampton in 1369 prior to recrossing to Gascony; although he headed the list of knights, he brought just two esquires and no archers to the muster.[75] Aubrey seems to have become quickly a man of some influence with the Prince, becoming his secretary by 28 September 1371, when the Pope, Gregory XI, wrote to Aubrey, along with various others such as the king and the prince in order to try and obtain the release of Roger de

---

[72] Printed in 'Private Indentures for Life Service in Peace and War 1278–1476', eds M. Jones and S. Walker, in *Camden Miscellany XXXII* (Camden Society, fifth series, 3, 1994), 80–1; *CPR, 1367–70*, 57; *Catalouge des rolles gascon, norman et francois conserves dans le archives de la tour de Londres*, ed. T. Carte (2 vols, London, 1743), i, 155; *CPR, 1377–81*, 161 (an inspeximus and confirmation of various grants to him).

[73] Brinton, *Sermons of Thomas Brinton*, ed. Devlin, 355–6.

[74] He is simply Aubrey de Vere in his licence to cross the sea, but Aubrey de Vere, knight, in a property transaction on the latter date: *CPR, 1367–70*, 57; *CCR, 1364–8*, 491.

[75] E101/29/24; *CPR, 1367–70*, 256; D. Green, 'The Later Retinue of Edward the Black Prince', *Nottingham Medieval Studies*, 44 (2000), 141–51. Green notes the problems with the muster document, which has no date beyond a regnal year, and suggests that at least some of those recorded as mustering may not have been there, but given Aubrey was enfeoffed of estates in England in a private transaction in July 1369, it is probable he was in England at the time of the muster.

Beaufort, the pope's brother.[76] He was obviously considered to have influence with the prince, if the pope was writing to him, and in a position of trust as his secretary.[77] Aubrey also witnessed a charter of the Prince's at Berkhamsted in 1374.[78] Judging how much time Aubrey actually spent with the Prince is somewhat difficult, since few sources record that information. However, given the absence of any reference in the patent or close rolls between 24 July 1369 (an enfeoffment) and 13 July 1373 (a recognisance) it seems likely that he was with the prince in Aquitaine during 1369 and 1370, and probably returned to England with him in early 1371.[79] He was, after all, to abide with him for life.

Between 1370 and 1377 there are few sources that shed light on Aubrey's activities. It is in fact with the death of the Black Prince, and the succession shortly afterwards of his young son, that Aubrey, as with many of the prince's associates, became more influential, given that they formed the nucleus of the new royal household.[80] During the problems between Gaunt and the Londoners in 1377, Walsingham records that Aubrey, with Simon Burley and Lewis Clifford, were sent by the Princess of Wales to negotiate with the citizens on Gaunt's behalf.[81] He was at the same time appointed as one of the ambassadors to treat with France.[82] He was already in the circle around the young Richard, seen in the fact he gifted the king the charger on which Richard rode from London to Westminster for his coronation, for which gift he was granted £200 according to the Issue Rolls.[83]

In 1378 Aubrey served under John of Gaunt during the latter's fruitless expedition against St Malo. He indented alongside Sir John Devereux, his brother-in-law, for one hundred men at arms and a hundred archers, but in

---

[76] *Calendar of Papal Registers: Papal Letters*, iv (1362–1404), 96.

[77] Tout, *Chapters*, v, 379. The prince had more than one secretary, as John Fordham is also described as his secretary in 1370 and 1374.

[78] *CChR*, v, 241; R. Barber, *Edward, Prince of Wales and Aquitaine* (London, 1978), 231.

[79] *CPR, 1367–70*, 256; *CCR, 1369–74*, 577.

[80] Given-Wilson, *Royal Household*, 161–2; D. Green, 'The Household of Edward the Black Prince: Complement and Characteristics' in C. Woolgar, ed., *The Elite Household in England, 1100–1550* (Donington, 2018), 360–1. More generally, see D. Green, 'Edward the Black Prince and East Anglia: An Unlikely Association', in W.M. Ormrod, ed., *Fourteenth Century England III* (Woodbridge, 2004), 83–98; D. Green, *The Black Prince* (Stroud, 2001), 126–7.

[81] *Chronicon Angliae*, ed. Thompson, 126.

[82] *Foedera, Conventiones, Literae...*, ed. T Rymer (20 vols, 2nd edn, London, 1728), vii, 143; Holmes, *Good Parliament*, 163.

[83] E403/465, m. 19.

the end served with four other knights, 114 men-at-arms and 120 archers, and was paid for service for 169 days from April to September, for which a sum of £2,298 was due.[84] It may, in part, have been a result of the influence of Gaunt, as well as his position in the young king's household and his connections with the Black Prince, that led to him being appointed to the third of the continual councils for the day-to-day governance of England which took over in October 1378 during the Gloucester Parliament. The other members were the earls of Arundel and Suffolk, the bishops of Winchester and Bath and Wells, the bannerets, Sir Robert Hales and Sir Roger Beauchamp, and Sir Robert Rous and Aubrey as the two knights bachelor.[85] Aubrey attended for 113 days, being paid £37 13s 4d, at ½ mark per day.[86] This was considerably less than some of the clerical members of the council, and indeed the earls, and only Rous attended on fewer days. However, around this time he had acquired a further royal office that may have occupied a considerable amount of time and may explain his limited attendance on the council.

From the beginning of the reign some petitions were addressed to the king himself, and Aubrey, who became acting chamberlain, and the underchamberlain Simon Burley were responsible for dealing with them. It is difficult to date Aubrey's acquisition of this role precisely. He is certainly referred to as the king's chamberlain in a grant to him on 18 January 1381, and Tout dates his chamberlainship to the Northampton Parliament late in the preceding year.[87] However Tuck has made a case that Aubrey was acting chamberlain since the beginning of the reign.[88] The chamberlain's role in dealing with petitions during the minority varied a little from that when the king was an adult. Under the latter, petitions granted by the king were passed to the great chamberlain if present, or to his deputy if not, to then be passed to the chancery. During a minority the responsibility seems to have devolved to the chamberlains themselves for dealing with these grants. Whether they actually granted the petitions themselves is unclear, but their signatures appear on petitions, and they

---

[84] E364/13, rot. C; E101/68/7/162; E101/36/39, mm. 3–5; Sumption, *Divided Houses*, 325–7. Devereux had married Aubrey's sister, Margaret, daughter of the seventh earl of Oxford. Margaret left Aubrey a silver cup in her will of 1397: BL, Lansdowne MS 1, fol. 62 (no. 24 in the original numbering system).

[85] N.B. Lewis, 'The "Continual Council" in the Early Years of Richard II, 1377–80', *EHR*, 41 (1926), 250; Saul, *Richard II*, 30.

[86] Baldwin, *King's Council*, 123.

[87] *CPR, 1377–81*, 564; Tout, *Chapters*, iii, 356, 406; iv, 346; v, 212n and see vi, 48–9.

[88] Tuck, *Richard II*, 42–3; A. Tuck, 'Richard II's System of Patronage', in F.R.H. Du Boulay and C.M. Barron, eds, *The Reign of Richard II. Essays in Honour of May McKisack* (London, 1971), 5–6.

seem then to have passed them to the council for approval or straight to the chancery for direct action. Even before the appointment Tuck argues that de Vere and Rous, another household man, used their position to 'ensure that the court's business was dealt with by the council'.[89] For example twenty clerks were presented to benefices in early 1379, and Aubrey acted as 'intermediary between the king and the officers of state', and he also at the same time steered a petition from Sir Thomas Percy through the council, which states that it was done on the information of Aubrey de Vere.[90] Another warrant from 1380 from the king to the chancellor notes that a petition had been granted and that in the absence of the secretary and the signet, the seal of Aubrey de Vere had been attached.[91] He signed another and endorsed it 'to the council' in 1380.[92] His heightened status is apparent in his witnessing seven royal charters between 1379 and 1382 as acting chamberlain or chamberlain.[93]

Aubrey's position was strengthened in that as a member of the continual council he could help influence the direction of patronage and policy, and as a senior member of the household the same was true. As Tuck says 'The appointment of de Vere to the council can only have strengthened household influence at the centre of government, and if anything militated against increased conciliar supervision of the household' and Aubrey was 'primarily responsible for the assertion of power of the royal household'.[94] Even after the end of the continual councils, Aubrey remained involved in government. A document from the spring of 1381 names the members of the king's council as the Archbishop of Canterbury (the chancellor), the treasurer, the keeper of the Privy Seal, the acting chamberlain, Aubrey, the chief justice of the Common Pleas, and a few others.[95] These were then the major officers of state, but does show the exalted company that Aubrey was then keeping. Aubrey was able to act as patron and intercessor on occasion: it was on his information that the Londoner Paul Salisbury acquired a pardon, having taken advantage of the uprising of 1381 to pursue his own ends.[96] It is unlikely that it was Simon Burley who, as the Appellants later

[89] Tuck, *Richard II*, 3.
[90] SC8/236/11793.
[91] SC8/185/9204.
[92] SC8/223/11135.
[93] C53/157, m, 23 (*CChR*, v, 258, no. 19); C53/158, mm. 5, 8 (*CChR*, v, 274–6, nos. 2, 4, 8); C53/159, m. 13 (*CChR*, v, 276–7, nos. 20, 21, 22).
[94] Tuck, *Richard II*, 43, 48.
[95] E207/6/10; Tuck, *Richard II*, 48.
[96] *CPR, 1381–5*, 30–1; A. Dunn, *The Peasants' Revolt. England's Failed Revolution of 1381* (2nd edn, Stroud, 2004), 85.

claimed, was responsible for introducing Robert de Vere into the king's circle and getting him patronage in his early years.[97] Aubrey was equally well placed, and had a far better motivation – a close friendship between his nephew and the king would lead to his family's advancement and possibly to his own, although the latter did not in the end actually happen.

Aubrey also served as an ambassador, being involved in the negotiations concerning the king's marriage with Anne of Bohemia, alongside Edmund, earl of Cambridge, and Hugh de Segrave, the ambassadors being appointed on 2 May 1381. The negotiations were successful, as the treaty was ratified on 29 August 1381, and the marriage took place on 20 January 1382.[98] In September 1383 he was at Calais with a retinue of four knights, five esquires and twenty archers, and he stayed on there as on 4 October 1383 he was involved in ambassadorial negotiations again, when he, John Devereux, captain of Calais, William de Elmham and William de Ermyn were appointed to negotiate the arrangements for a high level meeting between English and French ambassadors.[99] Nor did his military activities cease. He submitted a complaint to the king and council in December 1383 of negligence by a number of safekeepers of the sea by which he lost a ship, men-at-arms, and equipment to the value of 400 marks, the ship being on the way to reinforce and revictual Calais before the arrival of the duke of Lancaster there.[100] Aubrey was also in demand as a feoffee throughout his active career, both with high profile individuals, such as Henry Percy, earl of Northumberland, and Sir Edward de Berkeley, and amongst the Essex gentry.[101]

For all the fact that Aubrey had good connections on campaign and in government with John of Gaunt, there occurred in the spring of 1382 an unpleasant incident that may have soured relations. A dispute broke out between the inhabitants of Stony Stratford and Passenham. The west side of Stony Stratford, which is divided by the River Ouse, was part of Aubrey's manor of Calverton, while the fair and market of the town were also part of the manor's

---

[97] *WC*, 276–7.
[98] *Foedera*, ed. Rymer, vii, 290–5; Tout, *Chapters*, iii, 383.
[99] E404/13/87, unnumbered, *sub* 10 September; *Foedera*, ed. Rymer, vii, 412.
[100] SC8/214/10696. He struggled to get the defendants to Chancery where the case was to be heard: SC8/214/10692-10706.
[101] *CPR, 1367–70*, 256, 293; *1374–7*, 26; *CCR, 1374–7*, 107–9, 111, 121; *CPR, 1377–81*, 447, 525; *CCR, 1381–5*, 395; C143/396/17. For his actions as a feoffee for Lady Mohun and on behalf of his sister-in-law, Elizabeth Courtenay, see S.J. Payling, 'Legal Right and Dispute Resolution in Late Medieval England: the Sale of the Lordship of Dunster', *EHR*, 126 (2011), 25–6. As a feoffee for his brother-in-law, Sir Nicholas de Louvain, see *Register of Simon Sudbury*, ed. Logan, 134–7.

appurtenances.[102] Passenham, on the east side of the Ouse, was a Lancastrian manor; John of Gaunt had given it to his young son and heir, Henry, earl of Derby, as the first stage of a landed endowment. The dispute became serious enough that Derby sent sixty bowmen to arrest the malefactors from Stony Stratford; Aubrey's response was unknown. While such trouble amongst tenants did not necessarily lead to animosity between manorial lords, the fifteen-year-old Derby's decision to send bowmen was an overreaction and an escalation that caused him trouble. Derby's trusted servant, Hugh Waterton, had to be sent to the king to tell him that he had been misinformed about the dispute. As Given-Wilson has pointed out, that almost certainly meant Aubrey or perhaps de Vere had told their side of the story to the king and presumably painted Derby in a negative light.[103] McFarlane argued that 'Derby never obtained justice against de Vere from the partial Richard', though that seems to accept the Lancastrian side of the story (and all this is known only from duchy of Lancaster accounts) overly readily, and in fact how the dispute was resolved is unknown.[104] Whether this had any role in the decision that Derby took to oppose Robert de Vere in 1387, as McFarlane suggested, or Aubrey's expulsion from the court in 1388 is not clear.

During the late 1370s and early 1380s, while prominent at court and in government, Aubrey was building up his local landed interests. His cash annuity from the Black Prince, confirmed by Richard II, was by stages converted into a series of life holdings of royal manors in Essex. In part exchange for the grant at the stannary of Cornwall of £100, he was granted on 1 February 1378, the custody of the castle at Hadleigh, the manor of Thundersley, and the profits of the town and market at Rayleigh, all Essex, rendering 10 marks as was customary.[105] He was then granted the custody of the parks of Rayleigh, Hadleigh and Thundersley on 25 June 1379.[106] On 1 August 1380 he was granted the Essex manor of Eastwood, and the profits of the honour of Rayleigh.[107] Finally on 18 January 1381 he was granted the reversion of the bailiwick of

---

[102] *The Victoria County History of Buckingham*, ed. W. Page (5 vols, London, 1905–20), iv, 476–82.

[103] DL28/1/1, fols 8v–9v; Given-Wilson, *Henry IV*, 34–5; Tuck, *Richard II*, 80.

[104] K.B. McFarlane, *Lancastrian Kings and Lollard Knights* (Oxford, 1972), 20–1.

[105] *CPR, 1377–81*, 112. Part of this grant became subject to a law suit with the prior of Merton as late as 1397: JUST1/1503, rot. 15-16d.

[106] *CPR, 1377–81*, 371.

[107] Ibid., 542. The grant was cancelled because he was granted instead the manor of Liston, but this was later surrendered to Hugh de Segrave, and the first grant seems to have come back into force since he was holding them at his death. *CPR, 1381–5*, 120; *CIPM*, xviii, 60.

Rochford hundred in Essex.[108] He was still receiving £22 18s 6½d from the stannary of Cornwall as the residue of the grant of £100 from that source.[109] He did however surrender the Stewardship of Wallingford and its honours to Hugh de Segrave on 12 April 1382. The total value of these grants was £115 7s 5d, which, with the 50 marks still paid from the manor of Newport, which he remained in possession of, comes close to the £173 he had earlier in his career, without the Wallingford grant. The lands in practice may in fact have been worth more, and it was preferable to have the grants in the form of land rather than cash given the value attached to the ownership of land at this period. It is interesting to note that it was at the height of his influence that he was able to exchange cash grants for land, and that he managed to group them together, achieving a certain territorial influence in south-east Essex, which allied to his prominence and connections at court, made him a potential force in the area.

It was probably also in the autumn 1381 that he finally married: he was already over forty, which was late for a first marriage. His wife was Alice, daughter of Walter, Lord Fitzwalter, and the latter's spouse Eleanor Percy. The marriage is not well documented, and can be pieced together only from scattered sources.[110] However, it makes sense of an otherwise inexplicable series of recognisances, all enrolled on 12 October 1381, between Aubrey and Lord Fitzwalter.[111] Two, for 1,000 marks and 100 marks, were by Fitzwalter to Aubrey, and one for 300 marks was by Aubrey to Fitzwalter; none contain details or conditions. These complicated negotiations presumably concerned the marriage portion and a jointure for Alice. The marriage portion was likely to have been somewhere between 550 and 1,100 marks, depending on whether the recognisances were for a similar sum to the actual payment or guaranteeing a smaller sum. Aubrey's bond to Fitzwalter was probably to enforce his settlement of land on Alice, and at least one manor was settled on her in jointure by February 1382, when Alice is mentioned as Aubrey's wife.[112]

---

[108] *CPR, 1377–81,* 564.

[109] *CPR, 1381–5,* 112; *CCR, 1381–5,* 169.

[110] Bodleian, Rawlinson B248, fol. 22v; JUST 1/477/3, m. 6v; CP25/1/29/87, no. 32; J. Enoch Powell, 'The Riddle of Bures', *EAH*, 3rd series, 6 (1974), 92–3.

[111] *CCR, 1381–5,* 87–8.

[112] Simon Payling has estimated the average dower portion for a baronial daughter as being in excess of 1,000 marks between 1300 and 1500: S. J. Payling, 'The Politics of Family: Late Medieval Marriage Contracts', in R.H. Britnell and A.J. Pollard, eds, *The McFarlane Legacy. Studies in Late Medieval Politics and Society* (Stroud, 1995), 26, and see more generally 21–47. I am indebted to Dr Payling for his suggestions on these transactions, including that the additional 100 m recognisance might have been for a small contingent eventuality, perhaps an additional jointure as more land came

This alliance made considerable sense for Aubrey since his life holdings of estates from the Black Prince were all in south-eastern Essex, not too far from the Fitzwalter seat at Woodham Walter, and a marriage for a younger son of an earl to a daughter of a baron was eminently respectable.

Aubrey also ventured into the property market in a complicated series of purchases by which he acquired the various manors within the parish of Dullingham in Cambridgeshire over the course of nearly twenty years. The first was the manor of 'Beauchamps' in Dullingham (Cambridgeshire) as early as 16 November 1368, when a group of feoffees, John de Sudbury, Clement Spice and Robert de Naylinghurst, clerk took possession from John de Meryet. One recognisance from Naylinghurst for £40 was enrolled.[113] Aubrey did not finally receive a quitclaim from Clement Spice until 13 July 1383.[114] It is possible that the feoffees paid at least some of the sum and kept possession of the manor until their debts had been paid. He purchased a further manor in Dullingham, 'Poyneshall', in the autumn of 1381. One payment, of 200 marks to John Kemp of Finchingfield, was recorded in two final concords, but three different men – perhaps Kemp's feoffees – released the manor on 21 December 1381 to Aubrey.[115] A third manor, 'Chalers' was acquired in stages between 1382 and 1386.[116] As late as 29 February 1388, he received a final quitclaim for two moieties of Dullingham from Clement Spice, Henry Sparke and William

---

to Aubrey through purchase, and may indeed relate to the purchase of Poyneshall in Dullingham in the autumn of 1381 which was settled jointly on the newly-weds in February 1382 (see n. 115 below). There is no extant return for Cambridgeshire in Alice's inquisition *post mortem*, and no other jointure property is mentioned: *CIPM*, xviii, nos 485–8.

[113] *CCR, 1364–8*, 491.

[114] CA, K604/T/20; *CCR, 1381–5*, 385.

[115] CP25/1/29/87, nos 32, 35; CP40/483, rot. 326; CA, K604/T/18; *Pedes Finium*, ed. W. Rye (Cambridge Antiquarian Society Publications, 1891), 132. The first fine (no. 35) was for Aubrey alone in Michaelmas 1381, the second (no. 32) for Aubrey and Alice, and the heirs of Aubrey in February 1382. Each mentions 200 marks as the consideration for the property but it is more likely one replaced the other, with the adjustment being to ensure the joint tenure of Aubrey and his new wife. This fine was not noted by *The Victoria County History of Cambridge and the Isle of Ely*, ed. L.F. Salzman et al. (10 vols, London, 1938–2002), vi, 160–3, whose account of the manorial descent of the various moieties of the manor contains one or two inaccuracies. Kemp acknowledged a debt of 100 marks to Aubrey in the summer of 1381: C241/167/8.

[116] CA, K604/T/21, 27; *Victoria County History Cambridge*, vi, 161–2. For a complicated arrangement regarding potential villeins in Dullingham, see *Calendar of Select Pleas and Memoranda of the City of London, 1381–1412*, ed. A.H. Thomas (Cambridge, 1932), 188–9.

Stuteville, clerk, although this may either have been a re-enfeoffment, or given the date, coinciding with the Merciless Parliament and his expulsion from the royal court, for the better security of both parties.

A further landed purchase was also in train. By the autumn of 1387 he had agreed to pay 800 marks for purchase of the manors of Langdon and Amys, both in southern Essex, from Richard Palmer.[117] This was a rather opportunistic purchase. Palmer's title to Langdon was dubious as Aubrey, Lord Fitzwalter, and others had been appointed on 6 December 1384 to enquire into an allegation that the manor had been seized into crown hands by the county escheator who, it was alleged, was beheaded by Palmer during the 1381 revolt and Palmer had subsequently seized the lands.[118] Presumably the allegation was false and certainly Palmer was able to prove his title to Langdon in King's Bench by February 1387, but perhaps feeling discretion was the sensible option or perhaps financially struggling after the legal battle, he sold it to Aubrey, who in 1387 would have thought himself in a good position to defend any legal challenge.[119] These purchases were not hugely valuable but did make a nice addition to his landed estates. Langdon, unvalued in Aubrey's Inquisition *post mortem*, was producing £13 14s 4d in 1442–3, and Amys' value is unknown, though at twenty years purchase price, it was probably about the same again.[120] Dullingham was valued at £18 5s 9d in the same source. Thus, by the late 1380s, with these purchases, family estates and royal estates in his hands for life, he was probably earning in total around £220 per annum from land.[121]

There is, however, no evidence on which to base any assessment of the personal relationship between Aubrey and his nephew Robert de Vere. Whether Aubrey spent much time with his nephew in London or at his ancestral home of Castle Hedingham is unknown. The only time they can be placed together after 1381 is in the army that invaded Scotland in 1385. However, politically they were aligned. Aubrey's long service to the Black Prince transferred into loyalty to the Prince's son, and Aubrey may

---

[117] *Calendar of Select Pleas and Memoranda*, ed. Thomas, 133, an acquittance for £100 in part payment of 800 marks; *CCR, 1385–9*, 423, 428–30, 485; *CCR, 1389–92*, 288, the latter being a quitclaim to Aubrey by Palmer and two others of the manors.

[118] *CPR, 1381–5*, 503.

[119] KB145/3/10/1 contains a royal order to the justices of King's Bench to restore the manor to Palmer, dated 3 February 1387; the case was pleaded in the Michaelmas term of 1385: KB27/498, rots. 3ff.

[120] Essex Record Office, Chelmsford, D/DPr 138, m.1.

[121] Values from *CIPM*, xviii, 57–60. He also acquired temporarily the manor of Wigpet in Arkesden, Essex, through a grant by Sir William de Walton in August 1376: C146/2501; C146/878. It was not in his hands by his death in 1400: *CIPM*, xviii, 57–62.

have played some role in introducing de Vere into the king's inner circle. If Aubrey was far less prominent at court after he was replaced as chamberlain of the household by Simon Burley, he was still expelled from the court by the Lords Appellant in 1388, and he maintained connections with prominent courtiers, including Sir Simon Burley and Sir John Devereux, in the mid-1380s.[122] He was also a likely ally at a local level, and could be trusted to look after the de Vere interests in Essex, something that would have been increasingly necessary given the trajectory of de Vere's career.

※

There were some weaknesses in Robert de Vere's position as he approached his majority in the early 1380s. His mother's control of about half of the estates of the earldom of Oxford significantly weakened his financial position, and as she was not yet forty by the time of his majority in 1383, she might, in the absence of serious illness, be expected to live some time. Conversely, illness and violence had carried off potential allies in his mother-in-law, Isabella, maternal relative, William Ufford, earl of Suffolk, and his godfather, Simon Sudbury before they could significantly aid his career. Yet, overall, his prospects were bright. Should he outlive his mother, the estates of the earldom were more than adequate, worth in the region of £1,200 p.a., and his wife's lands would add a few hundred pounds more, even if he was not heir to a vast estate, unlike his contemporaries Thomas Mowbray, earl of Nottingham, or Henry, earl of Derby. In his uncle Aubrey, he had both a local ally and a relative at the heart of the minority regime, well connected and influential, and also embodying a tradition of distinguished service to the Black Prince, which clearly had its resonance in the early years of the reign of the Prince's son. De Vere himself had embarked on a career of service, on campaign in France in 1380–1 and in local government and peace-keeping in 1381–2. Lastly, the building blocks for a good relationship with the king were already in place; he seems to have spent much time at court growing up, and he had proved his loyalty, and perhaps courage as well, in acting with the young king during the dramatic days at the height of the Peasants' Revolt. It was the way this factor, his relationship with Richard II, developed that in large part transformed his career from conventional to unusual, but the other factors – his comital inheritance, family connections, promising beginnings in royal service building on a family tradition, and a courtly upbringing – emphasise the key point that he already had all the ingredients necessary for a successful career as a late medieval earl.

---

[122] CA, K604/T/25, 27; His expulsion, along with many others, is mentioned in some of the major chronicles: see for example *WC*, 230–1.

Table 1. Estates of de Vere family, 1383 (Essex unless otherwise stated)

Manors in Robert de Vere's Hands*	
Castle Hedingham	£20
Sible Hedingham	£20 (IPM 1417)
Bourehall	£6 (IPM 1417)
Little Yeldham	£14
Doddinghurst	£20
Fingrith	£20
Downham	£15 (IPM 1417)
Bures Giffard	£5 6s 8d
Great Canfield	£50 (IPM 1417)
Stansted Mountfitchet	£15 6s 8d
Steeple Bumpstead	£20 (IPM 1417)
Helions Bumpstead	£44 (IPM 1417)
Tilbury	£15
Beaumont (Bernhams)	£6[†]
Badlesmere (Kent)	£13 7s[‡]
Castle Camps (Cambs.)	£21 6s 8d
Kensington (Middlesex)	£33
Lyonshall (Heref.)	£33 6s 8d**
Cockfield (Suffolk)	£13 6s 8d
West Whetenham	£4[††]
Total	£368 18s 4d

* List of properties taken from *CFR, 1377–81*, 13 (except Helions Bumpstead, Tilbury, Beaumont, Badlesmere, Lyonshall and West Whetenham). Value of the manors in Robert's hands unless otherwise stated from Earl Aubrey's inquisition *post mortem* in 1400: *CIPM*, xviii, 57–62. 'IPM 1417' is Earl Richard's: *CIPM*, xx, 201–7. There is incomplete set of valuations for many of Robert's estates in the escheators' account rolls after his fall: E357/9, rot. 41; E357/10, rot. 1d., 4d., 13d., 14d., 19d., 20, 24, 44.

[†] Beaumont was granted to John Humbelby and John Revell for life by Robert on 1 September 1383: E357/10, rot. 19d; *PPC*, i, 89; *CFR, 1383–91*, 242; *CIM, 1387–93*, 91; *CIPM*, xviii, 59; *CFR, 1383–91*, 242; *CPR, 1385–9*, 548, 556. This was one manor in the parish, known as Bernhams; Aubrey held the other, the manor of Newhall: C143/4017/27; P. Morant, *The History and Antiquities of Essex* (2 vols, London, 1768), i, 485.

[‡] No contemporary source states in whose hands the manors of Helions Bumpstead and Badlesmere were during this period, but given that the holdings of Countess Maud, Elizabeth Courtenay, William Wingfield and Aubrey de Vere are better

documented than Robert's they seem most likely to have been in the earl's hands. Badlesmere certainly was in Aubrey's hands in 1400: *CIPM*, xviii, 58–9.

** Lyonshall had been enfeoffed to Countess Maud in 1371 (E326/12895), but the transfer apparently never took place as Sir John Burley had custody of the manor during Robert's minority in the 1370s at an annual farm of 50 marks: *CPR, 1377–81*, 137. Robert sold it at some point before August 1384 to Simon Burley: *CPR, 1381–5*, 447; *CIM, 1387–92*, 132.

†† *CPR, 1396–9*, 149; for discussion, see below, pp. 212–13.

Manors in Other Hands

Dower of Countess Maud*	
Lavenham, 'Overhall' (Suffolk)	£44 9s 10d
Lavenham, 'Netherhall'	£8
Aldham, with Hellond (Suffolk)	£55
Great Hormead (Herts.)	£34 3s 3d
Earls Colne	£27 3s 4d
Great Bentley	£22 (IPM 1417)
Land in Cowley (Bucks.)	40s
Great Abington (Cambs.)	£34 6s 8d
Ringwold and Charlton (Kent)	£16
Old Romney/Langport (Kent)	£21
Kingsdown (Kent)	40s

* The grant of dower is *CCR, 1369–74*, 271–2; values are from her receiver-general's account, 1386–7; BL, Harleian Roll N3. See also her inquisition *post mortem* in 1413: *CIPM*, xix, 376–80. The dower also included four advowsons, Hedingham Priory, Colne Priory, Lavenham and Aldham, with a total value of £56. 4d. p.a.

Jointure of Countess Maud	
West Dean (Sussex)	£10
Chesham (Bucks.)	£42
Welles (Herts.)	£15
Whitstable (Kent)	£40
Fleet (Kent)	£40
Bockingfield (Kent)	£16
Laughton and hundred of Shiplake (Sussex)	£60
Ramsey	£30

Westwick (Herts.)	£38
Preston (Suffolk)	£13 6s 8d
Wigston Magna (Leics.)	£33 6s 8d
Frating	£11 13s 4d
Hedingham Vaux	£10
Cruswiche	£6 13s 4d*

* This is the first reference to this manor belonging to the de Veres. See *CIM, 1387–93*, 91.

Maud's Inheritance	
Wrabness	£17 6s 8d
Total Maud (dower, jointure and inheritance)	£649 9s 9d

In jointure of Elizabeth, widow of John*	
Whitchurch (Bucks.)	£40
Mendham (Suffolk)	£10 13s 4d
Aston Sandford (Bucks.)	£10
Swaffham (Cambs.)	£10
Total	£70 13s 4d

* *CIPM*, xvii, 262–3. See above, p. 57.

In hands of Sir William Wingfield*	
Market Overton (Rutland)	£20†
Langley and Bradley (Berks.)	£14‡
Milton and Paston (Northants.)	£10 13s 4d
Total	£44 13s 4d

* *CIPM*, xiii, 96–7; xvii, 262–4, 400; *CPR, 1348–50*, 541; *1364–7*, 62; *1385–9*, 549; *CIM, 1377–88*, 26–7, 209. Market Overton was held by Wingfield for life, with remainder to countess Maud for life, and then to the male line of the de Veres: LR14/562. Langley and Bradley were held with reversion to the earl and his heirs (the heir being Aubrey at Wingfield's death).

† Value from *CIM, 1387–93*, 131 and E357/9, rot. 22d. Nottingham University Library, Mi 6/170/87 is a mutilated account of the manor in 1410–11, then in countess Maud's hands. Gross revenue from assize rent, demesne land and profits of court was £15 4s 5d, £5 6s 8d, and 17s respectively, totalling £21 7s 1d. Arrears were running at £13 4s. 3d. The expenses section is lost. I am indebted to Dr Maureen Jurkowski for this reference.

‡ *CIM, 1387–93*, 35.

In hands of Aubrey de Vere*	
Saxton (Cambs.)	£13 6s 8d †
Calverton (Bucks.)	£26 13s 4d
Beaumont (Newhall)	£2
Crepping	£11
Total	£53

* Aubrey was holding Calverton in tail male, with a remainder to Robert de Vere; Bodleian, Rawlinson B248, fol. 34r. Whitchurch, Aston Sandford, Saxton and Mendham were after the death of Elizabeth to be held in tail male by Aubrey with a similar remainder: *CIM, 1387–93*, 34; *CIPM*, xvii, 262–3. The manor of Beaumont had been enfeoffed to Maud, wife of the seventh earl in joint tenure, with a reversion after her death to Aubrey: Bodleian, Rawlinson B248, fol. 34r. Perhaps by a similar means Aubrey acquired Crepping, which was recorded as being in his possession in 1382 though it is not included in his inquisition *post mortem*: C143/401/27; *CIPM*, xviii, 57–62.

† There was some confusion over Saxton. It was part of the original enfeoffment to Elizabeth in 1341, and her inquisition *post mortem* states that she died seised in 1395, with remainder to Aubrey: *CPR, 1340–3*, 254; *CIPM*, xvii, 263. However, there were grants to Aubrey in reversion after the death of his mother, the dowager Countess Maud, wife of the seventh earl, in 1360 and 1366, and in the latter year, after Maud died, the escheator was ordered to deliver the manors of Saxton and Calverton to Aubrey: Bodleian, Rawl. B 248, fol. 35r; *CIPM*, xii, 61; *CCR, 1364–8*, 242–3. Elizabeth, apparently, released her life interest in the manor to Aubrey in 1371: CP25/1/288/49, no. 722. Had he granted it back to her for life?

In hands of the Pichard family*	
Easton Hall	£4 14s 7d

* Easton Hall had been granted to Nicholas and Elizabeth Pichard by the seventh earl of Oxford. Elizabeth was still alive at de Vere's fall in 1388: *CIM, 1387–93*, 92. Valuation taken from Earl Aubrey's *post mortem*: *CIPM*, xviii, 57–62. Edward Pichard was a household servant of Countess Maud in 1389 and 1391: Longleat MS 442, rot. 1; *CPR, 1388–92*, 407. He held half a knight's fee in Castle Hedingham of Earl Aubrey in 1400: *CIPM*, xviii, 61.

3

Politics, Court and Patronage, 1381–5

And the same tyme, Kynge Richard made þe Erle off Oxenforde and Ser Michael de la Poole & other flateres cheefe off his counsel, and be thayme wasse gouerned.

(*An English Chronicle*, entry under the seventh regnal year, 1383–4[1])

Robert de Vere's minority formally ended in January 1383 and indeed it was not until March of that year that, having proved his age and given homage and fealty to Richard II, eleven escheators were ordered to give him seisin in his father's estates.[2] However, he had been acting as an adult for two years before that in his own eyes and those of the crown, and he may well have had possession of his estates before formal seisin. Because his family estates were centred on Essex, he was appointed to a string of commissions in the aftermath of the Peasants' Revolt in 1381; that county had been one of the two most important in the rebellion.[3] Despite being a major Essex landowning family, the de Vere estates had not been targeted during the rebellion.[4] However,

---

[1] *An English Chronicle, 1377–1461*, ed. W. Marx (Woodbridge, 2003), 8.

[2] *CCR, 1381–5*, 254.

[3] For Essex in the Peasants' Revolt, see particularly the various essays in W.H. Liddell and R.G.C. Wood, eds, *Essex and the Great Revolt of 1381* (Chelmsford, 1982); H. Eiden, 'Joint Action against "Bad" Lordship: The Peasants' Revolt in Essex and Norfolk', *History*, 83 (1998), 5–30; L.R. Poos, *A Rural Society after the Black Death: Essex 1350–1525* (Cambridge, 1991), 231–40.

[4] The research of Liddell, Wood and Eiden has identified seventy-seven places in Essex where court rolls were burnt and a further eight-two where other incidents of unrest were recorded. Only three were on de Vere manors – Beaumont, Sible Hedingham and Wrabness – of the twenty-two manors in the county in the hands of de Vere or his mother. It was the manor of Sir John Argentein at Steeple Bumpstead rather than the de Vere manor there that was attacked (Liddell and Wood, *Great Revolt*, 87) and likewise it was not the de Vere manor that was targeted at Stanstead Montfichet but another in the same vill. Given the correlation between the burning of court rolls and grievances of lordship, this is striking. This suggests that the family were not seen as oppressive landlords or particularly unpopular, and is in contrast to other members of the nobility such as the countess of Hereford and the Princess of Wales, who saw

on 10 July 1381 he had been commissioned to array the men of the county of Essex against the insurgents, on 1 August he was appointed to a commission of Oyer and Terminer in Cambridgeshire and Huntingdonshire, on 8 October another commission was issued to deal with insurgents coming into Essex from Kent to incite further rebellion, and on 14 December he was named as a commissioner to preserve peace and deal with unlawful assemblies in Essex.[5] In each he was the second named commissioner, behind the king's uncle, Thomas, earl of Buckingham, and ahead of other prominent Essex landowners, such as Lord Fitzwalter and Aubrey de Vere. Predating any of these commissions, Thomas Walsingham states that the earl of Buckingham and Sir Thomas Percy, the earl of Northumberland's brother, were sent into Essex in late June to deal with the remaining rebels, and it was forces led by these two men that defeated and killed up to five hundred of them at Billericay on 28 June.[6] De Vere is not named, but as the king was in Essex between 22 June and 8 July, de Vere may well have been with him, and it is not impossible he was also with Buckingham, under whom he had served in Brittany until two months previously, at the defeat of the rebels.[7] Further commissions to de Vere followed in 1382, one relating to an illegal entry into the manor of Bradwell, others to

---

more widespread attacks on their manors, or almost all members of the commission of the peace and the county administrators, who were targeted and in the case of the escheator and sheriff, killed and abducted respectively: Eiden, 'Joint Action against "Bad" Lordship', 12–15; Liddell and Wood, *Great Revolt in Essex*, 85–98. Aubrey de Vere suffered more – there was trouble at his manor of Hadleigh, and his auditor, Nicholas Davenant, was beheaded at Brentwood on 12 June: Liddell and Wood, *Great Revolt*, 90; A.J. Prescott, 'Essex Rebel Bands in London', in Liddell and Wood, eds, *Great Revolt*, 58. See also A. Ford, 'The Essex Sessions of the Peace and the "Peasants' Revolt" of 1381', *EAH*, 4th series, 10 (2019), 142–8. Recent research has tended to emphasise discontent with local and national government and high taxation rather than seigneurial repression and villeinage as the most important motivating factor for the rebels: M. Bailey, *After the Black Death. Economy, Society and the Law in Fourteenth Century England* (Oxford, 2021), 283–325; idem, *The Decline of Serfdom in Late-Medieval England: from Bondage to Freedom* (Woodbridge, 2014). For a new case study, see M. Xu, 'Analysing the Actions of the Rebels in the English Revolt of 1381: the Case of Cambridgeshire', *Economic History Review*, 75 (2022), 881–902. An older study reaches the same conclusions for Essex: N. Brooks, 'The Organisation and Achievements of the Peasants of Essex and Kent in 1381', in H. Mayr-Harting and R.I. Moore, eds, *Studies in Medieval History Presented to R.H.C. Davis* (London, 1985), 247–70.

5 *CPR, 1381–5*, 73, 76, 79, 85; BL, Add. Ch. 15249.
6 *SAC*, i, 514–17; *WC*, 12–13.
7 W.H.B. Bird, 'The Peasant Rising of 1381: the King's Itinerary', *EHR*, 31 (1916), 124–6. He is, however, not mentioned in a Wardrobe account covering June to

enquire regarding the death of the escheator of Essex, to deal with treasonable insurrections and an appointment to the commission of the peace in Essex.[8] While it is not possible to say how much involvement the underage earl had in many of these commissions, he did sit in person in July 1382 on the commission relating to Bradwell.[9]

Five years younger than de Vere, Richard II was an adolescent or young man throughout the period of his active career. The initial continual councils appointed to govern when he succeeded to the throne in 1377 at the age of ten ended in 1380 when he was just fourteen. As Mark Ormrod has argued, this would not have been sanctioned by parliament 'had there not been a clear sign of the king's ability and willingness… to undertake at least some of the functions of an adult ruler'; this was confirmed by the promise shown in his actions during the Peasants' Revolt, followed shortly by the important life-cycle event of his marriage to Anne of Bohemia in January 1382.[10] Yet parts of the same political community that encouraged or allowed this to happen then, almost immediately after the king took up some functions of ruling, began to criticise the king's decisions and methods. Such criticism continued until the crisis of 1386–8, when restrictions were actually placed upon Richard's exercise of his royal rights and duties.[11] These mixed messages from the political community, in addition to Richard's sensitivity to criticism, as well as the difficult circumstances – military, fiscal and political – in which he took up the reins of power, were at the heart of the problems of the 1380s.

September 1381 which notes payments to the earls of Buckingham, Kent, Salisbury, Warwick, Derby and Suffolk for resisting the rebels: E101/400/1, m.1.

[8] *CPR, 1381–5*, 136, 139, 196, 198–9, 244, 246, 253.

[9] See below, p. 204.

[10] W.M. Ormrod, 'Coming to Kingship: Boy Kings and the Passage to Power in Fourteenth-Century England', in N.F. McDonald and W.M. Ormrod, eds, *Rites of Passage. Cultures of Transition in the Fourteenth Century* (York, 2004), 35, 38; Dodd, 'Fiction of Majority Rule', 144–5.

[11] Criticism was made of the royal household and of the chancery, exchequer, and the machinery of justice, and their leading personnel, by the parliamentary Commons from the aftermath of the Peasants' Revolt onwards, though this was not directed at the king initially: see W.M. Ormrod, 'The Peasants' Revolt and the Government of England', *Journal of British Studies*, 29 (1990), 23–7; Saul, *Richard II*, 80–2. It does, however, demonstrate the difficult political atmosphere that Richard inherited from the onset of his reign, and the way both the Good Parliament and the Peasants' Revolt resonated in the politics of the 1380s.

Robert and Richard

Contemporary writers were fascinated by how, as they saw it, de Vere maintained such control over the king. The less extreme saw the king as 'fervently loving him', but the more malicious attributed other causes, and in particular one made the damaging accusation of a homosexual relationship between the two. The only explicit allegation of a sexual relationship between de Vere and Richard was, predictably, by Thomas Walsingham. He accused the two of sharing obscene familiarities ('familiaritatis obscene') in the context of de Vere's promotion from marquess of Dublin to duke of Ireland in 1386, as a way of explaining why a man who, in Walsingham's opinion, was no better than his peers should have been so raised.[12] Walsingham also prefaced the remark, probably first composed in the late 1390s, with a partial disclaimer of 'it is said'. However, in a case of slinging as much mud as possible in the hope of some sticking, Walsingham also hinted that de Vere's influence over the king was being maintained by the *maleficiis* of a certain friar. While the translation of that word in the standard edition of the St Albans Chronicle is 'wickedness', the word strongly suggests black magic rather than just the friar's moral outlook. Given this passage related to de Vere's divorce from his wife and marriage to Agnes Lancecrone, it is unsurprising no reference to homosexuality is made in this context, but also shows Walsingham's finely tuned instincts as what would damage Richard's reputation most at any given point in his narrative.[13] However, what has been printed as the *Cronica Maiora* in the St Albans Chronicle was a later revision of his earlier chronicle, written around 1388 or a little after, and the earlier text makes no mention of either black magic or obscene familiarities.[14] This revision process further weakens the veracity of any claim of homosexuality or genuine belief in black magic on the part of the chronicler. Furthermore, Walsingham had no particular inside source that would lend any credence to such allegations. It was also the only time he made the accusation of homosexuality, rather than it being a running theme through his narrative; it has been noted that Walsingham generally did not have much interest in this particular strategy of defamation.[15] All in all, Walsingham's addition of a (qualified) allegation of 'obscene familiarities' must be treated with real caution.

---

[12] *SAC*, i, 798–9.

[13] *SAC*, i, 822–3.

[14] The earliest text is *Chronicon Angliae*, ed. Thompson, 372; Stow, 'Richard II in Thomas Walsingham's Chronicles', 82–7.

[15] W.M. Ormrod, 'Knights of Venus', *Medium Aevum*, 73 (2004), 296–7.

No other source directly alleges a sexual relationship between the two men, though Knighton's chronicle is allusive when he describes de Vere, de la Pole and others as 'unmentionable seducers of the king'.[16] Thomas Favent's *Historia* describes how de Vere – with de la Pole, Burley, Tresilian and Brembre – blinded the king by 'adulations, lascivious words and praises'.[17] However, there was a distinct tendency to criticise the court for its sexual misrule – to which de Vere's liaison with Lancecrone must have contributed – and sexual deviancy was linked by contemporaries to political disorder. Walsingham's famous passage about the knights of Venus rather than of Bellona (Mars), quoted at the opening of Chapter 1, is merely the most famous of such critiques, linking courtly behaviour with sexual misrule.[18] Walsingham in this passage was not suggesting homosexuality but too much heterosexual intercourse, which by implication robbed knights of their martial inclinations.[19] Nonetheless, it was a contemporary critique, being composed around 1388 or a little later, and as Mark Ormrod notes 'it was both convenient and increasingly credible to represent the untrustworthiness of Richard's friends by associating them loosely with a more general trend away from martial pursuits and towards the cultivation of the courtly elements of chivalry'.[20] Other contemporary sources discuss sodomy, notably the contemporary poem *Cleanness*, and at least one literary scholar has discussed this poem in connection with de Vere and Richard, but the link is tenuous.[21]

Modern historians have tended to dismiss the allegations of homosexuality, Nigel Saul has argued that the allegation of obscene familiarity is likely to be 'baseless'.[22] However, Michael Bennett does not dismiss the story out of hand, noting, for example the childless state of Richard himself, and a number of his closest associates, including de Vere.[23] While this is entirely correct, the counter-argument is that Richard seems to have had a happy marriage with Anne of Bohemia, and evidence has come to light that the royal marriage

---

[16] *KC*, 392.

[17] Favent, 'History or Narration', 233.

[18] For discussion, see Federico, 'Queer Times', 35–41; Ormrod, 'Knights of Venus', 297–8.

[19] Ormrod, 'Knights of Venus', 294–5.

[20] Ormrod, 'Knights of Venus', 293. See also N. Saul, 'A Farewell to Arms? Criticism of Warfare in Late Fourteenth-Century England', in C. Given-Wilson, ed., *Fourteenth Century England II* (Woodbridge, 2002), 131–45.

[21] E.B. Keiser, *Courtly Desire and Medieval Homophobia* (London, 1997), 150, 226 n.6.

[22] Saul, *Richard II*, 121.

[23] M.J. Bennett, *Richard II and the Revolution of 1399* (Stroud, 1399), 71.

was a sexual one and not chaste; the childlessness was not through lack of trying.[24] Furthermore, de Vere's scandalous abduction of Agnes Lancecrone, with whom he presumably had a sexual relationship, and married shortly after, to the absolute detriment of his own interests, would also suggest heterosexual attraction, as well as a desire for an heir. No definite conclusion can be reached on the question as to whether there was a homosexual relationship between the two men; there is now no evidence to prove it one way or the other. However, on balance, it is rather less likely than was the case with Edward II and Gaveston and Despenser, on which there was considerably more contemporary comment.

The alternative is that the relationship was, as Saul suggests, a 'close friendship and no more'.[25] De Vere was brought up at or around the court, and Richard must have known him from a young age. Froissart noted that the king loved de Vere with 'his whole heart, they having been brought up together'.[26] Almost exactly five years older than the king, an age gap that would have allowed shared experiences and outlook but gave de Vere that edge of knowledge and maturity, it might have encouraged Richard to look up to him in a way the king might not have done to boys closer to his own age, notably Henry Bolingbroke and Thomas Mowbray. It has already been shown that de Vere was present supporting Richard at two major formative events of the young king's life, his coronation in 1377 and the revolt of 1381, and the effect of these on Richard should not be underestimated. There is also evidence that de Vere owned courtly skills which would also have helped: being brought up at court and being a few years older than the king would have availed him nothing if by word or deeds he could not pass muster as good company for Richard.[27] Another factor that might have aided the closeness of the two was the service that the de Vere family had done to the Black Prince over the preceding decades. Aubrey's close service as retainer and secretary to the Prince has already been noted, but Robert de Vere's grandfather, Earl John, had probably been one of the commanders of the Prince's division at Crécy and he had certainly fought with distinction

---

[24] For Anne's efforts to conceive and the evidence that the couple were actively trying to produce an heir, see K.L. Geaman, 'A Personal Letter Written by Anne of Bohemia', *EHR*, 128 (2013), 1090–4; eadem, 'Anne of Bohemia and her Struggle to Conceive', *Social History of Medicine*, 29 (2016), 224–44.

[25] Saul, *Richard II*, 121.

[26] Froissart, ed. Johnes, ii, 70.

[27] For hints of de Vere's courtly skills, see below, pp. 188–9.

at the Black Prince's greatest moment of glory, the battle of Poitiers.[28] Sir William Wingfield also had close connections with the Black Prince before moving into the service of Robert's father, Earl Thomas.[29] Distinguished family service would have been part of the foundation of the relationship between Robert de Vere and the Black Prince's son.

There is also evidence that Richard wanted to, and did, spend time in de Vere's company. The first evidence for this is from an undated royal signet letter to the chancellor, Michael de la Pole, given at Castle Hedingham.[30] The most likely date is during the king's lengthy sojourn in East Anglia between late May and early July 1383, and if so, it is early evidence of good relations between de Vere and Richard.[31] There is plenty of other evidence for the king making an effort to spend time with him. During his preparations for the Irish expedition, de Vere was at Bristol, one of the embarkation ports, and the king came to join him, reaching the town on 13 July 1386, and staying a week.[32] De Vere, along with others like Nottingham and Lancaster, had an apartment of his own at the royal palace at Eltham, and in winter 1386 as part of the renovations at Kings Langley, new chambers were added for de Vere and Nottingham.[33] He also had a chamber within the palace of Westminster.[34] At the Salisbury Parliament in 1384 the king celebrated mass, according to the Westminster Chronicler, in de Vere's apartments.[35]

While it demonstrates de Vere in Richard's company rather than Richard seeking him out, a different type of source suggests that they spent time together, and interestingly from an early date. Two petitions were endorsed by the earl of Oxford between 1380 and 1383 in his capacity of great chamberlain of England, an office confirmed in the preparations for Richard's coronation

---

[28] For Crécy, see D.S. Green, 'The Household and Military Retinue of the Black Prince' (2 vols, unpublished PhD, University of Nottingham, 1998), I, 71.

[29] Ibid., II, 154–5.

[30] C81/1339/55. It was written to the chancellor, de la Pole, but not addressed to him as the earl of Suffolk, so it must postdate the start of his office on 13 March 1383 and pre-date his promotion to earl on 6 August 1385.

[31] Saul, *Richard II*, 470.

[32] C81/1352/34; Saul, *Richard II*, 155 and see appendix, 471.

[33] E101/473/2, mm. 13, 16; R.A Brown, H.M. Colvin, and A.J. Taylor, eds, *The History of the King's Works* (6 vols, London, 1963–82), ii, 935, 976. He is not among those noted as having a chamber at Sheen in which work was being done; these included John Holland, Ralph Stafford, Simon Burley and Nicholas Slake: E101/473/2, m. 8.

[34] 1351 E101/473/2, m. 20.

[35] *WC*, 68.

in 1377. While the importance of this office as regards royal favourites has been discussed above, and a closer analysis of the key role it played for de Vere will be undertaken below, these two petitions show him in the king's company and potentially exercising influence much earlier than is usually thought. The first is a petition requesting a cancellation of a subsidy assessment by the master of the hospital of Writtle, Essex, dated to around 1381.[36] This is not a question of Oxford necessarily exercising good lordship to a local hospital, as the manor of Writtle was in the hands of Thomas of Woodstock, while the hospital was a papal foundation.[37] The second, dating probably from 1383, was a request by William Montagu, earl of Salisbury, requesting the appointment of commissioners to deal with a case in the Court of Chivalry: Oxford is named as one of the desired commissioners, alongside the earls of Arundel and Stafford, but he endorsed the petition 'le roy lad grantee' and signed it with his comital title.[38] A further early indication of a good relationship between the two can be seen in a grant on 10 January 1382 by the king's signet letter confirming to de Vere a charter of Henry I's granting to de Vere's ancestor, the first earl of Oxford, the great chamberlainship of England.[39] While a confirmation might have been expected and need not be seen in terms of patronage, such an authorisation indicates the king's personal initiative, aged just fifteen, and is one of the earliest examples of the use of the signet; it did not otherwise become a significant tool for the king to use until late 1383, when there was a rapid rise in its employment by the king.[40]

In fact, it seems most plausible that Richard found in de Vere someone a little older, a little more sophisticated and grown-up. As an earl, de Vere was a natural companion of the king and this association would have been reinforced by his presence at the two most crucial formative moments of Richard's early reign, his coronation and the dangerous days at the height of the Peasants' Revolt.[41] If de Vere was much around the court in the 1370s while still a minor

---

[36] SC8/223/11102, dated on the guard to 1385 but by the Ancient Petitions project to c. 1381 (see the comments on the National Archives online catalogue).

[37] *Victoria County History Essex*, ii, 200–1; Morant, *Essex*, ii, 62–7, although the earls of Oxford did have a feudal overlordship of one of the smaller manors in the parish (ibid., 67).

[38] SC8/224/11168. For dating, see the comments on the National Archives online catalogue for the document. For discussion on the background to the case, see J.L. Leland, 'Richard II and the Counter-Appellants: Royal Patronage and Royalist Politics' (unpublished PhD, Yale University, 1979), 26–31.

[39] CPR, *1381–5*, 65.

[40] Saul, *Richard II*, 109–10; Tout, *Chapters*, iii, 404–5; v, 206–7.

[41] See above, pp. 51, 53–4.

as a result of his wardship being held by the king's aunt, Isabella, and thereafter was regularly in the king's presence, notably in his role as chamberlain, this is likely to have reinforced the relationship. By 1383 or 1384, when criticism was made of Richard's government, ministers and policies, de Vere, closely linked to, and beneficiary of, some of those policies, backed Richard wholeheartedly, the political alignment supplementing the personal connection. From de Vere's point of view, it is impossible to know if he genuinely liked the younger boy or whether, perhaps, he saw in him someone to exploit, manipulate and benefit from. The possibilities are not mutually exclusive. It is worth noting, though, that as events placed them together in an ultimately violent confrontation with an opposing faction, de Vere was prepared to risk his life on behalf of Richard's kingship and his own position. This was not a foregone conclusion, as is demonstrated by Thomas Mowbray, earl of Nottingham, initially also close to Richard, choosing a different course and going into full-blown opposition in 1386–7.

There is a sense in some modern writing that Richard had a limited pool of potential friends and that de Vere was not the first choice. Steel argues that in choosing his friends among the nobility 'in singling him [de Vere] out as his special friend and companion the king had had little choice' as only Mowbray, Bolingbroke and de Vere were of a similar age to him. This is of course true, but Mowbray seems to have enjoyed much favour at court until jealousy of de Vere drove him into political opposition, and Derby was not ignored, although he is less likely to have been close to Richard, given the uneasy relations between the king and Gaunt.[42] However, from what is known of Richard it seems highly unlikely that he would have been forced into elevating a worthless incompetent, as Steel characterises de Vere, simply through necessity. Nigel Saul takes a different tack, arguing that in the early 1380s Richard enjoyed the company of many younger men, and he may not have had a single favourite, 'but if there was someone who enjoyed a primacy in his affections', it was Sir Ralph Stafford, heir to the eponymous earldom. Stafford was killed in a brawl on the Scottish expedition of 1385, but Saul offers no detailed evidence of why he should be considered the closest to the king in the early 1380s, though he is not alone in arguing that Richard's relationship with Stafford may have paralleled that of de Vere and certainly Richard was deeply upset by Stafford's death, as the Westminster Chronicle records.[43] The reason that the chronicler gives for the king's grief is that Stafford had been 'a contemporary and comrade in the heyday of his own youth'; such a

---

[42] Steel, *Richard II*, 112; Saul, *Richard II*, 123, 181; Goodman, *Loyal Conspiracy*, 29.

[43] Saul, *Richard II*, 120–1; Leland, 'Richard II and the Counter-Appellants', 59.

characterisation would fit de Vere just as well.[44] Saul discusses also Thomas Mowbray, earl of Nottingham, and while his characterisation of the primary reason for Mowbray's defection to the Appellants – jealousy of de Vere – may well be right, he states that de Vere supplanted him in the king's favour in the mid-1380s, and contrasts Mowbray's wealth and a 'virtually guaranteed' place at court with de Vere's position.[45] As has been argued, de Vere's birth guaranteed him a place at court just as much as Mowbray, his wealth has been understated, and in redating the closeness between de Vere and Richard to 1381 or before, rather than to 1384–5 when the flow of patronage to him increased significantly, a much more long-standing friendship between the two is posited. De Vere did not need to supplant Mowbray or Stafford in the king's affections because he was already there and to suggest otherwise is an unduly negative reading of de Vere. None of this need mean that de Vere was the king's sole or paramount friend in the early 1380s, and Saul is surely right that Richard had a number of close companions. Yet that circle narrowed with Stafford's death and Mowbray's increasing alienation from the king until by 1387 de Vere was the king's primary friend amongst the nobility, in contrast to the king's older allies – minister and tutor – in de la Pole and Burley, and other companions drawn from the socially less distinguished chamber knights.

Some historians have argued that Richard II had an unusual view on the nobility, and that de Vere was favoured and promoted to the marquessate and the dukedom as part of a policy towards the nobility. Tuck notes the unusual attitude towards the nobility in the creation of de la Pole as earl of Suffolk: 'The more we bestow honours on wise and honourable men, the more the crown is adorned with gems and precious stones.'[46] He also argued that Thomas of Woodstock's elevation to the dukedom of Gloucester, accompanied by the grant of £1,000 in customs revenue over which the king had control, rather than in land, shows a different attitude to the link between land and status compared to Edward III. This is, however, unconvincing, since not only was very little land available for patronage in 1385, but it was also common practice in Edward III's reign; for instance Ingelram de Coucy and Isabel were granted 1,000 marks in tail male 'until they should be provided of an equivalent in lands and rent', which was in practice never fully realised.[47] Nevertheless, Tuck argues that Richard attempted to create a group of nobles

---

[44] *WC*, 122–3.

[45] Saul, *Richard II*, 122–3.

[46] *Report from the Lord's Committees Touching the Dignity of a Peer of the Realm* (5 vols, London, 1829), v, 62, 64–5; Tuck, *Richard II*, 84; Saul, *Richard II*, 284.

[47] *CPR, 1364–7*, 156; *1367–70*, 16.

bound to the crown by common interests, by loyalty created by extensive endowments, and by grants of titles according to principles which differed sharply from previously.[48] This latter, it must be said, is not evident from the patent for de Vere's marquessate. This rehearses de Vere's qualities, birth and deeds: 'considering the noble birth, strenuous probity and excellent wisdom of his beloved cousin Robert de Vere, earl of Oxford, and willing that that an excellence of name follow upon the magnificent deeds of this earl, and that the bestowal of means and honour accompany the exaltation of his name'.[49] There is little unusual in this, given that he had the inherited the title and lands of the earldom of Oxford through his bloodline, and the praise of his qualities and deeds was conventional enough; it stands in contrast to the more unusual language used in the patent that created de la Pole earl of Suffolk in the same parliament.[50] The promotion to the marquessate was novel, as was the grant of the whole of Ireland, but as will be argued below this may well have been an innovative solution to a long-standing problem for English kings. There was no need to bind de Vere to the king by grants or endowments, since they had seemingly been close friends for several years. De la Pole's creation, on which so much of this argument is based, was an exception, given his humbler origins and the need to justify this great elevation in social status. Given-Wilson, discussing the promotions to the marquessate and that of de la Pole to earl of Suffolk, argues that there was 'a concern that the higher ranks of the nobility – traditionally a warrior class – were being infiltrated by men with little expertise in warfare'.[51] De Vere may well have been resented for rising above his station to marquess, but as his lineage was so old, his family tracing its descent back to one of the Conqueror's companions, there could have been no argument that his place at court and alongside the king as a member of the higher nobility was deserved on his blood alone, while his wife's ancestry was even more distinguished. His lack of military experience was relative only, given that by the time he was twenty-three he had campaigned both in France and Scotland, and was a result of his own comparative youth. The elevations of de Vere and de la Pole are not comparable, given their differing lineages.

---

[48] Tuck, *Richard II*, 71–2.
[49] *PROME*, vii, 1385 Parliament, no. 17.
[50] Tuck, *Richard II*, 84.
[51] Given-Wilson, 'Richard II and the Higher Nobility', in Goodman and Gillespie, eds, *Richard II and the Art of Kingship*, 118.

Patronage

The distribution of royal patronage was frequently a major political issue in the later Middle Ages. It did not, by any means, define the entire political system but was clearly of importance in the polity. In 1971, Anthony Tuck wrote that 'the exercise of patronage... was a powerful means of building support and exclusion from patronage was a powerful incentive to political action, but none the less it is possible to exaggerate its political importance... not every political crisis was provoked by "outs" trying to get "in"'.[52] As has been discussed, patronage formed part of the traditional allegations against favourites, both as they enriched themselves, but also as this led to the impoverishment of the crown. It was precisely this aspect of the grants to de Vere that the Appellants focussed on the parliament of 1388. De Vere, Pole and Neville,

> have ensured that our lord the king, without the assent of the realm, or their desert, has given them, at their instigation, various lordships, castles, towns and manors, both those annexed to the crown and others, like the land of Ireland, and Oakham with the forest of the same, and other lands which were the Lord Audley's, and other great lands to the said Robert de Vere, duke of Ireland... whereby they have been greatly enriched and the king has been impoverished, having nothing by which to support himself and bear the charges of the kingdom, except by imposing and taking imposts, taxes and tributes from his people, to the disinheritance of his crown and the destruction of the realm.[53]

It is interesting that the critique of royal favourites in general, and Richard's court circle in particular, should have had so lasting an impact, and the type and language of such allegations as were made against them should still pervade the historiography of the period. Why, as Chris Fletcher argues, should the granting of Robert de Vere's duchy of Ireland, or Simon Burley's role in Kent 'be portrayed as "patronage" rather than as the distribution of resources to fulfil certain military functions'?[54] A role such as Burley's constableship of Dover Castle had to be occupied – it had significant military responsibilities – and there was no expectation that the role would be left vacant and the salary retained by the crown.[55] The way they exercised such offices, and Burley

---

[52] Tuck, 'Richard II's System of Patronage', in Du Boulay and Barron, eds, *Reign of Richard II*, 3.
[53] *PROME*, vii, 86.
[54] Fletcher, *Richard II*, 9–10.
[55] Tuck argues that (some of) the nobility would have aspired to this office and that it made them suspicious of royal policy towards France: *Richard II*, 76. For his conduct in local government in Kent, see Saul, *Richard II*, 163–4.

at Dover and in Kent seems to have generated considerable criticism, is a different point. The permanent alienation of land, in particular, through grants in tail male was undoubtedly controversial, but the pool of such lands was fairly limited, and as will be discussed de Vere received few such grants. From the point of view of the political nation it was important to ensure reasonable returns for the crown in any such grant and that a balance was maintained between individuals and groups without the king being seen to favour overly any person or faction. This was true from the king's point of view as well but there was another principle at stake for him – his ability to make grants as he saw fit. It is thus important to recognise this was not just about 'patronage' but about the broader issue of the king's ability to rule without undue restrictions being placed upon his prerogative. Patronage was a symptom and not a cause of the political crisis of the mid-1380s.

There were political problems arising from Richard's use of patronage before de Vere began to receive much from him. According to Walsingham, Richard, Lord Scrope, the chancellor, refused to comply with the king's desire to accede to requests made of him from the Mortimer estates which had fallen into the hands of the crown through the death of the earl of March in December 1381, saying he was impoverishing himself with such wasteful grants. Richard, furious, dismissed Scrope after the latter refused to change his stance. Walsingham's later, hostile, take on this episode has been rightly questioned by Fletcher, but he also notes that contemporaries may have interpreted Scrope's dismissal at the time as the chancellor trying to protect the king from himself, in line with parliamentary rhetoric from the Good Parliament onwards.[56] Thus, the scene was already set, before de Vere really entered onto the stage, for one of the issues that was to dominate de Vere's career and the politics of the mid-1380s. Battlelines were already being drawn between the king, who thought he could dispose of offices, lands and other perquisites in his hands as he saw fit, and others who wished to limit his power to do so. However, for the next few years, with Michael de la Pole as chancellor and the king acting personally through use of the signet, Richard had real control over the disposal of his resources.[57]

De Vere's career after he reached his majority was, in part, defined by the patronage that Richard II gave to him. As noted, Saul has argued that he was driven by financial necessity because his family was one of the poorest of the titled nobility. He continued that 'while de Vere was in the ascendant few others were able to gain access to the king's favour. He lapped

---

[56] Fletcher, *Richard II*, 90–5. For a different interpretation, see Saul, *Richard II*, 111–2.
[57] Roskell, *Impeachment of Michael de la Pole*, 34–5.

up offices, wardships and grants of land and generally, as Froissart put it, "bore all the rule around the king."[58] The main evidence for the claim of the difficulty in maintaining the rank of earl comes from the wording of two royal grants. The first was in October 1382 and conveyed the lands of the de Coucy inheritance in England to de Vere and Philippa, which was done 'in consideration of their not having land or other maintenance to support their estate'. This was accurate, as de Vere was still under age, and had not formally taken possession of his ancestral inheritance; it need not reflect on their financial circumstances in reality or after he formally reached his majority. De Vere's own petition for the de Coucy estates, to which the grant was a response, makes no mention of poverty, and simply rehearses Philippa's claim to inherit the lands held by her father.[59] More supportive of the claim of poverty was a further grant in 1384 of the castle and fee-farm of Colchester, which was justified on the basis that he did not have sufficient means to maintain his estate of earl during his mother's lifetime, as she occupied 'a great part of his inheritance as it is said'.[60] As noted above, Maud had half of the estates that would have descended to de Vere, though by 1384 his income ought to have reached the minimum level required to support an earldom, in part through possession of the de Coucy estates, so while the justification of the grant was technically accurate, it may have been designed more for public consumption than reflecting the real situation.

The de Coucy estates are central to the proper assessment of the patronage granted to de Vere. Worth about £350 p.a. on inquisition *post mortem* values, they comprised fourteen manors in Westmorland, Cumberland, Lancashire and Yorkshire.[61] After the start of the Hundred Years' War these estates had been seized as belonging to a French national, and they were granted to John de Coupland and Joan his wife, but the reversions were granted in August 1363 to de Coucy, then in England as a hostage for King John II of France. Already high in Edward III's favour, as this grant suggests, he married Edward III's eldest daughter, Isabella, in 1365. The lands were granted to Ingelram, Isabella

---

[58] Saul, *Richard II*, 121.

[59] *CPR, 1381–5*, 177; SC8/145/7223.

[60] *CPR, 1381–5*, 44; C81/486/3326. It is not known if de Vere petitioned formally for the grant, and therefore what wording – if any – he used.

[61] See Map 2 above, p. xvii. They were a moiety of the lordship of Kendal, Holme and Casterton in Westmorland, Lyneside in Cumberland, Ashton, Warton, Carnforth, Wyresdale, Scotforth, and Whittington in Lancashire, and Coghill, Thornton in Lonsdale, Middleton Tyas and Kneeton, in Yorkshire: *CPR, 1396–9*, 583. Only Kendal, Thornton, Middleton and Kneeton are mentioned in her inquisition *post mortem*: *CIPM*, xix, 356–8.

and the heirs of their bodies, and a further letter patent was issued stating that their children, wherever they were born, were capable of inheriting in England.[62] Joan de Coupland did not die until 1375 but Isabella complained in 1377 that she had been unjustly ousted from the most important of the estates, the lordship of Kendal, by Alice Perrers, a complaint that was upheld.[63] After de Coucy's return to his French allegiance on the accession of Richard II, and his resignation of all his English honours, the estates had been taken into the king's hands once more, and trustees were granted the estates on Isabella's behalf until her death in 1382. Shortly afterwards, de Vere, married to Isabella and de Coucy's daughter, petitioned the king for these estates on 25 October 1382 on the basis of their grant to Ingelram and Isabella and the heirs of their bodies, and argued that they should descend to his wife.[64]

It could be argued that the grant of the de Coucy lands was royal patronage, and this might justify Saul's claim that 'access to royal patronage was essential to [de Vere's] well-being'.[65] The Appellants in 1388 made the accusation that Simon Burley caused the king to grant the de Coucy lands to de Vere, and received the manor of Lyonshall (Herefordshire) in payment.[66] They may even have been aware of the wording of a royal letter patent which rehearsed the gift of Lyonshall by de Vere to Burley in fee simple.[67] However, Lyonshall was actually sold to Burley for 400 marks, and the sale took place (probably) nearly two years later than the de Coucy grant.[68] Any grant to de Vere and Philippa

---

[62] *CPR, 1396–9*, 583.

[63] J. Bain, 'Petition of the Lady Isabella, Countess of Bedford', *The Archaeological Journal*, 36 (1879), 174–6.

[64] SC8/145/7223; *CPR, 1345–8*, 226; *1377–81*, 174–5; *CIPM*, xiv, 107; *CP*, ii, 69–70; Green, *Lives of the Princesses*, iii, 198–206.

[65] Saul, *Richard II*, 121.

[66] *WC*, 244–5, 276–7; *PROME*, vii, 114–15.

[67] C81/1342, no. 42; *CPR, 1381–5*, 447. The signet letter authorising a grant under the great seal is dated 3 August 1384 and adds an additional judicial franchise to the lordship. No date is given for de Vere's grant but it would make sense for it to be not long before Burley asked for additional rights.

[68] *CIM, 1387–92*, 132 (no date given for the sale); *CPR, 1381–5*, 447. The manor was thoroughly peripheral to de Vere landed interests (see Map 2 above, p. xviii, no. 19 on map). It was worth just under £30 p.a. according to Earl Thomas's inquisition *post mortem* in 1371: C135/222, no. 13. The sale was thus on advantageous terms for Burley – close to ten years purchase price rather than nearer to twenty which was the normal market rate – although the fact it was isolated and distant from all other de Vere estates may in part explain the sale and the terms. The Burley family had also long had an interest. Simon's older brother, Sir John, had had custody of the

obviously depended on royal favour since the lands had been temporarily in the king's hands due to de Coucy's return to his French allegiance, and indeed there might have been a case to split the lands between Philippa and her sister Mary as co-heiresses, though that would also have made Philippa co-heiress to the de Coucy lands in France. However, in practical terms that would have been nearly impossible, and given Philippa's residency in England and Mary's in France, contrary to Ingelram and Isabella's implicit plan to divide their lands between their two daughters along national lines. Thus, Philippa had a very good claim to them as de Coucy's co-heiress, but the practice of providing for royal kin was also long established – Philippa was Edward III's granddaughter – and in this case she was especially needful as de Vere was not in possession of most of his estates. Although de Vere petitioned in 1382 claiming Philippa's hereditary right, it was the practice of providing for royal kin that formed the formal justification. Isabella herself petitioned for these lands in 1377 to support herself and Philippa and de Vere, and the grant in 1382 explicitly gives as a reason for the grant of the de Coucy lands that they were 'especially to support the said Philippa, the king's kinswoman'.[69] Certainly there were no complaints at the time that this grant was extravagant, and was done surely in part as Philippa did have a very good claim to them in her own right, even if that was not highlighted in the grant.

Aside from the de Coucy estates, it has been alleged that grants and privileges were showered on de Vere 'seemingly without limit'.[70] Up to the autumn of 1385 this is doubtful. Both the de Coucy lands, and a grant in July 1384, which gave de Vere the custody of Colchester Castle, the hundred of Tendring which pertained to it, and the fee-farm of the town for life, were arguably legitimate inheritances.[71] Colchester had been granted to the first earl of Oxford and his heirs in July 1142 by the Empress Maud, and de Vere therefore actually had a good hereditary claim to it, although no source survives to show whether he

---

manor during de Vere's minority in the 1370s at an annual farm of 50 marks: *CPR, 1377–81*, 137.
[69] SC8/95/4710, 4711; *CPR, 1381–5*, 177.
[70] Saul, *Richard II*, 182.
[71] *CPR, 1381–5*, 442.

knew this or not.[72] The value of the castle and hundred was estimated at £20 in 1388, that of the fee farm £35 in 1365.[73]

There were, therefore, until autumn 1385, only three grants that were purely a result of royal favour. In June 1384, and then under amended terms on the same day as the Colchester grant, 17 July 1384, de Vere was assigned the custody of the lands of the son and heir of Thomas, Lord Roos of Helmsley, during his minority. While this superficially appears very lucrative, two factors meant it was much less so. The heir, Sir John de Roos, was already over eighteen, and therefore the grant was of short duration. Moreover, of the entire Roos estate at the death of Lord Thomas, by far the largest proportion was either of the inheritance of Beatrice, Lady Roos, widow of Lord Thomas, or had been enfeoffed to joint tenure with her and therefore was excluded from the grant of the wardship of the estates. In practice this left only eight manors in Yorkshire, Lincolnshire and Leicestershire, worth some £200 per annum.[74] The initial grant specified that de Vere was to render at the exchequer a sum for the support of the young lord and his household to be agreed between him and the council; the July amendment altered the terms by stating that he did not have to render anything for the wardship (including for Roos's upkeep).[75]

The second, and more controversial, piece of patronage was granted in March 1385 when the castle and lordship of Queenborough in Kent was bestowed on de Vere. The grant was for the life of de Vere and of Richard II, but then had the very unusual clause that if de Vere were to die first, the premises were to revert to the crown but if Richard were to die first, de Vere was to have the property in tail male. The grant then ends with the extraordinary phrase, 'The

---

[72] *CPR, 1381–5*, 442; *CCR, 1381–5*, 462; *Red Paper Book of Colchester*, ed. Benham, 151. The king's esquire, George Felbrigg, had previously held Colchester, but surrendered it to de Vere, being compensated the next day by the grant of £40 from the fee farm of Norwich; *CCR, 1381–5*, 459–60; *CIM, 1387–93*, 91; SC6/1092/3; *CPR, 1381–5*, 542, 576. For the hereditary claim: *CP*, x, 201. The warrant does not mention any claim but there is apparently no surviving petition: C81/494, no. 3325. A century later, the thirteenth earl of Oxford was well aware of his hereditary right: *Letters and Papers, Foreign and Domestic of the Reign of Henry VIII*, eds J.S. Brewer, R.H. Brodie and J. Gairdner (23 vols in 38, London, 1862–1932), i, p. 28, no. 12, citing C66/610, m. 4; E36/182, m. 44.

[73] *CIM, 1387–93*, 91; SC6/1092/3.

[74] *CFR, 1383–91*, 42 (C81/485, no. 3293); *CPR, 1381–5*, 442 (C81/486, no. 3327); which contains the usual clauses regarding maintenance of the estates; *CIPM*, xvi, 11–19; xx, 114–18; C.D. Ross, 'The Yorkshire Baronage' (unpublished DPhil, University of Oxford, 1950), 106–7. The value given above is derived from a later inquisition, that of William Lord Roos, d. 1414; *CIPM*, xx, 76–80.

[75] *CFR, 1383–91*, 42; *CPR, 1381–5*, 442.

curse of God and St Edward and the king on any who do or attempt aught against this grant.'[76] The grant went on to add that this curse was the custom of the king's progenitors in their charters to Westminster Abbey.[77] There are two possibilities as to why such a remarkable and personal addition was made to a formal grant. The sensitivity of the donation may have been less about its revenue potential than the fact the castle at Queenborough had been built in the 1360s at a total expenditure of more than £20,000, and in the most recent style – cylindrical and concentric – by Edward III and named after Queen Philippa.[78] It was therefore modern, expensive and royal, and granting it out from the crown lands was likely to be unpopular. In practice, though, it is worth noting that the castle had suffered extensive damage to six towers of the inner ward and some of the chambers within as a result of an earthquake in 1382. De Vere clearly took on responsibility for repairing the castle, as two months after the grant four men were ordered to take labourers, carpenters and others to repair the earl's castle at Queenborough at the cost of the earl.[79] This might have rendered the grant less lucrative than it appeared, and it is not known how much de Vere spent. Clearly, however, the job was not completed, as substantive repairs were still required in 1393.[80] De Vere may well have had intentions of spending time there as he acquired the chace and warren on the isle of Sheppey, where Queenborough was situated, for himself and his heirs in August 1385 from the king.[81] Yet, this grant was also about de Vere undertaking a military function rather than just benefitting from Richard's largesse.

The other possible explanation for the curse was that Queenborough, among many other manors, had been enfeoffed to the performance of Edward III's will, with the intention it go to the endowment of one of the three religious houses the old king wished to support. As Given-Wilson has shown, by 1382, a compromise had been reached by which only some of these manors were to be used for this purpose; this compromise was a result of the over-generous nature of the grant, on which both Richard, many of his advisors and the royal

---

[76] *CPR, 1381–5*, 542; C81/1344, no. 74.

[77] C81/1344, no. 74. No specific charter is mentioned in the signet warrant. This was not the only occasion the king included such a curse – a grant of £1,000 per year to the king of Armenia in February 1386 included an almost identical phrase: *CPR, 1385–9*, 110.

[78] *History of the King's Works*, ii, 793–804.

[79] *CPR, 1381–5*, 576.

[80] *History of the King's Works*, ii, 803.

[81] C81/49, no. 3709. This was not enrolled on the patent rolls. The grant was given at Newcastle upon Tyne on 19 August after the army returned from Scotland.

council clearly agreed, and legal tussles had broken out over this issue well before any grant to de Vere.[82] Nonetheless, the grant in 1385 might have been thought to be potentially insecure for de Vere and the curse was to warn off legal challengers.

The last favour was shown on 23 July 1385, when he was granted, in tail male, the castle and lordship of Oakham, with the forest of Rutland and the office of the sheriff of Rutland.[83] This grant certainly might have aroused some irritation. The lordship had been held by the Bohun earls of Hereford and Essex, and the daughters and co-heirs of the last earl were married by the date of the grant to Thomas of Woodstock and Henry Bolingbroke, son of John of Gaunt. Both might have had expectations of the lordship. However, it had been in crown hands for some time since the lordship had been granted in tail male to the Bohuns and therefore Richard was fully entitled to grant it to whoever he wished since the male line had died out in 1373. Richard had also made use of the lordship as a source for two royal annuities totalling more than £100, which again rendered it significantly less lucrative.[84]

It is difficult to put a figure on the exact revenue potential of the patronage given to de Vere in these two years. Excluding the de Coucy estates, the Roos wardship was worth £200 p.a. but only for two and a half years, Colchester and its appurtenances £55 p.a. for life,[85] and Oakham was assessed at the clear value of £37 in 1388, though this would subsequently rise once annuities assigned on its revenues expired.[86] The total value of this patronage in 1384–5 was £292 p.a. in addition to the income from Queenborough, for which no extant contemporary valuation can be located. Overall, while sizeable, the level of patronage hardly

---

[82] C. Given-Wilson, 'Richard II and his Grandfather's Will', *EHR*, 93 (1978), 320–37, and for Queenborough, 327–8.

[83] *CPR, 1385–9*, 14.

[84] *The Victoria County History of Rutland*, ed. W. Page (2 vols, London, 1908–36), ii, 5–27. For the annuities, see n. 86 below.

[85] A payment of £20 for the castle of Colchester and the hundred of Tendring for the half year following de Vere's forfeiture by Walter atte Lee is E364/28, rot. 6.

[86] Oakham was a valuable manor – profits were £150 gross in 1381–2 (SC6/964/9) and £115 net in 1383 (E364/17, rot 4d.), while it was extended at £134 7s 5d in 1388 (E357/9, rot. 22d). However, Richard II had assigned two pensions of £100 annually to Sir Richard Stury and £6 13s 4d to Henry Chaundler from its revenues: *CIM, 1377–88*, 210; there is a duplicate copy of the original inquisition in Northamptonshire Archives, FH/426/7. An account during de Vere's tenure (SC6/964/10) is partly illegible and lacking totals. The manor of Langham, worth £96 18s 2d p.a., would have fallen to de Vere as lord of Oakham on the death of Joan, Countess of Hereford: E357/9, rot. 22d.

seems to be immoderate, so how objectionable was this to the rest of the political community? There seems little policy in the patronage: the grants were scattered from Yorkshire to Kent and were not designed to establish him in a new local power base. Historians have criticised the grants of Queenborough, Oakham and Colchester on the grounds of them giving offence to local landowners, by intruding a courtier into established local society.[87] Yet the grants were all in areas, Kent, Essex and Rutland, where the de Veres already held land. He and his family had been Kentish landowners for three generations, and as co-heirs of the Badlesmere family were representatives of a well-established Kentish noble family. De Vere held only the manor of Badlesmere in that county, but his mother held in dower and jointure seven others. Kent was not their primary area of interest, but they certainly had a well-established and not unimportant stake in the county. The family also held the wealthy manor of Market Overton in Rutland. Colchester was in the de Vere heartland of northern Essex, and the only man who might also have had expectations of this grant was Gloucester, albeit de Vere had a hereditary claim to it. Saul states that 'the position of the de Vere interest so close to his own constituted a threat to Gloucester's position in the county', while Tuck argues that Richard II's patronage had had the effect of raising up de Vere and Pole as 'territorial powers' in the region where Gloucester's interests and residence lay.[88] Gloucester had married Eleanor, one of the co-heiresses of the Bohun family, earls of Hereford and Essex, and had his major seat at Pleshey, some fifteen miles from de Vere's Castle Hedingham. At least one historian has described Essex as Woodstock territory, asserting that only Aubrey de Vere, intermittently serving on the quorum for the commission of the peace in Essex, could exert even marginal influence on behalf of Richard II there.[89] Yet, in assessing the question of spheres of interest, it needs to be understood that the ancient de Vere territorial stake in Essex was far greater than that of Gloucester, who held only six manors in the county, considerably less than the total de Vere holding of twenty-one manors, fifteen held by de Vere, and six by his mother.[90] It can hardly have been a foregone conclusion that

---

[87] See for example, Saul, *Richard II*, 163.

[88] Saul, *Richard II*, 179; Tuck, *Richard II*, 102.

[89] S. Mitchell, 'The Knightly Household of Richard II and the Peace Commissions', in M.A. Hicks, ed., *The Fifteenth Century II: Revolution and Consumption in Late Medieval England* (Woodbridge, 2001), 50.

[90] *CIPM*, xvii, 378; xx, 204–6; BL, Harleian Roll N3. While he stood to inherit more estates whenever his mother-in-law, Countess Joan, died (this did not happen until 1419), these would be split with the other co-heiress, Mary, countess of Derby, and it cannot be presumed that Gloucester could exploit Countess Joan's influence in the county during her lifetime.

Gloucester would have enjoyed the dominant position in Essex during de Vere's majority, despite his royal blood, and indeed he might well have struggled to do so with such a small territorial stake.[91]

Thus, before the grant of the lordship of Ireland, royal patronage to Robert de Vere, while substantial, was not vast, nor did it impinge to any great extent on other spheres of influence, with the possible exception of Gloucester. Nor was de Vere the only person to benefit in this way. Certainly at a little over £300 per annum, this patronage was rather less than Michael de la Pole was promised when he was created earl of Suffolk in 1385, which was £500 per year in land, while by 1385, Edward III's youngest son Thomas, duke of Gloucester, was in receipt of £2,000 a year of royal annuities to support his titles.[92] If the de Coucy lands were a legitimate inheritance, then de Vere was in possession of lands of his own patrimony and that of his wife worth perhaps £800 annually, and had expectations of inheriting lands worth nearly as much again. His financial situation was not as problematic as has been suggested, and there was no economic necessity for him to receive vast amounts of patronage. His coffers are unlikely to have been overflowing, but he should not have had to struggle to maintain his rank. Given also that de Vere's income at this stage in his life was diminished because of the various burdens on his estates, the granting of some patronage seems entirely justifiable, especially given the legitimate reason of provision for the support of his wife, a granddaughter of Edward III. The curse concerning Queenborough, which is the only strictly contemporary evidence suggestive of objections to this patronage, implies perhaps that there had been complaints. Surely, however, it was not so much the value of the patronage in itself but rather the frequency of the grants not just to de Vere but also to others in the court circle such as de la Pole and Burley, that may have been offensive to other magnates and perhaps especially to Gloucester who was so dependent on royal largesse. Moreover, the economic conditions and the financial position of the crown, given the strain of the war, meant that the disposal of patronage was politically more sensitive than it might otherwise have been. Some might also have taken note of the fact that three castles – Colchester, Queenborough and Oakham – had been granted to de Vere in little more than a year in tail or for life, and the first two were certainly of strategic significance in the defence of the realm and the control of a major town close to the coast.

---

[91] For a similar dismissal of Richard's patronage disrupting Appellant interests, see Gundy, *Richard II and the Rebel Earl*, 103–6.
[92] Saul, *Richard II*, 121; *CPR, 1377–81*, 60, 66–7; *1381–5*, 177; *1385–9*, 55.

Politics

In the first half of the 1380s, English politics was dominated by the war with France. This is not to say there was a united front amongst the English against their enemies across the channel. In fact, fault lines ran deep within England as to whether peace or war was the best policy, and if the latter, whether intervention in northern France and the Low Countries would be more effective than opening a second, southern, front against the French by intervening against their allies, the Castilians. Both policies had been tried in the early years of Richard's reign without any success. Buckingham's expedition in northern France and Brittany in 1380, in which de Vere had participated, was followed by an expedition by Buckingham's brother, the earl of Cambridge, to Portugal in 1381 as a preliminary to an attack on Castile. This immediately ran into difficulties, and John of Gaunt, the leading advocate of the 'way of Spain', sought funding for a second expedition. Parliament, generally suspicious of Gaunt's self-interest, given his claim to the throne of Castile, rejected the necessary funding. Cambridge found the Portuguese had negotiated a settlement with Castile behind his back and was forced to return home in humiliation in the autumn of 1382. The pendulum swung again to action closer to home and, in particular, to the 'way of Flanders'. An opportunity had arisen to exploit differences between the pro-French count of Flanders, Louis de Mâle, and the pro-English townsmen of the great Flemish cities, whose prosperity depended on the wool trade with England. Yet the expedition launched in 1383 took a surprising form – a crusade against the count who was on the other side of the papal schism – and led by a bishop, Henry Despenser of Norwich. Despite some early successes, Despenser was forced to retreat in the face of a far superior French force, and the crusade was abandoned. Thus, three expeditions in four years had failed to deliver any notable successes while emptying the exchequer and provoking a massive popular uprising in 1381 which was certainly sparked by royal taxation, even if it had other causes as well.

In all of this Richard had little active role. There was certainly some discussion as to whether he should campaign in person on Despenser's expedition in 1383, and part of the charge against the bishop during his impeachment in the parliament of October 1383 was that he had caused the council to lay aside plans for an expedition led by Richard or by Gaunt. However, as Saul has pointed out, the exchequer could not have afforded the bigger costs required for a royal expedition, and the bishop's option was far cheaper. Saul also argues Richard seems to have shown little enthusiasm himself to take part.[93] It is worth

---

[93] Saul, *Richard II*, 104.

noting that Richard does not seem to have been against the war in general. Just a year earlier, he had declared his firm purpose to lead an expedition to France at a great council in 1382; this foundered as parliament refused to grant sufficient taxation to fund it in the aftermath of the Peasants' Revolt.[94] There were also a string of cogent reasons why the king should not lead a campaign in 1382–3, but as Fletcher has pointed out, Richard may well have been keen to do so, to prove his manhood, his fitness to rule and to throw off any remaining restrictions on him as king.[95] Richard seems to have been keen to go to the bishop's aid in Flanders at a great council which met to deliberate on the matter in September 1383 but the council advised against it and, as the Westminster Chronicle put it, 'in this way his purpose was thwarted'.[96]

It is, perhaps, from this point that it is possible to see the emergence of tensions between the king and his circle and some of the nobility. The Westminster Chronicle notes that during the parliament of autumn 1383, perhaps coincidentally the first one to which de Vere was summoned as earl of Oxford, 'a serious quarrel arose between the king and the lords temporal, because, as it seemed to them, he clung to unsound policies and for this reason excluded wholesome guidance from his entourage', and that he ought to listen and follow their advice.[97] Richard's response was to say that he was unwilling to be led exclusively by their advice, but he was content to accept the guidance of his council. The Chronicler ought to have qualified his remarks slightly – it was not the whole of the Lords temporal against the crown, as many lords were part of the royal council and the king's entourage. It is also incorrect to criticise Richard for not consulting widely in these years; it was a great council that advised him not to go to Flanders for example. However, the accusation that he listened too much to those much around him and that their advice was 'unsound' was to become one of the touchstones of politics over the next few years. Richard won this round as, in the words of the Westminster Chronicler, he 'acted with great shrewdness and discernment' in parliament and he was able to reject any formal imposition of additional council on him. Yet the problem remained that some outside his inner circle – notably Gaunt and Buckingham – felt their advice was not being followed, and that it should be by right of their royal blood and their experience.

It is hard to be precise about de Vere's place in this. It is likely that he was one of those whose unwholesome guidance was rebuked but none are named

---

[94] Fletcher, *Richard II*, 98–9.
[95] Fletcher, *Richard II*, ch. 6.
[96] *WC*, 48–9; Fletcher, *Richard II*, 108–13.
[97] *WC*, 54–5.

in the Chronicle's account of the parliament.[98] It is simply unclear what policy he might have urged on Richard in 1383 – whether to campaign or not – and whether Richard sought to follow that advice. Yet the fault-lines were clear, and the politics of Richard II's minority began to take a darker turn in 1384 from differences of opinion over the right foreign policy to serious disagreements about domestic policy coupled with increasing hostility between these factions within the polity itself.

The hostility first openly manifested itself at the Salisbury Parliament of spring 1384. During the parliament, a Carmelite friar, one John Latimer, told King Richard that Gaunt was plotting to kill him.[99] According to the Westminster Chronicle, Richard immediately ordered that Gaunt be put to death. The nobles present declared that he could not be condemned without trial, to which the king agreed. The friar stated that William, Lord Zouche, had knowledge of the affair as well. Richard ordered the friar into custody, but Sir John Holland, personally close to Gaunt, intercepted the party and took the friar off to interrogate under torture. Although so broken in body that he died a few days later, he did not retract his allegation and refused to admit 'he had been suborned by some prominent person' and while his accusers hoped 'the fear of pain would speed his disclosure of his principal's name' their efforts were in vain. Zouche denied any knowledge of the matter and was absolved of any charge, and Gaunt hurried to the king and 'disposed so brilliantly of the slur upon him that the king thenceforward regarded him as cleared'.[100] As Saul suggests, Zouche is unlikely to have been deeply involved, and the friar might have been acting on his own account, or indeed was mad – he certainly seems to have shammed insanity when his allegations against Gaunt were not immediately acted upon.[101] However, there is circumstantial evidence that de Vere might have been involved. The Westminster Chronicle alleged that the friar first spoke to Richard after leaving mass in de Vere's apartments. Two historians have used another account, that of the Monk of Evesham, to further implicate de Vere, stating that the friar asserted that there was a worthy esquire of the earl of Oxford's who was deeply involved and would support his accusation. However, this seems to be based on a mistranslation of the Latin, which actually has the friar asserting that a worthy esquire of the county of

---

[98] There is no record of any disagreement on the parliament roll itself, as the editor notes: *PROME*, vi, 321.

[99] R. Copsey, *Biographical Register of Carmelites in England and Wales 1240–1540* (Faversham, 2020), 178–80.

[100] *WC*, 74–7.

[101] Saul, *Richard II*, 132; *WC*, 70

Oxfordshire would support the accusation; the nameless esquire went on to excuse himself upon oath.[102] Saul found the involvement of de Vere plausible, asserting 'if anyone at court was implicated it was… likely to have been Robert de Vere'.[103] Tuck argues that there was a possibility that Oxford used the friar to undermine Gaunt's standing at court and with the king, but found it more likely to represent hostility between the friar (and friars more generally) and Gaunt. Likewise Gaunt's biographer, Anthony Goodman, notes the hostility towards Gaunt by the friars and argues the significance of the affair 'may have been to demonstrate to the king's close friends, such as Oxford, how dearly he longed for his uncle to go'.[104] It is noteworthy that Walsingham, deeply hostile to de Vere, did not mention him in connection to the episode, either as instigator or advisor to the king; in his account the king apparently took advice from two clerks of his chapel, Nicholas Slake and one unnamed other, who advised him to discuss the matters with the duke.[105] Overall, then, de Vere's involvement in any plot seems rather unlikely.

Another plot was, apparently, hatched in order to arrest and murder Gaunt in mid-February 1385. The Westminster Chronicle describes how at a tournament in Westminster 'a plot was hatched on the concluding night by some of the nobles (with the king's approval, it was said), to murder the duke' but he got wind of it and made his escape.[106] At a reconciliation on 6 March between the king and the duke, brokered by Joan of Kent, the duke was persuaded to abandon 'the resentment he had nursed against some of the nobles who were intimate with the king. These were the earls of Salisbury, Oxford and Nottingham: there were others who were not yet able to win from him the favour of forgiveness.'[107] The implication is unclear here. Were the three earls forgiven by Gaunt because they had not been involved in a plot, whereas others had been? Or Gaunt forgave them in public, perhaps as a result of their status, but they were no more or less involved against him than

---

[102] *Historia Vitae et Regni Ricardi Secundi*, ed. G. Stow (Philadelphia, PA, 1977), 81–2. The Latin has 'quod fuit quidam ualens armiger de comitatu Oxon' qui erat testis et conscius predictorum.' Tuck translated this as an esquire of the earl rather than of Oxfordshire: *Richard II*, 93; Saul, *Richard II*, 132. However, the county rather than the earl is surely to be preferred, and the former is used in the collection of source material by A.K. McHardy, ed., *The Reign of Richard II* (Manchester, 2012), 117.

[103] Saul, *Richard II*, 132.

[104] Tuck, *Richard II*, 93; Goodman, *John of Gaunt*, 100.

[105] *SAC*, i, 722–7.

[106] *WC*, 110–1.

[107] *WC*, 114–15.

others who he did not need to forgive? Other chroniclers, such as Walsingham and the Monk of Evesham, simply accuse the men around the king without naming any, although Walsingham perhaps implies de Vere (and others) when he stated that 'the young king and his youthful associates plotted his [Gaunt's] death'.[108] Saul, while suggesting that Salisbury was not involved, is prepared to believe that 'Oxford and Nottingham were probably the main culprits' while both Tuck and Goodman also accept the probability of these two men being involved, though Tuck suggests it might have been competition between the two men rather than cooperation between them.[109] According to a French narrative of Richard II's downfall, Mowbray confessed in 1398 to a previous plot to murder the duke for which Gaunt forgave him; this would fit well with the episode of February 1385.[110]

Yet, there is no really authoritative evidence that Robert de Vere was involved in either plot. If he was, then it was likely to have been that of 1385 rather than 1384. The connection with the latter is weak and made weaker still when the Monk of Evesham's account is shown not to name de Vere at all. All the narrative accounts cited above were written after de Vere's downfall in 1388 which may have influenced their depiction. While a plot in 1385 is plausible, the format alleged by the chronicler – the outright murder of Gaunt – was highly unlikely, given Gaunt was the second most powerful man in the realm (and de facto heir to the throne). Perhaps the fabrication of a conspiracy by Gaunt to kill the king (as seems to have been alleged in 1384), for which treason he could be quickly executed, was meant. Such a course of action by the king's friends was not inherently impossible: royal uncles were to fall to such accusations in 1397 and in even more closely aligned circumstances in 1447. Saul argues the two young earls were jealous of Gaunt's standing, his greater weight in council and his vast wealth. Goodman suggests de Vere's motivation more generally against Gaunt was in pursuance of his rivalry for territorial power in Essex against Gaunt's brother, Thomas, duke of Gloucester.[111] Yet an indirect local rivalry seems an unlikely motivation. In fact, the episode might be more plausibly linked not to jealousy on the part of Oxford, Nottingham – or indeed Salisbury – or a local rivalry on de Vere's part, but to national politics. The Westminster Chronicle directly links the episode of February 1385 with a bitter argument over foreign policy in a council meeting. There Gaunt

---

[108] *SAC*, i, 50–1; *Historia Vitae*, ed. Stow, 85–6.

[109] Saul, *Richard II*, 134; Tuck, *Richard II*, 95–6; Goodman, *John of Gaunt*, 102.

[110] *Chronique de la Traison et Mort de Richart Deux Roy Denglettre*, ed. B. Williams (RS, London, 1846), 147–9; Given-Wilson, *Henry IV*, 112.

[111] Saul, *Richard II*, 134; Goodman, *John of Gaunt*, 284.

and his brothers argued in vain against the rest of the council for an invasion of France, and then stalked out when it was rejected, vowing, to the great displeasure of the king and council, that he would not aid the king unless he crossed to France. Gaunt was an obstacle to the policies of those close to the king and to that of the king himself. If a plot against Gaunt existed in February 1385, it is most likely that men close to the king – perhaps including Oxford – were acting with the tacit approval or even on the instruction of the king. A reading of Richard's immediate decision to execute the duke before being persuaded otherwise in 1384 and the more explicit statements in the chronicles that the plot of 1385 was hatched with the king's approval or indeed was his in the first place, could certainly mean the author of the policy was Richard himself.[112] Clearly, these episodes were murky in the extreme, but it is not unlikely that Gaunt felt threatened and that threat was linked to those close to the king, including de Vere. It would explain, in part, why de Vere was so disliked by the Appellants and chroniclers.

Less serious but a better evidenced episode that is suggestive of faction and perhaps of de Vere's growing unpopularity is the accusation made by Walter Sibille against Robert de Vere of maintenance and denial of justice. The accusation is recorded on the parliament roll of November 1384 and was later recorded in detail on the close rolls; there were subsequent parliamentary petitions relating to the original law suit (which did not involve de Vere) in 1390 (November), 1391 and 1394. Its origins lay in legal proceedings between Walter Sibille, a London merchant, and two East Anglian knights, Nicholas Twyford and William Coggeshall.[113] Both parties were summoned before the council, and an Oyer and Terminer commission was granted to Walter and a special assize to the knights, in which Walter was, according to his version, 'condemned in £800 for property not exceeding the value of 8s. a year, great number of his goods and chattels were taken away, and he suffered other damage and grievance, and that by the maintenance of the said earl [of Oxford] as he supposed'.[114] Sibille accused de Vere of maintenance to no less a person than John of Gaunt, and when Sibille was brought before the lords in parliament at de Vere's suit, he continued to 'suppose' de Vere's involvement. De Vere denied any maintenance in parliament and invoked the statue of

---

[112] Fletcher puts forward a different argument, that the king might have initially believed the friar's accusations against Gaunt in the context of the disagreements over foreign policy and his close involvement in the peace negotiations under discussion which were ultimately rejected: *Richard II*, 124. He does not speculate, however, on whether the friar was acting alone or in conjunction with others.

[113] The next few sentences are based on *PROME*, vi, 387; *CCR, 1385–9*, 44, 234–5.

[114] *CCR, 1385–9*, 234–5.

defamation of peers. Three days later, Sibille was brought back into parliament, retracted his accusation and threw himself on the mercy of the king and the earl. Sibille was then convicted of defamation and damages of 500 marks were granted to de Vere. Sibille was then committed to prison until he paid.[115] He was released under surety for a few weeks in the winter of 1384–5 with de Vere's assent but not fully set at large until April 1387, but then 'with the assent and at the prayer of Robert de Veer'. It is not stated there that de Vere had been fully paid, which suggests some leniency.[116]

Clearly neither the parliament roll or the close roll should be taken at face value. The case could be seen another of de Vere's iniquities and of the increasing unpopularity of the regime – de la Pole was accused of a similar crime in the parliament of April 1384 – and at least one historian has accepted the allegations, noting it was thanks to de Vere's 'dubious methods' that Coggeshall had been awarded a staggering £800 in damages. However, there are grounds for considering Sibille a troublemaker and that perhaps de Vere was in fact the aggrieved party.[117] Inevitably most of the documents relating to the case, notably those of the special assize and the Oyer and Terminer, have not survived, but perusal of the extant case in King's Bench offers a somewhat different perspective to that put forward by Sibille. The original case was heard at Henhowe in Suffolk shortly after Michaelmas 1384.[118] The case concerned whether a free tenement and 1,000 acres of moorland, certainly worth rather more than the 8s annually, that Sibille alleged, pertained to the manor of Landwade in Cambridgeshire, owned by Sibille, or in Exning, just over the border in Suffolk, held jointly by Twyford and Coggeshall. Moreover, at this first pleading Sibille did not turn up, and the case was awarded to Twyford and Coggeshall, with damages of £40. Sibille, when he did finally turn up to quash outlawry proceedings started against him, rather than presenting his arguments as to his right to the land, proceeded to indulge in legal time wasting, firstly pleading an error in the process, then that the original assize should not have taken place at Henhowe, which he alleged was a field in a marsh, but at the county town of Ipswich, and then that the justices' commission had expired.

---

[115] The fifty marks noted in *PROME*, vi, 388 is a mistranslation of 'quingentas', unusually for such an excellent edition.

[116] *CCR, 1385–9*, 234–5.

[117] C. Rawcliffe, 'Parliament and the Settlement of Disputes by Arbitration in the later Middle Ages', *Parliamentary History*, 9 (1990), 331; R. Bird, *The Turbulent London of Richard II* (London, 1949), 56–60.

[118] KB27/498, rots. 52, 61. There is also a considerable amount of material relating to the case collected in the King's Bench Recorda file for 8 Richard II, none of which mentions de Vere at all: KB145/3/8/1.

Such specious delaying tactics – Henhowe was in fact a regular venue for common law hearings – forced the case to be brought before the council, and more effective commissions were issued. Far from just being the injured party, Sibille was accused by Twyford in a separate case in the court of Common Pleas of stealing ten oxen, forty head of cattle and 200 ewes, worth together £44, from Exning.[119] It would be an understandable, if ill-judged, tactic – or even an outburst of anger or frustration – amidst the ruin of a legal case, to blame a powerful peer of maintenance. Moreover, the sources do not suggest that de Vere was connected at all with Twyford, although William Coggeshall had made the earl a feoffee in June 1384.[120] De Vere was well within his rights to plead defamation, given no evidence was put forward by Sibille to support his allegation of the earl's maintenance, and the political context provides a possible explanation. It is possible, if unproveable, that Sibille made his accusation as part of an attempt to get Gaunt to back him in a difficult legal case by alleging the involvement of a political rival. He would then have been forced to retract the accusation, as he did not have any evidence, when Gaunt did not back him. Sibille himself had only just been cleared of a malicious accusation of treason in connection with the 1381 revolt and given this and the entanglements of London politics with court politics – Gaunt and John of Northampton versus the court and Nicholas Brembre[121] – to try and involve Gaunt may have been a course that presented itself readily to the Londoner.

Disagreements over foreign policy continued throughout 1384 and 1385 amongst the political elite. On the one hand, the French were making great strides in the Low Countries – Philip, youngest son of John II of France, succeeded to the county of Flanders on the death of his father-in-law, Count Louis, in January 1384 – at the expense of English allies and to the serious detriment of English strategic interests.[122] On the other, the taps of taxation were running at little more than a trickle in the aftermath of the Peasants' Revolt in 1381 and as a result of war weariness after more than fifteen years of unsuccessful conflict since 1369. Three of four parliaments between 1381 and 1383 refused any grant of taxation, while only limited grants were made in the two parliaments of 1384. Over Christmas 1383 serious negotiations for peace with France led by the duke of Lancaster took place, and consideration was

---

[119] CP40/499, rot. 222d.

[120] For which, see below, p. 208.

[121] See below, p. 107. For more overtly political defamation cases, see M. Hanrahan, 'Defamation as Political Contest During the Reign of Richard II', *Medium Aevum*, 72 (2003), 259–76.

[122] For English policy over these years, see Saul, *Richard II*, ch. 7.

given to them in the spring parliament of 1384. A further round of negotiations broke down by the summer, however, and it was clear that whatever the financial situation some further military efforts would be required. Ironically, it was the French who decided English military strategy. They landed around 1,600 troops in Scotland in summer 1384 as part of a two-pronged strategy to attack England; neither the Scottish nor the cross-channel prong achieved much that year, but the threat of simultaneous invasion from north and south remained. It became the English strategy to deal with the threat from Scotland first, though not without some debate as the arguments at the great council of February 1385 between the royal uncles on the one side and the majority of the councillors on the other demonstrated. In what was actually a reasonable solution to the need to raise a large army but without sufficient revenue from taxation to do it, a feudal summons was issued. This was probably initially intended to raise money – scutage in lieu of military service – but cash was never raised as a result of opposition to this outmoded demand. Instead, a very large army of perhaps fourteen thousand men mustered at Newcastle towards the end of July 1385. Most served at the king's wages, though some savings were made by virtue of it being a feudal summons.[123]

Robert de Vere served in person. The best estimate of his retinue is that it consisted of two knights, 118 squires and 200 archers.[124] Aubrey de Vere was also present, with a retinue of three knights, seventeen squires and thirty archers.[125] Both of them were under contract rather than serving under feudal terms;

---

[123] For the debate over this, see J.J.N Palmer, 'The Last Summons of the Feudal Army in England, 1385', *EHR*, 83 (1968), 771–5; N.B. Lewis, 'The Feudal Summons of 1385', *EHR*, 100 (1985), 729–43; Palmer's response in the same volume (743–6) is convincing.

[124] E403/508 m. 19; N.B. Lewis, 'The Last Medieval Summons of the English Feudal Levy', *EHR*, 73 (1958), 19, 23. The Issue Roll does not record the size of the retinue, but does record the sum paid for it – £457 6s. 8d. Lewis compared the standard wage rates with the estimate of the retinue given in a near-contemporary document, the Order of Battle (BL, Cotton Nero D VI, fols 91v–92r, printed in S. Armitage-Smith, *John of Gaunt* (London, 1873), 437–8), and notes that the payments work out correctly. The figure is also the same for de Vere (but not other retinues) in College of Arms, London, M16 bis, fol. 73v. Three other documents giving the size of de Vere's retinue survive, two recording 220 men-at-arms and 200 archers (BL, Harleian MS 309 and Ashmole MS 865), and one 200 men-at-arms and 200 archers (Harleian MS 369); see N.H. Nicholas, 'An Account of the Army with which King Richard II Invaded Scotland in the Ninth Year of his Reign, A.D. 1385', *Archaeologia*, 23 (1829), 16. All three would seem to contain too high an estimate of the men-at-arms, consistent for all the major retinues on the expedition.

[125] Lewis, 'Last Medieval Summons', 18.

while these contracts do not now survive, they were listed by the antiquarian William le Neve in the early seventeenth century and were seen by Dugdale, who noted that both were for forty days only.[126] It is noteworthy that de Vere's retinue was larger than all but four contingents – the three uncles of the king, Lancaster, Cambridge and Buckingham, and the forces led by the Percy family – and was indeed greater than three of the future Appellants, the earls of Arundel, Warwick and Nottingham, while Derby did not lead a contingent. Oxford's retinue formed part of the king's division, alongside those of the earls of Cambridge, Stafford, Arundel, Warwick and Salisbury.[127]

As a sensible precaution before a major expedition, in early June de Vere made a major settlement of his estates, specifically of twelve manors held in chief, including Castle Hedingham, and nine manors not then in his hands.[128] His feoffees were the bishops of Winchester and Worcester, Hugh, earl of Stafford, Sir Simon Burley, Sir Robert Tresilian, John Lancaster, Henry English, Walter de Skirlawe, keeper of the Privy Seal, and three clerks, Richard Medford, Nicholas Slake and John Ripon.[129] Only the petition to enfeoff these lands has survived, and not the enfeoffment itself, so its terms are unknown. Some provisions for the performance of a will (it is likely that he made one around this time, but none survives), the payment of debts and for the good of his soul could be presumed, but there was also the vexed question of the succession of the estates and earldom. At this date Robert de Vere and Aubrey were each other's heirs male, and there was no other male de Vere alive except for a very distant cadet line established in the twelfth century. Aubrey and Robert would have known Aubrey's wife, Alice, was pregnant – the future eleventh earl of Oxford, Richard, was born on 16 August 1385 – but there was no guarantee the child would be male or would survive birth and infancy.

---

[126] BL, Stowe 440, fol. 22v; W. Dugdale, *The Baronage of England*, 2 vols (London, 1675–6), i, 194.

[127] *WC*, 124–5.

[128] *CPR, 1381–5*, 556; SC8/255/12738 (petition for licence to enfeoff). Neither document mentions the fact that de Vere held only the reversions to Earls Colne, Great Bentley, the two manors in Lavenham, Aldham and Abington, which were in his mother's hands, and Langley and Bradley which was held for life by Sir William Wingfield. Also enfeoffed were the manors of Calverton, held in tail male by his uncle Aubrey, and Saxton held either by his aunt Elizabeth with reversion to Aubrey or by Aubrey himself (see above, p. 74). These latter two may be included here as Robert de Vere may still have been his uncle's male heir before the birth of Aubrey's son and eventual successor in the earldom, Richard. See above pp. 57–8, 71–4 for more details of the estates.

[129] For discussion of the feoffees, see below, pp. 209–11.

What de Vere would have wished for, in the event of disaster overtaking the English army and both their deaths, is not known.

The expedition to Scotland caused some controversy at the time and has done so subsequently. The English army crossed the border looking to bring the Scots to battle. Predictably, the Scots had no intention of fighting a big English army and avoided contact, instead stripping the countryside of food. After burning a few abbeys, the army arrived at Edinburgh to find the city deserted. All the major chroniclers state that Richard ordered the Scottish capital to be destroyed by fire.[130] Then there seems to have been a disagreement over future strategy. Froissart records that, after the sacking of Edinburgh and various other towns, the duke of Lancaster and others wanted to go south and fight the Scots who were raiding Cumberland. However, de Vere, who 'had at the time all the heart and the counsel of the king' persuaded the king to return home, stating not only the danger from the Scots but also hinting darkly at treason.[131] A slightly different version is given by both Thomas Walsingham and the Monk of Westminster who state that Gaunt wanted to go north and raid beyond the Firth of Forth and destroy the whole of Scotland.[132] Given the terms on which the force was raised, under contracts for forty days, an extended expedition either north past the Firth of Forth, or chasing raiders around the border, was not a realistic plan. The expedition had achieved its limited objectives, a reprisal for Scottish raids and the sacking of the Scottish capital, and was never intended to be of a long duration, which the English exchequer could not have afforded. Both the Westminster Chronicle and Walsingham place the rejection of Gaunt's plan as the king's initiative and do not mention his receiving counsel. De Vere's advice, if he gave any, was sound if he suggested returning south, even if it offended Froissart's chivalric sensibilities, and several modern historians agree, including Gillespie, who goes on to note that 'even the bad can give good advice!'[133] The

---

[130] *WC*, 128–9; *SAC*, i, 760–1; Froissart, ed. Johnes, ii, 53. For the campaign, see A.J. McDonald, *Border Bloodshed. Scotland, England and France at War, 1369–1403* (East Linton, 2000), 87–91; Sumption, *Divided Houses*, 544–57.

[131] Froissart, ed. Lettenhove, x, 395–6. Froissart gives the speaker as 'le conte d'Asquesuffort'. This is Oxford (made clear by the description of the duke of Ireland as 'qui jadis fut nommé le conte d'Acquessufort', in ibid., xiv, 32) and not the earl of Suffolk as incorrectly translated by Thomas Johnes: Froissart, ed. Johnes, ii, 54. See also Goodman, *Loyal Conspiracy*, 127; J.L. Gillespie, 'Richard II: King of Battles?', in idem, ed., *The Age of Richard II* (Stroud, 1997), 144.

[132] *WC*, 128–30; *SAC*, i, 762–5. This version of events is accepted by Goodman, *Loyal Conspiracy*, 127, Gillespie, 'Richard II: King of Battles', 144 and Fletcher, *Richard II*, 137, but not by Saul, *Richard II*, 145.

[133] Gillespie, 'Richard II: King of Battles', 144.

English army thus marched south again, with the king crossing back onto English soil just two weeks after leaving it.[134] Historians have generally been critical of the expedition, but it might be noted that the symbolic burning of the enemy capital was not an insignificant achievement and in the straitened financial circumstances of an army raised for just forty days, little more might be expected.

During the campaign there was a further grant to de Vere that is rather indicative of much about his career and his relationship with Richard. On 26 July 1385, while the army was at Durham, a royal signet letter was issued granting de Vere that 'wherever for the present expedition he may lodge, he may for himself and his retaining grind before all others at the mill nearest his lodging'.[135] Possibly even reflecting a practical incident on the campaign when his men struggled to gain access to a mill, such a grant can only have done two things. It would have annoyed all who heard it, both de Vere's peers and their men, who would have to give precedence to de Vere's servants. It also demonstrated both de Vere's and Richard's lack of judgement. De Vere should not have asked for this and Richard should not have granted it. However petty the subject matter was, it demonstrated, even flaunted, the paramountcy of de Vere around the king.

Royal Court and Household

One aspect of de Vere's career, and of his relations with the king, is now impossible to reconstruct. Very few records of the royal council survive between 1383 and 1389, and it is therefore impossible to say how deeply de Vere was involved in governmental decisions. It seems likely that he would have attended on a regular basis, when at court. He can be seen as being present at council twice in July and August 1384 during proceedings against the failed London mayoral candidate, John of Northampton.[136] Northampton, who had the sporadic support of John of Gaunt, and who had been mayor in 1381–3, had been defeated by his rival, Nicholas Brembre, at the election of 1383, when it is clear that the king gave his backing to Brembre. Northampton was to allege that Brembre had packed the Guildhall with his supporters. In early 1384, Brembre had Northampton arrested on a charge of sedition, and disturbances after his arrest made the crown take a keen interest in the case.[137]

---

[134] For the duration of the campaign, see Lewis, 'Last Medieval Summons', 15–16.

[135] *CPR, 1385–9*, 13.

[136] C49/87, mm. 12–14.

[137] Saul, *Richard II*, 132–3; C.M. Barron, *London in the Late Middle Ages. Government and People, 1200–1500* (Oxford, 2004), 148–9; P. Strohm, 'Northampton [Comberton], John (d. 1398)', *ODNB*.

The Westminster Chronicle says that de Vere interceded on Northampton's behalf with the king against the interests of Nicholas Brembre, who was to fall with de Vere in 1388, but the story seems unlikely.[138]

As has been remarked above, one regular accusation against royal favourites was that they controlled access to the king and denied it to those who ought to have access or enriched themselves through receipt of bribes to allow people to see the king. Robert de Vere, as great chamberlain, had the ultimate responsibility for controlling access to the royal chamber and the king's presence. Simon Burley was the under-chamberlain or chamberlain of the household.[139] It has been generally assumed that the senior hereditary officers of the royal household, of whom the great chamberlain was one, were only occasionally present to exercise their duties and usually only on special occasions, and it was the household staff who were the ones who carried out most of the duties of the office.[140] Insofar as the hereditary officers were almost exclusively members of the upper nobility and had significant other responsibilities, this was normally true. Further backing is given to the role of the great chamberlain at court as being just occasional in the Black Book of the royal household, composed nearly a century later, which states that the 'grete chaumbyrlayne of Inglond comithe to this courte at the v principall festes of the yere'.[141] However, there might be individuals among the great officers of state who were much more frequently around court and who chose to exercise such offices in person. Where the 'permanent' member of the household staff was an ally – and in the case of the chamberlains in the 1380s Burley and de Vere were politically aligned – there was real potential to exercise control over the key functions of the office. Already during Richard's earliest years on the throne Burley has been described as controlling the staff and operations of the king's chamber, and 'was soon to make that place the "power house" of the curialist party'.[142]

It is, of course, difficult to disentangle the normal duties of the chamberlain – whether exercised by the great chamberlain or the chamberlain of the household – from the type of activities criticised by contemporaries. The chamberlain, by definition, controlled access to the king's chamber, and to

---

[138] *WC*, 184–5; Bird, *Turbulent London*, 87–8.

[139] Tout, *Chapters*, vi, 45–50.

[140] Vale, 'Courts', in Fletcher, Genet and Watts, eds, *Government and Political Life in England and France*, 26.

[141] *The Household of Edward IV: The Black Book and the Ordinances of 1478*, ed. A.R. Myers (Manchester, 1959), 101.

[142] Roskell, *Impeachment of Michael de la Pole*, 22.

some extent therefore, the business conducted there. As Chaplais has said 'in the late-fourteenth and early-fifteenth centuries it was not unusual for the intermediary between the king and petitioners to be the royal chamberlain, who either signed or endorsed the petitions which had been granted'.[143] In particular, this was true of the more informal discussions of petitions and bills. There is an interesting depiction in the *Ryalle* book of the first two Lancastrian kings after dinner on days they did not keep state leaning on cushions against a cupboard or sideboard of the great chamber for an hour or more to receive bills and petitions of whosoever might come.[144] It has been estimated that Henry IV dealt with approximately four thousand petitions a year, at an average of ten or more a day.[145] Not all, or perhaps even most, would have been dealt with in this type of informal setting, but the scale and importance of petitions is clear as is the potential for the involvement of the chamberlain and others around the king. While the *Ryalle* book does not mention the chamberlain, it was surely when the king dealt with matters in his chamber that the written evidence of the chamberlain's involvement was produced. Certainly, advice produced for Henry VI in the 1440s – in an effort to control the indiscriminate flow of patronage and careless granting of petitions – noted that the king should sign a petition or 'commaunde his chamberlain to subscribe it or take it to his secretary'.[146] The chamberlain may well have scrutinised petitions or petitioners before passing them onto the king for consideration. Thus, the fact that, as will be discussed below, there is evidence of Robert de Vere signing petitions and endorsing royal decisions should not be taken as unusual. There are many instances of the involvement of intermediaries in the transmission of authorised petitions, before, during and after Richard II's reign, as Maxwell-Lyte has shown.[147] As Gwilym Dodd has discussed, from 1399 onwards there are a considerable number of documents in the National Archives series E28 signed by the

---

[143] Chaplais, *Piers Gaveston*, 102.

[144] *The Antiquarian Repertory*, ed. F. Grose (4 vols, London, 1807–9), i, 314, dated and discussed by D. Starkey, 'Henry VI's Old Blue Gown: the English Court under the Lancastrians and Yorkists', *The Court Historian*, 4 (1999), 1–28.

[145] A.L. Brown, 'The Authorization of Letters under the Great Seal', *BIHR*, 37 (1964), 154.

[146] *PPC*, vi, 318.

[147] H.C. Maxwell-Lyte, *Historical Notes on the Use of the Great Seal of England* (London, 1926), 144–7, 151–2.

chamberlain.[148] Yet, it was a very short step from being the intermediary or gatekeeper to being influential in the decision to grant or reject a petition. As Vale has put it 'the petitioning process... did not always involve two parties: it could be a three-party nexus', whether through bribery, mutual co-operation or the enlisting of one with the king's ear.[149]

De Vere was allowed to exercise the office of great chamberlain at the king's coronation in 1377 and in January 1382 had the office confirmed upon him by a royal *Inspeximus* under the signet, a very early example of the use of the most personal of the royal seals, and one which may indicate that de Vere was in the king's company when it was granted.[150] There is clear evidence that when present Robert de Vere does appear to have exercised this office in person, at least on some occasions, rather than letting his deputies in the royal household do the work. There are six extant petitions in the National Archives series SC8 that bear his signature. Two have been discussed already in the context of the early relationship between de Vere and Richard.[151] The remaining four probably represent two separate periods when de Vere was exercising his office in the king's presence. While dating can be problematic for such petitions, resulting actions in the records of chancery suggest that two petitions were authorised in late February or early March 1385 and two in late April or early May the same year.[152] None related to de Vere's own dependents or allies, as far as can be ascertained. Two related to a case before the court of the constable and marshal of England brought by Roger Doket and relating to a ransom of a French prisoner. While the petitions, which sought to overturn a judgement by the deputies of the constable and marshal, might have been a minor annoyance to the holders of those offices, it cannot be classed as a genuinely political problem. Indeed, while the constable, Thomas of Woodstock, was not close to de Vere or Richard, the marshal, Thomas Mowbray, was very much part of the court circle at this stage.[153] In addition, there is evidence of two further grants

---

[148] G. Dodd, 'Patronage, Petitions and Grace: the "Chamberlains' Bills" of Henry IV's Reign', in G. Dodd and D. Biggs, eds, *The Reign of Henry IV. Rebellion and Survival, 1403–1413* (York, 2008), 105–35.

[149] Vale, 'Courts', in Fletcher, Genet and Watts, eds, *Government and Political Life in England and France*, 36.

[150] *CCR, 1377–81*, 2; *CPR, 1381–5*, 65.

[151] SC8/223/11102; 224/11168. See above, pp. 81–2.

[152] SC8/224/11153 (late April–early May 1385: cf. *CCR, 1381–5*, 545), 11159 (early March 1385, cf. *CPR, 1381–5*, 592), 11160 (late February 1385, cf. *CPR, 1381–5*, 593), 11199 (early May 1385, cf. *CPR, 1381–5*, 598).

[153] *CPR, 1381–5*, 592, 598.

where Oxford was present, also from the early months of 1385. One is amongst the warrants for the Great Seal, and is particularly noteworthy as the petitioner was Geoffrey Chaucer, asking to exercise an office in the customs of London by deputy. This was granted by the usual formula of endorsing the petition 'The king grants this', and this was written by de Vere, who also signed the document.[154] The resultant letter patent was issued on 17 February. The second concerned a bill presented by Thomas Mowbray, earl of Nottingham, which was granted by the king, and 'sealed by the earl of Oxford, his chamberlain' in January 1385, though not in this case signed.[155]

Thus, we have eight examples of de Vere signing or sealing royal decisions on petitions sent to the king in his office as royal chamberlain, and almost certainly in the royal presence. Six of these were from the early months of 1385. Did de Vere simply temporarily alter his practice in these months and sign a number of bills or is this all or most of the bills he handled over the course of his active career? There was nothing particularly noteworthy about the king's movements in those months – he was generally at Eltham, Sheen or Westminster, so there is little to indicate that he was without access to particular seals or personnel. If eight is not a sizeable sample, it is worth noting that there are only thirteen such bills or petitions amongst the Ancient Petitions signed by Simon Burley.[156] Between the two, they must surely have been present when hundreds, perhaps thousands, of petitions were seen by the king; that both rarely signed them probably hides the fact they were involved in handling – and perhaps influencing – a great deal more business.

Such a personal presence would, of course, have given the chance for him to attempt to use his influence concerning the distribution of patronage. It has certainly been assumed that the favour and ready access he had to the king led to benefits for his clients and dependents.[157] That de Vere had some influence is attested by three grants to members of his affinity that are enrolled as being at his supplication and a further grant at his supplication to a significant local figure perhaps outside his affinity.[158] One grant, at the supplication of the earl,

---

[154] C81/1394, no. 87; *CPR, 1381–5*, 532. For discussion, see J.R. Hulbert, 'Chaucer and the earl of Oxford', *Modern Philology*, 10 (1913), 433–7.

[155] SC8/226/11272. This was enrolled 10 January 1385: *CPR, 1381–5*, 529.

[156] Dodd, 'Richard II and the Fiction of Majority Rule', 158.

[157] Tuck, *Richard II*, 80.

[158] The figure beyond his affinity was John Doreward, for whom a ratification of descent of estates to him was made at the instance of de Vere, 8 May 1386: *CPR, 1385–9*, 150. For Doreward, see below, pp. 208–9. De Vere also mainperned for the good behaviour of John Lancaster in the office of Sheriff of Wiltshire, 12 October

on 10 January 1385 was to his esquire, John de Routh, of the wardship and marriage of heir of William Lylle of Sussex, worth 20 marks; another was to a servant of the marquess of Dublin, Martin Medritz, of the fee-farm of Ilchester, Somerset, extended at £8, at a yearly rent of £6 on 16 July 1386.[159] The third was the promotion of John Ripon to archdeacon of Wells on 1 December 1386.[160] A licence in November 1385 to Woburn Abbey, described as being of the advowson of the king's kinsman, Robert de Vere, to acquire land in mortmain may also have been at his supplication; although no mention was made of any intercession, he had been with the king two days earlier.[161] The exemption of his close servant, Henry English, from serving on juries, assizes and other offices on 10 April 1386 was sandwiched between grants to de Vere in relation to the ransom of John of Blois on 8 and 11 April, and while there is no direct evidence to say de Vere was present, it is likely he was and he may well have taken the opportunity to obtain a favour for his servant.[162] There are eight other documents, comprising one grant, one exemption and six pardons, enrolled as being at his supplication to men who cannot otherwise be linked to de Vere over the four years between 1383 and 1387.[163] One other possible example, not

---

1383: *CFR, 1383–9*, 6. This may have been the start of the relationship with one of his most significant servants and retainers. For Lancaster, see below, pp. 205–6.

[159] *CPR, 1381–5*, 516; *1385–9*, 201. Medritz may have been a Bohemian – he is certainly assumed to be so by A. Simpson, *The Connections between English and Bohemian Painting during the Second Half of the Fourteenth Century* (London, 1984), 48. The grant was made at Bristol Castle while de Vere was with the king: C81/1352, no. 36.

[160] C81/494, no. 4149. That the grant was at the supplication of de Vere did not make it onto the Patent Roll, nor did a number of other details; C66/322, m. 5; *CPR, 1385–9*, 246.

[161] *CPR, 1385–9*, 75 (4 Nov. 1385); C53/161, m. 14 (2 Nov.)

[162] *CPR, 1385–9*, 132, 133, 136 (C81/492, nos 3947–9).

[163] *CChR*, v, 301 (Richard Duffield, grant of free warren to, at request of the marquess of Dublin, 1385); *CPR, 1381–5*, 233 (Robert Archer of Rowenhale, exemption for life from jury services, etc., at supplication of the earl, 1 March 1383); 238 (John Audeyn of Essex, pardon to, at supplication of earl, for his part in 1381 rising, notwithstanding parliamentary judgement against him, 16 March 1383); 399 (Pardon to John Halsham for rape, at supplication of earl, 7 June 1384); *CPR, 1385–9*, 289 (Walter atte Hall, of Knipton, Leicestershire, pardon to, at supplication of the duke of Ireland, for all felonies, 6 April 1387); 292 (Pardon to Ralph of the Hul, at supplication of the duke, for breaking Oakham prison and abjuring the realm, 7 April 1387); 299 (Ralph Corbyn of Chester, pardon to, at supplication of duke, for a murder, 5 May 1387); 347 (Thomas Wodyngfield, esquire, pardoned for a death, at the supplication of the duke, 20 July 1387). A further undated pardon to a R. de D. for the death of E. de G. is noted at being at the supplication of the king's 'uncle'

noted at being at his supplication, is doubtful: in a pardon granted to John Malweden of Walden, Essex, on 5 April 1387 described as 'a servant, so he says, of our most dear cousin, the duke of Ireland', for a killing by misadventure.[164] Taken together all these examples certainly attest his influence at court but the small number does not suggest a complete control over the distribution of royal patronage and grace. It may, of course, be only part of a wider network of sponsorship and influence that de Vere maintained through his friendship with the king which the sources do not record.

Most of the pardons were not overtly political in any way, though there was one high profile case amongst them. John Halsham had committed the spectacular crime of abducting Philippa, daughter and co-heir of David, earl of Atholl, and wife of Sir Ralph de Percy, younger son of the earl of Northumberland, by February 1384. Percy brought complaints against him and claimed damages of £3,000, and a commission of Oyer and Terminer was issued. However, writs of *supersedeas* were issued in May as 'the king desires to find a remedy by way of agreement touching the debates between the said parties'.[165] By 7 June, however, a pardon had been issued to John for rape and all other felonies at the supplication of Robert de Vere, and this was followed a month later by a further pardon to Halsham at the supplication of the earl of Nottingham for all rapes, murders, homicides and felonies.[166] One wonders if this was competitive pardoning by Oxford and Nottingham or if there was a more prosaic reason (had the first pardon been insufficient and the second, more comprehensive one, needed to cover the full catalogue of Halsham's crimes?). While Halsham and Philippa did subsequently marry, the previous marriage to Ralph Percy, then aged in his later teens, apparently being annulled, the actions of de Vere and Mowbray were likely to have gained them a certain level of enmity from Ralph and by extension his powerful father, the earl of Northumberland.[167]

The exercise of such influence with the king was not condemned by contemporaries, unless done to excess or through more corrupt means, and

---

the duke of Ireland: Edinburgh University Library, MS 183, fol. 83v. This is a copy of the original signet letter, and it is not known if the mistake is 'uncle' for 'cousin' or whether uncle is correct, and the duke meant is in fact one of Lancaster, York or Gloucester.

[164] C81/495, no. 4250 ('sicome il dit'); *CPR, 1385–9*, 291.

[165] *CPR, 1381–5*, 423–4; *CCR, 1381–5*, 452 (quote).

[166] *CPR, 1381–5*, 399, 439; *CCR, 1381–5*, 459, 571; *CPR, 1385–9*, 421.

[167] For some detail on the case, see H.P. South, 'The Question of Halsam', *Proceedings of the Modern Language Association of America*, 50 (1935), 362–71.

should not be by historians. Any influence exercised on behalf of dependants or connections would have been categorised as good lordship, that crucial and widely accepted concept, while influence exercised on behalf of unconnected people could be classified as giving counsel if there is no evidence of bribery.[168] De Vere, as an English earl as well as chamberlain, had every right to give such counsel. There was no criticism of counsellors or others about the king labouring to Henry VI for the expedition of any bill for someone else in conciliar guidance issued around 1444, just an order that he (or she) write their name on the bill 'so that it may be known at all tymes by whoos meanes and labour everi bille is'.[169] Likewise, the inclusion of the name of a patron on a pardon was made a statutory requirement in 1353.[170]

It is worth placing de Vere's activity in terms of pardoning in context. Helen Lacey's work on the royal pardon lists the number of cases where formal intercession was recorded. De Vere – with seven (perhaps six) – is not in the top ten, which was headed by Queen Anne (seventy-one), John of Gaunt (sixty-two) and Henry Percy, earl of Northumberland (fifty-three), but included Nicholas Exton, mayor of London (twenty-nine) and a man who was never close to the king, Richard, earl of Arundel (seventeen).[171] The earl of Derby obtained seven pardons for murder in a single year in 1387–8.[172] While de Vere's short career may account for his absence from the top ten, it is indicative that he did not ever match the key individuals as an intercessor.

Similar conclusions might be drawn from the witness lists to the royal charters. As Chris Given-Wilson has remarked, witness lists at this date might indicate the witness's presence at the grant or more likely at the sealing of the grant in chancery a few days later, but probably do indicate some participation in the process, unlike the fifteenth-century lists which become standardised and occasionally provably inaccurate.[173] There were forty-three royal charters issued between de Vere's coming of age early in

---

[168] G. Dodd and S. Petit-Renaud, 'Grace and Favour: the Petition and its Mechanisms', in Fletcher, Genet and Watts, eds, *Government and Political Life*, 263–9; H. Lacey, *The Royal Pardon: Access to Mercy in Fourteenth Century England* (York, 2009), ch. 4.

[169] *PPC*, vi, 317.

[170] Lacey, *Royal Pardon*, 48–9.

[171] Lacey, *Royal Pardon*, Appendix 4.iii, 213–32. Lacey notes (226) a pardon granted at de Vere's supplication in 1378 which cannot be traced in the patent rolls.

[172] Leland, 'Richard II and the Counter-Appellants', 200 and see more generally ch. 3.

[173] C. Given-Wilson, 'Royal Charter Witness Lists, 1327–1399', *Medieval Prosopography*, 12 (1991), 39; *The Royal Charter Witness Lists 1426–1516*, ed. J. Ross (List and Index Society, 316, 2012), xviii–xxii.

1383 and summer 1385, of which he did not witness a single one.[174] A further thirty royal charters were issued between summer 1385 and the end of 1387, two of which were to de Vere; of the remaining twenty-eight, de Vere was a witness to thirteen – a substantial number but by no means all – which is indicative of a regular presence and a prominence but not a dominance at court.[175] Compared, for example, with the younger Despenser, who witnessed a high level of charters – 73 per cent and 83 per cent in the last two years of Edward II's reign – de Vere was an infrequent witness.[176]

A further source also suggests that he was not constantly around the king nor frequently whispering in his ear for a particular course of action. Some chancery warrants were actioned on the basis of information received by the king from a named individual, almost certainly verbally. Not a single one refers to information from de Vere himself. Amongst those who are named as supplying information between 1381 and 1389, Thomas Holland, earl of Kent, appears once, the bishop of London four times, a number of those with household or ministerial appointments appear once, including Simon Burley, Michael de la Pole, Richard Medford, the king's secretary, John Beauchamp, keeper of the jewels, and Aubrey de Vere (in 1381).[177] De Vere is thus conspicuous by his absence.

Lastly, of course, the chamberlainship offered the opportunity to acquire favours not for dependants or others but for de Vere himself. It is not easy to show that he presented requests for himself in his guise as chamberlain. Dodd has pointed out that:

> hardly any examples exist of private petitions presented to the king in parliament from the notorious royal favourites of the late medieval period. Piers Gaveston, Robert de Vere… and William de la Pole… did not accrue their wealth and position by public requests to the king for his favour:

---

[174] C53/159, mm. 1–2 (*CChR*, v, 280–1, nos 1–7); C53/160 (*CChR*, v, 282–99). Unsurprisingly, he did not witness any earlier than his formal majority.

[175] C53/161 and C53/162, m.26. The numbering to 29 in the *CCHR*, v, 300–7, omits one charter between 7 and 8. De Vere witnessed that one and numbers 1, 3, 4, 6, 7, 8–10, 21, 23, 24, 29. He was the recipient of numbers 2 and 25.

[176] *The Royal Charter Witness Lists of Edward II (1307–1326)*, ed. J. Hamilton (List and Index Society, 288, 2001), x–xi. Gaveston, by contrast, was not a regular charter witness when present in England.

[177] *CPR, 1381–5*: Bishop of London: 27, 28; Aubrey de Vere: 31; Hugh de Segrave: 57; Sir Walter atte Lee: 61; Michael de la Pole: 100; Simon Burley: 512. *CPR, 1385–9*: Kent: 51; Medford and Beauchamp: 179; Bishops of Winchester and Bath: 401; Bishops of London and Winchester: 445; Bishop of London: 480.

instead they gained preferment by exploiting the private access they enjoyed to the king in his chamber.[178]

There is one surviving parliamentary petition from de Vere – for the de Coucy lands – and it is not clear how public requests outside parliament might be.[179] While some may well have been informal in the chamber, others may have been in more public settings. Certainly, some started with a written request and all created a paper trail. Moreover, particularly with Richard II, it is highly likely the king initiated grants.

Up to the summer of 1385, it would be rather hard to define de Vere as a royal favourite using the checklist compiled in Chapter 1. Certainly, he was a close friend of the king, though not the only one, but did not owe either his presence at court or his role as great chamberlain to the king's favour. He did not abuse the law for his own ends. There is little strictly contemporary evidence that he enjoyed an objectionable amount of royal favour; de Vere certainly never established a vice-like hold over royal patronage. Nor did he seriously influence the exercise of royal grace, control access to the king nor was constantly present at court, as far as the sources show. The perception that he did before 1385 postdates the period itself and derives from both later chronicle accounts and the proceedings against him in 1388. Perhaps he took the king's part, and perhaps exceeded his mandate, in plotting against John of Gaunt – the jury remains out – but he also gave good service and good advice in the expedition against Scotland, as a great magnate was expected to do. It was not until the autumn of 1385 that his role and his service became more unconventional.

---

[178] G. Dodd, *Justice and Grace. Private Petitioning and the English Parliament in the Late Middle Ages* (Oxford, 2007), 216.

[179] SC8/145/7223.

4

Ireland, 1385–7

> The king 'gave and granted to the same marquis the land and lordship of Ireland, with rights and jurisdiction high and low, and authority simple and mixed, and [all] royal rights… and all other things which pertained and could pertain to the king's royalty, to have and to hold of the lord king and his heirs for the entire life of the same marquis.
>
> (The grant of Ireland as recorded on the roll of the Parliament of 1385[1])

The Grant of Ireland

Richard had returned from Scotland to London by 3 September as writs were sent out on that day summoning parliament to meet on 20 October. When it convened, it was a long and tempestuous assembly. Richard and his ministers faced a barrage of criticism over royal grants, the handling of taxation and royal finance more generally. The Westminster Chronicle states that one of the commons' petitions was that royal grants that had been imprudently made be revoked, although this was rejected, in part through the opposition of John of Gaunt, who was a consistent upholder of the royal prerogative.[2] This petition has not survived but two other documents from the commons, designed to subject exchequer and household spending to external review and restrict royal patronage, have done. Richard, amidst the criticism, much of which accused him of ill-advised use of patronage, was forced to make concessions, including allowing a committee of four men to supervise royal finances after the parliament was dissolved.[3]

Richard had also, while on campaign in Scotland, enacted a round of promotions amongst the peerage. Unproblematic were the promotions of the royal earls of Buckingham and Cambridge to the dukedoms of Gloucester and York, but more controversially Michael de la Pole was promoted to be earl of

---

[1] *PROME*, vii, 1385 item 17.

[2] *WC*, 146–7.

[3] *PROME*, vii, 2–3, 28–9; Palmer, 'Impeachment of Michael de la Pole', 96–101; idem, 'The Parliament of 1385 and the Constitutional Crisis of 1386', *Speculum*, 46 (1971), 477–90.

Suffolk, and probably John, Lord Neville, was to be earl of Cumberland and Simon Burley to be earl of Huntingdon. The latter two had been dropped by the time of the summons to parliament were issued, but the other three were enacted during that assembly. Yet it was the fourth promotion that was the most striking. Robert de Vere was granted a new title, marquess of Dublin, and this was given substance on an unprecedented scale in parliament by the grant of the rule of the whole of Ireland for life, and all royal rights in the lordship, excepting only liege homage.[4] By 1385 Robert de Vere was undoubtedly the most powerful of the small group of men close to the king and his promotion and the grant of royal rights in Ireland made that manifestly clear. The grant also changed the trajectory of de Vere's career.

There is no evidence that de Vere's promotion was amongst those initiated during the Scottish campaign. The first record evidence of the plan dates to 12 October 1385 and records a grant of land to de Vere, upon whom the king 'wishes shortly to bestow the title of marquess of Dublin, to hold without rent until he has conquered Ireland and can hold it in peace'.[5] Yet the formal grant came very late in the parliamentary proceedings – on 1 December – despite the other promotions, including that of Michael de la Pole, being confirmed nearly three weeks earlier. This, it has been suggested, was because it was controversial.[6] While this was probably true, the idea of the promotion and grant may have come later than the others, which were first considered in the summer of 1385; de Vere's grant was likely a product of discussions in the autumn. It was also a grant that was a great deal more complicated than a simple promotion in the peerage, as it had significant financial and administrative implications, involving as it did the effective rule of Ireland; the delay may have been as much working through the various aspects of the grant than anything else.

The marquessate was the first ever granted in England, and indeed few were to be created in the following hundred years. It is unclear where the idea came from. In 1384 the marquis of Pont-à-Mousson, son of the duke of Bar, married Mary de Coucy, de Vere's sister-in-law, so it is feasible de Vere, taking inspiration from this, was the initiator, but marquis was a more common title in the Imperial lands, which Queen Anne would have been well aware of, so it may have been Richard or Anne's idea.[7] While the promotion of de Vere to

---

[4] *PROME*, 1385 parliament, item 17.
[5] *CPR, 1385–9*, 115; C81/490, no. 3763.
[6] *PROME*, vii, 2; Palmer, 'Parliament of 1385', 479.
[7] M.J. Bennett, 'Richard II, Queen Anne, Bohemia: Marriage, Culture and Politics', in P. Brown and Jan Čermák, eds, *England and Bohemia in the Age of Chaucer* (Cambridge, 2023), 28.

a new rank was unexpected, some action on the situation in Ireland was not. The English lordship had been in decline since the invasion by the Bruces in 1315, and despite occasional attempts by the English crown to alleviate the situation, such as the expedition by Lionel, duke of Clarence, in 1361, it was in a weak position in the early 1380s. The greatest Anglo-Irish landowner, the earl of March, who held a significant part of the lordship of Ireland as earl of Ulster and lord of Connacht, was a minor after the death of Earl Edmund in 1381 and the situation seemed highly precarious. Before his death, Edmund Mortimer had made considerable efforts to assert his power over the O'Neills, perhaps the most dangerous opponents of the English. But after 1381, Niall O'Neill, king of Tyrone, was able to attack the royal castle at Carrickfergus in 1384, and Louth, just north of Dublin, was threatened.[8] To the south Brian O'Brien of Thomond remained a formidable opponent, in part through his web of alliances with other families.[9] This genuine set of threats formed the context of an appeal to the king by the Anglo-Irish in a letter of 1385, even if one discounts the usual hyperbole of such appeals. The prelates, lords and commons of Ireland claimed that without help 'in this next season there will be made a conquest of the greater part of the land of Ireland' by the native Irish. They asked that the king should come in person for 'the rescue and salvation' of his seigneury, and that if the king should not come 'which God forbid', they urged that 'the greatest and most trustworthy lord of England' should come in his place.[10] Nonetheless, while not directly responding to this entreaty, as it arrived after the grant to de Vere, the king, as Nigel Saul states, 'was well aware of the general movement of opinion in the province'.[11] This appeal to Richard was not also without its immediate political context. The king's lieutenant in Ireland, Sir Philip Courtenay, was not popular, and the powerful earl of Ormond was manoeuvring to have him replaced. Ormond was at the English court in the autumn of 1385 and it is possible that Richard sought his advice on de Vere's appointment.[12] Nor was a substantial effort to support the

---

[8] B. Smith, *Crisis and Survival in Late Medieval Ireland. The English of Louth and their Neighbours, 1330–1450* (Oxford, 2013), 77-8; K. Simms, *Gaelic Ulster in the Middle Ages. History, Culture and Society* (Dublin, 2020), 134-5.

[9] E. O'Byrne, 'O'Brien (Ó Briain), Brian Sreamach', *Dictionary of Irish Biography*, accessed online 14 September 2023.

[10] *Statutes and Ordinances and Acts of the Parliament of Ireland from the Reign of King John to that of Henry V*, ed. H.F Berry (Dublin, 1907), 485–6.

[11] Saul, *Richard II*, 274.

[12] *WC*, 140–1, for Ormond being knighted by the king at Westminster on 9 November 1385. For the political situation in Ireland, see the excellent discussion by P. Crooks, 'The "Calculus of Faction" and Richard II's Duchy of Ireland, c. 1382-9', in

Anglo-Irish lordship, funded by English resources, against precedent; after Lionel of Clarence's expedition, two substantial forces were dispatched under William of Windsor in the 1370s, funded by the English exchequer, and, of course, Richard himself was to go twice to Ireland in the 1390s.[13]

Nonetheless, it is worth stressing the novelty of what Richard granted de Vere in autumn 1385. All royal possessions in the lordships, all feudal rights, all jurisdictions, all income, all patronage of religious institutions, the right of appointment of all officials, and the right to mint coin in the lordship were included in the grant.[14] Letters patent and close were issued in the name of the marquess of Dublin and not the king, the only time that occurred between 1272 and the Commonwealth period.[15] There is no obvious earlier parallel to this grant. While the grant was of a palatinate in all but name, and perhaps Richard had the example of the creation of the palatinate of Lancaster in 1351 in mind, Ireland was different. Rather than a single county within England, it was a separate dominion of the crown and comprised rights over four counties at the smallest extent, and potentially over a far larger area and on a grander scale, if English power could be asserted. Perhaps the only comparable grant was that of Aquitaine to John of Gaunt in 1390, by which the duchy was potentially to be separated from the English royal line.

It is worth considering the possibility that Richard had drawn inspiration from an earlier lieutenancy in Ireland. Edward II had appointed Piers Gaveston as lieutenant of Ireland instead of sending him into a dishonourable exile in June 1308. Moreover, Gaveston had received vice-regal powers for the duration of his lieutenancy, being empowered to appoint and remove justices, sheriffs and other officials, and the right of presentation to churches. Gaveston's appointment was during pleasure, de Vere's for life, and de Vere certainly had considerably more powers conferred on him, yet there are similarities, and it is also clear that

---

N. Saul, ed., *Fourteenth Century England V* (Woodbridge, 2008), 101–4 and Saul, *Richard II*, 270–3. For the more general situation, J.F. Lydon, *The Lordship of Ireland in the Middle Ages* (Dublin, 1972), 202–6, 215–32, and also S. Egan, 'Richard II and the Wider Gaelic World: A Reassessment', *Journal of British Studies*, 57 (2018), 221–52, in which de Vere's lordship could be seen as a forerunner to Richard II's serious attempt to reverse the ebb tide of the English lordship in Ireland (251).

[13] S. Duffy, *Ireland in the Middle Ages* (Basingstoke, 1997), 151–65.

[14] *PROME*, vii, 1385 item 17.

[15] I owe this point to Dr Peter Crooks. There is no phrase that explicitly gave the right to de Vere, it presumably being covered by the grant of 'all other things which pertain… to our regality' (*PROME*, 1385, item 17). The grant of the dukedom did not enhance de Vere's powers in Ireland, the two grants being nearly identical (*Report on the Dignity of a Peer*, v, 79–81).

Richard II had considerable interest in the reign of his great-grandfather and closely identified with him. This fascination began not after Richard II was nearly deposed in 1388 but by 1383, and in 1385 – the same year as de Vere was granted Ireland – he petitioned the pope for Edward II's canonisation.[16] Gaveston's lieutenancy in Ireland was successful in military terms, which Richard might also have been aware of. The idea of appointing a trusted friend and subject to run the lordship of Ireland with extraordinary powers was common to both, even if de Vere's appointment went further than Gaveston's.

Perhaps predictably, the English chronicles focus on the personal aspects of the new title rather than the political and strategic reasons behind the associated grant of Ireland. Walsingham described the outraged reaction of the assembled nobility to de Vere's promotion: 'other earls took offence at this because they considered that he had received from the king a position which was superior to theirs, and they were especially indignant that it was not for his greater learning or military prowess that he was regarded as more important than they'.[17] In contrast, the Westminster Chronicle simply neutrally recorded the promotion, noting that a marquess was superior to an earl and less than a duke, 'so that the king caused him to be seated in parliament above the earls'. Knighton noted the conferring of the title, without passing significant comment.[18] For once Walsingham may actually be closer to the truth, despite the silence of other chronicles on the subject. There was likely to have been a reaction against the novelty of the title, but it is striking that the criticism as recorded by Walsingham was about the title of marquess not the far more important grant of the king's rights in Ireland. These can perhaps be teased out separately.

On the novelty of a marquessate, a later comment may be instructive. John Beaufort, earl of Somerset, was created marquess of Dorset in Richard II's mass promotions of 1397. Demoted by Henry IV in 1400, along with others, his restoration as marquess was requested in a commons' petition in 1402. Somerset's response was recorded on the parliament roll:

> the said earl, kneeling most humbly, prayed the king that as the name of marquess was an alien name in this kingdom, he did not wish him to bestow

---

[16] For Gaveston's appointment and his successful term as lieutenant, see Hamilton, *Piers Gaveston*, 53–66. For Richard II and Edward II, see C. Given-Wilson, 'Richard II, Edward II and the Lancastrian Inheritance', *EHR*, 109 (1994), 567–70. For the petition of 1385, see *WC*, 158–9.

[17] *SAC*, i, 781.

[18] *WC*, 144–5; *KC*, 338.

the name of marquess in any way, because never again by the king's leave did he wish to bear or accept for himself any such name in any form.[19]

Such suspicions of innovation amongst the political elite may well have been genuine, but this disavowal of Ricardian innovation suited (and may well have been urged by) Beaufort's half-brother, Henry IV.[20]

Yet, if there was disapproval of either the grant of Ireland or the novelty of the title, the charter roll records that two dukes – Lancaster and York – and five earls, Arundel, Stafford, Salisbury, Nottingham and Suffolk, witnessed the grant, alongside two archbishops, two bishops and others, which would hardly indicate wholesale rejection by the political community, and would normally suggest the opposite.[21] While some caution must be taken with the witness lists, the fact it was done in parliament may well indicate that those who witnessed the sealing also witnessed the grant itself. Further clarifications and grants on 3 January, relating to his new coats of arms and that the marquess could collect money from Irish landowners who did not contribute to its defence as per the statute of 3 Richard II, also stress that the grant of the marquessate was done with the assent of the prelates, dukes, other peers and the community of the realm in parliament.[22] De Vere was also admitted to the order of the Garter, participating at the chapter in April 1386; while the sovereign was clearly influential in choosing members, it was hard to impose a candidate entirely through royal will, since member knights supplied the king with a list of names to choose from, and this suggests also some acceptance of de Vere within circles not closely aligned with the court.[23]

One reason that the grant may have caused resentment – and the direct evidence for such a reaction is, as shown above, rather thin – was the idea that Ireland was an inalienable possession of the crown. Peter Crooks has noted that the only previous occasion that Ireland was (temporarily) granted out

---

[19] *PROME*, viii, 164–5.

[20] Given-Wilson, *Henry IV*, 439–50. See also C. Given-Wilson, 'Rank and Status among the English Nobility, c. 1300–1500', in T. Huthwelker, J. Peltzer and M. Wemhöner, eds, *Princely Rank in Late Medieval Europe: Trodden Paths and Promising Avenues* (Ostfildern, 2011), 97–117, esp. 100.

[21] C53/161, mm. 12, 13; *CChR*, v, 301. Others named included Hugh Segrave, treasurer, Walter Skirlawe, keeper of the privy seal and bishop-elect of Coventry and Lichfield, and John de Montagu, steward of the household.

[22] C66/320, m.1; the assent clause is omitted in the calendar: *CPR, 1385–9*, 78–9.

[23] G.F. Beltz, *Memorials of the Order of the Garter* (London, 1841), cliv. For a summary of the procedure, see P.J. Begent and H. Chesshyre, *The Most Noble Order of the Garter. 650 Years* (London, 1999), 197–8.

of the king's direct control was in 1254 when Henry III gave it to the future Edward I, though on the grounds it would not be separated from the crown of England.[24] Richard's grant did retain the paramountcy of the crown in title, given the reservation of liege homage to the crown, and could, of course, be revoked, while the grant was also for de Vere's lifetime only rather than in perpetuity. Yet the extent of the governance given to Robert de Vere was novel, and greater than any since 1254. The problem of inalienability merged with another allegation brought against de Vere in the Merciless Parliament which alleged that the traitors around the king encouraged the latter to make de Vere king of Ireland and to send letters to the pope to that effect, to the detriment of the king, the Irish and the disinheritance of the crown of the kingdom of England.[25] Walsingham, writing somewhat later but probably deriving his idea from the records of the parliament, alleged that the grant of the dukedom in 1386 was with the intention that 'he should later be raised from duke to king, if fortune favoured him'.[26] Although Crooks rightly argues that this cannot be lightly dismissed, given Richard's novel dealings with Ireland, the fact the first source formed part of the hostile twisting of recent events to create charges of treason in the Merciless Parliament of 1388, and the second source was the inimical Walsingham, means the charge must remain at best unproven and at worst unlikely.[27] It is interesting a similar accusation was made of the intention to make an English nobleman king of Ireland in regard to Thomas Holland, duke of Surrey, in 1399 by Adam Usk; the chronicler adds Richard planned to do this in Dublin on 13 October 1399 and murder a number of leading Englishmen at the ceremony. This latter detail seriously undermines the veracity of the former, and means the idea of raising an Englishman to king of Ireland perhaps became, temporarily, a stock charge against Richard.[28] There

---

[24] Crooks, 'Calculus of Faction', 95–6. See also J.F. Lydon, 'Ireland and the English Crown, 1171–1534', *Irish Historical Studies*, 29 (1995), 281–94; B. Hartland, 'Policies, Priorities and Principles: the King, the Anglo-Irish and English Justiciars in the Fourteenth Century', in B. Smith, ed., *Ireland and the English World in the late Middles Ages: Essays in Honour of Robin Frame* (Basingstoke, 2009), 131. For the use of the doctrine of inalienability of royal dominions against the crown, see Rosenthal, 'Baronial Rebellions', 603.

[25] *PROME*, vii, 87.

[26] *SAC*, i, 799; Neither the Westminster Chronicle nor Knighton's Chronicle mention it.

[27] Crooks, 'Calculus of Faction', 96.

[28] *Chronicle of Adam of Usk*, ed. Given-Wilson, 76–7. Alastair Dunn also supports the idea of Holland being raised to king, noting a set of payments for substantial repairs to the great hall of Dublin Castle in 1399 and the grant of a coronet formerly

is nothing in Richard's record that suggests he would have wished to divest himself of his title over Ireland, nor is it likely that de Vere could have been made a subordinate king to Richard as *dominus Hiberniae*, albeit a number of the native Irish rulers did call themselves king, which was something that by the fourteenth century the English crown had become increasingly adverse to.[29] Richard, indeed, seems to have had a heightened view of kingship and his royal status compared to many other kings, and creating a subject his equal in title does not fit the persuasive reading of his 'lofty conception of his office'.[30] Moreover, the reaction amongst the English political community of making de Vere a king would surely have been more toxic even than it apparently was when the titles of marquess and duke were conferred on him.

One other argument that has been made about the grant of Ireland to de Vere also needs to be considered. This takes the line that the grant was not so much about Ireland but a strategic move for Richard in terms of English politics. Tuck has advanced a two-pronged case. He argues that de Vere's appointment 'was widely assumed in England to be evidence that Richard intended to develop Ireland as a bastion of royal power, closely linked with Cheshire and North Wales where de Vere and other favourites already held important office'.[31] Yet this is problematic: de Vere's appointment as justice of Chester was two years later than the grant of Ireland, and while John Beauchamp of Holt was appointed justice of North Wales the same month as de Vere's marquessate was conferred, the politically neutral Edmund, duke of York, held the Chester office, which hardly suggests the building of a royal power base. Indeed, it might be asked as to why Richard might have thought he needed a royal power bastion along these lines at this time. Although there was criticism of royal policy in the parliament of 1385, Richard could not have foreseen the challenge to royal power of the impeachment of the chancellor, the establishment of the commission and the rising military tensions that occurred from the summer of 1386 to the autumn of 1387. The second strand of Tuck's argument was that de Vere had, in the previous three years, been trying to undermine the influence of John of Gaunt and enhance his own standing. By creating him marquess of Dublin and then duke of Ireland, Tuck

---

belonging to the earl of Arundel: 'Richard II and the Mortimer Inheritance', in C. Given-Wilson, ed., *Fourteenth Century England II* (Woodbridge, 2002), 169. For the use of coronets amongst earls and dukes, see below, p. 227.

[29] R. Frame, 'Two Kings in Leinster: The Crown and the Mic Mhurchadha in the Fourteenth Century', in T.B. Barry, R. Frame and K. Simms, eds, *Colony and Frontier in Medieval Ireland. Essays Presented to J.F. Lydon* (London, 1995), 156–7.

[30] Saul, *Richard II*, 339–44 (quote 339).

[31] Tuck, 'Anglo-Irish Relations', 24.

argues, and with the grant of palatine powers, Richard 'gave him equality of status with Lancaster and placed [him], nominally, above the other two royal dukes, York and Gloucester'.[32] In support of his hostility to Gaunt, he cites only the two plots of 1384–5; as has been discussed, the first of these is deeply problematic in terms of de Vere's involvement. Yet only with the dukedom the following year did de Vere equal the status of the royal dukes, and that was surely as much about Richard's reaction to the restrictions placed on him in 1386 as seeking to match de Vere with his uncles in 1385.

The grant of Ireland has been criticised as entirely unrealistic, as the 'task of subduing the country was beyond him' and therefore 'the grant of the title was a shrewd means of conferring on de Vere the shadows and trappings of power without its substance'.[33] However, there are a number of reasons for taking the grant of the lordship of Ireland to de Vere more seriously than it has usually been. As mentioned above, Richard was well aware of the difficult position of the Anglo-Irish, and the promotion came in the context of strategic discussions concerning the lordship of Ireland in the autumn of 1385 with the earl of Ormond and others. There is nothing in Richard II's record either before or after to suggest that he would treat one of the appanages of his crown in anything other than a serious manner, and certainly not as a plaything to increase his friend's standing. Richard in fact was more concerned with his lordship of Ireland than most medieval English kings and was later the first English monarch to set foot in Ireland since King John. More generally, he had a wider and more 'British' view of his kingship and dominions than most English kings.[34]

Therefore, the idea that this was not a serious venture should be dismissed. Much of this comes with hindsight, of knowing the project failed – and struggled in some respects to get off the ground – but as will be argued that was largely because of the problems of English politics rather than because it was never designed to be a realistic project, or that it was all about buttressing Richard's domestic position, not about Ireland. Clearly the appointment of de Vere was taking a risk if the project was designed as an answer to the problem of the English lordship of Ireland rather than about enhancing de Vere's status. Many of the higher nobility would have disapproved of a relatively young man given such a responsibility and promoted in the peerage. In their view, it should have been an appointment and grant for a king's younger son, like Gloucester, or for a man with military experience, like Arundel, albeit

---

[32] Tuck, 'Anglo-Irish Relations', 24–5.

[33] Tuck, *Richard II*, 82.

[34] M.J. Bennett, 'Richard II and the Wider Realm' in Goodman and Gillespie, eds, *Richard II: the Art of Kingship*, 187–204.

service in Ireland did not have the chivalric allure or opportunities for gain of service in France. Furthermore, de Vere had no Irish lands; the manor of Inchiquin and the town of Youghal, the only Irish estates the family had ever acquired, had been granted in 1367 to James, second earl of Ormond, by Earl Thomas.[35] Yet, to put a more positive case, de Vere was not totally lacking in military reputation and administrative experience as Tuck alleged.[36] He had considerable acquaintance with military matters for a man of only twenty-four, having served on campaign in France and Scotland, and was probably involved in the suppression of the 1381 revolt. Administrative experience he may – or may not – have been lacking in, although he had been the head of a noble estate for a few years by the date of his appointment, but either way there were existing, established, administrative channels in Ireland to work through, as well as his own council. From Richard's point of view, if this was a serious plan, de Vere was the perfect candidate for the appointment, given that as a close personal friend he was entirely trustworthy, and also solely dependent on royal favour for his position. He was, presumably, in Richard's eyes a better candidate than someone like Gloucester, of royal blood, ambitious, and perhaps a potential threat as lord of a conquered, and pacified, Ireland. It is also worth stressing the minority of the greatest Anglo-Irish landowner, Roger Mortimer, earl of March, who would presumably have filled the position of lieutenant of Ireland during the later 1380s had he been of age, as he did through most of the 1390s. His absence created a vacuum. However, while during March's minority de Vere's lordship would not have impinged on the Mortimer interest, the fact the grant was for life might have seriously circumscribed Mortimer power and damaged their interests in the longer term. It may be one explanation for the prominent role the young earl's illegitimate kinsman, Sir Thomas Mortimer, played at Radcot Bridge: he was looking after the family interests as well as serving the earl of Arundel, a leading Lord Appellant.[37]

The whole project of de Vere's lordship was imaginative, ambitious, if ultimately unsuccessful, but it should not be taken lightly. Did it have a chance of actually imposing effective English rule on Ireland, through de Vere's agency? De Vere was given the governance of Ireland, and as will be discussed shortly, a large sum to pay for a substantial army, as well as the possibility of a political and territorial base from which he could continue to raise troops, and consolidate any gains made. It had the advantage of not being intended

---

[35] *Calendar of Ormond Deeds*, ed. Curtis, ii, 101–2.
[36] Tuck, 'Anglo-Irish Relations', 24.
[37] I am grateful to Dr Patrick McDonagh of Trinity College, Dublin, for discussing this with me.

to be a short-term expedition, such as Richard II's was to be in 1394–5, which, while it overawed the Irish in the short term, achieved very little in the long term, forcing him to return just four years later. While English arms did not have a distinguished record in Ireland in the fourteenth century, not least as evidenced in Clarence's expedition in 1361–2, a standing army of 1,500 men, for two years at least, in addition to any forces to be raised in Ireland itself, with good military leadership, might have achieved results. The fact that the plan never fully got off the ground does not mean that the whole enterprise was unrealistic or doomed to failure, and it should not be dismissed as a whim of Richard's or an attempt by de Vere to enhance his status without any intention of exercising his powers in Ireland.

Resources

De Vere required material resources to make his new grant of the rule of Ireland a practical proposition and reassert English power in the lordship. As has been noted, Tuck has suggested that it was never intended to be realistic, but this flies in the face both of Richard's attitudes to the dominions of the crown and what was ultimately to happen in terms of financial support of de Vere's position in Ireland. More intriguing is Palmer's suggestion that the parliament of 1385 'refused the money necessary to make de Vere's title more than a nominal one'.[38] Palmer states that Richard had promised de Vere royal financial support to the tune of £45,000, and that the commons in the parliament would have looked at this as the equivalent of one and a half parliamentary subsidies. However, this places the cart before the horse. Palmer reached the figure of £45,000 through a calculation of the wages of 500 men-at-arms and 1,000 archers over two years, the army that was to make de Vere's power in Ireland real. Yet, this army was not mentioned in the grant of the lordship of Ireland in parliament, which was far more general in noting only the grant of most royal rights and revenues in Ireland, that de Vere was to pay nothing for two years, and then 5,000 marks a year, and while the 'conquest of the land' over those two years was mentioned, the specifics were not. They were not directly stated until March 1386.[39] Moreover, there is no evidence that the Commons refused a grant of taxation for Ireland. In the opening address to the Commons, the chancellor did not request anything for Ireland directly, merely noting the need to sustain the kingdom in foreign war. The resulting grant of taxation made in the parliament – one and a half fifteenths and tenths

---

[38] Palmer, 'Parliament of 1385', 479.

[39] *PROME*, 1385 Parl., item 17; *CPR, 1385–9*, 123: College of Arms, London, MS Vincent 65, fol. 44.

– was to be split, according to its terms, between Gaunt's expedition to Spain, the keeping of the seas and the marches of Scotland, and to assist the English ally in Flanders, the city of Ghent.[40] There was no mention of Ireland either way. While the purpose of the parliament roll was not to record matters of disagreement, the Westminster Chronicle also does not record any suggestion of a request for taxation for Ireland.[41] Instead, then, of assuming that taxation for an army for Ireland was refused, it might be better to assume that the specific plans for the army came later, and that Richard and those around him realised that it was highly unlikely taxation would be granted directly for Ireland. It would have come lower in the priority list than activities on the continent, the keeping of the seas and the border with Scotland, probably for both court and parliament. Therefore, the king and his circle did not ask for support for Ireland explicitly. It might also be that Richard assumed he would have much less opposition in the 1385 parliament than he faced, and that he had anticipated greater taxation revenues, and their unrestricted use, from which he could subsidise de Vere in Ireland. When a more limited and more restricted parliamentary grant arrived, a new plan had to be formulated.

Some revenues from Ireland would, of course, accrue to de Vere that could be used for military forces. On 3 January 1386, de Vere was granted the right to the profits of those who held land, offices, benefices or other holdings in Ireland and refused to contribute to its defence, penalised by a statute of 3 Richard II, and, moreover, the right to have all sums of money due from the king's officers in Ireland – implicit in the grant in parliament but confirmed explicitly.[42] Yet such dues in Ireland were not sufficient to pay for more than a small fraction of the cost of an army – it has been calculated that revenues accounted for at the Irish exchequer averaged just under £2,500 p.a. over the period 1368–84 – and it did not take long for an additional source of revenue to be found.[43] On 23 March 1386 de Vere was granted the right to negotiate and collect the ransom of John of Blois, claimant to the duchy of Brittany. It was only at this point that specifics relating to an army for Ireland were mentioned. The grant of the ransom was explicitly to pay for 500 men-at-arms (at 12d a day and 40s regard per quarter) and 1,000 archers (at 6d a day) for two years, and if the ransom exceeded this sum, he was to account for the surplus.[44] Two

[40] *PROME*, vii, 4–7 (items 2–5, 10).
[41] *WC*, 136–49.
[42] *CPR, 1385–9*, 78–9.
[43] H.G. Richardson and G.O. Sayles, 'Irish Revenue 1278–1384', *Proceedings of the Royal Irish Academy*, 62 (1962), 87–100, at 94.
[44] *CPR, 1385–9*, 123.

later amendments were made to these terms – the first on 8 April 1386 that he could have the ransom without rendering anything for it, and the second three days later that he would account for any surplus but if the ransom was insufficient or it was not paid in time, the king bound himself to pay the deficiency.[45]

The assignment of the ransom of John of Blois, whenever it could be negotiated, was thus four months after the initial grant of Ireland. The ransom could not yield immediate resources but was potentially lucrative in the long term.[46] It was also politically controversial. Blois, son of Charles of Blois, and count of Penthièvre, was the potential heir to the duchy of Brittany. His father, the French-backed claimant to the duchy, had been captured at the battle of La Roche-Derrien in 1347. In 1356, as sureties for the payment of Charles's ransom, his sons John and Guy were sent to England. In the meantime, John of Montfort, the English-backed claimant and de facto duke of Brittany, had distanced himself from Edward III and Richard II, and the situation had become considerably more confused. Put simply, the release and ransom of John of Blois was favoured by those, such as Richard II, looking at the option of a negotiated settlement with the French, while the more pro-war party, which comprised most of the future Lords Appellants, did not want his release. Diplomatic negotiations between the English, French, Duke John of Brittany and the pro-Penthièvre faction further muddied the waters as far as ransom negotiations were concerned.

The ransom was granted to de Vere on 23 March, but the transfer of the prisoner was delayed. De Vere appointed three men to be his special attorneys to receive John of Blois on 30 June 1386 and custody was transferred thirteen days later.[47] Even then, there were clearly difficulties. John, duke of Brittany, was to allege in 1393, amongst other complaints to the royal council, that it had been agreed in the tenth year of Richard's reign (22 June 1386–21 June 1387) that there was to be no release of John of Blois without the duke's agreement, but that it had happened anyway.[48] It is highly likely that some on the royal council or the commission of 1386 had made this offer, despite not formally

---

[45] *CPR, 1385–9*, 132, 136.

[46] For John of Blois, see M. Jones, 'The Ransom of Jean de Bretagne, count of Penthièvre: an Aspect of English Foreign Policy 1386–8', *BIHR*, 45 (1972), 7–26 on which most of the next two paragraphs are based.

[47] The appointment of the attorneys is in TNA, temp. editorial ref. X-box 4278, and is noted in the account of the expenses for the keeping of Blois up to the handing over to de Vere's custody in E364/25, rot. 9. See also Jones, 'Ransom', 12 n.2, 15.

[48] *PPC*, i, 48.

having the power to forbid his ransoming.[49] It is therefore no surprise that Blois's release formed the twenty-third article of the accusations levelled at the Appellees in the Merciful Parliament of 1388:

> the said traitors Robert de Vere, duke of Ireland, Alexander, archbishop of York, and Michael de la Pole, earl of Suffolk, on the advice and prompting of the aforesaid Robert Tresilian and Nicholas Brembre, accroaching to themselves royal power, caused to be freed John of Blois, heir of Brittany, who was a prisoner and the treasure of our said lord the king and his kingdom, without the assent of parliament and of the great council of the king, and without warrant, to the great strengthening of the adversary of France, and to the great injury of the king and the kingdom, and contrary to the aforesaid statutes and ordinances made in the last parliament.[50]

The last reference was to the commission of 1386 which had the power to enquire into royal grants, but not to stop them; the grant also predated the appointment of the commission.[51] The allegation was not found to be treasonous by parliament, and the king had every right to ransom a royal prisoner if he so chose, although politically it might be a mistake. The accusation, of course, omitted the facts that the release was for a large ransom and explicitly for funding an expedition to Ireland. Palmer also alleged that Blois's release had been forbidden by the parliament of 1386 but again there is no evidence that this was the case.[52] To some extent, Walsingham supports the lack of any prohibition. Discussing the ransom of John of Blois which de Vere was given to 'recover by force the domain in Ireland which the king had given him', the nobles and commons in the Wonderful Parliament of 1386 were enthusiastic that he crossed to Ireland, 'preferring that the kingdom should lose all that money than that they should have this man's presence in the kingdom, leading the king astray as he was and making a fool of him'.[53] He linked parliament accepting de Vere having the ransom to a condition that he cross to Ireland by Easter 1387. However, the grant was a year earlier than that (March 1386), so his chronology is incorrect. Whether he picked up an echo of discussions in parliament in autumn 1386 to encourage de Vere to cross the Irish Sea remains a possibility.

---

[49] Saul, *Richard II*, 166–7, demonstrates that the commission interfered in foreign diplomacy even though its terms of reference only related to domestic affairs.

[50] *PROME*, vii, 91.

[51] 10 Ric II, c1: *Statutes of the Realm*, ii, 39–43.

[52] Palmer, 'Parliament of 1385', 488.

[53] *SAC*, i, 802–3.

What is undeniable is that whether because domestic opposition made it difficult to proceed or that the negotiations over the ransom with French authorities inevitably took time, given that ultimately nineteen French noblemen stood surety for various sums as part of the ransom, it was not until 1 October 1387 that a sum of 120,000 francs (approximately £19,000) was agreed upon, of which 78,000 arrived in Calais by November 1387.[54] It is also possible that negotiations only made significant progress when Richard was in regular contact with the French court, which he is known to have been in the summer of 1387, and de Vere made use of these ongoing negotiations to complete the process of agreeing the ransom. Given the French were preparing a massive invasion of England from spring to autumn 1386, this was not the ideal time for an English nobleman to be negotiating with France over a ransom. Either way, it should be noted that the ransom was neither sufficiently timely nor sufficiently lucrative to pay for the army he was meant to have sent in 1386.

Another grant to de Vere was also explicitly to help pay for the task of imposing his rule there. The patent rolls record that on 12 October 1385, shortly before he was granted the lordship of Ireland and made marquess of Dublin in parliament, he was assigned the reversion of fourteen manors in Cornwall, Devon and Somerset, which Sir James de Audley held for life, and which were to have reverted to the king at his death, which in the event was on 1 April 1386. He was to hold them without rent until he had conquered Ireland and held it in peace. The following February there was a further grant of Audley lands totalling six manors, seven advowsons, and two Devon hundreds on the same terms.[55] De Vere made one or two visits to the West Country in 1385–6, presumably to visit his new properties, and he stayed at Minehead and Dunster Castle in Somerset where the costs of his entertainment, given as separate payments of 10s and £6 1s 5d, were defrayed by Lady Mohun.[56] The

---

[54] Jones 'Ransom of Jean de Bretagne', 18–19.

[55] *CPR, 1385–9*, 112–13, 115; *CCR, 1385–9*, 70; E357/9, rots. 15, 36d. The February grant contained one manor already granted. See Map 2 above, p. xvii, for the estates.

[56] Somerset Archives, DD/L/P/31/2, accounts of the bailiff of Carhampton hundred, 1381, 1383–99, *sub anno* 10. No dates are given within the regnal year for the entertainment. This entry led Maxwell-Lyte into an error in dating the grant of the Audley estates to early 1385, having misdated the visits to the West Country to the 1384–5 regnal year. However, the visits are in the relevant bailiff's account clearly dating from Michaelmas 1385 to Michaelmas 1386, confirmed by the fact that de Vere was given his title as marquess of Dublin in the account, which he did not hold in the 1384–5 regnal year: H.C. Maxwell-Lyte, *A History of Dunster and the Families of Mohun and Lutterell* (2 vols, London, 1909), ii, 448. Aubrey de Vere had acted as a feoffee for Lady Mohun and her late husband a decade earlier, so good relations between the families might be assumed: CP40/459, rot. 92d.

estates had previously been granted to John Holland, earl of Huntingdon, in December 1384. Holland later argued that he had lost the Audley lands 'by reason of the influence of certain men at court ill-disposed to him' who had forced him to renounce his interests.[57] This, of course, was gross opportunism – the lands had been lost, alongside all his other properties, because of his murder of the son of the earl of Stafford in July 1385. The additional grant to de Vere in February 1386 was a couple of weeks after Stafford acquired a pardon; Leland has suggested his acquiescence in the transfer to de Vere was part of the price for the pardon, though given Stafford's only title was through royal grant, and the February grant was an extension of an earlier one, this may be overstating the connection between the two.[58]

Such grants could lead to difficulties, however, and they could be used for other purposes than intended. De Vere lost the manor of Staunton as it had been incorrectly granted to him, a grant by Audley to one William Gambon in fee simple having been confirmed by Edward III; summoned to show his case in chancery, de Vere did not appear, perhaps because he had no title except by this erroneous royal grant, and therefore lost the case by default.[59] By autumn 1387, in rather different political circumstances, de Vere secured a life annuity of £100 to John, Lord Beauchamp, on four of these manors.[60] Claimants to the Audley lands sprung up after de Vere's fall, all claiming he had wrongfully occupied them. That was because seven of these manors, alongside Queenborough, were among those enfeoffed by Edward III for endowment of his royal religious foundations, and the abbey of St Mary Graces by the Tower petitioned in 1388 for these and other property. Yet, it was not just Richard II who considered that they were at the disposal of the crown – it was during the ascendancy of the Appellants that they were regranted to John Holland, earl of Huntingdon, and it was not until Henry IV's reign that they were eventually granted to the abbey of St Mary Graces.[61] A more opportunistic claimant was Nicholas Audley, son of James, who claimed that his father had enfeoffed them for the benefit of his heirs, though this claim was clearly problematic. More interestingly, Audley asked for them at farm stating that the duke of Ireland and his ministers had wasted and

---

[57] SC8/129/6431; *CPR, 1385-9*, 99, 112, 114; Leland, 'Richard II and the Counter-Appellants', 67–8.

[58] Leland, 'Richard II and the Counter-Appellants', 68.

[59] *CPR, 1385-9*, 332.

[60] *CPR, 1385-9*, 364.

[61] St Mary Graces: SC8/20/989; *CPR, 1385-9*, 539. For petitions of c. 1400, see SC8/325/E711A; SC8/324/E658. For discussion, Given-Wilson, 'Richard II and his Grandfather's Will', 330–1.

destroyed them.[62] There was certainly some exaggeration here, given the £100 annuity being assigned on just four of these manors in the autumn of 1387, and references to substantial cash receipts in 1387 were included in inquisitions in 1388. Only occasional notes were made in those inquisitions of lack of upkeep of the estates, for instance at Dartington, where the residence was rundown, and at Bovey Tracey where the fences of the park were broken.[63] However, he had only had custody of the lands for less than two years by the date of his forfeiture and the neglect may well have predated his tenure.

The Audley lands were certainly valuable. Inquisitions and extents after de Vere's fall record extents for some of the manors, totalling £392 10s 3d p.a.[64] Four manors granted in one or other grant in 1385–6 have no valuations amongst these accounts. Fourteen of these estates were granted to John Holland, earl of Huntingdon, after de Vere's forfeiture, and were valued at £400, which is reasonable; add in the four missing manors and the advowsons, and £500–£600 annually seems a reasonable estimate. The Westminster Chronicle went a little higher, estimating the lands as being worth 1,000 marks per annum.[65] However, wealth generated from land was for the long term, and the estates could not generate the cash reserves necessary to fund an army for a campaign in the short term in 1386 or 1387, unless they were to be sold, something all peers were reluctant to do. Thus, the grant, while generous of Richard – and which formed part of article five against de Vere in the Merciless Parliament of 1388 – was not fit for the purpose it was explicitly given.

Even taken all together, the sources of revenue available were substantially insufficient and also tardy for the purposes of paying an army in 1386–7.

---

[62] SC8/222/11058. Dated to between 1386 and 1388 by the evidence of the bishop of Ely's term as chancellor, it seems certain to have been early in 1388 after de Vere's fall.

[63] *CIM, 1387–93*, 4.

[64] Inquisitions are *CIM, 1387–93*, 3–4, 89–90, though the inquisition for Fremington is in bad condition, while that for South Molton is illegible; others lack details through damage. There are enrolled accounts with extents in E364/28, rots. 3–4. Extents from the accounts rather than the damaged inquisitions have been preferred. The annual values given are Barnstaple £13 16s 4d, Fremington £111 12s 10d, Combe Martin £13 15s 7d, Holsworthy £14 16s 7d, Bovey Tracy £43 3s 10d, Dartington £50 10s 8d, Langacre £30 16s 2d, Tackbeare 40s, Blagdon £34 6s 8d and Norleigh 40s. Two bailiffs accounts for 1388–9 record income from West Lydford of £36 4s 11d net, and £33 4s 5d excluding arrears: SC6/826/13. Some of the estates are mentioned in Audley's inquisition *post mortem*, printed without valuation in *CIPM*, xvii, 72–7, the valuations are in E152/6/243, nos 1 & 2. These are South Molton £20, Holne, £6 13s 4d, Nymet Tracy £10, Staunton £2 13s 4d, and the two Devon hundreds of South Molton and Fremington valued together at 60s.

[65] *CPR, 1385–9*, 495; *CIPM*, xvii, 72–7; *WC*, 188–9.

Theoretically, if de Vere had realised all the potential income from the ransom and the Audley lands, he would have had £20,000 over two years to raise and pay an army of 1,500 men. He also had income from the revenues paid into the Irish exchequer, from rents, farms, escheats and customs and two loans, which, according to the unfortunately rather brief account of Robert Crull, treasurer of Ireland, totalled £4,868 between April 1386 and May 1388. Of this sum £2,453 was spent on the wages of his force.[66] There may have been more from Irish sources, such as the revenues of lands in wardship in Ireland, such as the Mortimer estates, less all the necessary expenses. However, when combined these revenue streams would not have close to covering the wages of the army, which, according to the standard rates of pay entered in the patent granting him the lordship of Ireland, would have come to £44,500 over two years.[67] The grants to him totalled half the amount needed. Moreover, the vast bulk of the income – the Blois ransom – could not realistically have come in time to pay for the summer campaign of 1386 even before attempts to stop its realisation by the commission after the Wonderful Parliament. While some money was granted from the English exchequer for military wages in 1386 and 1387, as will be discussed below, it was not nearly enough to pay for what had been agreed, despite the king promising to cover any deficiency.[68]

It is worth noting that the sums granted to de Vere for his governance of Ireland, though frequently seen as excessive, were not out of proportion to other lieutenants of Ireland during Richard's reign. Gloucester was promised 32,000 marks over three years – while maintaining a force of 500 men compared to de Vere's envisaged army of 1,500 – and Surrey 11,500 marks per annum in 1398; perhaps only Mortimer, promised 20,000 marks over three years in 1379, was less well-provided for.[69] Richard was, of course, far more concerned with Ireland than almost all medieval English kings, but it is worth noting that the principle of supporting English arms in Ireland from the English exchequer had been accepted since Lionel of Clarence's expedition of 1361, and a minimum of around £2,667 expenditure on the defence of Ireland was thought necessary even in less difficult circumstances in 1410 and 1433.[70]

---

[66] E364/32, rot. 6d.; *Irish Exchequer Payments, 1270–1446*, ed. P. Connolly (Dublin, 1998), 544–5.

[67] *CPR, 1385–9*, 123.

[68] See below, p. 138. For the commission, see Saul, *Richard II*, 161–70.

[69] For these figures, see Tuck, 'Anglo-Irish Relations', 18, 27 n. 88.

[70] R. Frame, *English Lordship in Ireland, 1318–1361* (Oxford, 1982), 333–4; Given-Wilson, *Henry IV*, 474; *PPC*, i, 350 (£2,667 in 1410); ii, 8 (4,000 marks in 1411);

De Vere's duchy of Ireland, then, was unlikely to benefit him in terms of military power or financial profits in the short term. None of this meant, though, that it was not a serious project, that it was unrealistic, or that de Vere and Richard treated Ireland as a mere plaything. It was the circumstances of English politics and the problems of governmental finance that hampered the project from the beginning. If de Vere had won at Radcot Bridge and Richard had triumphed over his domestic opposition and enhanced his authority, it is possible that with significant financial backing from the ransom payments in late 1387 and revenue from an exchequer fully back under royal control, the duchy of Ireland might have become a viable proposition once more. The position of the Anglo-Irish would have been enhanced by a powerful lord backed by royal favour and a substantial armed force and de Vere would have had revenues, patronage and recruiting avenues to draw upon to be a force in both English and Irish politics.

The Duchy of Ireland: Military Forces and Administration

Why, one might ask, if this was a serious project, did de Vere not go to Ireland himself? He certainly intended to, as one of the first grants concerning Ireland gave a date for his arrival in February 1386, but a draft appointment of Sir John Stanley as deputy for a year was made on 20 March.[71] No more than a week later than Stanley's appointment, and very feasibly the same day, an indenture was sealed between de Vere and the king, in which it was agreed that 200 men-at-arms and 600 archers were to serve in Ireland in de Vere's name, though under Stanley, at a standard rate of pay. The indenture does not survive but it is clear that it was agreed that this force would be paid for by the exchequer, as this was what happened.[72]

While this could certainly be read as de Vere not treating Ireland as a serious responsibility needing his presence in the lordship, the appointment of Stanley as a deputy and the halving of the military force reflected the political circumstances of 1386 rather than de Vere's attitude. In fact, it may well have been Richard who began to have second thoughts about sending his most

---

J.L. Kirby, 'The Issues of the Lancastrian Exchequer and Lord Cromwell's Estimates of 1433', *BIHR*, 24 (1951), 133.

[71] C47/10/24/8; is a draft appointment of Stanley dated 20 March at London. Although the phrasing of the appointment shows evidence of alteration, the duration of one year is clear. See also *CPR, 1385–9*, 125, 131; *CCR, 1385–9*, 49.

[72] The indenture is referred to in a number of payments on the issue rolls, and while no date is mentioned for the sealing of it, the first payment under it was issued on 27 March 1386: see below, p. 138.

trusted friend and supporter away for two years or more. One chronicler says that the de Vere was 'setting out for the ships in Wales', but the king 'would not dismiss him, but detained him'.[73] Had the king told de Vere to go, the latter would have had little choice, but the growth of political opposition during late 1385 and early 1386, and the narrowing of Richard's circle after the earl of Nottingham married Arundel's daughter, moving him away from the king, may all have encouraged Richard to keep de Vere close by him. More specifically, the invasion scare that lasted from spring to autumn in 1386, and in the response to which de Vere was involved, must have encouraged Richard to keep him in England. The threat of a French invasion was closer during 1386 than at any time during the Hundred Years' War to this date, and a truly formidable army was assembled at Sluys for this purpose. In the event the French failed to sail, but the threat caused serious panic in England throughout the year, and de Vere, as a southern and eastern English landowner as well as a leading magnate, was involved in the preparations to resist the expected onslaught. He was appointed to a commission of array 'in view of the imminent invasion' on 14 May 1386 in Essex. It was shortly before this, on 16 April, that letters were sent to the peers of the realm and to others in the king's retinues concerning the need to resist the French. More generally from late March a flow of orders relating to coastal defence began, relating especially to Kent, but also to other coastal counties in the south. These dates tie in rather well with the appointment of John Stanley as de Vere's deputy in Ireland on 20 March.[74] Given the apparently dangerous situation is it surprising that Richard wanted a man he trusted close to hand, to say nothing of his retinue? The latter was gathered and arrived in London on 20 September, when it was thought the invasion was imminent. De Vere's retinue was very sizeable indeed, totalling two bannerets, sixteen knights, 180 esquires and 400 archers and was second only in size to that of Henry, earl of Derby, who was in temporary charge of his father's Lancastrian domain.[75] It is noticeable, that even with conspicuous royal favour, de Vere was unable initially, like every other lord, to claim adequate wages from the exhausted exchequer. He was paid only £31 2s on 26 October, which was less than four days wages. It was this general

---

[73] Thomas Otterbourne, 'Chronicon Rerum Angliae', in *Duo Rerum Anglicarum Scriptores Veteres*, ed. T. Hearne (Oxford, 1732), 168.

[74] Saul, *Richard II*, 152–6; *CPR, 1385–9*, 82, 176; E403/511, cited in J. Sherborne, 'The Defence of the Realm and the Impeachment of Michael de la Pole in 1386', in J. Taylor and W. Childs, eds, *Politics and Crisis in Fourteenth Century England* (Gloucester, 1990), 102, and see more generally, 101–6.

[75] E403/515, mm. 7, 12. Sherborne, 'Defence of the Realm', 107 incorrectly records the retinue as sixteen knights, 120 men-at-arms and eighty archers.

problem that led to the attack on de Vere's ally, Chancellor de la Pole, in the 'Wonderful Parliament'. However, as with all the other lords, he was later paid in full, the Issue Roll recording on 5 December 1386 a payment of £334, albeit a tally of £100 had to be reassigned on 23 February 1387.[76]

Once the invasion scare had ended, there is evidence of a fresh intention for de Vere to cross to Ireland – on 12 November 1386 two commissions were issued to the sheriffs of Dublin and Meath and others to inquire as to where 200 quarters of wheat, 300 crannocks of oats, 100 cart-loads of hay and sixty cart-loads of straw ('littere') might be found and purveyed for the marquess' use, to be paid for by him, as he 'is coming to Ireland'.[77] This second spate of preparation, coinciding with his promotion to the dukedom of Ireland, was almost certainly derailed by the attack in the concurrent Wonderful Parliament (1 October–28 November) on Richard II's ministers, which deprived Richard of control over many aspects of his government and meant he could not afford to part with his closest ally. Even then, between February and April 1387, five protections were issued to men going to Ireland in the company of de Vere, including the treasurer of Ireland, Robert Crull, and John Newton, esquire, who was one of de Vere's inner circle; a further protection in June 1387 was also for service in the company of de Vere. It was only on 20 July that the idea of the duke going to Ireland in that year was formally abandoned when Sir Robert Hereford, already in Ireland, had a protection issued for his service in the company of Sir John Stanley, deputising for de Vere for a second year.[78]

Despite his personal absence, de Vere was involved in the administration of his new lordship, and the organisation of the military force that set out for Ireland and arrived by the late summer of 1386. De Vere's governance of Ireland, although nominally dating from his promotion on 1 December 1385, took some time to take effect. The previous lieutenant in Ireland was still issuing grants under the Irish seal on 14 April 1386, but a document enrolled in the Irish chancery states that the governance of Ireland came into de Vere's hands on 19 April[79]; de Vere's council in England appointed Prior Richard White of the hospital of St John Jerusalem as justiciar of Ireland, and he was sworn into that office on that same day. He served in that office until Sir John

---

[76] E403/515 mm. 7, 12, 21. Some retinues are not given explicit numbers – notably that of the duke of Gloucester – but de Vere was paid more substantially more than Gloucester, which would suggest a larger retinue (ibid., mm.1, 4, 5, 7-9, 12, 14, 21, 26).

[77] *RPC*, 136, nos 193–4; https://chancery.tcd.ie/document/Patent/10-richard-ii/224; https://chancery.tcd.ie/document/patent/10-richard-ii/225.

[78] *CPR, 1385–9*, 278, 341.

[79] *RPC*, 134, no. 125.

Stanley, de Vere's lieutenant, arrived at the end of August. However, the crown had been issuing writs to de Vere as if he had already taken up his post earlier than April 1386; a mandate was issued to de Vere or his justiciar in Ireland at the end of January to ensure Alexander, bishop of Ossory, rendered an account in the exchequer.[80]

As discussed above, the agreement made between de Vere and the king in March 1386 specified that a force of eight hundred men was to travel to Ireland and to serve for half a year. This was indeed what happened. Musters were taken in Burton (Cheshire), Liverpool, Conway and Bristol in late June or early July by various royal officials, including Thomas Saville, a royal serjeant at arms, and de Vere and the king reached Bristol by 13 July presumably to oversee the final stages of preparation and embarkation.[81] The mustered forces included contingents led by de Vere's lieutenant Sir John Stanley and the earl of Ormond, and totalled 766 men, a little under the total envisaged.[82]

It was the English exchequer which paid over sufficient cash to cover the wages of the reduced force in 1386. A payment of £2,000 was made on 27 March 1386 to John Lancaster and Robert Crull towards the wages and regard of 200 men-at-arms and 600 archers as well as 400 marks for the costs for their passage to Ireland, another was made for £500 on 9 April, a further one of £1,200 on 9 June, another of £1,633 6s 8d followed on 25 June, and a final one of £300 was paid on 6 September: these totalled £5,633 6s 8d.[83] This is almost exactly the sum that would be expected: at the rates of pay set out in the grant of Ireland, 200 men-at-arms at 12d a day and 40s regard per quarter and 600 archers at 6d. a day total £5,375; 400 marks to cover the shipping costs brings that total to £5,641 6s 8d.

The much-reduced force (800 rather than 1,500) that went to Ireland should also not be read as de Vere's lack of interest in his lordship. Firstly, the primary source of revenue envisaged to fund the larger force was not to be realised until November 1387. It must have been understood that to find £22,250 to fund the force for a year from the spring of 1386 onwards was a political and fiscal impossibility; a force of half the size and half the duration was considerably

[80] E159/162, Hil. Term Recorda, rot. 24d.

[81] The muster rolls have not survived. The account of Thomas Saville, a royal serjeant at arms, for his expenses for the Bristol muster, for which he was paid for twenty-six days from 9 June to 5 July is E364/24, rot. 3d. For the other musters, Nicholas Vernon and John Wodehouse, chamberlain of North Wales, were appointed on 18 June: *CPR, 1385–9*, 163. For de Vere and Richard, see above, p. 81.

[82] *CPR, 1385–9*, 91, 125–6, 128, 130, 156, 157, 158, 163, 188–9.

[83] E403/511, mm. 28, 31; E403/512, mm. 8, 10–11, 21. A payment on 2 June 1386 of £300 levied on the revenues of Chester was cancelled (E403/512, m. 6).

more realistic. It is impressive that de Vere was able to secure what he was owed for the reduced force that did serve from the overstretched exchequer. The other explanation of the smaller army was that the difference between the envisaged and the actual force was de Vere's own retinue was missing. De Vere himself had not gone to Ireland and indeed was leading a force of 600 men during August 1386 to resist the French invasion, almost the number he would have needed to complete his initial obligation of 1,500 men.

Stanley's smaller force was delayed and did not reach Ireland until August, but again this reflects not on de Vere but on the fact there were also no fewer than three calls on the limited English naval resources during the hectic summer of 1386. Alongside de Vere's force, a larger expedition under John of Gaunt intended to try and realise his claim to the Castilian throne was a huge maritime commitment, and there was a third priority, as ships were required to serve against the expected French invasion. On 28 March 1386, William Whitheved, esquire, and others was appointed to provide ships and arrest mariners in the port of Bristol, those for the duke of Lancaster's expedition excepted. Stanley, William Frodesham and others were appointed in North Wales, Furness, Copeland and the counties of Cheshire and Lancashire, and in April further orders were issued for the ports of Bristol, Bridgewater, Chepstow and Axewater.[84] In fact the demand proved too great and both expeditions to Castile and Ireland were delayed.[85] The fact that any force at all reached Ireland that summer was impressive.

A further payment for military forces in Ireland of £466 13s 4d was made by the exchequer on 14 May 1387.[86] Given this was made under the commission imposed on Richard by the Wonderful Parliament, it is a little surprising that any was made at all. The issue roll of that date recited an indenture between the king and de Vere identical in terms of numbers of men and other conditions to that recited in the payments made in 1386, with the exception of the change of title from marquess of Dublin to duke of Ireland. It is possible that this reflected no more than the exchequer clerk updating the title and not including the fact that the indenture was made while he was still marquess, but it could also represent a new indenture made between the duke and the king in the spring of 1387 for 800 men to serve under Stanley in Ireland for half a year. There was also a steady trickle of grants of protection for men going to Ireland

---

[84] *CPR, 1385–9*, 131. Whitheved was of Bromsgrove in Worcestershire: *CPR, 1385–9*, 272. He served in Ireland with a retinue of eight men-at-arms and twelve archers: ibid., 126, 163.

[85] Roskell, *Impeachment of Michael de la Pole*, 70.

[86] E403/517, m. 4.

after the main force had left. Between September 1386 and December 1387, a further twenty-five grants were issued, including one knight, Robert Clifton, one esquire, Robert de Eure, and one abbot, of Vale Royal.[87] There were also numerous revocations of protection for men who had fraudulently acquired them, and then had not gone: they totalled twenty-six, compared to the 110 who acquired them between early 1386 and late 1387.[88] Nonetheless, there was military activity in de Vere's duchy of Ireland in 1387. While there was just this single small payment from the English exchequer, the account of Robert Crull, treasurer of Ireland, covering 1386–8 records military expenditure of £2,453. This may well mainly represent spending in 1387, when there was almost no other source of funding available beyond de Vere's personal revenues or loans.[89]

The Irish patent rolls do not themselves now survive, but in the nineteenth century the Record Commission calendared the patent rolls for the tenth year of Richard II's reign (June 1386–June 1387).[90] They record 234 actions made in the name of the marquess of Dublin.[91] They show that de Vere played a rather greater part in the governance of Ireland than has previously been recognised. Only 105 of the 234 items of business state by what authority the grant was made. Of these fifty-one were specifically acknowledged to have been done either by the lieutenant, Stanley, on his own authority, by the council in Ireland, or by both. However, the rolls also record a number of actions that were undoubtedly de Vere's. These included the presentation of Master Maurice Sweetman to the church of Fethard, a grant that was given at Oxford on 12 August 1386 and was witnessed by the marquess himself as he accompanied the royal court.[92] The second was a grant of the manor called Blackcastle (in Navan, County Meath) to the lieutenant, Stanley, for

---

[87] *CPR, 1385–9*, 210, 214, 223, 232, 240, 278, 280, 312, 341, 352, 355, 377. These also included two clerks, one spicer, one drover, one vintner and one taverner.

[88] Revocations are ibid., 199, 211, 219, 234, 249, 252, 257, 274–5, 277, 285, 337, 450.

[89] E364/32, rot. 6d.

[90] *RPC*, 131–7.

[91] This is, of course, problematic, as de Vere was made duke of Ireland in October 1386 on the resignation of his marquessate, but not a single one of the administrative actions recorded here use his ducal title. It seems most likely that the various seals of his administration in Ireland were not updated: an order in April 1388 to Irish officials to cease using and destroy the great seal of Robert de Vere, late marquess of Dublin, would rather suggest that was the case, given the otherwise consistent use of his ducal rank in English government documents: *CPR, 1385–9*, 441. If so, it is odd that he did not change his seals as de Vere clearly had pride in his ducal title (see below, pp. 231–2).

[92] *RPC*, 130, no. 9.

life, which was given by a letter under the signet of the marquess on 27 June 1386. Five other grants were given under the signet of the marquess, which was surely present wherever he went. Two more grants were made 'by letters of the lord marquess himself', one 'by letters of the marquess in England' and one 'by letters of privy seal of the lord marquess himself'.[93] Moreover, his council in England seems to have been involved in the administration, making at least one appointment, that of Richard White as justiciar.[94] We can say then that De Vere himself made at least twelve grants. Also indicative is a petition to the Merciless Parliament by John Ross, bishop of Down, for ratification of his temporalities which he had been granted by de Vere in March 1387 having done fealty to him, and which was delivered to the bishop by John Stanley, the duke's deputy. This is clear evidence of – at the very least – the paperwork being done by the duke's administration in England.[95] The appointment of the earl of Kildare to intercede in the quarrel between the earls of Desmond and Ormond was done when the marquess himself heard of the dispute.[96] The seriousness of the dispute would certainly have meant de Vere would have been consulted.

There are also twenty-nine grants which are enrolled as being done by either 'letters of privy seal', or 'by letters of the privy seal of the marquess'. Given that the privy seal was in Ireland, it is probable that these were grants made in Ireland, but we cannot be sure that the initiative did not come from de Vere personally in every case. Moreover, 128 grants do not give an authorisation clause, mostly just reciting a formula such as 'The marquess assigns/concedes/grants' or some similar variation. It is tempting to say that de Vere was not involved but without the original documents it is impossible to be sure, especially since it is perfectly clear that a number of Anglo-Irish went to England to petition the marquess. We know of at least five who set out to seek favours from de Vere, including William Frodesham, admiral of Ireland.[97] There were a party of Irishmen on pilgrimage under safe-conduct from the king and the duke of Ireland in Aylesbury in early 1388, and again they may have sought out the duke in person.[98] These may well just be the tip of the iceberg – one historian of Ireland has described the 'constant traffic

---

[93] *RPC*, 131–7, nos 35, 39, 46, 47, 60, 61, 121, 144, 233, 234.
[94] Tuck, *Richard II*, 82.
[95] SC8/216/10751; *CPR, 1385–9*, 413.
[96] *RPC*, 137, no. 220.
[97] *RPC*, 133–7, nos, 68, 76, 103, 192, 217. Frodesham had brought a retinue of twelve men-at-arms and thirty-six archers in 1386 to Ireland.
[98] SC8/148/7385.

of messengers, petitioners and envoys' across the Irish Sea throughout the later Middle Ages.[99] There may have been more who sought out the duke of Ireland in England, and we know nothing of any less formal channels which would have involved de Vere himself – did his lieutenant seek his advice or authorisation on a regular basis? How much correspondence was there between the duke and Dublin?

The brief account of Robert Crull, treasurer of Ireland, between April 1386, the beginning of direct rule by de Vere in Ireland, and May 1388, can give a little insight into de Vere's administration.[100] It is however, not without its problems, not being rendered until ten years later, and containing at least one significant error, dating Robert de Vere's forfeiture to the start of the Wonderful Parliament (1 October 1386) rather than the Merciless Parliament (February 1388).[101] Receipts from customs and lands totalled £4,556 15s 6d, and loans from John Carloll (£93 6s 8d) and Robert, archbishop of Dublin (£218) added just over £300. The loans suggest at least some buy-in to de Vere's regime by senior local figures. £1,100 was paid in fees and wages to the senior figures in the Irish exchequer, chancery and judiciary, and to two of the leading Anglo-Irish peers, the earls of Kildare and Ormond. But defence was the main priority. Walter Eure acted as the main treasurer for the wages of Stanley's force, and received £2,453 10s 9d in three payments, again undated in the summary account. Works costing just over £36 were carried out to the castle at Dublin. A further £586 15s 10d was given as payments or reward to John Darcy, constable of the castle of Rathmore in Limerick and several others, English and Irish, through the advice of the Irish administration, and military service might be presumed here. Not mentioned explicitly in the account but known from other sources was a payment of £40 to the earl of Desmond from the revenues of Ireland for expenses – presumably military – in Munster.[102] Fees were paid to Art MacMurrough, self-proclaimed king of Leinster, and

---

[99] P. Crooks, 'Representation and Dissent: "Parliamentarianism" and the Structure of Politics in Colonial Ireland, c. 1370–1420', *EHR*, 125 (2010), 17.

[100] What follows is drawn from E364/32, m. 6d, a summary account of Robert Crull for these two years, which was not drawn up until 22 Richard II (1398–9). It is summarised and translated in *Irish Exchequer Payments*, ed. Connolly, 544–5.

[101] For the accounting, see D. Johnston, 'Chief Governors and Treasurers of Ireland in the Reign of Richard II', in Barry, Frame and Simms, eds, *Colony and Frontier in Medieval Ireland*, 109–10.

[102] *A Roll of the Proceedings of the King's Council in Ireland for a portion of the Sixteenth Year of the Reign of Richard II, A.D. 1392–3*, ed. J. Graves (RS, 69, 1877), 126–8. The petition by Desmond was that payment had been partly assigned on a tally from the revenues of the city of Cork, and the mayor and bailiffs of the city had refused

Gerald O'Byrne, described as captains of the Irish nation, totalling £48 13s. MacMurrough was granted an annuity of 80 marks per annum, but this was clearly not paid in full during Crull's account.[103] A payment of £214 12s 6d was made to Alexander, bishop of Meath, the chancellor, Edward Perers and Thomas Everdon, lieutenants of the treasurer, for the wages of their soldiers, ordained by the council of the marquess, to resist their Irish enemies. No date is given for this payment, but it was probably after Stanley's return to England in 1387 when the bishop of Meath took over as de Vere's deputy.[104] After some other expenses, Crull's outgoings totalled £4,883 17s 7d, an overspend of £15 15s 5d, though the loans of more than £300 made the account seem more balanced than it was.[105] The account, of course, does not indicate exactly how much input de Vere had into the financial decisions or the authorisation process. Here, though, the priorities of the Dublin administration and the marquess/duke were the same. Defence had to be of the highest importance, given its criticality to those in Ireland and the fact that any hint of military defeat would only serve to give ammunition to de Vere's critics in England.

The governance of Ireland did not, of course, exist in a vacuum, and was subject not only to the politics of Richard II's court in England but the politics of Ireland as well, and Peter Crooks has ably demonstrated the interlocking nature of these forces.[106] The key Irish factor was the ongoing power struggle between the earls of Ormond and Desmond, which had needed arbitration before de Vere's appointment and would do so again in 1387. Ormond, as has been noted, was a key supporter of de Vere's administration, assuming that it would benefit his interests; relations with the previous lieutenant, Sir

---

to pay. The payment, which was during the time of the marquess of Dublin, is not dated any more specifically.

[103] MacMurrough was the chief target during Richard II's campaign in 1394, though he submitted quickly enough to the king, being an 'astute politician': R. Frame, 'Mac Murchadha, Art Caomhánach [Art Kavanagh MacMurrough; called Art Mór Mac Murchadha], d. 1416/17', *ODNB*; Frame, 'Two Kings in Leinster', 155–75; E. O'Byrne, *War, Politics and the Irish of Leinster, 1156–1606* (Dublin, 2003), 103–19. For the 80-mark fee, see *RPC*, 131, no. 42

[104] Tuck, 'Anglo-Irish Relations', 26.

[105] There is other evidence of an administration keen to exploit its limited resources. The abbot of Tintern was sued by de Vere's administration at a Wexford quarter session for £42 4s 2½ d, part of a pension due for the Irish holdings of Canterbury Cathedral Priory. However, the abbot was able to show Irish exchequer tallies to prove he had paid it and was discharged: Canterbury Cathedral Archives, CCA-DCc-ChAnt/I/246.

[106] This paragraph is based on Crooks, 'Calculus of Faction', particularly 105–13.

Philip Courtenay had recently soured. Courtenay, in high dudgeon about the manner of his dismissal, was elected as an MP to the Wonderful Parliament of 1386, and during the Commission's term of office in late 1386 and 1387, was able to extract a measure of revenge and the Irish administration (and de Vere's duchy) somewhat undermined. It is no coincidence that it was in March 1387 that reports of great discord between Ormond and Desmond were recorded, as they took matters into their own hands and de Vere (perhaps on the advice of his Irish officers) appointed the earl of Kildare to try and patch up the quarrel.

De Vere's deputy, Stanley, landed at Dalkey on 31 August 1386, and on 18 September he held his first great council in Dublin Castle, at which he showed his patent of appointment.[107] Stanley seems to have been active enough, moving around as far as Tristernagh, County Westmeath.[108] He also paid considerable attention to the affairs of Ulster, Meath and Connacht, which were in the hands of de Vere because of the minority of the earl of March. Edmund Savage was reappointed as steward of the liberty of Ulster in de Vere's name in October 1386 with the substantial annual fee of 80 marks, Richard Calf as sheriff of the Crosslands of Ulster the same month, and Robert, son of Adam FitzEustace, as sheriff of Antrim in February 1387 during pleasure.[109] He was also able to extract a grant of taxation from the commons of the county of Dublin of 1d a head in aid of war at some point during 'the time of the marquis of Dublin'.[110] The one criticism that could be levelled against Stanley was that he failed to lead a major campaign against the Irish. He had not landed until September, which was late in the year to undertake a lengthy campaign, but some military activity did take place. Two rebel leaders were raiding in the marches and the commons of Fingal granted a subsidy to maintain guards against them before 26 October when Sir Richard Talbot, sheriff of Dublin, and others were appointed to lead forty 'hobellar et sagittar' against the rebels for fifteen days.[111] However, more military activity might have been expected given the fact that Stanley had more than 700 men with him. Indeed, the

---

[107] *RPC*, 131, no. 31; Tuck, 'Anglo-Irish Relations', 25.

[108] *RPC*, 127, no. 238; 131, no. 42; 134, no. 49; 135, no. 160; 136, no. 191; 137, nos 217, 220, 216; A.J. Othway-Ruthven, *A History of Medieval Ireland* (London, 1968), 320.

[109] *RPC*, 131, nos 48, 50; 133, no. 115. Savage was, however, rather independently minded: K. Simms, 'The Ulster Revolt of 1404 – an Anti-Lancastrian Dimension', in Smith, ed., *Ireland and the English World*, 145.

[110] National Archives of Ireland, EX 2/4/1/16, accessed through the Virtual Record Treasury of Ireland.

[111] *RPC*, 136, no. 191. Light horsemen and archers.

military situation in 1387, as the exchequer money dried up, was difficult, and the sheriff of Meath and the bishop of Sodor were empowered to treat with the Irish in Meath and Ulster respectively, with the intention of concluding local, temporary, truces.[112]

It is not clear how John Stanley came to be de Vere's choice as his deputy in Ireland. The younger son of a minor Cheshire knight, he had accumulated military experience in Gascony from the early 1370s, where is just possible that he became known to de Vere's uncle Aubrey in the service of the Black Prince, and in 1372 in Robert Knolles' campaign, where he may have served under Thomas Trivet. He was also in the garrison in Cherbourg under Thomas Holland, earl of Kent, in 1385. As Morgan notes, 'the basis of his preferment is far from clear: either military experience and reputation, or perhaps more likely, a connection with the king's chamber knight, Sir Thomas Trivet'.[113] This is certainly possible, given de Vere's role as great chamberlain, the senior role in the king's chamber. Stanley seems to have been a good choice in most respects for de Vere's deputy in Ireland; his reappointment as lieutenant of Ireland by Henry IV and Henry V – he died in Ireland in 1414 – suggests real competence and expertise.[114]

De Vere also made a shrewd appointment of Robert Crull as treasurer of Ireland. It is unlikely that de Vere had much prior knowledge of Crull, though as rector of Stepney in Middlesex and a royal clerk since the 1370s, their paths may have crossed.[115] However, it may well have been on the recommendation of Aubrey de Vere as he, Crull and others had acted together in a case in the court of Common Pleas in 1381 concerning land in Essex.[116] Crull was at the time of his appointment as treasurer and war treasurer on 20 March 1386 – the same date as Stanley's appointment as lieutenant – also a canon of St Patrick's Cathedral in Dublin and a prebendary of Swords

---

[112] Smith, *Crisis and Survival*, 77–8; College of Arms, PH 15172, pp. 38–9; *RPC*, 136, no. 207, 211.

[113] P. Morgan, *War and Society in Medieval Cheshire 1277–1403* (Chetham Society, 3rd series, 34, 1987), 172–3.

[114] For a summary of his career, see M. Bennett, 'Stanley, Sir John (c. 1350–1414)', *ODNB*. He seems to have been deeply unpopular amongst the Irish.

[115] Rector since 1368: *The Victoria County History of Middlesex*, ed. W. Page et al. (13 vols, London, 1911–), xi, 73; King's clerk: *CCR, 1369–74*, 510. If he was Irish, Irish clergy in England were not uncommon: V. Davis, 'Irish Clergy in Late Medieval England', *Irish Historical Studies*, 32 (2000), 145–60.

[116] CP40/483, rot. 108d.

in the same city.[117] However, he is known to have been in England in January of that year, transacting Irish council business alongside the archbishop of Dublin and the bishop of Ossory, and it is probably in this context that he met de Vere and clearly impressed him sufficiently to be appointed to the role.[118] Crull gave long service as treasurer of Ireland, serving until 1399, which suggests his administrative abilities were of a good order.[119] He also contributed six men-at-arms and twenty-four archers to the force that travelled to Ireland under John Stanley in the summer of 1386.[120] It may well have been to protect his English interests at Stepney that he acquired letters of protection before travelling to Ireland in May 1386 and again in March 1387.[121] De Vere also appointed William Frodesham, esquire, as admiral of Ireland by October 1386.[122] Frodesham, and his brother, Thomas, a chaplain, who accompanied him to Ireland, may have come to de Vere's notice through their connections with de Vere's leading servant, Sir John Lancaster. It was by Lancaster's mainprise the two brothers received the custody of the alien priory of Tickford in Buckinghamshire, for which they were to pay an annual rent of 40 marks, as confirmed by a royal signet letter of March 1385.[123] Frodesham served in Ireland with a retinue of twelve men-at-arms and thirty-six archers, and was involved in impressing ships in north-west England to transport de Vere's troops across the Irish Sea.[124] Sir Robert de Hereford was another who served in Ireland, having had previous experience of doing so, and was already well-versed in the politics and governance of the lordship, as he had married the dowager countess of Ormond by 1383.[125] Sir Edward Perers, deputy treasurer to Crull, had had experience in Ireland since the late 1370s, while Sir John Shriggley, appointed escheator, clerk of the markets and keeper of weights and measures in Ireland during de Vere's

---

[117] The appointment is noted at the beginning of his account for 1386–8 in E364/32, rot. 6d.

[118] *CPR, 1385–9*, 91.

[119] Johnston, 'Chief Governors and Treasurers of Ireland', 109–10.

[120] *CPR, 1385–9*, 163.

[121] *CPR, 1385–9*, 155, 156, 278.

[122] *RPC*, 135, no. 177; 136, no. 192.

[123] *CPR, 1381–5*, 554; *1385–9*, 201.

[124] *CPR, 1385–9*, 125, 131, 163.

[125] Crooks, 'Calculus of Faction', 100; *CPR, 1381–5*, 403; *1385–9*, 125, 130, 144, 278, 341; *CCR, 1381–5*, 372, 467.

marquessate, married into Meath society.[126] These men, closely connected with the earl of Ormond, filled the intermediate ranks of de Vere's administration, but were also acceptable to the Anglo-Irish community rather than being outsiders. It is worth noting that by 1391 the three most senior posts in Ireland, justiciar, chancellor and treasurer, were held by Stanley, the bishop of Meath, and Crull, who had filled these roles under de Vere, which suggests competence and experience amongst these men.[127]

※

None of this activity in the government of Ireland came to the attention of Henry of Marleborough, whose near-contemporary chronicle of Ireland ended with his death in 1421. He did not mention de Vere's appointment or promotion but simply the duke of Ireland's military resistance at Radcot Bridge to the peers who had risen 'against those that were of the side of Richard the second', his defeat and escape, all of which was described in a neutral tone.[128] Robert de Vere's innovative duchy of Ireland entirely escaped his notice. Perhaps to the English in Ireland, in retrospect, it felt like nothing had changed. It is clear that much of the administration was carried out by Stanley and the council, as would be expected in de Vere's absence. Certainly, the mechanisms for government were available in Ireland to continue without his direct input. A mandate was issued in April 1388, four months after de Vere's exile, to the key members of the Irish administration, the king's justiciar, the keeper of the great seal and the treasurer of the exchequer. It noted that they had in error continued to use de Vere's great seal, privy seal and other seals of his, and had displayed his standards against Irish rebels, and ordered that these symbols of his lordship should be destroyed.[129] Yet the evidence shows that de Vere did carry out some administrative duties, and kept most of the more important decisions for himself. De Vere's lordship of Ireland was a serious project derailed by external factors. The lack of parliamentary taxation for the project, and the limited funding available from the exchequer, meant innovative financial measures had to be taken, which could not deliver sufficient cash and would be tardy in any

---

[126] Crooks, 'Factionalism and Noble Power', 209–10, 213–14.

[127] Crooks, 'Factionalism and Noble Power', 198–9. For Stanley's indenture of appointment, muster of his retinue as justiciar (100 men at arms and 200 archers) and other documents, see E101/247/1 and E101/41/18.

[128] 'Henry Marleburrough's Chronicle', in *Ancient Irish Histories*, ed. J. Ware (2 vols, Reissued Dublin, 1809), ii, 14.

[129] *CPR, 1385–9*, 441.

case. Political opposition, particularly in the Wonderful Parliament may, ironically, have made it more likely that de Vere had to stay by Richard's side, despite Walsingham's assertion that nobles and commons were enthusiastic he crossed to Ireland. It could be argued that de Vere actually made a decent attempt at doing a difficult job in trying circumstances.

5

Downfall, Exile and Death, 1386–92

[Neville, de Vere, de la Pole, Tresilian, Brembre] the governors and most intimate counsellors of the king, were leading wicked lives, deceiving the aforesaid king, attending to the business of neither king nor kingdom, but continually appropriating to themselves the fruits of their iniquity through their evil deeds.

(Thomas Favent on the court circle in his history of the Wonderful Parliament[1])

The 'Wonderful' Parliament of 1386 to Summer 1387

The Parliament of 1386, which saw the impeachment of the unpopular chancellor, Michael de la Pole, earl of Suffolk, was the most problematic to date for Richard II and his friends.[2] It also coincided with Robert de Vere's greatest promotion. On 13 October 1386, on the resignation of his marquessate of Dublin, de Vere was created duke of Ireland.[3] Thomas Walsingham, as he did with the grant of the marquessate the previous year, stated that the nobility objected: 'other nobles and barons secretly grumbled, and were indignant at the desire for such promotion in so unremarkable a man, who had no more to commend him than others did in nobility of birth or in his endowment of other virtues'.[4] There is nothing implausible in this reaction, but it is interesting that Walsingham notes secret grumbling, since the act, assuming the charter roll is

---

[1] T. Favent, *Historia sive Narracio de Modo et Forma Mirabilis Parliamenti…*, ed. M. McKisack in *Camden Miscellany XIV* (Camden Society, 3rd series, 37, 1926), 1.

[2] As *PROME*, vii, 31 n.1 notes, the label 'wonderful', deriving from Favent's tract, was probably meant to be applied to the Parliament of 1388 rather than this one, but the name has stuck.

[3] *CChR*, v, 307. Mitchell has noted that the date of de Vere's creation as duke, 13 October, was the principal feast day of the Confessor and perhaps Richard was seeking the sanction of the Confessor (and of St Edmund, whose arms of three crowns were the same as those of Ireland) for his actions: S. Mitchell, 'Richard II: Kingship and the Cult of Saints', in D. Gordon, L. Monnas and C. Elam, eds, *The Regal Image of Richard II and the Wilton Diptych* (London, 1997), 118.

[4] *SAC*, i, 798–9.

correct, was witnessed by three of the future Appellants, Gloucester, Arundel and Nottingham, as well as the duke of York, four other earls, three archbishops and four bishops. This was more, in fact, of the higher nobility than the grant of the marquessate in the previous year and in different circumstances this might be used as evidence of the assent of the political community.[5] It is also noticeable that other chroniclers, notably Knighton and the continuator of the *Eulogium*, report the promotion without comment.[6] Chris Given-Wilson has suggested that, as it was not enrolled on the parliament roll, the grant may have been done at Eltham, where the king was, rather than in parliament itself and that it was as unwelcome a promotion as chroniclers imply.[7] Although it is not included in the parliament roll, the royal charter of creation states that it was done by the king in parliament, so the venue and context of the creation is therefore a little unclear.[8]

The grant has been noted as being the first of a dukedom to someone outside the immediate royal family, which is accurate, though it might be remarked that de Vere did have some royal blood, as he was descended from Henry III, and he had, of course, married Edward III's granddaughter, Philippa de Coucy. However, neither his birth nor his achievements to date in his twenty-four years would have led to such an elevation in this way without royal favour. Walsingham certainly noticed this. In the context of the grant of the dukedom, the Monk of St Albans stated that 'the king was very devoted to him, and greatly respected and loved him', which is unarguable. The sentence then went on to add that this was 'not without the ignominy, it is said, of an impure relationship', though arguably the Latin – 'familiaritatis obscene' – requires a stronger and more literal translation as 'obscene familiarities', which is, as discussed above, far more difficult to prove.[9]

Although the Wonderful Parliament of 1386 was famous for the impeachment of Michael de la Pole, he may not have been the initial target. One source, preserved in Sir Walter Scott's *Somers Tracts* and purporting to be a transcript of a history of the parliament, states that the Commons proposed

---

[5] C53/161, m.1. The other earls were Salisbury, Devon, Northumberland and Suffolk. The ecclesiastics were the archbishops of Canterbury, York and Dublin, and the bishops of London, Winchester, Ely and Durham. The only other named witness was John de Montagu, steward of the household.

[6] *KC*, 352–3; *Continuatio Eulogii*, ed. Given-Wilson, 55. A missing leaf in the MS of the Westminster Chronicle means the promotion is not discussed: *WC*, 184n.

[7] *PROME*, vii, 32.

[8] C53/161, m.1; *CChR*, v, 307.

[9] *SAC*, i, 798–9. See above, pp. 78–80.

to remove de Vere on account of his overweening influence with the king. However, they then thought it better to attack de la Pole, who was easier to remove, partly because he 'was the steersman of the ship of state' as chancellor but also 'he was out of danger of being pittyed, which the duke of Ireland, as earl of Oxford, was not'.[10] This last point presumably refers to de Vere's ancient lineage and higher social status. The overall idea that de Vere was the first target of the parliament is almost impossible to accept on this evidence. In the form in which it now survives 'the narrative was clearly composed during the reign of Charles I with a view to proceedings against Buckingham', another royal favourite under attack in parliament.[11] While it may have been based on a contemporary source – the editor notes only that it was translated from a manuscript source in the University of Cambridge – and Taylor argues that there is a 'substratum of facts' which indicates this, there are a number of issues with the source. Aside from the analogous position of the two royal favourites (de Vere and George Villiers, duke of Buckingham) which colours the narrative, it has very long reported speeches by a representative of the commons and by Michael de la Pole in response, which are not reported anywhere else. More specifically in regard to de Vere, it states his overweening arrogance, which provoked the Commons to desire to lance it before they shifted their aim to de la Pole, was caused by his creation of duke of Ireland. However, as noted, his elevation to the dukedom occurred on 13 October, almost two weeks after the assembly opened. Yet almost all the more contemporary sources for the parliament suggest that the attack on de la Pole followed hard on the heels of his opening address and therefore the source's chronology and argument are faulty.[12] Palmer contends that the attack by the Commons was about finance and financial mismanagement more than anything else, and de Vere was only tangentially connected with this, unlike de la Pole, the chancellor, John de Fordham, the treasurer, who was also dismissed, and the king himself.[13] Despite these flaws, Nigel Saul, while acknowledging the problems with it, argues the source 'carries the ring of verisimilitude' and that 'almost certainly the impeachment of de Vere was one of the options considered'.[14] Yet it is hard to know on what grounds de Vere could have been impeached in 1386. De la Pole was accused of misconduct of government and of personal financial

---

[10] *Somers Tracts. A Collection of Scarce and Valuable Tracts...*, ed. Sir Walter Scott (13 vols, 2nd edn, London, 1809–15), i, 15–16.

[11] J. Taylor, *English Historical Literature in the Fourteenth Century* (Oxford, 1987), 272.

[12] See the introduction to the parliament by Given-Wilson in *PROME*, vii, 31–3.

[13] Palmer, 'Impeachment of Michael de la Pole', 98–9.

[14] Saul, *Richard II*, 160.

peculation in his role as chancellor; de Vere did not hold such office by which he could be held to account.[15] Any treason charges drawn up at the beginning of the parliament of 1386 would have been complete fabrications: of the fourteen charges found to be treasonable in 1388, eleven related to events that occurred during the parliament of 1386 or in 1387, two were totally generic and only one, the grant of Ireland, might have been applicable in October 1386.[16] Overall, then, the idea that de Vere was the first target of the 1386 parliament has little to commend it.

The parliament of 1386 imposed unprecedented restrictions on Richard and his conduct of government, and indeed set the scene for the showdown of late 1387. It not only saw the impeachment and dismissal of Michael de la Pole, and the appointment of a much less sympathetic chancellor as far as Richard was concerned, Thomas Arundel, bishop of Ely, but the appointment of a commission which effectively removed from Richard the ability to run his own government. The commission was to investigate and reform the royal finances, had significant judicial powers, and included the new chancellor, treasurer and keeper of the privy seal, appointed by parliament not the king. It was to remain in place for a year, until 19 November 1387, and in return Richard received only one fifteenth and tenth in direct taxation and an extension of indirect taxation on wool until Christmas 1387. It largely removed Richard's ability to make grants of patronage, as Ormrod has shown, and this aspect can be demonstrated in the timing of two grants relating to Robert de Vere.[17] The first was the ransom of John of Blois which was not finalised until October 1387 and the initial instalment not paid until 23 November 1387, at the end of the commission's term. A grant of the king's castle of Berkhamsted for a year to de Vere was dated 1 November 1387, eighteen days before the commission was to expire, but which could presumably be implemented afterwards.[18] There were no grants to de Vere while the commission was in force from November 1386 to November 1387. As Ormrod has asked, 'Could it be that this restriction of patronage was the true cause of Richard's vindictive pursuit of the commissioners both in 1387 and later in 1397?'[19] Not all of the commissioners were hostile to Richard.

---

[15] For the charges, see *PROME*, vii, 37–8 and for discussion, see Roskell, *Impeachment of Michael de la Pole*, 57–185; Palmer, 'Impeachment of Michael de la Pole', 96–101.

[16] *PROME*, vii, 102.

[17] For an excellent dissection of the remit, performance and results of the commission, see W.M. Ormrod, 'Government by Commission: the Continual Council of 1386 and English Royal Administration', *Peritia*, 10 (1996), 303–21.

[18] *CPR, 1385–9*, 366.

[19] Ormrod, 'Government by Commission', 319.

If Alexander Neville, archbishop of York, was not already close to Richard at the time the commission was established as several sources suggest, he would shortly become so, while the archbishop of Canterbury and Bishops Wykeham of Winchester and Brantingham of Exeter should not be seen as either directly hostile to the crown or closely associated with its most vociferous detractors.[20] However, several commissioners were leading critics, notably Gloucester, the earl of Arundel, his brother, Thomas, bishop of Ely, and Richard, Lord Scrope, whom the king had dismissed as chancellor in 1382.[21]

Indeed, for all the contemporary and modern commentary on de Vere taking the lion's share of the available patronage, almost all of the grants he received between being created marquess of Dublin in December 1385 and his downfall in December 1387 related to Ireland and were connected to the task of making that effective. There were only two landed grants not explicitly connected to Ireland and neither were permanent ones. Early in 1386, with the assent of the council, he was granted the manor of Kennington, without rent, on 3 February for eight years and sixteen days later for life. The other dated to 1 November 1387 when he received a grant for one year of the castle of Berkhamsted for his residence.[22] Kennington was one of the Black Prince's favourite residences, having built a substantial palace there, so it was a grant of an impressive house close to London and of some personal significance to Richard, the Black Prince's son, who had spent some of his childhood there. De Vere certainly used Kennington, as documents written on 20 and 21 October 1386 are dated there.[23] Quite why de Vere needed another substantial residence formerly belonging to the Black Prince at Berkhamsted and less than 30 miles away from Kennington a year later is not obvious. Yet it was explicitly for 'his own and his family's abode' and came with the right to take as much fuel within the wood and park as was necessary for his household. De Vere was at Berkhamsted the previous Christmas and it may be he took a liking to the place; the commission's control of royal patronage may be the reason the grant was only for a year, and had Richard triumphed over his opponents in December 1387 the grant might have been extended.[24]

---

[20] Davies, 'Episcopate and Political Crisis', 664–7.

[21] Saul, *Richard II*, 162–3; Tuck, *Richard II*, 100; Fletcher, *Richard II*, 154.

[22] *CPR, 1385–9*, 115, 117, 366.

[23] E368/159, rot. presentaciones 2.

[24] *CPR, 1385–9*, 366. For his use of it at Christmas 1386, see below, p. 205, n. 16. The fairly paltry sum of just over £5 had been spent on repairs and works to Berkhamsted over the previous few years: E101/473/2.

The appointment of the commission in November 1386 made matters more difficult for Richard and those around him, and Robert de Vere was no exception to this. The most important matter related to Sir Philip Courtenay, the previous lieutenant of Ireland, who petitioned that by de Vere's appointment to the lordship of Ireland his term of office had been interrupted, that he had lost his income there, and that his goods and chattels in Ireland had been unlawfully seized.[25] An order was made by the council on 28 February 1387 to de Vere and his Irish administration to restore Courtenay's own goods and the profits of Ireland due at Easter 1386. This was somewhat harsh on de Vere. It was in response to a royal order, warranted by the king himself, in March 1386, that Courtenay had been arrested and his goods seized, and he was ordered on his allegiance not to depart Ireland.[26] The grounds were Courtenay's alleged misconduct while in office, and the allegations against him came from the Anglo-Irish rather than being some malicious plot by de Vere. Courtenay had been deeply unpopular as the king's lieutenant in Ireland and demands for his removal from office predated de Vere's appointment.[27] Saul states that de Vere was ordered to pay a fine of 1,000 marks to Courtenay. However, the entry in the issue rolls only notes that the sum was agreed by the council and not who was to pay it and the payments noted by Saul – £275 6s 7d in September 1388 and two in December of that year for £266 13s 4d and £66 13s 4d – postdate de Vere's fall, so the duke, if he paid anything at all, presumably handed over no more than £125.[28]

Richard found the restrictions placed on him by the commission a source of immense frustration and while he remained in or around the capital his household was open to the scrutiny of the commission, which had the reduction of household expenditure as one its aims. Therefore, from the second week of February 1387 he set off on a series of 'gyrations', as Knighton described them, around the country, not returning to Westminster until November, when the commission's term of office was to expire.[29] Although occasionally back in the south-east – for instance for the St George's day celebrations at Windsor – much of the king's time was spent in the midlands and the north-west. How much time de Vere spent with the king during his travels is less clear. He can be definitely placed with the king on only four occasions: at Reading in May, Lichfield in June, Shrewsbury in early August, and at Nottingham on

[25] CCR, 1385–9, 232.
[26] CCR, 1385–9, 49.
[27] Crooks, 'Factionalism and Noble Power', 181–7; Saul, *Richard II*, 165, 273–4.
[28] E403/519, m. 24; E403/521, mm. 7, 9.
[29] KC, 400–4; Saul, *Richard II*, 171–3; Tuck, *Richard II*, 108–10.

25 August. The latter two were the venues for great councils, while the visit to Lichfield related to the installation of Richard Scrope as bishop.[30] He was probably with the king at Leicester in mid-September and certainly was with him on 10–11 November when the king returned to London. On the other hand, not entirely reliable evidence – from the charter rolls and from the Chester Eyre rolls – has him apart from the king in March and in October, and perhaps places him at Nottingham when the king was at Leicester in September.[31] It is certainly not clear that he spent most of the year constantly in the king's company, though we might well speculate that he was in close contact with, and undertook regular sojourns in the company of, the king. His lack of constant attendance is suggested by other evidence. He was with the king at Reading on 8 May 1387, and there was a little flurry of minor grants at his supplication or to his servants on 5, 10 and 13 May; was this because he had just arrived in the king's company and de Vere had a number of favours to ask of Richard which the latter was happy to grant?[32] A similar pattern emerges in early April; while there is no direct evidence that de Vere was with the king at Nottingham, a pardon to one of his servants and two further at his supplication on 5, 6 and 7 April is rather suggestive of his arrival there, but again perhaps not of constant attendance on the king.[33]

While Richard left London on his 'gyrations', the earl of Arundel undertook a successful naval action off Margate in March 1387, taking the Franco-Flemish wine fleet, comprising sixty-eight ships with, apparently, 8,000 tuns of wine, which were sold on the cheap in England, as a shameless and effective bid for popularity.[34] Walsingham records the actions of the 'king's companions', de Vere, de la Pole, Burley and Richard Stury, denigrating Arundel's achievements by stating he had attacked merchants and that it would have been more profitable to preserve their love for England. He goes on to describe that when Arundel and Nottingham came to visit the king, they

---

[30] Staffordshire Record Office, LD30/2/2/1, fol. 15; Bennett, 'Richard II and the Wider Realm', 193. The queen, Michael de la Pole, Lords Basset, Beaumont and Zouche, Sir Simon Burley, Sir John Beauchamp and many other laymen were there, alongside the archbishops of York and Dublin, and the bishop of Chichester.

[31] For de Vere's movements, see Appendix, p. 245.

[32] *CPR, 1385–9*, 299, 301 (Fitzmartin), 303 (Bole).

[33] *CPR, 1385–9*, 289, 291, 292.

[34] *WC*, 182–5. For Arundel and the naval war, see Given-Wilson, 'The Earl of Arundel, the War with France and the Anger of King Richard II', 28–32; A.R. Bell, 'Medieval Chroniclers as War Correspondents during the Hundred Years War. The Earl of Arundel's Naval Campaign of 1387', in C. Given-Wilson, ed., *Fourteenth Century England VI* (Woodbridge, 2010), 171–84.

were received with sullenness, and 'the duke of Ireland not only refused to look at the two earls, but would not even speak to them'.[35] If accurate, this petty and petulant display would give support to the modern descriptions of de Vere as embodying everything that was objectionable about Richard's court.[36] Yet, this depiction must be treated with real care. Earlier in the same paragraph as Walsingham's description of de Vere snubbing the militarily successful earls was his famous description of the king's companions as being more knights of Venus rather than of Mars/Bellona, and how they made no effort to inculcate knightly qualities in the king. What better way to make the point than to show a response of sullen resentment to a martial achievement? The description of de Vere is thus part of the rhetorical strategy in the immediate context of the passage, and part of a more general portrayal of the king and his councillors as seeking peace through the 1380s that at least one modern historian has taken serious issue with. It cannot be taken as a literal description. Walsingham took a further additional swipe at de Vere, adding immediately after his refusal to speak to the earls, saying 'perhaps he envied them their integrity which he was unable to imitate'.[37] It is telling that other chronicles – without a similar rhetorical point to make – do not record any such reaction by the king, de Vere or others in this context.[38]

Perhaps the most important action taken by Richard while he travelled around the country was the delivery of the famous questions to the judges.[39] These were addressed to the assembled justices of England at two councils at Shrewsbury and Nottingham in August 1387. The questions were carefully crafted to elicit answers that established that the actions taken by the Wonderful Parliament had infringed the liberties and prerogatives of the crown. The judges agreed that the establishment of the commission had been derogatory to the regality of the crown as it was against the king's wishes, and indeed it was under duress, as Richard later claimed, given the implicit threat of deposition. Answers to further questions established that judges thought that parliament could not impeach a minister of the king without his consent

---

[35] *SAC*, i, 812–15.

[36] Tuck, *Richard II*, 115.

[37] *SAC*, i, 814–15. For Richard and war see Fletcher, *Richard II*, esp. ch. 7.

[38] *WC*, 182–5; *KC*, 388–91.

[39] For the legal and constitutional position of the judges and the questions addressed to them, see S.B. Chrimes, 'Richard II's Questions to the Judges, 1387', *Law Quarterly Review*, 72 (1956), 365–90; D. Clementi, 'Richard II's Ninth Question to the Judges, 1387', *EHR*, 86 (1971), 96–113; Tuck, *Richard II*, 116–17; Saul, *Richard II*, 173–5; Fletcher, *Richard II*, 162–3.

and therefore that the judgement on Michael de la Pole was erroneous and revocable. The judges further concluded that those responsible should be punished as traitors. Taken together it was, as Saul has described it, 'the most remarkable statement of the royal prerogative ever made in England in the Middle Ages'.[40] Although, perhaps, the punishment of those responsible as traitors was legally questionable, almost every other point made was within the bounds of the law and hard to argue with from a legal standpoint. Politically, however, it was an extreme position. While it provided Richard and his allies with a firm ideological platform with which to proceed against his enemies, it was provocative and a threat to his opponents. For that reason, Richard initially kept the judges' answers quiet. His actions in regard to the judges also fit with a letter to an official at the papal court, dating from around this period, in which he sought a sentence of papal excommunication against all opponents of his crown and its liberties and prerogatives.[41]

While Robert de Vere was present at both of the councils to which the judges were summoned – Knighton records his presence at both, and his seal and that of his servant John Ripon were attached to the statement issued on 25 August at Nottingham – it is, as always, very hard to say what his input into this policy was.[42] It is more likely that it was the experienced Michael de la Pole, the target of the Wonderful Parliament, or the Chief Justice of King's Bench, Robert Tresilian, by this stage firmly attached to Richard's side, who were the authors of the policy. Later evidence is equivocal about his involvement. The article by the Appellants in 1388 regarding the questions to the judges certainly indicted Tresilian and de la Pole but also named de Vere, Neville and Brembre as the instigators.[43] Almost all the justices later claimed, under examination in parliament, that they had had been coerced by Archbishop Neville, de Vere and de la Pole, while Knighton states that Sir Robert Belknap had been compelled by de Vere and de la Pole and they had threatened him with death if he did not comply.[44] Other justices claimed later, while in the Tower, that they had been pressured by Bishop Rushook, Richard's confessor.[45] As Saul argues, it certainly suited all the judges to claim during the Merciless Parliament that they were coerced, but there is no evidence of it during the

---

[40] Saul, *Richard II*, 174.
[41] Edinburgh UL, MS 183, fol. 106v; *Diplomatic Correspondence of Richard II*, ed. E. Perroy (Camden Society, 3rd series, 48, 1933), 52.
[42] *PROME*, vii, 93; *KC*, 392–3.
[43] *PROME*, vii, 90, 91–3 (articles 18, 25).
[44] *PROME*, vii, 107; *KC*, 394–5.
[45] *KC*, 394–5; *WC*, 316–17.

councils at Shrewsbury or Nottingham.[46] Indeed, rather than accept the plea of coercion and mitigate their punishment, all the judges were found guilty in parliament and condemned to death, but were pardoned their execution after intervention by the archbishop of Canterbury and other bishops.[47]

The Divorce

More than any other action, de Vere's repudiation of his wife, Philippa de Coucy, for Agnes Lancecrone, a servant of the queen, brought him into disrepute. Most contemporary chronicles record a condemnation of the action, except, oddly, that of Henry Knighton who does not mention it at all. Walsingham provides a succinct and well-honed description in which de Vere:

> divorced his wife, a noble and beautiful girl, the daughter of Isabella, who was herself the daughter of the illustrious King Edward. He married another girl who had come with Queen Anne of Bohemia and was said to be a saddler's daughter of decidedly low rank and ugly. This, therefore, provided a great opportunity for scandal to spread. The name she was given in common parlance was 'Lancecrona'.[48]

Froissart, by contrast, describes her as 'a tolerably handsome pleasant lady', which seems more plausible, given what de Vere risked for her.[49] It is also worth at this stage dispelling one idea about Lancecrone. It is very unlikely that she was low born, despite Walsingham's jibe. It is inherently unlikely that a saddler's daughter was in the train of any noblewoman, let alone Queen Anne of Bohemia, and she must have been of gentle or noble birth. She is described in a patent roll entry as a damsel of the queen's chamber, which suggests a certain social status.[50] Another of Anne's attendants, who married Sir Simon Felbrigg, was Margaret, daughter of the duke of Teschen.[51] Agnes

---

[46] Saul, *Richard II*, 174. Goodman is neutral regarding the extent to which coercion of the judges was likely: *Loyal Conspiracy*, 20–1.

[47] *PROME*, vii, 111.

[48] *SAC*, i, 822–3. This passage is identical to that in *Historiae Vitae*, ed. Stow, 105, except for the spelling of Lancecrone, there given as 'Lamicienu'. See also *WC*, 190–1; Otterbourne, 'Chronicum Rerum Angliae', 167; Clarke and Galbraith, 'Deposition of Richard II', 167.

[49] Froissart, ed. Johnes, ii, 271.

[50] *CPR, 1388–92*, 20. The Westminster Chronicle describes her as a Bohemian chamberwoman of the queen, which is a little less clear cut as to her rank: *WC*, 189–91.

[51] Saul, *Richard II*, 92n, 335. A fine brass of the pair survives at Felbrigg church in Norfolk. The marriage perhaps took place around 1395 (Bennett, 'Richard II,

has been identified as German, rather than Bohemian, and possibly of a German noble family called Landskron.[52] However, her social status must also not be overstated. Geaman's recent biography of Anne of Bohemia states she was a countess, but this is based on Johnes' mistranslation of Froissart, which states that she was 'one of the queen's damsels, called the Landgravine'.[53] Geaman takes 'Landgravine' to mean a title, 'roughly equivalent to a countess', however it is surely a rendering of her surname of Lancecrone, confirmed by the French 'qui se appelloit la Lancegrove'.[54]

Even if 'tolerably handsome' and not of low birth, there is no possible explanation for de Vere's extraordinary actions except for complete infatuation on his part with Agnes and/or serious personal problems between de Vere and Philippa. Concerning the latter, the most reliable of the chronicles notes: 'he grew to detest her'.[55] There is little evidence for the relations between the two, but the lack of children after eleven years of marriage (although both were well under age at the time of the union) may well have been a factor. Yet, there was no material gain for divorcing Philippa, and indeed he would have lost the de Coucy lands as a result of doing so, although his financial position by 1387 was secure, as was his place in the king's affection. He does seem to have developed a passionate attachment to Lancecrone, given the extraordinary circumstances by which she came into his company. A pardon was issued to John Banastre of Farington (Lancashire) and William de Stanley of the Wirral (Cheshire), Sir John Stanley's brother, for breaking prison after being arrested on suspicion, 'when staying with Robert de Vere, late duke of Ireland, of having, at his command, with others, abducted Agnes Lanchecron, late damsel of the Queen's chamber'.[56] It is hard to know if the phrasing used of

---

Queen Anne, Bohemia', 21, 38). See also J.D. Milner, 'Sir Simon Felbrigg, K.G.: the Lancastrian Revolution and Personal Fortune', *Norfolk Archaeology*, 37 (1978), 84–91. For the likely identification of Margaret, wife of Sir Nicholas Sarnesfield, as Bohemian, see D. L. Biggs, 'Patronage, Preference and Survival: the Life of Lady Margaret Sarnesfield, c. 1381–c. 1444', in L.E. Mitchell, K.L. French and D.L. Biggs, eds, *The Ties that Bind. Essays in Medieval British History in Honor of Barbara Hanawalt* (Farnham, 2011), 143–58.

[52] For this, see *CP*, x, 231–2n, and Halliday, 'Robert de Vere', 79. Froissart describes her as a German lady: Froissart, ed. Johnes, ii, 264.

[53] Froissart, ed. Johnes, ii, 271.

[54] K. Geaman, *Anne of Bohemia* (Basingstoke, 2022), 99; Froissart, ed. Lettenhove, xii, 261.

[55] *WC*, 188–9.

[56] *CPR, 1388–92*, 20, dated 5 March 1389. The full patent roll entry and authorising warrant add no further detail as to the date of the abduction or the circumstances:

abduction (the Latin is 'abduxit') in the pardon is simply legal language or if it might suggest that Agnes was unwilling.

When and where the abduction happened is confusing, however. The Dieulacres Chronicle stated that he brought Agnes to Chester.[57] Given-Wilson suggested that the abduction to Chester therefore may have occurred in mid-July 1387 when the king was there, which is feasible, although it would have predated Robert de Vere's appointment as justice of Chester, which took place in September.[58] However, the pardon issued to Banastre and Stanley notes that after the abduction took place at an unknown place, those abductors came to the king's household at Henley-on-the-Heath, where they were arrested and sent to prison in Winchester Castle.[59] Richard was at Henley-on-the-Heath in Surrey in May and June 1386, but not as far as is known in 1387.[60] It may well be that the report of the Dieulacres Chronicle (written after 1400) that he brought Agnes to Chester refers to a visit in the autumn of 1387, when certainly de Vere, and very probably Agnes, were there, rather than after the abduction itself, and this would also explain various goods that probably belonged to Agnes being found in Chester.[61] On balance, it seems more likely

---

C66/327, m.19; C81/1504, no. 5122.

[57] Clarke and Galbraith, 'Deposition of Richard II', 167; for recent discussion of the chronicle, see P. Morgan, 'Historical Writing in the North-west Midlands and the Chester Annals of 1385–88', in G. Dodd, ed., *Fourteenth Century England IX* (Woodbridge, 2016), 121–6. For the most detailed study of medieval abduction see C. Dunn, *Stolen Women in Medieval England. Rape, Abduction, and Adultery, 1100–1500* (Cambridge, 2013).

[58] Given-Wilson, *Henry IV*, 42.

[59] The calendar does not include the crucial detail that the royal household was at Henley and it was not just the place where Banastre and Stanley were arrested, but it is clear in the warrant for the Great Seal and on the Patent Roll itself ('post abductionem illam ad hospicium nostrum declinarunt apud Henle in le Heth arestati et ad prisonam nostrum Castri Wyntoniensis ducti'): C81/1504, no. 5122. See also C66/327, m. 19; *CPR, 1388–92*, 20. No legal proceedings against the two men can be found in either the rex side of King's Bench (KB27/KB29) or in the gaol delivery rolls (JUST 3) in 1386 or 1387.

[60] Saul, *Richard II*, 470–1. According to Saul's itinerary, the closest Richard was in 1387 to Henley was in January at Easthampstead in Berkshire, nearly forty miles away.

[61] The chronicle reports Agnes being brought to Chester immediately before discussing the Radcot Bridge campaign: Clarke and Galbraith, 'Deposition of Richard II', 167. Interestingly, a Chester chronicle covering 1385–8, edited by Philip Morgan, which shares some similarities with Dieulacres, does not mention Agnes being brought to the city: Morgan, 'Historical Writing', 125–8. Among de Vere's goods seized at Chester were 'two new saddles for Bohemian ladies, worth £3, and one old

that Agnes was abducted in May or June 1386. By this time de Vere already had connections with the Stanley family and may have been seeking men not clearly part of his own household to undertake the deed to avoid being directly implicated. If this redating of the event is correct, there may then have been a sexual, adulterous, scandal – the fact there was an arrest suggests word had spread – in 1386 well before the more shocking scandal of a formal divorce, which probably dates from 1387.

The strong balance of the evidence is that there was a formal divorce between de Vere and Philippa and that he then remarried Lancecrone. The question arises as there is no surviving ecclesiastical proceedings relating to a divorce, so we are forced to rely on other evidence.[62] The editors of the Dieulacres chronicle suggest that no divorce took place as the Westminster Chronicle says that de Vere 'in conjugem nefarie copulavit'.[63] However, this statement in the latter chronicle is due to the chronicler's earlier assertion that de Vere's servant, John Ripon, had used false witnesses to gain the divorce. The weight of the chronicle evidence is, however, that he did secure the divorce as Walsingham, Froissart and the Westminster Chronicle agree that he did.[64] This is confirmed by a previously unremarked detail in the records of the crown. The warrant under the privy seal for the grant of the castle of Berkhamsted for a year on 1 November 1387 states that it was for de Vere's use and for the use of the king's 'dear and welbeloved cousin, Agnes, duchess of Ireland, his [de Vere's] wife'.[65] Interestingly, when this grant was enrolled on the patent roll,

---

saddle in the Bohemian style, worth 20s', as well as one pair of 'bedes', a rosary, for the lady and a great set of pearls bound or wrapped in a couvrechief, which are most likely to have belonged to Agnes rather than Philippa: E36/66, f.7; E101/631/13.

[62] There are no references in the *Calendar of Petitions to the Pope, I: 1342–1419*, ed. W.H. Bliss (London, 1896) or *Calendar of Papal Letters, vol. 4: 1362–1404*, eds W.H. Bliss and J.A. Twemlow (London, 1902). The registers of the Papal Penitentiary do not survive earlier than the fifteenth century. Those of the papal chancery do but have not been calendared. It is also clear that not every petition, successful or not, was entered in the registers: P.D. Clarke, 'Petitioning the Pope: English Supplicants and Rome in the Fifteenth Century', in L. Clark, ed., *The Fifteenth Century XI. Concerns and Preoccupations* (Woodbridge, 2012), 42–3. I am very grateful to Professor Clarke for discussing this episode and possible sources with me.

[63] *WC*, 190–1, translated as 'the iniquity of taking to wife'; Clarke and Galbraith, 'Deposition of Richard II', 167.

[64] *SAC*, i, 822–3 (the Latin used is 'repudiaret', translated by the editors as 'divorced'); Froissart, ed. Johnes, ii, 264; *WC*, 188–9, 404–5.

[65] C81/498, no. 4563 ('nostre treschere et tresame Cousine Anneys duchesse dirlande sa compaigne'); C66/324, m. 10 ('pro mora sua et familie sue'); *CPR, 1385–9*, 366, where 'familie' is translated as family rather than household.

the wording was changed to being for the use of de Vere and his household, perhaps indicating disapproval or circumspection amongst the chancery clerks. Nonetheless, this formal reference on the warrant proves beyond doubt that de Vere had sought and achieved a divorce. The Westminster Chronicle states that in 1389 the divorce between the two was then declared null and void by the pope. A royal grant on 18 October 1389 notes Philippa's husband as de Vere, which suggests the marriage to Lancecrone had been made void by that date.[66] There was no need to divorce Philippa if he did not intend to marry Lancecrone. Froissart states that de Vere divorced Philippa and took another wife, to which the king and queen assented, and 'pope Urban had, at their entreaties, sent from Rome a dispensation for the marriage'.[67]

It is, however, impossible to prove whether Richard played any role in securing the divorce since much of Richard II's diplomatic correspondence with the pope at this period had disappeared.[68] Moreover, no record of the promulgation of the divorce or its cancellation appears in the register of the archbishop of Canterbury, the most likely English ecclesiastic to have been involved or informed by the pope, nor in the less likely places of the registers of the bishop of London (if his primary residence was either the court or Castle Hedingham in Essex) or the bishop of Winchester (Kennington).[69] While it would have been a stretch to claim that de Vere was resident in the jurisdiction of Archbishop Neville of York, he did of course hold land there in right of his soon-to-be ex-wife, and as an ally at court, Neville might have been a good diocesan to use, but his register has little material after 1384.[70]

It is very difficult to date the divorce or remarriage as no chronicle source gives such a date, though both had taken place by 1 November 1387 as is made clear by the reference to Agnes as duchess of Ireland in the grant of Berkhamsted. The Westminster Chronicle places its discussion of the episode

---

[66] *CPR, 1389–92*, 117.

[67] Froissart, ed. Lettenhove, xiv, 33; Froissart, ed. Johnes, ii, 408.

[68] *CP*, x, 231n.; *Diplomatic Correspondence*, ed. Perroy, vii.

[69] Lambeth Palace Library, Reg. Courtenay I–II. There are no surviving act books of the Court of Arches for the 1380s, although it is unlikely the case would have been pleaded in the Canterbury court as well as the papal one. London: London Metropolitan Archives, Ms 9531/5 (Register of Robert Braybrooke, 1382–1404); Winchester: *Wykeham's Register*, ed. T.F. Kirby (2 vols, Hampshire Record Society, 1896–9).

[70] Borthwick Institute, York, Register 12, helpfully digitised and (at time of writing) partly calendared at https://archbishopsregisters.york.ac.uk/browse/registers; D.M. Smith, *Ecclesiastical Cause Papers at York: the Court of York 1301–1399* (Borthwick Texts and Calendars 14, 1988).

at a convenient place in the narrative (after the appointment of Robert de Vere as justice of Chester in September and the release of John of Blois in November), but then returns to discussion of events in the summer of 1387 concerning John of Gaunt's campaign in Spain.[71] If we were to take the date of abduction and marriage as summer 1387, which, as discussed, is less likely than early summer 1386, there is the additional difficulty of timing for the confirmation of the divorce from the pope. John Ripon, de Vere's emissary to the curia, witnessed Richard II's questions to the judges in late August 1387, and could not have travelled to Rome, procured the papal pronouncement and returned to England between then and late October. In fact, Ripon must have gone rather earlier. He was – as discussed below – made archdeacon of Wells on 1 December 1386, and as the previous incumbent seems to have made a resignation and been deprived of the office in Rome as well as in England, there is the possibility that Ripon was at the Curia in late 1386 achieving this and returning at some point in the first half of 1387. Dr Richard Rouhale, an experienced diplomat, left London on a mission to Rome on 10 September 1386, to undertake secret negotiations 'touching the state of the king and the kingdom'. The timings would work very well for Ripon to accompany him to transact private business for de Vere. Two of Richard II's favoured clerks, Henry Bowet and Richard Clifford, were also in Rome in the spring of 1387; it is not clear if they were part of the same embassy as Rouhale, but it is also possible Ripon accompanied them if they travelled separately.[72] If so, then the scandal of the divorce must have broken before the summer of 1387 but, probably, a year or so after the abduction of Agnes.

What is not clear is on what grounds Robert de Vere was able to divorce Philippa. Even the most detailed and authoritative contemporary chronicle, that of the Monk of Westminster, does not explain the stated reasons. The chronicle says that de Vere 'sent the clerk John Ripon to the Roman curia to secure a divorce ("ad divorciandum") terminating the marriage – a task at which he worked to such an effect that through perjured witnesses, hired for the purpose, he came away with the pronouncement of a sentence of divorce'.[73] However, grounds for annulment in the late Middle Ages were extremely limited: non-consummation of the marriage, a prior marriage or contract, duress – in this case being forced

---

[71] *WC*, 188–91.

[72] Rouhale: E403/512, m. 20 (quote); E364/21, rot. D (he did not return from Rome until December 1387); Bowet and Clifford: *Diplomatic Correspondence*, ed. Perroy, 50–1. No particulars of accounts, naming members of the party, survive for either mission nor are other members of the party named in the Issue Roll.

[73] *WC*, 188–9.

to be married while under age – and consanguinity (or an inadequate papal dispensation for this) were the primary ones.[74] It seems unlikely that the marriage between de Vere and Philippa had not been consummated after more than ten years of matrimony, albeit Philippa was only twenty years old in 1387.[75] The young age of the two when they were married in 1376 would have made it unlikely for either to claim a prior betrothal or marriage. The two were not closely related; their only common ancestor was Henry III, some five generations prior for both parties, and therefore beyond the four degrees of consanguinity prohibited by the church. There might have been grounds that the two had been married before the canonical age of consent – Philippa was nine in 1376 and Robert only just fourteen – and in canon law fresh consent after that age was reached was required. However, the fact de Vere and Philippa had cohabited for more than a decade after the marriage and seven years after Philippa reached the canonical age of consent for women (twelve) would have rendered the plea ineligible as 'continued cohabitation itself was sufficient to make a valid marriage'.[76] In fact, the 'perjured witnesses' might suggest a claim of non-consummation rather than a technical issue. The other possibility was a spurious claim of consanguinity but that was far easier to disprove by enemies than non-consummation and such shaky grounds would have put at risk the legitimacy of any future children de Vere might have had with Agnes Lancecrone or anyone else.

Robert de Vere was not completely heartless towards Philippa. Later sources confirm that he had given her, at an unspecified date but probably around the time of the divorce, 100 marks a year for life from his estates for the expenses of her chamber.[77] While this was not particularly generous, he would also have been well aware that the Coucy estates in England would be hers as well. They had been granted to them both for life in 1382 but he cannot have expected to have any claim on them after his divorce. She would not therefore be destitute but comfortably off in the short term, yet divorce from Duke Robert would have left her demoted from a duchess to a mere lady, as well as socially and publicly humiliated. Given the absence of any hint of her

---

[74] B. Wells-Furby, *Aristocratic Marriage, Adultery and Divorce in the Fourteenth Century* (Woodbridge, 2019), chap. 3, and pp. 61–2 for brief discussion of Robert and Philippa. For discussion of the principles (though none of the studies below mention de Vere and Philippa), see R.H. Helmholz, *Marriage Litigation in Medieval England* (Cambridge, 1974), ch. 3; S.M. Butler, *Divorce in Medieval England. From One to Two Persons in Law* (Abingdon, 2013), ch. 1. More generally, F. Pedersen, *Marriage Disputes in Medieval England* (London, 2000); W.P. Müller, *Marriage Litigation in the Western Church* (Cambridge, 2021).

[75] For discussion, see above, p. 48.

[76] Butler, *Divorce*, 24.

[77] C81/508, no. 5591; *CPR, 1388–92*, 117; *1381–5*, 177, 314.

feelings towards her husband, it cannot be known if she was also emotionally hurt by his rejection of her.

It was also noted by chroniclers that Countess Maud took Philippa's side against her son, and this can be confirmed by two later pieces of evidence. A payment of £100 was made to Maud on 16 May 1388 'of the king's special grace and the advice of the council and for the compassion he has for the state of his cousin Philippa consort of Robert de Vere... for the costs and expenses of the said countess for the sustentation of the said Philippa for past times ("retroactis temporibus")'.[78] Clearly then Maud had taken Philippa into her care, though whether at the time of the divorce or in the aftermath of Radcot Bridge is not clear. Countess Maud's household account of the summer of 1389 records that the duchess paid £56 13s 4d in part payment of an annual £113 6s 8d to Maud for her expenses for her 'suiournac[ione]', her stay, residence or sojourn in Maud's household.[79] The size of the payment, its annual nature and the vocabulary used in the account indicate a semi-permanent stay with her mother-in-law. Although Philippa's estates were confirmed to her during the Merciless Parliament, their exclusively northern nature meant she would have been without a residence in the south of England and easy access to the court, so there may have been a practical aspect to residing with Countess Maud, alongside any emotional or social bond.

What is most surprising about this episode is the fact that Richard did not join in the disapproval of the action. Presumably, de Vere sought the king's acquiescence in the matter beforehand, as otherwise he risked a great deal. For de Vere to repudiate a member of the royal family so close in blood to the king, was, as indeed the royal uncles took it, an insult to the Plantagenet line, and one might have expected Richard, who had a highly developed sense of the majesty of the crown and of his lineage, to have taken this badly. The Westminster Chronicle states that de Vere's action was certainly in the 'face of the queen's unremitting protests'.[80] That Richard did not react in the same way can only be attributed to the strength of the friendship between himself and Robert de Vere. Had Richard been creating his own loyal nobility to glorify the king, then this would have been the moment to abandon de Vere from this enterprise. It seems unlikely that Froissart's famous comment on this episode, that Richard consented to de Vere marrying Agnes because he 'was so blinded by the duke of Ireland that, if he had said black was white, the king would not have said to the contrary', was an accurate reflection of the relationship, but

---

[78] E403/519, m. 10; E403/521, m.11.
[79] *WC*, 190–1; Longleat, MS 442, m.1d.
[80] *WC*, 190–1.

there must have been a very close bond between them to survive an action that brought some disrepute on the royal family and scandal on de Vere.[81]

Chester and the Autumn of 1387

Further evidence of the trust that Richard II had in Robert de Vere, but also of the deteriorating political situation, is seen in the king's appointment of the duke to the positions of justice of Chester on 8 September 1387 and then justiciar of North Wales on 10 October.[82] The Westminster Chronicle adds the castle of Flint to the grants, but no other source substantiates this.[83] It is not clear, however, that de Vere made Chester his headquarters as has been suggested by Clarke.[84] In favour of the idea is the fact that Lancecrone was probably there and de Vere had a significant amount of household goods at Chester, which were seized after Radcot Bridge.[85] However, these may simply have been left there as unnecessary baggage when de Vere set out in mid-December for the campaign that ended at Radcot Bridge. He cannot have been in Chester for more than three weeks in the late autumn, as he only left London between 17 and 19 November and came north solely to take leadership of the royalist army, which he led south as soon as he could to support the king.

Richard was clearly looking for support during his gyrations and to consolidate his gains appointed de Vere to these two posts. It was surely only really at this point, with the judges supporting his position and the end of the powers of the commission of 1386 in sight, that Richard began to consider the possibility of a military showdown with his most vociferous opponents. He must have felt vulnerable well before this – the duke of Gloucester and Bishop Arundel had none too subtly brought up the prospect of deposition if he did not return to the Wonderful Parliament of 1386 after departing in high dudgeon to Eltham[86] – but his confidence had been bolstered by the strategy that sent him around his kingdom to loyalist areas to build support, and with his ideological position backed by the judges. It is evident that de Vere's role in Richard's strategy was central and of a military nature. The accumulation

---

[81] Froissart, ed. Johnes, ii, 264.

[82] *CPR, 1385–9*, 357; *31st Report of the Deputy Keeper of the Public Records* (London, 1870), appendix, 254; *36th Report of the Deputy Keeper of the Public Records* (London, 1875), appendix II, 494.

[83] *WC*, 186–9.

[84] Clarke, 'Forfeiture and Treason', 68.

[85] See below, pp. 225–8.

[86] *KC*, 360–1.

of military resources in his hands over the past few years was striking. It has already been shown that three castles (Colchester, Queenborough and Oakham) had been granted to him in 1384–5, and two more were added to his portfolio in 1386–7: Kennington on the south bank of the Thames, which must have had at least rudimentary defences, and the castle of Berkhamsted in Hertfordshire.[87] Both were within easy reach of London. The grant of Ireland, whose military resources were potentially vast if not easily realisable in the short term, enhanced his recruiting pool. This was then followed by the justiciarships of Chester and North Wales which certainly gave de Vere the prospect of raising a substantial force quickly. Almost certainly none of the grants until that of Chester in September 1387 were made with the idea of raising royalist troops against rebellious nobles in mind, but they could have been taken collectively in that way from the autumn of 1385 onwards by opponents. It was to de Vere, then, and not the more senior Michael de la Pole or Simon Burley, that Richard entrusted much of his actual military resources, though he would have had strong hopes of active support from London and from loyalists all over the country.

Walsingham twice imputes a desire by de Vere to murder the duke of Gloucester in 1387. The first was after the former's criticism of de Vere's divorce and the second in the context of the Nottingham council of August 1387, when he suggests de Vere and the king were wandering around Wales plotting the deaths of Gloucester, Warwick, Arundel, Nottingham and Derby. This latter group, the future appellant lords, were of course by this stage not obviously allied together.[88] The Monk of Westminster also suggests a plot against Gloucester but places it at Windsor on St George's day in 1387. However, he does not name names but only blames certain wicked and evilly disposed persons who stirred the king up against Gloucester, who apparently had to

---

[87] Albeit the *History of the King's Works*, ii, 967–9 does not mention any outer defences at Kennington. Berkhamsted had had some repairs to its defences during the years immediately preceding the grant to de Vere: E101/473/2; *History of the King's Works*, ii, 562–3. It is just possible there is an echo of this in Gower's *Cronica Tripertita* where de Vere 'delinquent, naked, he relinquished every fort… the Boar found no support in all his castles' pride': *Poems on Contemporary Events*, 257. However, a marginal note in the poem states that de Vere had taken up castles as his family emblem, which the editor then links to Chester, and states that the term is being used here to refer to his followers: ibid., 257, 337. It is highly unlikely de Vere used this allusive emblem. He did quarter the arms of Chester with those of Oxford, but the arms of Chester did not use castles, while the evidence of standards seized at Chester after Radcot Bridge showed his use of his arms and those of Ireland: see below, p. 232.

[88] *SAC*, i, 822–3, 824–5.

make a hasty departure after dinner to escape the plot.[89] The Westminster Chronicler, more sober and more cautious, may have been reporting rumours or some murky incident, but Walsingham seems to have been making up plots when it suited his narrative strategy to denigrate de Vere and Richard's circle.

Richard remained distant from the capital in early autumn 1387 and de Vere was, according to Knighton's chronicle, with the king and queen at Leicester Abbey overnight on 15 September.[90] By early October, Gloucester seems to have learned of the questions to the judges and their answers at Nottingham in late August. Given the incendiary nature of what had transpired there, this was the spark that initiated the military preparations of the king's opponents. Gloucester, according to Walsingham's chronicle, remained outwardly loyal, swearing an oath before the bishop of London and others that he had never plotted to harm the king but 'that he did not look upon the duke of Ireland, whom the king loved, with any favour, nor indeed did he wish to do so in the future, for this man had dishonoured not only his own kinswoman, but the king's, and it was his firm intention to punish him for this'.[91] As Walsingham tells it, the king had already mustered troops and it was only after the king had dismissed the bishop of London, who had reported Gloucester's oath and stated purpose, that Gloucester allied himself with Arundel, Warwick and Derby. However, military preparations by the opposition lords had almost certainly begun earlier. In early November, Richard ordered the earl of Northumberland to arrest Arundel at his castle of Reigate in Surrey, but it was already strongly held; Arundel then marched to Haringey, north of London, to join with Warwick and Gloucester on 13 November.

Three days earlier, the king had made a grand ceremonial entry to London, and then moved out of the city again to Westminster, with the Westminster Chronicle recording the detail that the king, de Vere, the archbishop of York and de la Pole all processed barefoot from Charing Mews to Westminster Abbey.[92] Exchanges of letters followed between the king and his opponents, but Richard and his inner circle seem to have been surprised by the speed of the opposition's military build-up and held an urgent council meeting to discuss how to deal with the situation. The king did not have the military forces to match those in arms against him since they had already mustered a significant body of men. Walsingham reports that Alexander Neville was keen to muster the royal household troops alongside the citizens of London

---

[89] *WC*, 184–5.

[90] Though there is some doubt over this: see Appendix, below, p. 245.

[91] *SAC*, i, 826–9.

[92] *WC*, 206–9; *KC*, 400.

and attack the rebels.[93] Calmer counsel prevailed and Richard suggested that the lords come under safe conduct to Westminster to discuss matters with him.[94] On 17 November, the lords met the king at Westminster and appealed de Vere, Neville, de la Pole, Tresilian and Brembre of treason, having made the same accusation in a letter to the Londoners four days earlier.[95] Richard had to compromise and say that the appeal would be heard in the next parliament, scheduled for February 1388, and he took all parties into his protection. It gave Richard and his allies a breathing space. Neville and de la Pole fled ignominiously, according to the chronicles, but de Vere did not.

Richard had not returned to London to seek a military confrontation with Gloucester and his allies; he had returned to prepare for and then attend a major diplomatic meeting with the king of France at or near Calais in late November. Fletcher makes a strong case that this was not the secret peace policy at least one historian has suggested. Not only had preparations been long in the making but Gloucester was written to on the subject as if well aware of the policy in early December by the duke of Burgundy.[96] Still less should the wild but contemporary accusations that Richard sought to ally with the French, having sold Calais to them in return for military support, be believed; the chronicle accounts were clearly based on Appellant propaganda both before Radcot Bridge and during the Merciless Parliament.[97] Five articles of the appeal of 1388 specifically relate to the negotiations with the French. Articles 28 and 29 stated that the Appellees advised the king to destroy the Appellants with the help of the French king and article 30 that the Appellees had caused the king to promise he would surrender Calais and the fortresses in the Pale, Cherbourg and Brest to Charles VI. The next article stated that the two kings, the Appellees and the Appellants would all meet at Calais (further evidence the Appellants were not unaware of the peace initiative) and there the Appellants would be put to death and the last that safe-conducts were procured from the French for the king, de Vere, Sir John Salisbury (a chamber knight executed in the Merciless Parliament) and Sir John Lancaster,

[93] *SAC*, i, 830–1.

[94] A small sum (22d) was allocated for works to the king's 'sedis', seat or perhaps throne, in Westminster Hall 'against the coming of the duke of Gloucester and other lords', presumably on this occasion: E101/473/2, m. 19, undated.

[95] *KC*, 410–12; *SAC*, i, 834–5.

[96] Fletcher, *Richard II*, 164–71. For an alternative view, see Palmer, *England, France and Christendom*, 105–21.

[97] *SAC*, i, 830–1, 842–3; *KC*, 404–7; *WC*, 204–7, though the latter is more reasoned in its coverage, and links the rising of the Appellants to the proposals for peace, though again this may be in hindsight after the Merciless Parliament.

de Vere's most dedicated follower.[98] This of course puts the most unfavourable spin imaginable on an initiative that was in keeping with English diplomacy of the last decade – of alternating aggression and seeking peace – and certainly was neither an attempt to enlist French aid against domestic enemies nor the capitulation Walsingham describes.[99] The date of the projected meeting is not known, but must have been after the end of the commission's term in late November. It is no coincidence that this was exactly the same time that the first instalment of John of Blois's ransom was paid to de Vere (19 November) and that Blois was released, reaching the French court by early December.[100] Presiding over the transfer of the ransom and the release of the prisoner would have been one of the set pieces of the projected Anglo-French summit. It also explains in part why de Vere and Sir John Lancaster were so prominent in the safe-conducts: they were at the heart of one major aspect of the business that was to be conducted.

Several chronicles suggest or hint at a plot to murder the duke of Gloucester around this time. Apparently, there was a plot to intercept Gloucester, Warwick and Arundel at Charing Mews as they rode to a meeting with the king on 17 November. Walsingham does not in fact charge de Vere with this – oddly given his earlier allegations on this subject – but instead, in a somewhat garbled account of a conspiracy, puts the blame on a chamber knight, Sir Thomas Trivet and on Nicholas Brembre. Knighton also mentions the ambush, but does not mention any individuals in connection to it, although the ambush was, in his account, prepared partly in the archbishop of York's house at York Place, which rather implies Neville's involvement.[101] Perhaps the only indirect link to any involvement by de Vere is that the parliament rolls accuse John Ripon of being the messenger that delivered the order to arrest Gloucester.[102]

Having been appealed of treason by the Appellants before the king on 17 November, de Vere did not waver in his loyalty to the king, despite the accusations of Knighton's chronicle. Knighton relates that de Vere fled to Chester at some point after 19 November, dressed as a soldier with a bow and a quiver of arrows; it was only when Richard 'deprived of the company of his intimates, and especially of the duke of Ireland, was sadly cast down and unable to bear their absence' sent urgently to the duke and commissioned

---

[98] *PROME*, vii, 95–6.

[99] For the diplomatic situation that inclined France, Castile, Scotland, and indeed John of Gaunt to peace, see Palmer, *England, France and Christendom*, 106–9.

[100] Jones, 'Ransom', 19; Palmer, *England, France and Christendom*, 108.

[101] *KC*, 412–15.

[102] *PROME*, vii, 94.

Thomas Molyneux to raise a force that de Vere came south again.[103] However, as Geoffrey Martin, editor of the chronicle, notes, nothing is less likely than de Vere fled to Chester for safety and was then urged to return by the king. Clearly de Vere's role was in fact that of the military leader of the royalist forces Richard had been preparing to raise if need be over the course of 1387 and while de Vere probably moved swiftly and perhaps incognito from Westminster to Chester it was not flight but to prepare for a military confrontation.[104] If the accusations in the Merciless Parliament are to be believed de Vere had with him both letters from the king and a royal standard; this would suggest at least some hasty planning and co-ordination between the king and the duke.[105] Letters to array troops in Cheshire probably arrived before de Vere did, as expenses for messengers to men to prepare to go to the king were paid in the chamberlain of Chester's accounts on 19 November.[106]

De Vere did not disappoint in raising royal forces, and it was from Chester that the royalist army at Radcot Bridge was recruited. On the face of it, the fact that an army that is usually estimated at 4,000–5,000 men was raised at short notice would reflect well on de Vere. Certainly, efforts were made by him – for example, two messengers were sent with letters from the king and the duke to leading men of Cheshire on 6 December as part of the recruiting process.[107] However, much of the successful recruitment related to factors outside his direct control. He had, of course, been justice of Chester for only three months by the time he led the army south; the previous chief justice, Edmund, duke of York, was a far less ardent royalist than de Vere. Part of the successful recruitment lay in the close ties between Cheshire and the crown and the long tradition of military service by Cestrians to the Black Prince and in the wars of Edward III, to which should be added Richard's active recruitment in the region during his gyrations of 1387, though direct evidence of that is lacking.[108]

---

[103] *KC*, 416–19; *SAC*, i, 832–5.

[104] *KC*, 419, n.3.

[105] *PROME*, vii, 98.

[106] SC6/773/3, m. 1d.

[107] SC6/773/3, m.2d. The letters were to Sir Ralph Vernon, Sir John Haukeston, Peter Legh and his brother John. The same membrane also shows that de Vere had also left some of his household at Chester. Prests were issued at Chester for £31 for his household expenses on 11 November when de Vere himself was in London, while cash payments of £13 6s 8d and 114s 11d were made on the 5th (ibid., m. 1d.).

[108] M.J. Bennett, *Community, Class and Careerism. Cheshire and Lancashire Society in the Age of Sir Gawain and the Green Knight* (Cambridge, 1983), 203–8.

A second factor aided recruitment in Cheshire and, in particular, in neighbouring Lancashire. Sections of the communities in both counties had become disaffected with John of Gaunt's lordship in the region. Simon Walker's work on the Lancastrian affinity has shown that there were some men from prominent families 'who had been prevented, by their exclusion from Gaunt's affinity, from achieving the position in county society for which their birth had apparently fitted them'.[109] There were others who had served Gaunt but for one reason or another had lost favour. Richard Massy of Rixton had refused to serve Gaunt in Spain and lost his annuity as a result. Sir Ralph Radcliffe had been removed from the shrievalty of Lancashire in 1387 for pecuniary irregularities and had a definite grievance. Both were probably with de Vere at Radcot Bridge. There are other examples.[110] Perhaps only a third factor relating to recruitment had much to do with de Vere and even then somewhat indirectly. A number of leading Cestrians served in de Vere's duchy of Ireland, under Sir John Stanley: men such as Sir Gilbert Halsall and Sir Robert Clifton, both of whom were also not in favour with Gaunt.[111] Stanley himself, though not at Radcot Bridge, was a Cheshire and Lancashire landowner, and at odds with the duke of Lancaster.[112] Some others serving in Ireland are noted as men of Cheshire and Lancashire.[113]

Not all Cheshire turned out for the king. Philip Morgan has pointed out that various Cheshiremen had to pay fines for pardons in 1397 for aiding the Appellants, so the county elite were not entirely united; that reflected on Richard and Sir Thomas Molyneux, de Vere's lieutenant, as well as de Vere. Likewise, the undersheriff of Flintshire, Hywel ap Tudur ap Ithel was indicted for taking 300 marks from de Vere to raise forty men at arms and 700 archers,

---

[109] S. Walker, *The Lancastrian Affinity, 1361–99* (Oxford, 1990), 169, and more forcefully stated, idem, 'Lordship and Lawlessness in the Palatinate of Lancaster, 1370–1400', *Journal of British Studies*, 28 (1989), 325–48.

[110] See Walker, *Lancastrian Affinity*, 168–70. For eight Lancashire and Cheshire men summoned before the council in January 1388, almost certainly for support of de Vere at Radcot Bridge, and including Radcliffe, Massy, Halsall and Clifton, see *CCR, 1385–9*, 393. Some of these men were bound over in the Palatinate of Lancaster: DL37/3, rot. 24d.

[111] Walker, *Lancastrian Affinity*, 169; McFarlane, *England in the Fifteenth Century*, 32.

[112] For Stanley, see Bennett, *Community, Class and Careerism*, 215–17.

[113] From Cheshire: Adam Bellyster and Peter Bygayn alias Cornewaill. From Lancashire: Henry de Bradesshagh, Thomas del Eues, John del Hulle, William de Lynhales, Thomas Molyneux, Robert Pilkington, John del Ridgate, Walter Robinson, John Shepherd, John Sotherton, Richard Walscroft: *CPR, 1385–9*, 156, 189, 232, 377. Searched via www.medievalsoldier.org/dbsearch/.

who failed to muster.[114] This is, in fact, the only indication of payment to the troops; so any others must have been made out of whatever funds de Vere and Richard had been able to scrape together in November 1387, or more likely the promise of future payment.[115]

The leading agent in all the recruitment that took place in the autumn of 1387 rather proves the point that de Vere had little to do with this. Sir Thomas Molyneux had long-held grievances with Gaunt dating back to the murder of Richard Molyneux in 1369 and the support offered to the murderer by one of the duke's officials. Molyneux pursued violent revenge and sustained his position within Gaunt's sphere of influence despite his opposition to the duke. However, he was also vice-justice of Chester by 1381, an acting justice of Flint by 1385, and constable of Chester Castle, while being a scion of a long-established Lancashire family, so had long-held connections with Cheshire and Lancashire society, and was in an excellent position to raise troops in the north-west.[116] He had letters of protection to serve in de Vere's lordship of Ireland in June 1386, though there is no evidence that he went.[117] De Vere reappointed him as vice-justice of Chester and Flint in September 1387.[118] Molyneux was described as the 'leading counsellor' of the duke at Radcot Bridge by the Westminster Chronicle.[119] Thomas Favent levelled charges of coercion against de Vere concerning the raising of troops. As Simon Walker has noted, it is not necessary to believe them to understand how the well-connected Molyneux was able to tap into royalist and anti-Gaunt factions within Cheshire and Lancashire society to raise a substantial force.[120] It was done through de Vere's authority as justice of Chester, primarily by Molyneux, and de Vere may not have been much more than a figurehead as far as the

[114] Morgan, *War and Society*, 189–91; CHES25/8, rot. 36.

[115] SC6/775/13. The Appellants alleged that the king had promised to pay all the troops, though presumably in arrears: *PROME*, vii, 98.

[116] For Molyneux, see Walker, *Lancastrian Affinity*, 165–7; J.L. Gillespie, 'Thomas Mortimer and Thomas Molineux: Radcot Bridge and the Appeal of 1387', *Albion*, 7 (1975), 165–9.

[117] *CPR, 1385–9*, 156. He did not bring a separate retinue to the main muster on 18 June and it is unlikely, though possible, that a man of his standing would have indented under Sir John Stanley: ibid., 163.

[118] CHES29/91, rot. 1.

[119] *WC*, 222. The Latin is 'precipuum consiliarium', translated as 'leading henchman' by the editors; this is a rather pejorative term here, and counsellor should perhaps be preferred.

[120] Favent, 'History or Narration', 234; Walker, *Lancastrian Affinity*, 168; Oliver, *Political Pamphleteering*, 132–5.

Cheshiremen were concerned. De Vere would have had no time to raise his own tenantry and retinue in Essex or, even if he had, to link with such a force as a result of the geography of the campaign. Given the size of the forces he led in 1385 and 1386 against Scotland and the threatened French invasion, this was a significant loss. When combined with the fact that he had little previous connection to Cheshire and seemingly not much direct involvement in the recruitment in the north-west, it would certainly be fair to say it was not really his army that he led at Radcot Bridge.

The Battle of Radcot Bridge

The army, having mustered at Flint and Pulford in the first week of December, moved south in the following week or so.[121] The plea roll of Chester has de Vere hearing cases on 3 and 10 December at Chester, which is plausible, but considerable care must be taken with the source given it also has him holding cases there on 7 January after he had fled the country.[122] The most strategically important of de Vere's castles in the south, Queenborough, was handed over to Degory Seys, an Appellant partisan deputed for the task by the council, for safe-keeping against the French, on 10 December. This may have been the date when reliable news of the muster reached London.[123] De Vere's army was substantial – Favent says 6,000, the Westminster Chronicle 5,000, Knighton says 4,000–5,000, the Register of Henry de Wakefield 4,000, while Walsingham just has 'a large force' and Henry of Marleborough 'many men'.[124] Philip Morgan has pointed out that these figures were in excess of the traditional Cheshire county muster, but bolstered by some household troops of de Vere and other royal well-wishers from Lancashire and North Wales, the lower end of the range, around 4,000, is plausible.[125] It also had the military arsenal at Chester to draw on.[126] In describing the muster and the march the

---

[121] Morgan, *War and Society*, 188.

[122] CHES29/91, rots. 2, 3, 6. The headings state that the cases were done 'coram', in the presence of, Robert, duke of Ireland, as justice of Chester.

[123] E403/518, m. 13.

[124] Favent, 'History or Narration', 239; *WC*, 220–1; *KC*, 420–1; R.G. Davies, 'Some Notes from the Register of Henry de Wakefield, Bishop of Worcester, on the Political Crisis of 1386–8', *EHR*, 86 (1971), 556; *SAC*, i, 836–7; 'Henry Marleburrough's Chronicle', in *Ancient Irish Histories*, ed. Ware, ii, 14.

[125] Morgan, *Cheshire*, 188.

[126] For some sense of the scale of the arsenal at Chester that de Vere's army must have drawn on, see the damaged dorse of SC6/773/2, which records more than ninety bows, 4,000 arrows and 3,000 quarrels for crossbows.

vitriol of several of the chroniclers really comes to the fore. Thomas Favent has de Vere 'with the devil his leader' raising troops, and then in rather confused imagery, 'his heart, foolish and hateful to God, grazed on vain hopes'.[127] Walsingham, describing the moments before de Vere saw the opposing forces, paints a picture of him 'riding high and haughtily upon his horse with the army he had mustered and believing that no one would venture to oppose him'; on spotting the opposition 'his heart failed him'.[128]

Clearly, however, it is important to move beyond the hostility of the chroniclers and analyse the strategic position in mid-December. De Vere's army, on leaving Cheshire, was aiming to link up with the king and (it was anticipated) a force of Londoners in or around the capital. This is made clear by a number of sources. Walsingham says de Vere's intention was to unite with the citizens of London to form a much stronger force, while the Westminster Chronicler places a speech in the earl of Warwick's mouth about the duke trying to reach the king.[129] When de Vere left for Chester, he would have had good expectations of support from the Londoners, as Nicholas Brembre, the former mayor, had promised exactly this. Knighton's chronicle has the mayor of the city, Sir Nicholas Exton, promising 50,000 men and the Westminster Chronicle records the mayor and citizens of London on 28 October stating they would stand with the king.[130] The citizens had taken an oath to uphold Richard against all his enemies earlier in the month.[131] There is some evidence that although the Londoners did not, at the critical moment, rally behind the king, opinion in the city was divided. Indeed, the capital shut its gates on the Appellants in December, and as Dodd has pointed out the Londoner Thomas Favent clearly hushed up the extent of the royalist support in the city.[132] Richard's resentment towards the city for its failure to support him in

---

[127] Favent, 'History or Narration', 239.

[128] *SAC*, i, 838–9. Froissart's narrative of the political manoeuvrings of the autumn of 1387 and the military campaign of Radcot Bridge is full of inaccuracies of chronology, of personnel, of geography, and is particularly full of invented speeches (mainly placed in the mouth of the duke of Gloucester) and cannot be relied on at all for this period: Froissart, ed. Johnes, ii, 263–74.

[129] *SAC*, i, 837; *WC*, 198.

[130] *KC*, 406–7; *WC*, 206–7.

[131] *Calendar of the Letter Books of the City of London H (1375–1399)*, ed. R.R. Sharpe (London, 1907), 314–15.

[132] Dodd, 'Thomas Favent', 411–12.

his hour of need was not assuaged until 1392, when, having extorted vast sums from the city, he restored their liberties after an extravagant royal entry.[133]

Other avenues for recruitment did not bear fruit either. Palmer has made the suggestion that de la Pole went to Calais in November to try and bring over part of the Calais garrison to bolster the king's forces. A garbled or deliberately distorted version of this was told by the Appellants, with Michael de la Pole escaping from England to Calais dressed in a ridiculous disguise.[134] De la Pole was unsuccessful in raising troops in Calais, however. Simon Burley was accused in the Merciless Parliament of summoning the mayor of Dover to him in November and ordering him to raise a thousand men to support the king against the Appellants.[135] Again, this seems not to have borne fruit. Mitchell notes the increasing number of chamber and household knights appointed to the Peace Commissions from the Peasants' Revolt onwards, reaching a peak in 1384–5 but continuing until the crisis of December 1387, although she also points out that none were appointed in 1387 to the traditional Fitzalan, Beauchamp or Lancastrian heartlands. Yet seemingly these royalists were unable to rally support for the king even in areas less closely associated with his opponents.[136] More specifically, Richard's recruiting drive over the spring, summer and autumn of 1387 was in the event largely unsuccessful.[137] Walsingham suggests as much when reporting that many, approached to support the king against the lords if required, replied that they could not oppose the lords, while others, 'who took the simple view that they were being hired, promised to be ready for a royal summons', but there seems to have been little support for the royalist faction in terms of boots on the ground.[138] In fact, given there seem to have been plenty who joined the Appellants, as the pardons of 1397 show, the balance of opinion amongst the land-owning

---

[133] A contemporary Latin poem by Richard Maidstone hints at this motivation as well: Richard Maidstone, *Concordia (The Reconciliation of Richard II with London)*, trans. A.G. Rigg and ed. D.R. Carlson (Kalamazoo, MI, 2003), 51. There were clearly other motivations, including financial ones, in 1392: see C.M. Barron, 'The Quarrel of Richard II with London 1392-7', in F.R.H. Du Boulay and C.M. Barron, eds, *The Reign of Richard II: Essays in Honour of May McKisack* (London, 1971), 173–201.

[134] Palmer, *England, France and Christendom*, 109–12.

[135] *PROME*, vii, 114.

[136] Mitchell, 'The Knightly Household of Richard II and the Peace Commissions', 48–51, 55.

[137] *WC*, 186–7; Given-Wilson, *Royal Household*, 214–15.

[138] *SAC*, i, 826–7.

and military classes was against Richard and his friends.[139] It is in this context that the oft-quoted speech of Ralph, Lord Basset, should be considered. It is recorded in Knighton's Chronicle that while he protested he would always be loyal to the king, but that if he had to go into battle, he wanted to be with the party that is true and seeks the truth, 'and that I am not going to offer to have my head broken for the duke of Ireland'.[140] While the speech may have been invented (and is qualified even in the chronicle as rumoured) and Basset, who was elderly, seems not to have stirred for either side in the event, it probably does capture the lack of enthusiasm for the royal cause. John Leland's work on the counter-Appellants, the nine men who brought the appeal in 1397, has shown too that there were reasons why some potential allies were not involved on the court's side in 1387. William Scrope was abroad at Cherbourg during the crisis while the loyalist Montagu family were busy with an unpleasant family quarrel between the elderly earl and his nephew and heir, John, who became earl in 1397. Two staunch royalists in the 1390s, Edward, earl of Rutland, and Thomas, Lord Despenser, were too young at fifteen to take part in the convulsions of 1387–8.[141] Henry Percy, earl of Northumberland, seems to have determinedly followed a middle course between royalists and Appellants throughout the crisis and the parliament that followed.[142]

In the proceedings against de Vere in the Merciless Parliament it was alleged that in de Vere's baggage there were letters from the king which stated that the king would meet him 'with all his own power and that with him the king would hazard his royal person'.[143] Whether or not these letters existed in this form, de Vere must have been expecting that the king would come to his aid, and this would have changed the complexion of the confrontation. An alliance of Cheshiremen, Londoners and the king with the royal household would have been formidable, and there would surely have been some reluctance amongst the Appellants and their followers to fight the king in person with his banner advanced. Why Richard, in the event, failed to come to the aid of his friend

---

[139] A recent study has emphasised this point: M.J. Bennett, '"Defenders of Truth": Lord Cobham, John Gower, and the Political Crisis of 1387–88', in Lutkin and Hamilton, eds, *Creativity, Contradictions and Commemoration*, 45–6. For the pardons imposed on those who supported the Appellants in 1397 more generally, see Goodman, *Loyal Conspiracy*, 35–41.

[140] *KC*, 406–7.

[141] Leland, 'Richard II and the Counter-Appellants', ch. 1.

[142] K. Towson, 'Henry Percy, First Earl of Northumberland: Ambition, Conflict and Cooperation in Late Medieval England' (unpublished PhD thesis, University of St Andrews, 2004), 92–7.

[143] *WC*, 266–7; *SAC*, i, 846–7.

is unknown, although cautious advice around the king would seem the most likely explanation. Goodman suggests that Brembre would have been keen to secure London, though ultimately this was of secondary strategic significance as events were to prove.[144] Richard's failure to move was a major factor in the collapse of the royalist position; he probably regretted it for the rest of his life.

However, all of this meant that it was not in de Vere's interest to fight during his march south; little support was coming in and only in conjunction with the king and, he would have thought, the Londoners would he have sufficient strength to win. He was thus aiming to avoid the Appellant forces and reach the environs of London and the king to reinforce his army and only then turn to attack those who he and Richard would have considered rebels. The Appellants, of course, wanted to intercept de Vere before he could reach the king and any reinforcements, and they therefore moved to place themselves between the duke and the king. It was only at this stage that three Appellants – Gloucester, Arundel and Warwick – became five, with Derby and Nottingham joining them at Huntingdon on 12 December.[145] They moved westward then to Northampton, which controlled the most obvious route for de Vere to take south to London, via Derby or Nottingham and then Leicester. De Vere, according to the Westminster Chronicle, having information of their movements, then turned south to Stow-on-the-Wold in Gloucestershire from where he could then hook east towards Windsor, where the king was.[146] But, according to the classic reconstruction of the campaign by Myres, the Appellants in turn had wind of his movements, and they took up positions in the Cotswolds to block his line of advance, and leave him with two options – to march down the Fosse Way towards Cirencester in the wrong direction, or to head towards the nearest bridge over the Thames in Oxfordshire at Radcot Bridge: the latter was a trap. Myres did an extremely skilful job of conflating two separate and incompatible accounts in the chronicles, making them into a coherent whole. Subsequent to his 1927 study, a third source came to light in 1971, which modern historians have adapted into the narrative

---

[144] As Goodman argues: *Loyal Conspiracy*, 30–1.

[145] Saul, *Richard II*, 187, based on *PROME*, vii, 408, 412.

[146] *WC*, 220–1, 224–5, has Richard at Windsor and moving to the Tower of London after Radcot Bridge; this is supported by the evidence of Wakefield's register which states de Vere was marching from Chester to Windsor to the king: Wakefield, 'Some Notes from the Register of Henry de Wakefield', 556. However, Goodman, *Loyal Conspiracy*, 32 has the move to London before Radcot Bridge, which would have made any effort to link with de Vere far harder.

of the campaign.[147] Instead of one climatic battle, the campaign comprised three skirmishes against the Appellants' forces which had divided in order to spring the trap. Each skirmish has one source, with that source having a connection to, or information from, the Appellant Lord whose skirmish they described, while each source ignores any other action. The three sources are the Westminster Chronicle, describing the action of the earl of Arundel, Knighton's Chronicle covers the skirmish of the earl of Derby, and Wakefield's Register notes that of the duke of Gloucester, derived from his information.[148] The composite modern reconstruction of the campaign has the Appellants spread out covering a number of different possible routes that de Vere could have taken from Stow-on-the-Wold. De Vere and his army ran into the forces of three of them, the first being the duke of Gloucester's troops in the vicinity of Moreton-in-Marsh (Saul has Bourton-on-the-Hill) on the morning of 20 December. Here, according to Wakefield's register, many of his men deserted.[149] Then de Vere encountered the forces of the earl of Arundel, probably at Burford on the River Windrush. Finally, he encountered the forces of Derby at Radcot Bridge, with the other Appellants coming up to the rear of his force. In one of the skirmishes Sir Thomas Molyneux was killed: Westminster has this in the engagement at Burford, and this is supported by the fact that the Molyneux's killers, Sir Thomas Mortimer and one William Curtis, his servant, who were charged with the murder in 1397 were both closely connected with Arundel and were likely to have been with him.[150] On the other hand, Knighton, who may well have been drawing on an eye-witness account, places the killing at Radcot Bridge.

Thus, the action was apparently spread over a considerable distance – it is fifteen miles from Moreton-in-Marsh to Burford, and a further ten from Burford to Radcot – and these were considerable distances for a medieval

---

[147] J.N.L Myres, 'The Campaign of Radcot Bridge in December 1387', *EHR*, 42 (1927), 20–33; Davies 'Some Notes from the Register of Henry de Wakefield', 547–58; Saul, *Richard II*, 188; Morgan, *Cheshire*, 188–9.

[148] It has been suggested that one possible source of information for the Westminster chronicler on the Merciless Parliament was John Scarle, connected to the earl of Arundel and indeed the chancellor of the duchy of Lancaster: A.K. McHardy, 'John Scarle: Ambition and Politics in the Late Medieval Church', in L. Clark, M. Jurkowski and C. Richmond, eds, *Image, Text and Church, 1380–1600: Essays for Margaret Aston* (Toronto, 2009), 68–93. It is not impossible, if he was a source for the parliament, that he also gave him information relating to Radcot Bridge.

[149] Davies, 'Some Notes from the Register of Henry de Wakefield', 557; Saul, *Richard II*, 188.

[150] Morgan, *Cheshire*, 188–9.

army. Given also the light would have faded early on a December afternoon, we might plausibly question if all three skirmishes occurred. But if they are accepted as happening, the question that faces the historian is what actually occurred at these? Should we believe the account of Wakefield that most of de Vere's army deserted at the first skirmish or dismiss that as implausible as surely Arundel's forces would have overwhelmed de Vere's in the second skirmish if that was the case? The Westminster Chronicler's account, making no mention of any previous skirmish, suggests that no fighting took place, with Arundel persuading de Vere's troops not to support traitors, and his troops 'demonstrated their peaceful intentions by holding up their bows and their other weapons'. They were then ordered to return home, helped on their way by the other Appellant lords appearing. De Vere, 'astonished at the sight this presented, and reckoning on the rout of the force under him' thus fled.[151] Myres argues that in fact de Vere brushed aside Arundel's forces, albeit no contemporary chronicle actually says this; his reasoning is that this source makes no mention of what happened at the final confrontation at Radcot Bridge, which suggests Arundel's forces never made it there because of the setback.[152] One obvious explanation for the absence of any statement regarding a success against Arundel in the chronicles is that the anti-Vere nature of the sources would suppress such information as this, and the Westminster Chronicle, from whom the skirmish with Arundel is known, took his information from a dependant of the earl, who would obviously wish to keep this quiet.[153] It would perhaps make some sense to think of the first two skirmishes as at least inconclusive and certainly not disastrous for de Vere, otherwise it is hard to imagine that his army would have made it as far as the third skirmish at Radcot Bridge itself. De Vere, of course, was trying to avoid a full-scale battle – his strategic objective was to get to the king and the capital, where he would be much stronger – so he may have tried to hustle his troops through rather than stay and fight. However, at Radcot Bridge, faced with the earl of Derby's troops ahead, and Gloucester's troops coming up behind and the bridge itself broken, and having lost (or be about to lose) Molyneux, the army disintegrated, and de Vere fled. This was probably in the dusk or full dark which would have aided his escape. He seems to have swum the Thames on horseback, leaving behind his armour, according to both Walsingham

[151] *WC*, 220–5.

[152] Myres, 'Campaign of Radcot Bridge', 31.

[153] *WC*, 220–3.

and Knighton, the former adding that it was initially thought that he had drowned.[154]

Several sources, including Knighton and Westminster, mention the fact that de Vere had the king's banner with him, and he had displayed it against the Appellants; this formed part of the thirty-ninth article in the Merciless Parliament, where it was described as accroaching royal power, and the display contrary to the estate of the king and his crown.[155] The use of royal banners was of considerable import: it denoted a state of open warfare between the crown and its opponents, and stood in some contrast to Edward II's refusal, for example, to display the royal banners in the Boroughbridge campaign of 1322, which designated his opponents as criminals rather than rebels.[156] The extent to which the display of the king's banner on 20 December – both in terms of raising battlefield morale for his troops, dismaying his opponents and defining the legal status of the combatants – was undermined by the king not being present is not clear, not least as the royalist army lost. The display of the banner was thus treated as a crime rather than those opposing it as committing treason. It seems most likely, when taken together with the letters that Richard seems to have sent to de Vere, that Richard had given or authorised him to use the royal standard, rather than de Vere taking it upon himself, having appropriated a standard (perhaps at Chester).

Perhaps the most surprising account of Radcot Bridge is that of Knighton, which describes de Vere in remarkably positive terms. When faced with the opposing army de Vere 'at once he stood his ground, ordered the king's banner, which he had ready, to be unfurled and raised upon a lance, and with an eager face and light-hearted mien ordered the trumpets and other musical instruments to sound, and with a cheerful voice exhorted his men to prepare for instant battle'. As he was preparing to fight the other lords led by Gloucester came up behind his force, and some of his men refused to fight; only then did de Vere decide to flee, which he did with 'wonderful daring'.[157] It is tempting to accept this as there was no reason for Knighton to be favourable to de Vere (and indeed he was not throughout the rest of his chronicle). It is certainly a contrast to Favent, who has the Cheshiremen 'leaderless' or Walsingham, who

---

[154] *SAC*, i, 840–1; *KC*, 422–3.

[155] *KC*, 420–1; *WC*, 220–3; *PROME*, vii, 98. The Westminster Chronicle adds that de Vere had the standard of St George as well.

[156] A. King, '"War,", "Rebellion" or "Perilous Times"? Political Taxonomy and the Conflict in England, 1321–2', in Ambühl, Bothwell and Tompkins, eds, *Ruling Fourteenth-Century England*, 113–32.

[157] *KC*, 420–3.

records (or rather invents) a direct conversation between the duke and the Cheshire troops designed solely to allow de Vere to be accused of cowardice.[158]

What is not known is the size of the Appellant forces, since, unusually, no contemporary offers an estimate. It seems likely that on their own resources, no single Appellant could have matched de Vere's army of perhaps 4,000, not even Derby, who was in temporary charge of the Lancastrian domains, given his father was abroad with a large army. As a comparison, for the expedition to Scotland in 1385, Gloucester, Arundel, Warwick and Nottingham mustered 1,978 soldiers, and Gaunt 3,000.[159] The admittedly difficult evidence from 1397–8, when Richard II virtually forced the south-east to sue for pardons for the help given to the Appellants indicates that this area may have supplied many additional men for the campaign. Forty-two knights and forty-two esquires from these counties sued for pardons, and there were fifty-seven individuals pardoned from Sussex alone, though this was Arundel's area of influence.[160] There was also support from beyond south-east England and East Anglia.[161] If this was the case then de Vere's force might have had a numerical advantage against any one of these forces, such as Arundel or slightly less certainly Derby, but when Gloucester and the other lords added their forces together, de Vere must surely have been significantly outnumbered in total. It is difficult to imagine that the Appellants would have been willing to divide their forces to the extent they did if their numbers were not large. It makes some sense, then, that de Vere's army could survive two skirmishes with the contingents of Gloucester and Arundel but faced with all the forces combining against him in the vicinity of Radcot Bridge, he was at a significant disadvantage.

Given this, it is not hard to excuse de Vere from the accusations of cowardice levelled against him in several of the chronicles. If he did not cover himself in glory, he seems to have kept his force together throughout what must have been a very difficult day until the end. Myres has described the Appellants' tactics and positioning as brilliantly conceived and brilliantly executed, and rightly so given the difficulty of co-ordinating the movements of so many forces.[162] De Vere was thus out-planned, probably outnumbered, and without the king's personal support, his position on the field at Radcot Bridge was hopeless and he knew it.

[158] Favent, 'History or Narration', 240; *SAC*, i, 838–9.

[159] Goodman, *Loyal Conspiracy*, 127.

[160] Goodman, *Loyal Conspiracy*, 36–40. For discussion, see also C.M. Barron, 'The Tyranny of Richard II', *BIHR*, 41 (1968), 8–9.

[161] Goodman, *Loyal Conspiracy*, 39.

[162] Myres, 'Campaign of Radcot Bridge', 25.

The 'Merciless Parliament' that met at Westminster on 3 February 1388 indicted de Vere, de la Pole and others of treason. This indictment provides the most extensive catalogue of de Vere's apparently unsavoury activities, totalling thirty-nine articles against him and the Appellees. There were three strands to the allegations. The first were generalised statements of the malign actions of the Appellees in dominating the king, causing evil government, and of engaging in active treason with the French, the second concentrated on the patronage granted to de Vere and others, and the third focused on the events of 1387, framing the actions of Richard's circle as treasonous. Some of the specific allegations put forward in the parliament can in fact be disproved.

The Appellants alleged that de Vere and others had caused the king to grant many lordships, castles, and manors such as Ireland, Oakham and the Audley estates to the duke of Ireland by which the king was impoverished.[163] This of course was neatly evading the truth – Oakham and the Audley lands were recent escheats to the crown, and Ireland had produced little for the English exchequer for decades. Royal impoverishment was hardly de Vere's fault, but rather due to the burdens of attempting to fight a war with France and Scotland, a policy the Appellants were determined to continue. Regarding the Audley lands, part of the complex issues relating to Richard's attitude to his grandfather's will, Chris Given-Wilson has pointed out that as the earl of Huntingdon received these lands back during the Merciless Parliament, 'it is difficult to see the attitude of the Appellants towards de Vere and Burley concerning their appropriation of the enfeoffed lands as a crusade for impartial justice; it was simply another stick with which to beat the hated courtiers'.[164] Moreover, in the judgement made in parliament, this allegation was not found to be treasonous.

The Appellants also made the accusation, in the proceedings against the king's former tutor Simon Burley, that he caused the king to grant the de Coucy lands to de Vere and received the manor of Lyonshall in Herefordshire in payment. This was inaccurate: Lyonshall was actually sold to Burley for 400 marks and perhaps a couple of years later than the grant of the de Coucy lands.[165] A further allegation did not stick either, this time concerning de Vere's appointment and conduct as justice of Chester. He was alleged to have 'without the usual commission from the king or other sufficient warrant, made himself justice of Chester'. The appointment, by royal letters patent, is however recorded in the recognisance rolls and plea rolls of Chester,

---

[163] *PROME*, vii, 86; *WC*, 244–5.

[164] Given-Wilson, 'Richard II and his Grandfather's Will', 335.

[165] *PROME*, vii, 114–15; *WC*, 276–7; see p. 89, above, for the sale.

granted by the king for life on the surrender of the same office by Edmund, duke of York.[166] However, the plea roll records authorisation by the seal of the exchequer of Chester, dated 8 September at Chester (the king was at Clipstone in Nottinghamshire that day), while the recognisance roll notes a warrant under the privy seal and the initial grant under the signet. It is possible that no copy of the grant was issued under the great seal of England; certainly it was not enrolled on the Patent Roll.[167] So, the Appellants may have had a technical point while the substance of the allegation – that de Vere made himself justice of Chester – was inaccurate. Three other specific allegations against de Vere were also not found to be treasonous by judgement of parliament. These were that the de Vere and the court circle were guilty of maintenance in quarrels, that de Vere accroached royal power in freeing John of Blois, without consent of parliament or council, to the strengthening of the French, and that de Vere and the others caused the king to build up a retinue and gave many badges.[168]

There were only two charges of treason focussing primarily on de Vere (rather than more collectively) which were allowed by the parliament. The first was the plan to make de Vere king of Ireland, for which this is the first evidence, and is almost certainly a fabrication, although there may have been fears of de Vere building up a royal military power-base there.[169] The second were the charges relating to Radcot Bridge.[170] The tortuous logic in this latter allegation, that de Vere, bringing an army to defend the king against his liegemen up in arms against him, was committing treason by working to the detriment and ruin of the king and the kingdom, shows in microcosm how difficult it was to indict a man so clearly enjoying royal favour of treason against the king and the realm using contemporary political ideas and terminology. It was not possible to separate the king and the realm in the written appeal of treason, though the Appellants were, in effect, arguing that de Vere had committed crimes against the realm but not against the king.[171]

---

[166] *PROME*, vii, 91; *WC*, 257 and n.; CHES29/91, rot. 1; CHES2/59, rot. 7 (cf. *36th Report of the Deputy Keeper*, Appendix II, 494). Tout, *Chapters*, v, 296–7, 367–8 discusses the use of the Chester seal by the Black Prince. The grant in October to de Vere of the justiciarship of North Wales was made under the Great Seal: *CPR, 1385–9*, 357.

[167] No warrant appears to survive under the signet or privy seal (C81/497; 1354).

[168] *PROME*, vii, 88, 91 (articles 13, 23, 24).

[169] See above, pp. 123–4. Tuck, *Richard II*, 83, dismisses the allegation as baseless.

[170] *PROME*, vii, 87, 98; *WC*, 268–9.

[171] Bellamy, *Law of Treason*, 209–10.

It is worth noting the centrality of de Vere to the proceedings in parliament. He is named in thirty-eight of the thirty-nine articles, the last of which related to him alone, and he formed the primary focus of many of the group charges. This is in contrast for instance to Alexander Neville who was not singled out in any charge.[172] A significant percentage of those named as exempted from the general pardon – his clerk, John Ripon, his chamberlain, Sir John Lancaster, his chancellor, John Fitzmartin, and his confessor, Richard Roughton – were closely connected to him, and the same is true of those expelled from court, including his uncle Aubrey de Vere, his first cousin John, Lord Beaumont, and his ambassador and attorney Sir Henry Ferrers.[173]

Exile

After swimming the Thames with his horse as his army disintegrated, de Vere seems to have made it to Windsor, where the Westminster Chronicle records that he had a discussion of sorts with the king before hurrying off to his castle of Queenborough in Kent, where he quickly found a ship and crossed overseas.[174] Degory Seys had been deputed by the council to undertake the safe-keeping of the castle as early as 10 December but had clearly not taken up the post in person immediately; he may well have been at Radcot Bridge. De Vere's flight from Queenborough was known at Westminster by 27 December when Seys was granted control of the castle and its armaments to the use of the king.[175] Froissart records that de Vere first arrived in Holland, and remained for a short time at Dordrecht, before being forced to leave by Duke Albert of Holland. Albert's reasoning was, according to Froissart, that he had no wish 'to act contrary to the will of his cousins in England, notwithstanding King Richard had written to him in his favour'.[176] This letter was presumably sent in the first month or two of 1388, when the Appellants were in control, and would indicate Richard took a risk on de Vere's behalf, given his difficult political position.

---

[172] Davies, 'Alexander Neville', 99.

[173] *PROME*, vii, 73; *WC*, 230–1. Beaumont's mother, Margaret, was the daughter of the seventh earl of Oxford. Beaumont and de Vere were almost exactly of an age, both were brought up in or around the royal court, and both were close to the king: Given-Wilson, *Royal Household*, 62; *CP*, ii, 61.

[174] *WC*, 222–5 ('habito colloquio aliquali'); the *Eulogium* confirms de Vere took ship from the Isle of Sheppey, on which Queenborough is situated: *Continuatio Eulogii*, ed. Given-Wilson, 63.

[175] *CPR, 1385–8*, 381. He later accounted for his keepership of the castle from 28 December: E364/22, rot. 6.

[176] Froissart, ed. Johnes, ii, 407.

Additional evidence that de Vere was very much on Richard's mind comes from the date on which Richard confirmed a grant by de Vere to a hermit in Colchester – 20 February 1388, in the middle of the Merciless Parliament.[177]

According to Froissart, who is almost the only source for most of de Vere's time in exile, the duke then moved on from Holland to Utrecht, a free town, from where the king of France sent for him. He obtained a safe-conduct and went thence to France. Froissart unfortunately does not give a date for this, nor does the Monk of St Denys, who also records de Vere's arrival. Froissart missed one further stage of his travels, given additional information is supplied by the arrangements for the collection of the ransom of John de Blois. In March 1388 de Vere wrote from Trier in Germany confirming a change for the receipt of the ransom from Calais to Paris. Trier, on the western border of Germany, is 215 miles south of Utrecht and not on the route to Paris, so it is also possible that Froissart erred in placing him at Utrecht rather than Trier. Nonetheless, he made his way to Paris probably by the summer of 1388.[178]

The king of France had summoned de Vere to gain more information on English affairs on the advice of his uncle, according to Froissart.[179] This suited de Vere well, of course, for a number of reasons. Given the pro-war policy of the Appellants, he had every reason to be as useful as he could to Charles VI, which was the justification for his summons. Many of the leading French nobles and courtiers owed de Vere instalments of John of Blois's ransom, while as the man responsible for releasing Blois, over which he had fulfilled his obligations, he was presumably in good odour with most at the French court. Lastly, according to the well-informed chronicler of the French court, the Monk of St Denys, Richard had written to Charles VI asking him to protect and support the exiles, again perhaps at some degree of risk to himself. Although de la Pole and Neville joined him in Paris, de Vere was the only exile mentioned by name in the chronicle of the Monk of St Denys, as 'the duke of Ireland surpassed the others in authority'.[180] The king received them and their few followers honourably, entertained them and lavished them with gifts, and ordered a tournament to be held to show his joy at their arrival.[181] Froissart also recorded de Vere's honourable reception: 'the duke was well received by the king and his uncles; and the king was desirous he would fix his residence in France and had a hotel appointed for him to live'. He added that the duke

---

[177] *CPR, 1385–9*, 405.

[178] Froissart, ed. Johnes, ii, 331; Jones, 'Ransom', 21–2.

[179] Froissart, ed. Johnes, ii, 331.

[180] *Chronique du Religieux de Saint-Denys*, ed. M.L. Bellaguet (Paris, 1839), i, 496–7.

[181] Ibid., 496–9.

made frequent visits to the king, who entertained him well, and he was invited to all the feasts, tilts and tournaments.[182]

Yet, there was a serious problem at the French court for de Vere which was the reason he did not ultimately take up permanent residence there. As Froissart relates, 'notwithstanding this duke [of Ireland] was so well received by the king, the lord de Coucy mortally hated him, and not without reason' for, although in other affairs 'he showed great good sense, honour, fair speech and great liberality', he had 'behaved infamously to the daughter of the lord de Coucy'.[183] It is noteworthy that on 12 July or 12 September 1388, a letter of de Vere acquitted Coucy of 10,000 francs for which he had been bound for Blois's ransom, as de Clisson had taken over the debt; it seems likely that Coucy could not bear to be under obligation to de Vere.[184] Froissart goes on to note that the Lord de Coucy, overruled on the initial decision to summon him to France, but high in favour with the king, prevailed on the latter over time to dismiss de Vere. The latter was allowed to choose a place to retire to and accepted the decision as he 'perceived they were tired of him, and that he ran daily risks, from the Lord de Coucy and from his relations'.[185] The implication here was of a possible attack or assassination, not impossible given the murder of the duke of Orléans in the streets of Paris fifteen years later.

The chronology of de Vere's sojourn in Paris is not quite clear. Froissart does not give a date for any of it directly, but the discussion of his retirement to Brabant is placed just before a passage concerning the king of France at Michaelmas 1389. What is not clear is whether de Vere was in Paris from the late spring or summer of 1388 to late summer 1389 or whether there were a series of visits interspersed by periods of residence elsewhere. A quittance for an instalment of the ransom paid on 1 November 1388 in Paris made by de Vere on 11 November does not note where he was, but a ten-day delay between payment and quittance may suggest that he was not in the capital but whether he was with the French court elsewhere or if he had gone to Brabant is not clear.[186] He can be located in Paris on two further datable occasions, both in

---

[182] Froissart, ed. Johnes, ii, 331.

[183] Froissart, ed. Lettenhove, xiv, 33 ('il fuist bien pourveu de sens, d'honneur et de parole plaisant et de grant largesse'); Froissart, ed. Johnes, ii, 331, 408.

[184] Jones, 'Ransom', 24n citing an MS in Nantes with a July date and *Mémoires pour servir de preuves à l'Histoire ecclésiastique et civile de Bretagne*, ed. P.H. Morice (2 vols, Paris, 1742–6), ii, 529, which has Saturday 12 September as the date of a quittance from de Vere to de Coucy for 10,000 francs, but does not mention Clisson.

[185] Froissart, ed. Lettenhove, xiv, 33–4; Froissart, ed. Johnes, ii, 408.

[186] Nantes, Bibl. Mun. MS. 1697; 1689, no. 14, cited in Jones 'Ransom', 21–4.

1389. Froissart places de Vere at a tournament celebrating the entry of Queen Isabeau to Paris on 22 June 1389.[187] A letter from Alexander Neville to John de Shirburn, abbot of Selby, says that de Vere, de la Pole and Neville came to Paris at the beginning of September 1389, a week before the death of de la Pole there on 8 September.[188] So it is not clear whether de Vere left the French court later in 1388 because of de Coucy's ire, and made at least two return visits after that date – certainly a possibility, given the king seemed to hold de Vere in good regard – or departed permanently only in 1389, which would fit better with Froissart's account.

Overall, there is a surprisingly positive portrayal of de Vere at the French court. While the chronicler of St Denys is neutral in his brief description, there is no hint of negativity about his comment on de Vere. Froissart, in contrast, is fulsome, particularly in comparison with the derogatory picture earlier in his chronicle. Indeed, he lists his qualities: good sense, honour, fair speech and liberality. These are stock phrases associated with good knights, but the application to de Vere is important, as Froissart had no need to praise him, and indeed had the hostile Lord de Coucy as a patron.[189] Hearsay at the French court before his arrival, recorded by Froissart, described de Vere as a 'gallant knight'.[190] Froissart also notes his participation at a grand tournament in Paris in June 1389 where 'the duke of Ireland tilted well', something that for the great chronicler of chivalry perhaps overcame other flaws.[191] Given de Vere had recently lost at, and fled from, Radcot Bridge, the comments on gallantry are interesting. Presumably, Richard had put a positive spin on the events in any letter to Charles VI and de Vere himself could revise the story to put himself in the best light, though as discussed above it may well be that he could tell the truth of the difficult campaign without shame. All of this suggests that de Vere made a good account of himself at the French court, and it is important to place this alongside the hostile picture of de Vere's personality given by the English chroniclers. The two are not mutually exclusive in some respects. Chivalrous skills exercised to gain ascendancy at court in England are not incompatible with making a good impression over a protracted period at

---

[187] Froissart, ed. Johnes, ii, 404.

[188] G.S. Haslop, 'Two Entries from the Register of John de Shirburn, abbot of Selby 1369–1408', *Yorkshire Archaeological Journal*, 41 (1964), 291.

[189] Froissart, ed. Johnes, ii, 397, 568, the first is where de Coucy is specifically mentioned as a patron.

[190] Froissart, ed. Johnes, ii, 331.

[191] Froissart, ed. Johnes, ii, 404.

the French court. However, it does demonstrate that de Vere was more than capable of an extended display of social skills and knightly talents.

De Vere chose Brabant as a place of retirement and asked the French king for a letter of recommendation to the duchess of Brabant, the king's aunt, which Charles VI provided. The chronicler goes on to say that de Vere was escorted by the king of France's officers to the city of Leuven, 'where he fixed his residence: he went, indeed, at times, to a castle near Louvain, which he had borrowed from a knight of Brabant'.[192] A city residence and a country retreat would certainly suggest de Vere was affluent and maintaining a high-status lifestyle. Archbishop Neville also settled in Brabant and is said to have served as a parish priest in Leuven, though on what evidence is unknown, and he predeceased de Vere by a few months in May 1392.[193] No further evidence has come to light on his time in Brabant, bar a single document relating to his burial and discussed below. There are a number of reasons for this lack of evidence. A large part of the archives of the Duchy of Brabant was destroyed in a fire at the city hall of Brussels in the late seventeenth century. The diplomatic correspondence of the dukes and duchess of Brabant does not seem to have survived. While there are surviving records, mainly charters from Brabant and financial and administrative records of the city of Leuven, which are now in Brussels and 's-Hertogenbosch, de Vere does not appear in them.[194] This may be the result of his informal status as an exile without diplomatic status, potentially leaving the duchess of Brabant in an awkward position, and if Froissart is correct, he borrowed rather than purchased property.

What happened to Agnes Lancecrone between 1388 and 1392 is entirely unknown and there are a whole range of possibilities. She may have stayed in Chester after the summer of 1387 or, having accompanied de Vere to London in November, she may have remained there when de Vere went north to Chester to raise troops. Did she accompany him from London on his flight to the continent and was she the reason he initially headed for Germany and

---

[192] Froissart, ed. Johnes, ii, 408.

[193] *WC*, 492–3; J. Raine, ed., *The Historians of the Church of York and its Archbishops* (3 vols, RS, 1879–94), ii, 424; R.B. Dobson, 'Neville, Alexander', *ODNB*.

[194] Research was undertaken in the city archive of Leuven and in the National Archives of Belgium in Brussels, as well as in digitised and print collections by Dr Aline Douma, and she was in correspondence with a number of archivists in Belgium on this subject. I am very grateful to Dr Douma for all her work. In addition, I searched printed primary and secondary works in the excellent collection on the Low Countries in the Institute of Historical Research in London, all to no avail. For the archives of the dukes of Brabant, see L.M.Th.L. Hustinx et al., *De archieven in Noord-Brabant* (Alphen aan den Rijn, 1980), xvii–xviii.

Trier (given she may have been a member of a German noble family)? Or since de Vere had formally married her, albeit the pope declared the marriage invalid in 1389, did he send for her once settled in France? Bringing her to the French court would have added insult to injury to the Lord de Coucy and would have been ill-advised; yet so was the marriage as a whole and can only be explained as sheer infatuation, which means it is not impossible that he did so. Alternatively, he may have waited until he settled in Leuven before bringing her from England. There is no evidence that she resumed her role with Queen Anne at court. Most modern authorities assume that they were separated permanently after Radcot Bridge and she returned to Bohemia. New research by Michael Bennett suggests that this was not the case, and that she was in England from at least 1393 onwards. His is an extraordinary piece of detective work.[195] Lady Agnes Arundel, wife of Sir William Arundel, nephew to the Fitzalan earl, made a will in 1401.[196] Alongside bequests to her late husband's family, and a request to be buried alongside her husband in Rochester Cathedral, she made bequests to five ladies, personal friends.[197] All five of these ladies were closely connected to Queen Anne, and three were probably or certainly Bohemian. Bennett has noted that the only Agnes known in the queen's service was Agnes Lancecrone. It seems likely that it was this Agnes who married Sir William Arundel. The timings work well too. The marriage to Arundel must have taken place before October 1393. If Agnes returned to England from Leuven after de Vere's death in November 1392 and threw herself on the queen's mercy, then a remarriage to a knight rising in royal service – William was to become a knight of the chamber by 1395 – would have been entirely in character with Richard and Anne's loyalty to their dependents and may have reflected Richard's devotion to his friend. Alternatively, if Agnes had stayed in England between 1388 and 1392, presumably in Anne's service, then the death of de Vere removed any possible impediment to a legal marriage to another, and a remarriage thanks to the queen's patronage would have been likely.

[195] What follows is based upon Bennett, 'Richard II, Queen Anne, Bohemia: Marriage, Culture and Politics', in Brown and Čermák, eds, *England and Bohemia in the Age of Chaucer*, 35–7. I am indebted to Professor Bennett for making me aware of his discovery, kindly sharing a draft version of the chapter with me, and subsequent correspondence on the matter.

[196] The will is Lambeth Palace Library, Register Arundel, I, fol. 183r-v.

[197] A tomb identified as theirs, though on fairly slight grounds, survives in Rochester Cathedral: W.B. Rye, 'Tombs of Sir William Arundel and Others in Rochester Cathedral', *Archaeologia Cantiana*, 13 (1880), 141–5. A 3D scan of the tomb can be seen at: www.rochestercathedral.org/research/brasses.

The other major question relating to de Vere's exile relates to the ransom of John of Blois. It is difficult to know how much of the ransom de Vere actually collected. 78,000 francs had been paid on 19 November 1387. This was probably still at Calais when he fled into exile after Radcot Bridge on 20 December; there would have been no advantage in moving it in late November when he was preparing for a military showdown, as it provided an insurance policy if things went wrong. On 1 January, one of de Vere's attorneys, John Newton, took receipt of the next instalment of the ransom, 10,000 francs (£1,580). Of these huge sums, de Vere appears to have lost only a proportion of a little under a third to the Appellants. One of the Appellant's servants, Janico Dartasso, was commissioned to take charge of the ransom on 30 December, and he arrived in Calais to seize what he could.[198] By late February, a sum of 22,441 francs and 4,858 'scutorum', coins, perhaps *écus*, which the exchequer calculated at an additional 5,466 francs – a combined total of £4,418 – was accounted for at the exchequer.[199] It is interesting that once again Richard tried to help his friend, since although Newton had been arrested by the authorities of Calais and Janico Dartasso on the latter's arrival, an order was made to release Newton on 20 April.[200] However, of the rest of the cash sum of the ransom, there was no account and presumably de Vere had been able to transfer most of what was in Calais to wherever he was in exile in January 1388 or to Paris. This suspicion is reinforced by the fact that the captain of Calais, William Beauchamp, was named by de Vere as one of his proctors for the collection of the next instalment of the ransom in his letter from Trier in March 1388, albeit de Vere may not have known of Dartasso's arrival and Newton's arrest.[201] Given de Vere, in mid-February 1388, had already been convicted of treason,

---

[198] C76/72, m. 17.

[199] E403/518, m. 23; E401/570, *sub* 2 March; E364/24, rot. 7d.; Jones, 'Ransom', 20.

[200] C76/72, m. 8; Jones 'Ransom', 20 and Palmer, *England, France and Christendom*, 111, say that Dartasso was arrested and released under pressure from the Appellants, but the order states that Newton was 'per vos [the Captain of Calais] ac dilectum armigerum Johannem Dartasso de mandato nostro… captum et arestatum' and that he [Newton] was to be freed and allowed to go within the kingdom of England without impediment (C76/72, m.8). It does not mention Dartasso being arrested. For Dartasso, see S. Walker, *Political Culture in Later Medieval England*, ed. M.J. Braddick (Manchester, 2006), 115–35.

[201] For Beauchamp, see C. Carpenter, 'Beauchamp, William, first Baron Bergavenny, c. 1343–1411', *ODNB*. His ambiguous political stance, as brother of one of the appellants, the earl of Warwick, yet one of Richard's chamber knights, is demonstrated by his murky role in connection with the ransom and de Vere. He, John Newton and John Olney made a substantial recognisance for £400 to two Londoners in 1393: *CCR, 1392–6*, 233.

sentenced to death and subject to the forfeiture of all of his lands and goods, the letter suggests some form of previous arrangement with Beauchamp. It is then all the more likely that he and Beauchamp had colluded in early January to move most of the ransom from Calais to a place of de Vere's choosing, perhaps with Beauchamp taking a cut. Why not all of it was moved is not clear; perhaps Dartasso arrived part way through a process which would have involved some considerable logistics.

In July 1388 de Vere claimed that he had still 42,000 francs left unpaid, although he said that he had lost some of the obligatory letters.[202] This was surely incorrect, as 10,000 had been received in January on top of the 78,000 in November of the original total of 120,000. However, apparently the French did not quibble with this, but the sum was bargained down to 27,600 francs (£4,370) in discussions in Paris in July 1388. The difference was an agreement made, according to Blois, under duress, of an additional 14,400 francs for his expenses while at Calais during the negotiations in 1387, which the king's uncles judging the case, the dukes of Berry and Burgundy, decided to discount but ordered the remaining sum to be paid.[203] Jones has noted a *vidimus* of November 1388 citing letters of de Vere in July 1388, renouncing any claims on 4,400 francs paid to his servants John Newton and John Lancaster and acknowledging receipt of 3,904 francs from the secretary of Oliver de Clisson.[204] Additional part payments of the remaining sum were made. 1,660 francs was paid on 1 November 1388 in Paris, while a further 6,000 francs was paid on 10 September 1389, as acknowledged by two Parisian merchants acting on de Vere's behalf.

In summary, at least 103,964 francs of the 120,000 originally agreed changed hands, and since the Appellants only apparently seized 27,907, the rest would seem to have been taken by de Vere and his servants. If this is correct, then de Vere received 76,057 francs (£12,093) of the ransom between November

---

[202] See Jones, 'Ransom', 23, and the sources in n. 4.

[203] Jones, 'Ransom', 23. Michael de la Pole was among those who gave their assent to the agreement suggesting de Vere and de la Pole were together throughout their exile until the latter's death.

[204] Jones, 'Ransom', 23–4. A box containing documents relating to the ransom was deposited in the exchequer in 1395–6 suggesting ongoing interest in what had been collected and when: *The Antient Kalendars and Inventories of the Treasury of His Majesty's Exchequer*, ed. F. Palgrave (3 vols, London, 1836), ii, 52. This was almost certainly 'les obligacions de Johan de Bloys' referred to in a letter of c. 1395 to the king's secretary by Robert Selby, treasurer of Calais, which he had brought over to England with him: *Anglo-Norman Letters and Petitions from All Souls MS. 182*, ed. M.D. Legge (Oxford, 1941), 54–5.

1387 and September 1389. There is some support for this in non-financial sources, specifically in Froissart, though clearly he did not know all the details. Froissart notes that on de Vere's arrival in Paris he had the wherewithal to live in state 'handsomely, for he had brought immense sums of money with him from England', and elsewhere added that he had 60,000 francs of the ransom waiting for him in France, with the other 60,000 as yet unpaid. He further alleged that de Vere had been depositing great sums of money at Bruges through the Lombards 'to be prepared for every event; for though he knew his power over the king of England, he was very much afraid of the nobles and the people'.[205] There is no source for this other than Froissart, and it seems most likely that Froissart may have created two great sums from the one generated by the ransom to make a rhetorical point regarding de Vere's influence over the king and his alleged enrichment at the latter's expense. However, the point regarding his lifestyle is key here to show that he had significant sums at his disposal. Nor was he apparently the only one of the exiles to have resources. While Walsingham states that Michael de la Pole left all his worldly goods to de Vere on his death in 1389, a letter by Alexander Neville the following year states that de la Pole had left him 20,000 pounds of gold to pursue a case at the papal curia.[206] As Tuck notes, even if this is taken as pounds of Paris (£4,000) or Tours (£3,000) rather than sterling, it suggests very considerable wealth, and the exiles appear to have, together, a great deal of money on which to live.[207]

These two sets of sources, the chronicler and the record evidence, are together convincing that de Vere had provided himself with money for a long time, and more so than the alternative picture painted by Walsingham and echoed by another later chronicler, John Capgrave.[208] They alleged that de Vere died in poverty in Leuven, with Walsingham adding that he lived there also in a state of mental anguish ('in mentis angustia rerumque penuria') which might be either a pleasing rhetorical device or wish-fulfilment on behalf of the Monk of St Albans.[209] The only other support for the idea of poverty comes from a pardon granted to his mother, Maud, who visited him in Leuven in 1391 and is said to have given him financial support. That she brought him money seems likely, as discussed below, but additional money to top up a fund that was

---

[205] Froissart, ed. Lettenhove, xii, 286; xiii, 99; xiv, 32; Froissart, ed. Johnes, ii, 279, 331, 408.

[206] *SAC*, i, 878–9; Haslop, 'Two Entries', 288–9.

[207] Tuck, 'Pole, Michael de la', *ODNB*.

[208] Froissart, ed. Lettenove, xii, 286; Froissart, ed. Johnes, ii, 279.

[209] *SAC*, i, 934–5; *The Chronicle of England by John Capgrave*, ed. F.C. Hingeston (RS, 1858), 254.

decreasing over time would surely have been welcome and sensible, since de Vere had to be planning for a long-term exile as a worst-case scenario. Froissart is a far more informed source for de Vere's life in exile than Walsingham, cloistered at St Albans.

Countess Maud received a pardon for crossing the sea to see her son without licence, along with two damsels and seven household servants, and for relieving him with certain gifts. The pardon to Maud was dated 10 May 1391; the same day the king granted Maud a licence to sell wood in her dower lands in Oxfordshire to the value of 400 or 500 marks 'for her better support'. The two acts are linked. Although separated by two membranes on the patent roll, the same privy seal warrant authorised both acts, separated by only a full stop.[210] The warrant notes that the licence was granted at the supplication of the countess and one might imagine this was done in person. The connection seems too much to be coincidental: Maud had provided financial gifts to de Vere and then asked the king for a pardon and to sell wood to the value of 400–500 marks. Surely this was to allow her to recoup what she had given to de Vere, which might therefore be presumed to be of the order of several hundred marks. This was a plea that Richard II would have been sympathetic to.

It was less than a year later that Richard made what was, in retrospect, his last public effort to reverse what had happened to his friend. On 15 February 1392, Richard asked a great council to overturn the banishment of de Vere and Neville. The 'temporal lords (and the ecclesiastics, too) were most emphatic in their insistence that Alexander Neville and the duke of Ireland should not be restored to their former positions and should on no account return to England to stay'.[211] The reason advanced by the lords was the need to silence popular murmurings. The lords present were the archbishops of Canterbury, York and Dublin, the dukes of Lancaster, York and Gloucester, the earls of Derby, Rutland, Arundel, Huntingdon, Devon and the earl Marshal, eight bishops, various royal officers and Aubrey de Vere, who might have been the lone voice in support of Richard's proposal. Richard was politically too weak at this stage to go against the combined will of the council, and he therefore 'graciously agreed to their demand and accepted that the banishment of the two from

---

[210] C81/525, no. 7226; C66/322, mm. 17, 19; *CPR, 1388–92*, 404, 407. The only peculiarity is the location given for the dower lands: she held none in Oxfordshire.

[211] *WC*, 484–7. The account is substantially confirmed by the minute from the council, printed in J.F. Baldwin, *The King's Council in England during the Middle Ages* (Oxford, 1913), 495. For discussion, see Saul, *Richard II*, 236, 255; Fletcher, *Richard II*, 209–10.

England should be permanent and should preclude any hope of return'.[212] Two possible explanations for this are either that Richard wanted the two to return, due to the friendship he bore de Vere especially, but the opposition was too strong, or that he wanted to make political capital out of his acceptance of the lords' veto, as the lords 'one and all expressed their deep gratitude' and 'the king was accorded full power to rule his kingdom as he pleased for all time to come'.[213] The explanations are not of course mutually exclusive.

Further evidence of Richard's continuing concern for his erstwhile friend is suggested by a letter written by the king at some point after de Vere's death. One 'Walter H' served as the duke of Ireland's cook while he was abroad, or so he said to Richard II; after the duke's death, he had lost his rents and all his goods and chattels, and because of his poverty, the king wrote to Countess Maud, asking her to grant Walter the office of keeper of her park at Bockingfield, Kent.[214] It is also perhaps suggestive that de Vere was not poor when in exile that his cook apparently had rents, goods and chattels, albeit there must have been something of a free-for-all when the duke died in exile without friends or relations present.

Death and Funeral

Robert de Vere died in Brabant on 22 November 1392, as was rehearsed in inquisitions taken in England in January and February 1393 as a result of a petition by Aubrey de Vere requesting the estates of the earldom of Oxford.[215] The manner of his death has caused some confusion. Otterbourne says that he died of injuries received in a boar hunt. Halliday argues that this may be due to a mistranslation of the family name, 'verres' being Latin for boar. However, the actual word used by Otterbourne is the more accurate 'aper' meaning wild

---

[212] *WC*, 486–7.

[213] Ibid., 486–7.

[214] *Anglo-Norman Letters*, ed. Legge, 64. Both All Souls MS 182, on which Legge's edition is based, and BL, Royal MS 10 B IX, fol. 5v which also contains a copy of the letter, only give 'Wautier H.' as the name. A Walter Helyon, a baker, was to serve de Vere in the Scottish campaign in 1385: C71/65, m. 9.

[215] *CIM, 1392–9*, 15; *CCR, 1392–6*, 43. The only hint of doubt as to the date comes from a commission issued on 5 August 1392 to investigate the values of the manors which were to revert to the crown after Maud's death because of the judgement in parliament against the late duke of Ireland. The 'late' probably refers to his forfeiture rather than his death, but it would be slightly odd timing to issue the commission otherwise: *CPR, 1391–6*, 167. August is the date used by Tuck, 'Robert de Vere', *ODNB*.

boar.[216] This then seems an unlikely confusion. It is possible, however that it was a play on a device: 'aper' is also used as a badge to describe de Vere by John Gower and the boar was certainly used later as a heraldic device by the family.[217] The only other chronicle which makes reference to his death states that de Vere 'stricken by illness, died after a short sickness'.[218] Between these two choices, it is impossible to know. He was just thirty at his death.

In death, as well as in life, Robert de Vere proved a divisive figure. The only document that has been identified that relates to de Vere in Leuven is a judgement made by the Prince-Bishop of Liège, John of Bavaria, in a dispute between St Peter's Church in Leuven and the Augustinian Friars in the city as to the rights to his burial and the associated fees.[219] St Peter's claimed he died within their parish and therefore they had the right, but that the body of the 'most illustrious and noble man, the former lord Robert duke of Ireland and earl of Oxford' had been taken by the Augustinian Friars. The Prince-Bishop ruled in favour of St Peter's Church, and his judgement was dated 5 July 1395, which can only have been a short time before the body was moved back to England, as he was reburied at Earls Colne on 22 November. It is possible that Richard II had already requested the body be moved and this brought the dispute to a head, given it had been more than two and a half years since de Vere's death. Regardless, the award in the dispute provides evidence for several aspects of the last phase of de Vere's life. It supports Froissart's evidence that he had settled in Leuven and lived there; St Peter's Church is right in the centre of the city. The fact that two religious institutions were squabbling over the rights to his burial, and that a fine of 1,000 silver marks was to be paid, strongly suggests that de Vere died in wealth rather in poverty. The document also notes that Sir John Lancaster was in the city in 1395 and clearly he seems

---

[216] Otterbourne, 'Chronicum Rerum Angliae', 181 ('percussus ab apro dum venaretur')

[217] *Political Poems and Songs*, ed. T. Wright (2 vols, RS, 14, London, 1859), i, 420; Gower, *Poems on Contemporary Events*, 255.

[218] 'Kirkstall Abbey Chronicles', ed. Taylor, 70.

[219] Rijksarchief Leuven, Archive of Saint Peter's Chapel, 1273/834, on which most of this paragraph is based. This document is discussed in Greatorex, *Robert de Vere*, 15–16 and is an excellent find. I am grateful to the Rijksarchief Leuven for supplying an image of the document and I have worked from this rather than the partial translation in Greatorex, 15–16. The latter unfortunately misidentifies Sir John de Lancaster as John of Gaunt. For a similar dispute over mortuary fees and the canonical fourth in the case of the burial of Edmund of Langley, see R.N. Swanson, 'An Ambivalent "First Yorkist": Edmund of Langley, Duke of York (d. 1402), in C. M. Barron and C. Steer, eds, *The Ricardian XXXIII. Yorkist People: Essays in Memory of Anne F. Sutton* (2023), 23–34.

to have been the man responsible for managing de Vere's affairs after his death. The document associates him with the Augustinian Friars – the losing side – and one wonders if this indicates that de Vere indicated a preference for the Friars for his burial (perhaps on his deathbed) and Lancaster was trying to carry out his wishes. While this is thoroughly speculative, it would connect with his use of friars as confessors during his lifetime.[220]

Shortly after de Vere's death, his uncle and heir male, Aubrey, petitioned for the earldom of Oxford and those of its estates to which he thought he was entitled through entails, which Richard II granted.[221] Most of these had been granted to Countess Maud by July 1388 at an annual farm of £310, later reduced to £217 p.a. because of annuities assigned on them.[222] Although Aubrey had been ordered to abjure the court in the Merciless Parliament of 1388, his record of service to the king and to the Black Prince – noted in the king's response to his petition – made him a less objectionable figure than de Vere to the Appellants and John of Gaunt. Despite his expulsion from court, Aubrey seems to have been at a royal council meeting as early as July 1388 in Oxford, where advice about a truce with the duke of Burgundy was given by a number of named councillors, including Aubrey.[223] He was certainly in sufficient favour to attend the royal council in February 1392 about his nephew's restoration. The response to the parliamentary petition after the latter's death stated that Richard was not obliged to restore the earldom as opposed to the estates – an entail meant that many of the estates should have descended to Aubrey legally at Robert de Vere's death as his heir male – but that the grant of the title was an act of grace.[224] Despite Aubrey's restoration to the earldom, many estates were lost to the family as a result of Robert's forfeiture, and a further raft were lost as a result of the actions of Countess Maud, with whom Aubrey had poor relations.[225] It was thus a weakened and shrunken earldom for the next forty years under Aubrey and his son Richard, the eleventh earl, and it was not until

---

[220] See below, p. 218.

[221] SC8/178/8874, though largely illegible; Aubrey's claims and the final concords on which those claims were based are set out in *CIM, 1392–9*, 14–15; *PROME*, vii, 230–1.

[222] *CFR, 1383–91*, 242; BL, Cotton Vespasian F XIII, no. 27; *CPR, 1388–92*, 117, 151. Expenses for valuing and extending the duke of Ireland's lands in Essex and Suffolk in 1388 by John Dautre and John Marcoll can be found in E364/21, rot. 4d.

[223] *CPR, 1385–9*, 502.

[224] *PROME*, vii, 230–1.

[225] For her partial dispersal of her dower and jointure estates and deteriorating financial position, see Ross, 'A Rich Old Lady Getting Poorer' (forthcoming).

the 1430s, after the twelfth earl married a very substantial heiress, that the landed estates of the earldom again reached the levels of the 1370s and 1380s.[226]

Philippa, always known as the duchess of Ireland, was by her husband's forfeiture not entitled to dower from his estates but was financially secure. Her parents' lands in England were enfeoffed to her use as early as 25 March 1388 after a petition in parliament, the annuity of 100 marks a year granted by de Vere was confirmed in October 1389, and on 21 August 1395 she was granted an annuity of 300 marks a year from the exchequer.[227] Occasional other grants from Richard followed, including the castle and manor of Moor End in Northamptonshire.[228] Her father wrote to her in 1389 asking about her welfare after de Vere's downfall and they met during peace negotiations at Amiens in 1392.[229] On the reversal of de Vere's forfeiture in 1397, she became entitled to dower and in 1398 an agreement was made with Aubrey. However, the large proportion of the estates of the earldom in Maud's hands meant Philippa's portion was limited to just three whole manors, a third each of two further manors and a rent, in total valued in her inquisition *post mortem* at just £107 6s 8d.[230] She was always treated with respect and played a role at courtly events, such as the arrival of Queen Joan of Navarre in 1401.[231] She did not outlive her mother-in-law, dying in September 1411 aged forty-four.

The postscript to Robert de Vere's death came in 1395, when Richard ordered his body to be brought from Leuven and to be reburied at the de Vere family mausoleum at Earls Colne Priory in Essex, the ceremony taking place on 22 November. Richard himself attended the event and indeed spent the huge sum of £233 6s 8d on the 'costs and expenses made about the exequies of Robert late duke of Ireland' as well as £58 5s 1½d in gifts and charity.[232] Walsingham states that the king, the dowager countess of Oxford,

---

[226] Ross, 'De Vere Earls', 25–30; Ross, *John de Vere*, 22–5.

[227] *CPR, 1385–9*, 423; *CPR, 1388–92*, 117; *CPR, 1391–6*, 620, 667; *PPC*, i, 12b, 89.

[228] *CPR, 1399–1401*, 273.

[229] *Foedera*, ed. Rymer, vii, 636; Green, *Lives of the Princesses*, iii, 227.

[230] *CCR, 1396–9*, 324; *CIM, 1392–9*, 14; *CIPM*, xix, nos 991–2. The right to dower was removed by the reimposition of the sentence of forfeiture under Henry IV in 1399, and it was not until the parliament of 1401 that she regained it by Henry's grant: C.D. Ross, 'Forfeiture for Treason in the Reign of Richard II', *EHR*, 71 (1956), 561–2n, 568–9; *PROME*, viii, 112–13. Under the aegis of parliament, she made an agreement with Earl Richard when he came of age in 1406: *CPR, 1405–8*, 297, 299, 311, 314; *PROME*, viii, 377.

[231] *PPC*, i, 132, 136.

[232] E403/554, m.12.

the archbishop of Canterbury, and many bishops, abbots, priors and other ecclesiastics were present but few temporal lords, 'for the hatred which they had conceived for him had not yet dissipated'.[233] This may be true, but no other source mentions this, and given Walsingham's unrelenting hostility to de Vere, the statement should be taken with caution. It is also interesting that the chronicler does not mention Philippa being in attendance, suggesting she had, unsurprisingly, not forgiven his scandalous treatment of her in 1387. Famously in Walsingham's account, Richard had the coffin, in which de Vere's embalmed body lay, opened so that 'he could gaze upon the earl's face and touch his fingers, which men say, were adorned with precious gold rings to be interred with his body'.[234] The latest version of the manuscripts, dating from after Richard's deposition and death, use the Latin verb 'tractare', to touch.[235] However, the version printed in the *SAC* uses the verb 'contrectare'. While this can mean touch – and was translated as that by the editors – it can also be used figuratively to mean 'consider', which seems in some way more likely, not least as 'considerare' was used two words earlier as Walsingham described Richard considering de Vere's face, and thus a synonym would be needed. Such an alternative reading would suggest that Richard was looking at the rings rather than stroking the fingers of a corpse three years dead – in most ways more likely. Walsingham's purpose in the passage is explicit in the next sentence, when he describes the king as showing his 'affection publicly for the dead man, as he had shown previously for him when alive'.[236] By strengthening his language in the touching of the corpse in the later versions of his manuscript, Walsingham was thus further denigrating Richard's character.

De Vere's tomb no longer survives. Earls Colne Priory was suppressed at the dissolution, but most of the de Vere tombs remained in the parish church, where they were in a poor state when visited by John Weever prior to 1631 and Daniel King in 1653, the latter making drawings of a number of them. Weever

---

[233] *SAC*, ii, 31.

[234] Ibid., ii, 31.

[235] *Historia Anglicana*, ed. Riley, ii, 219. This text is the Short Chronicle, probably dating originally from the mid- to late 1390s taken from Corpus Christi College Cambridge, MS 7, a manuscript dating from the early fifteenth century (*SAC*, i, lx-vii) but with later alterations. The *SAC* uses Bodley 462, also early fifteenth century (ibid., ii, xxvi–xxix), but perhaps composed in sections and therefore the 1395 entry may well have been composed before 1400. I am obliged to Dr Chris Fletcher for bringing the difference in Latin vocabulary to my attention. The episode has also been discussed by Stow, 'Richard II in Thomas Walsingham's Chronicles', 91.

[236] *SAC*, ii, 31.

describes briefly seven surviving tombs of male earls of Oxford (thirteen of the fourteen pre-reformation earls were buried there), but none seem likely to have been those of Robert de Vere. Though his father's tomb did survive, that of Robert appears to have been an early casualty of the dissolution of the priory and therefore no clue remains as to its form and imagery.[237]

---

[237] For a detailed description of the priory, the tombs and their subsequent history, see Fairweather, 'Colne Priory', esp. 289–91.

6

Affinity, Regional Influence and Lifestyle

'A coronet containing ninety pearls, five sapphires and five rubies',
priced at £300

(Item seized from Robert de Vere's goods after Radcot Bridge,
TNA, E401/570, under entry of 2 March 1388)

Local Influence in East Anglia, Officials and Associates

It was more than ten years after his father's death that de Vere reached his majority. As so often, this meant the dissolution of considerable elements of his father's affinity and connections. While some of Earl Thomas's household would have remained in the service of his widow, she continued to need household service throughout her son's lifetime and it is not likely many transferred to the household of her son; others would have dispersed into different employment. De Vere's household would have needed to be built from scratch in the years after 1380. Likewise, there was no guarantee that estate officers would remain unchanged through the minority, although the fact that the bulk of his familial estates were in the hands of two Essex landowners, Sir Thomas Tyrell and John James, might have allowed a little more continuity amongst the officers. Earl Thomas's more senior gentry connections were also likely to have either sought connections with other magnates in the intervening decade or not to need a direct patron. Thus, while there were traditions of service and residual connections in Essex in particular for de Vere to build from, a full reconstruction of an appropriate comital following would have been needed after a decade of minority and in the face of a wide variety of possible competitors for lordship.

There was considerable choice for those gentry seeking lordship in Essex and southern Suffolk where the bulk of the de Vere estates lay.[1] Walter, Lord Fitzwalter, primarily resident at Woodham Walter in central Essex, provided experience, if lesser wealth and status than an earl of Oxford, having served on a string of military expeditions since the late 1360s, mainly under Thomas of Woodstock and John of Gaunt, and it was under the latter's command that he

---

[1] C. Starr, 'The Essex Gentry 1381–1450' (unpublished PhD, University of Leicester, 1999), 56–8, 394–6.

died in Spain in 1386.[2] John Bourgchier, second Lord Bourgchier, was another experienced soldier with a military record stretching back to at least 1355. The family's primary residence at Halstead was less than five miles from the de Vere *caput honoris* at Castle Hedingham, although, like Fitzwalter, in normal circumstances Bourgchier would not have been in position to rival a de Vere earl of Oxford.[3] The most formidable alternative to de Vere lordship in the region was offered by Thomas of Woodstock, earl of Buckingham and from 1385 duke of Gloucester. Some seven years older than de Vere, Gloucester's formidability was in part because of his royal blood, political prominence and military experience, albeit the latter had not been conspicuously successful. However, he had acquired half of the estates of the Bohun earls of Hereford and Essex through marriage to Eleanor, co-heiress of the last Bohun earl. The Bohuns had been the other major magnate family in Essex for more than a century, though there is little evidence of earlier overt rivalry with the de Veres. Thomas of Woodstock had acquired the Bohun seat of Pleshey in Essex, but it is worth noting that he did not have extensive landholdings in the county – though he would have received more had he outlived his mother-in-law, Joan, countess of Hereford – and he was in part dependent on exchequer annuities rather than land to maintain his status. This must have hampered any effort to dominate the county or region.[4]

It is worth emphasising that the senior gentry in Essex had many connections with the resident peerage and care must be taken not to overstate their independence from the nobility. Ward's survey of the county community notes the followings of several of the major peerage families, while Starr's thesis on the Essex gentry posits an interlocking set of relationships, horizontal and vertical, between gentry, nobility and crown.[5] However, in the absence of evidence of a retinue roll or list of annuities paid by Robert de Vere or Thomas of Woodstock it is likely that the number and significance of the connections between magnates and gentry have been underestimated. Why should de Vere and Thomas of Woodstock have been unable to match Edward Courtenay, earl of Devon, who distributed his livery to seven knights and forty esquires, both retainers and members of the household, in 1384–5?[6] The earls of Devon were no richer than the de Veres or Duke Thomas, though they did have undisputed dominance of a county.

[2] *CP*, v, 477–80.
[3] *CP*, ii, 247; M. Jones, 'The Fortunes of War: the Military Career of John, second lord Bourchier (d.1400)', *EAH*, 3rd series, 26 (1995), 145–61.
[4] A. Tuck, 'Thomas [Thomas of Woodstock], duke of Gloucester', *ODNB*; Saul, *Richard II*, 178–9.
[5] J. Ward, *The Essex Gentry and the County Community in the Fourteenth Century* (Chelmsford, 1991), 17–19; Starr, 'Essex Gentry', ch. 3.
[6] Given-Wilson, *English Nobility*, 88–9.

Counties were important in terms of administration but not necessarily for lordship and landholding, particularly when there was little to distinguish between either side of a county boundary in terms of geography or tenurial differences. De Vere interests straddled both northern Essex and southern Suffolk.[7] Lordship in Suffolk was equally fragmented, with a chronological gap between the death of the last Ufford, earl of Suffolk in February 1382, and the rise of Michael de la Pole, who acquired the title and some of the Ufford estates in autumn 1385, but never fully established himself as a local leader before his fall. Thomas Mowbray, earl Marshal and earl of Nottingham was heir to the great estates of his grandmother, Margaret of Brotherton, in Suffolk and Norfolk, with its centre at the castle of Framlingham. However, he also faced the problem of building his retinue while many estates were in the hand of an elderly female relative and did not exercise a great deal of influence in Suffolk during the 1380s, despite receiving livery of his estates in 1383 when only seventeen.[8]

The fluid situation of lordship in the region would have given de Vere opportunities to build an effective following if he had been focussed on his locality and primarily resident there, as most of his predecessors had been. His landed base was potentially greater than any of the other magnate families in the region, albeit Mowbray's prospects in terms of landed estates across England as a whole outstripped his. However, unlike almost any earlier earls of Oxford, his interests – both landed and political – were notably wider than his family's traditional area of Essex, southern Suffolk and eastern Cambridgeshire. De Vere grew up at court or close to it with Isabella, countess of Bedford, he continued to spend plenty of time there from his majority onwards, and from 1385 his interests were enormously diversified with grants of lands in the West Country and Ireland and office in Cheshire. His comparative lack of interest in familial heartlands is reinforced through what can be reconstructed of his itinerary between 1385 and 1387 in the Appendix. While inherently predisposed towards his courtly activities as a result of the source material on which it has to be based – royal documents and chronicles – de Vere cannot be placed in East Anglia on a single occasion during those years. It was extremely hard for any peer to build and maintain a local following if he was not generally resident in the locality.

De Vere's East Anglian interests did not suffer directly from his increasing absence at court in the first year or two of his majority, with very little evidence

---

[7] See Map 1, above, p. xvi.

[8] R.E. Archer, 'The Estates and Finances of Margaret of Brotherton, c. 1320–1399', *Historical Research*, 60 (1987), 264–80; eadem, 'The Mowbrays, Earls of Nottingham and Dukes of Norfolk to 1432' (unpublished DPhil, University of Oxford, 1984). For discussion of local government in Norfolk and Suffolk, see R. Virgoe, 'The Crown and Local Government: East Anglia under Richard II', in F.R.H. Du Boulay and C.M. Barron, eds, *The Reign of Richard II* (London, 1971), 218–41.

for local problems among the legal records. Only two cases can be traced. The first, although pleaded in Hilary term 1387, dated to July 1382 when two men were accused by the duke's attorney, Henry Oundle, of breaking into his park at Castle Camps, Cambridgeshire, and taking away eight deer – the duke claimed damages of £100. The defendants, a chaplain, and one Walter Ongre from nearby Linton, defended themselves in part by claiming that it was not the duke's park at the time, he being underage and the manor being in the custody of the crown.[9] De Vere's attorney denied this but there was some legality to the defendants' case as, while he had been appointed to commissions and given grants of lands and office from 1381 onwards, he was not given formal seisin of his estates, including Camps, until March 1383.[10] The case was of sufficient legal interest to be discussed in the Year Books, although no verdict can be found. The other case occurred in Easter term 1384, when de Vere alleged that eight Suffolk men had broken his close and house at his manor of Cockfield, Suffolk, and taken away goods and chattels worth £20.[11] Both were of the type suffered by landowners throughout the later Middle Ages and neither were serious – as indicated by the former taking five years to be brought in court. There is little other evidence that has been found of any local disorder or attacks on his property in the south-east.

What then of de Vere's local influence? Of the twenty manors of his own inheritance that he held from 1383 onwards, fifteen were in Essex, and it might be expected that he would have played a leading role in the affairs of this county. Certainly, before the great grants after 1385 he can occasionally be seen to be active on a local level. In response to a commission issued in July 1382 concerning a dispute over the manor of Bradwell in Essex, he personally sat with his fellow commissioners in judgement at his mother's residence of Earl's Colne, only a few miles away from the disputed property.[12] Given he was not yet formally of age, this is an interesting early example of de Vere looking to exert his local lordship: one of the parties in the case was John Coggeshall, a member of a family with whom de Vere had connections. There were also a

---

[9] CP40/504, rot. 402; *Year Books of Richard II. 8–10 Richard II, 1385–7*, eds L.C. Hector and M.J. Hager (Year Books Series, 4, Ames Foundation, 1987), 320–3.

[10] *CCR, 1381–5*, 254.

[11] CP40/493, rot. 54d. The sheriff was unable to apprehend these men, and the case was postponed until the octaves of Trinity.

[12] KB27/486, rex rot. 16. The initial commission was on 11 April 1382 and included a number of men not named in the later commission, including his uncle Aubrey de Vere and Sir Simon Burley; *CPR, 1381–5*, 136, 196, and see for the continuing case 198, 199, 244, 478.

number of other commissions to Oxford while under age, though alongside other magnates, such as Thomas of Woodstock.[13]

After 1385 almost uniquely for a de Vere, Robert's local activities went well beyond the East Anglian framework of his predecessors, so much so in fact that when the crisis point of the clash with the Lords Appellant came, he found himself leading Cestrians against men from his heartland of Essex. This can be evidenced by looking at some of the men who can be identified as being closely connected with de Vere by 1385, and who could be confidently described as belonging to his affinity. Few of these men were from his familial region. Sir John de Lancaster was, despite the name, from Wiltshire. In October 1383 de Vere mainperned for the good behaviour of Lancaster in the office of sheriff of Wiltshire, which he was granted for life, though he was eventually replaced in 1385.[14] While the grant of the shrievalty has been linked to de Vere's influence and Lancaster identified as de Vere's chamberlain,[15] the first known connection between the two was de Vere acting as mainpernor in 1383, and he is not known to have served as de Vere's chamberlain until Christmas 1386, though it is possible he held the office earlier.[16] It is therefore rather unclear if the grant was through de Vere's influence. However, by 1385 Lancaster was de Vere's feoffee, and also had connections with Aubrey de Vere.[17] He served under the earl in Scotland in 1385 and mustered his retinue of twenty men-at-arms and sixty archers for transport to Ireland in June 1386.[18] He was also one of the duke's ambassadors for the ransom of John of Blois at Calais in November 1387; this could well have meant he missed Radcot Bridge. However, there were other consequences as a result of his close connection with the duke, as after de Vere's fall he was ordered to abjure the court. He shared de Vere's exile and in December 1388 a payment of 100s was made to Joan, his wife, in England to relieve her state and a more generous one of £20 in the following

---

[13] For the commissions concerning the aftermath of the 1381 revolt, see above, pp. 75–6 and also *CPR, 1381–5*, 134, 246, 253.

[14] *CFR, 1383–91*, 6, 101; see also *CPR, 1381–5*, 554, 589.

[15] See for example, Tuck, *Richard II*, 61; Gundy, *Rebel Earl*, 108, n. 36.

[16] SC1/43/80 is a letter by Lancaster to the clerks of the royal chancery asking for his master's fees that were due. These are likely to have included the fees from de Vere's office as great chamberlain, which were later recorded as £10 13s 4d for robes and 20m for the fee for the office: *Black Book*, ed. Myers, 101. The letter is dated from Berkhamsted on St Stephen's Day but no year is given. It must date from after de Vere's promotion to duke of Ireland in October 1386 but it is unlikely to be 26 December 1387 as de Vere had lost the battle of Radcot Bridge a few days earlier. However, de Vere was not granted the manor of Berkhamsted until November 1387, so perhaps he had use of it earlier or was staying there.

[17] *CPR, 1381–5*, 526, 556; *CCR, 1385–9*, 55.

[18] C71/64, m. 2; *CPR, 1385–9*, 163.

February noting John's adherence to the duke of Ireland.[19] A petition asking for his pardon was granted in January 1393 in parliament noting that the 'said John was overseas with Robert de Vere lately duke of Ireland, for the whole life of the said Robert' subsequent to the judgement in parliament against the duke.[20] The pardon was for a suit of the peace 'for evil governance and counsel about the person of our lord the king', and for all manner of treasons and offences.[21] Quite what had happened to Lancaster is unclear, as an entry in the Issue Rolls in December 1393 noted a payment of £50 related to the ransom of Lancaster, who was still, and had been for a long time, a prisoner in France. This seems to have released him, but he was still abroad, in a wretched state, in Paris in April 1396, though this was possibly on royal business, chasing up whatever remained of the Blois ransom, as he had been in correspondence with John of Blois.[22]

Sir John de Routh was a Yorkshire landowner and may have become connected with de Vere through the administration of the latter's de Coucy estates. He was described as the earl of Oxford's esquire in January 1385 when he was granted, at the supplication of the earl, the wardship and marriage of the heir of William Lylle of Sussex, worth 20 marks a year. After being knighted by February 1386, and appointed to provide horses for the Irish expedition, he was granted by de Vere in September the manor of Cockfield in Suffolk for life, worth £22 annually, rendering reasonable wages for six grooms for de Vere's stable.[23] Despite his possible presence at Radcot Bridge, he survived de Vere's fall with his career unscathed and twice sat as an MP for Yorkshire in 1394 and 1404.[24] He was forced to petition the king in 1390 for the manor of Cockfield, then occupied by Countess Maud. This may have been because the grant to Countess Maud of the farm of her son's estates after his fall merely noted a grant by patent of the duke of Ireland to Routh of £22 annually rather than the manor itself.[25] The countess fought Routh's restitution in the courts but lost.[26]

[19] E403/521, m. 11, 19. She had in March 1388 successfully petitioned for her husband's goods then in the keeping of the mayor of London, and worth £19 7s 8d: *CCR, 1385–9*, 380.

[20] *PROME*, vii, 230.

[21] *PROME*, vii, 231; *Preuves*, ed. Morice, ii, 529; *WC*, 301.

[22] E403/546, m. 16; *Anglo-Norman Letters*, ed. Legge, 66–7.

[23] *CPR, 1381–5*, 516; *1385–9*, 16, 248, 275; *CIM, 1387–93*, 41; E359/9, rot. 40. For his lands, see *CChR*, v, 301 (C81/492, no. 3920).

[24] *HoC*, iv, 239–41.

[25] SC8/250/12489; *PPC*, i, 89. It was also described as a grant of £22 by patent in a successful petition by Countess Maud for a reduction in the farm of de Vere's lands in a petition of c. 1389: BL, Cotton Vespasian F XIII, no. 27.

[26] The legal process is described in *CCR, 1389–92*, 267–8.

Only Henry English among de Vere's close circle was from East Anglia. Through his wife, Margaret, widow of Sir John Waweton, he had acquired land and rent in Steeple Bumpstead and Helions Bumpstead, both owned by the de Veres, and it may have been through this feudal tenancy that he came into the de Vere orbit, though his general landed interests in Cambridgeshire, southern Suffolk and northern Essex coincided with the territorial heartland of the de Vere family. He was already an experienced administrator in local government, having served as sheriff of Cambridgeshire in 1380–1 and 1384–5, and MP for that county in 1373, 1377, 1383 (October), 1384 (November) and later in 1390. He had acted in a Cambridgeshire property transaction with Aubrey de Vere in 1381 and in 1385 he was pardoned for the escape of felons during his shrievalty at the supplication of the countess of Oxford (though it is not specified whether that was Maud or Philippa).[27] He was the earl's feoffee in 1385, and together with John Bole, one of the duke's auditors, and others, received the profits of Colchester Castle and Tendring hundred from October 1386 to March 1388, and probably also of the manors of Great Canfield and Stansted Mountfitchet on de Vere's behalf.[28] He was the earl's steward, probably for all his Essex manors.[29] He was surprisingly appointed sheriff of Essex in 1389 immediately after de Vere's fall and then as escheator between 1390 and 1392.[30]

There were, of course, other connections amongst the Essex gentry, but it is perhaps striking that the more important of these gentry did not become too closely associated with de Vere. Perhaps the most prominent was Sir William Coggeshall. Eldest son and heir of Sir Henry Coggeshall, he was four years older than de Vere, and in a position to become one of the most prominent members of the Essex gentry; this promise he later fulfilled, being elected ten times as knight of the shire for the county between 1391 and 1422, and probably the richest member of the gentry in that county.[31] The biography of Coggeshall in the *History of Parliament* volumes states that by 1382 he had attached himself to Robert de Vere, but it is not clear from the sources mentioned there on what

---

[27] *HoC*, iii, 27–9; *CPR, 1381–5*, 573; C66/321, m. 22d.; C81/1345, no. 16; *CIPM, 1392–7*, 145 (though incomplete).

[28] *CPR, 1381–5*, 556; *CIM, 1387–93*, nos 116–17. No. 117 is fragmentary but it does seem as if he was acting as a receiver for these manors, one of which, Great Canfield, had been enfeoffed to him. See also Ward, *Essex Gentry*, 4.

[29] He certainly held the view of frankpledge at the manor of Stansted Mountfitchet in July 1386: JUST3/164, rot. 50.

[30] One Robert Brom was accused of lying in wait to kill him during his shrievalty, though this was less likely a result of English's political choices than of Brom's career as a serial criminal: *CPR, 1391–6*, 267.

[31] Starr, 'Essex Gentry', 55, 359–60.

grounds that date can be attributed, though he acted as a witness for Aubrey de Vere acquiring property in 1383.[32] It is correct in noting, however, that de Vere was clearly acting in a patronal capacity in 1384 when he paid the fee of five marks due to the hanaper for a royal licence for Coggeshall to enfeoff his estates. Oxford was appointed one of his feoffees, alongside Walter, Lord Fitzwalter, John Hawkwood the elder, John Doreward and others.[33] As has already been discussed, it was alleged that in the same year de Vere acted illegally in maintaining Coggeshall in his quarrel with Walter Sibille over land at Exning in Suffolk.[34] Even if the allegations were true – and the analysis offered above questions this – one man's maintenance was another's good lordship, and this may have been a rare example of de Vere acting forcefully on behalf of a member of his affinity. However, even these actions were not sufficient to bring Coggeshall fully into his orbit. He maintained connections with Walter, Lord Fitzwalter, who was closely associated with Thomas, duke of Gloucester, and by June 1388 at the latest, and perhaps earlier, with John, Lord Cobham, another supporter of the Appellants. There is certainly no suggestion that Coggeshall turned out to support de Vere at Radcot Bridge, despite his military experience amongst the *condottieri* in Italy, where he served in the White Company with Sir John Hawkwood. Certainly, William's uncle, Thomas Coggeshall, was standing with Thomas of Woodstock against de Vere at Radcot Bridge.[35]

A noncommittal attitude, similar to that of Coggeshall, was adopted by John Doreward, another wealthy member of the Essex gentry. He was still relatively early in his career in the 1380s, a career that would later lead to him twice becoming speaker of the House of Commons. Doreward was closely connected to the Coggeshall family, later marrying Sir William's daughter, and it was this connection that saw William make both Robert de Vere and Doreward feoffees of land in Essex and Cambridgeshire in June 1384.[36] De Vere proved useful to Doreward, as, at the former's instance, the king ratified the descent of the manor of Rawreth to the latter on 22 May 1386.[37] However, despite these promising beginnings, there is no evidence that de Vere was able

---

[32] *HoC*, ii, 617, and see 616–18 on which most of this paragraph is based. For Aubrey, *CCR, 1381–5*, 385.

[33] *CPR, 1381–5*, 433.

[34] See above, pp. 101–3.

[35] *HoC*, ii, 614–16.

[36] *CPR, 1381–5*, 433.

[37] *CPR, 1385–9*, 150.

to draw Doreward into the inner circles of his affinity and by 1387 he was also connected with the following of Thomas of Woodstock.[38]

Another Essex family that managed to balance the hostility between the two leading magnates in the county were the Feribys. Thomas Feriby, a clerk, was the chancellor of the duke of Gloucester, while Robert Feriby was, by the later 1380s, steward of the household of de Vere's mother, Countess Maud, and farmed her manor of Lavenham Netherhall in Suffolk between 1386 and 1388.[39] Yet another member of the gentry served both Countess Maud and an Appellant lord, though in this case he was Sir Peter Buckton, a Yorkshire knight. Buckton had long connections with John of Gaunt and was steward of Henry of Bolingbroke's household by 1390. He is named, however, as farmer of the countess of Oxford's Essex manors of Wrabness and Ramsey, and perhaps as officer of the countess's estates in 1386–8. While this connection seems unlikely, it would make sense as to why he was appointed to survey the countess's confiscated estates after her seditious activities in 1404.[40] Sir Roger Drury was another East Anglian with whom early connections with de Vere did not lead to fruitful support and indeed in this case almost the opposite. He mustered eighty men to serve de Vere in Ireland in June 1386, and there is no reason to suppose he did not go, but if he did he must have returned promptly as he served the earl of Arundel in the naval expedition of March 1387 and he supported the Appellants at Radcot Bridge in December of that year. Drury ought to have been a natural member of a de Vere affinity – his primary landholdings were in the liberty of Bury St Edmunds where the de Vere lordship of Lavenham and other holdings made the earls of Oxford the leading lay landholders – and he was Robert de Vere's distant relative by marriage, as his wife was descended from the sixth earl of Oxford. However, he was to serve against de Vere at the moment of crisis.[41]

An indication of de Vere's limited East Anglia connections – and strong courtly ones – can be seen in the enfeoffment he made of the core of his estates in June 1385 before the expedition to Scotland.[42] His feoffees were the bishops of Winchester and Worcester, Hugh, earl of Stafford, Sir Simon Burley, Sir Robert

[38] *HoC*, ii, 790.

[39] *HoC*, ii, 790; BL, Harleian Roll N3, passim. An Agnes Feriby sued Maud for £69 as late as 1412: CP40/605, rot. 55. A Robert Feriby was an esquire of the earl of Huntingdon by 1391; it is not clear whether this was the same man: *CPR, 1388–92*, 418; *1391–6*, 31, 46, 131. For Thomas, see *CPR, 1388–92*, 375; *CCR, 1389–92*, 497.

[40] BL, Harleian Roll N3, mm. 1, 3; Ross, 'Seditious Activities', 34. For his career, see *HoC*, ii, 404–7.

[41] *CPR, 1385–9*, 157; *HoC*, ii, 803–4.

[42] *CPR, 1381–5*, 556; SC8/255/12738. For details of the estates, see above, p. 105.

Tresilian, John Lancaster, Henry English, Walter de Skirlawe, keeper of the Privy Seal, and three clerks, Richard Medford, Nicholas Slake and John Ripon. Of the three clerks, two were striking in being very well connected at court. Medford and Slake were both clerks of the chapel royal (from 1375 and 1380 respectively) and were increasingly senior in royal service. Slake was by 1388 dean of the chapel royal and Walsingham described Richard turning to him for advice at the Salisbury Parliament of 1384 when a friar accused Gaunt of treason.[43] Slake witnessed de Vere's grant of an annuity of £100 to John Beauchamp of Holt in October 1387; his fellow witness was Richard Clifford, another clerk of the king, and later keeper of the Great Wardrobe.[44] Medford was the king's secretary from June 1385 and intimately involved in Richard's use of the signet as an instrument of government.[45] De Vere's feoffees, in fact, represented most of the really influential men at the centre of government: Burley was chamberlain of the household, Skirlawe the keeper of the privy seal, Tresilian the chief justice of King's Bench and Medford the king's secretary. In some ways this should not surprise: the point of an enfeoffment was to include men who could look after the estates for the purposes specified by the feoffor, and little adverse to de Vere's interests would get past these men. Perhaps only Michael de la Pole, the chancellor, matched these men in influence, and his absence is slightly surprising; that he was older than de Vere would not appear to be a reason, as Simon Burley was of a similar age to de la Pole but was included.

The earl of Stafford and the bishops of Winchester (William of Wykeham) and Worcester (Henry Wakefield) were all interesting choices as feoffees, as none were particularly closely linked to de Vere otherwise. Wykeham, former chancellor of England and a regular member of the royal council during Richard II's minority, was experienced and influential, but was very short to become closely associated with the opposition to Richard's government. He was a critic in the parliament of 1385, served on the commission of 1386, and was ultimately a 'firm, though discreet, supporter of the lords appellant'.[46] Wakefield, briefly treasurer of England in 1377, and bishop of Worcester since 1375, was a more surprising choice as he was not much as court during Richard II's reign and seems to have mainly been involved in his diocese, which was a long way from

---

[43] Saul, *Richard II*, 125–6; Given-Wilson, *Royal Household*, 175–6, notes that if Slake was indeed dean of the chapel royal as Walsingham describes him, it was only a very recent elevation: *SAC*, i, 722.

[44] C66/324, m. 11; J.L. Leland, 'Unpardonable Sinners? Exclusions from the General Pardon of 1388', *Medieval Prosopography*, 17 (1996), 183–4, 186–7.

[45] Saul, *Richard II*, 125–6; B. Golding, 'Medford [Mitford], Richard (d. 1407), *ODNB*.

[46] P. Partner, 'Wykeham, William', *ODNB*.

de Vere's heartland.⁴⁷ Hugh, second earl of Stafford, was twenty years older than de Vere, and while well connected with Gaunt, was not particularly close to Richard II, though his ill-fated eldest son Ralph (killed only a few weeks after the enfeoffment) was, and therein may lie the connection. Perhaps de Vere and Ralph were closer than has been realised, friends rather than rivals for the king's favour. Nonetheless, the lack of a politically aligned magnate – Michael de la Pole or Thomas Mowbray, earl of Nottingham, for example – is striking. The inclusion of the two retainers, Lancaster and English, is in itself unremarkable, as they may well have been expected to do most of the day-to-day administration of the estates if de Vere had died on the expedition. However, there was also a striking lack of East Anglia landowners – only Henry English was from the region – thus reinforcing the point that increasingly de Vere's associations were at court rather than in the traditional area of de Vere influence, and it was a very loyalist, royalist, group of feoffees.

It is hard to adduce much about another avenue to local influence, his relations with religious houses in the region. The de Vere family were patrons of several, notably the priory at Earls Colne, but also the priories of Hatfield Broad Oak and Thremhall, and the nunnery at Castle Hedingham, and it might be presumed that in the absence of evidence of conflict that these houses were on good terms with the representative of the founder family.⁴⁸ The manor of Earls Colne, with its mansion, however, was in the hands of Countess Maud, and the priory there was thus at one remove from de Vere. Meanwhile, the richest house in Essex (and fourth wealthiest in the country by the date of the Dissolution), St John's Colchester, was under the rule of Abbot Geoffrey Storey, who during Henry IV's reign proved so loyal to Richard II's memory that he went into rebellion with Countess Maud on Richard's behalf. However, to read back events nearly twenty years later into the mid-1380s and assume political alignment between the abbot and the earl would be dangerous.⁴⁹

So limited had de Vere's influence in his heartland become that as both sides began to recruit for the coming struggle in the late summer and autumn of 1387, the king

> sent into Essex, Cambridgeshire, Norfolk and Suffolk a serjeant at mace, who was commissioned to cause the more substantial and influential inhabitants of those counties to swear that to the exclusion of all other lords whatsoever they would hold with him as their true king, and they were to

---

⁴⁷ R.G. Davies, revised, 'Wakefield, Henry', *ODNB*.

⁴⁸ *Registrum Simonis de Sudbiria*, ed. Fowler, i, 86–8 (Thremhall), 89–93 (Hatfield), 163 (Earls Colne).

⁴⁹ *Victoria County History Essex*, ii, 96–7, 103–4.

be given badges… with the intention that whenever they were called upon to do so they should join the king, armed and ready.[50]

It would normally have been expected that de Vere would raise his home county, or elements of political society there, and this would have been considerably more effective than the serjeant, who was arrested without having achieved much. However, de Vere was, in the second half of 1387, focused on Cheshire. Roger Virgoe has noted that there was little concerted effort to fill key offices in Norfolk and Suffolk with royal allies in the mid-1380s as political tensions heightened.[51] Nor does it seem that the two family members primarily resident in Essex were able to bolster de Vere's influence there in any significant way. While Aubrey's landowning in the county was not that extensive, he did hold the castle and manor of Hadleigh on the Essex coast for life, was steward of the forest of Essex, and he seems to have played a prominent role in the administration of the county, being a regular Justice of the Peace and commissioner of array.[52] Yet there is no evidence that he moved to support his nephew in the autumn of 1387 when a showdown loomed. However, de Vere's movements – he was with the king in London and then made a swift departure for Cheshire – combined with Gloucester's presence at Pleshey in Essex and his muster at Haringey, on the Middlesex–Essex border, did not make it easy for any supporters of de Vere in Essex to join him. It is also hard to evaluate what role, if any, Countess Maud played in representing the family interest in Essex and Suffolk. She held six manors in Essex and four in Suffolk in dower and jointure and one more in the former county through inheritance, and seems to have been primarily resident at Great Bentley and Earls Colne in Essex; certainly a few prominent Essex gentry were associated with her estate administration. Equally, while she was unlikely to have abandoned her son, the Westminster Chronicle's statement that she cursed her son for his divorce of Philippa in 1387 means that she may not have been close to him at the crucial time.[53]

Beyond the men discussed above, it is only from occasional scraps of information that anything further can be gleaned about de Vere's local connections, and these were often to obscure individuals. For example, de Vere granted the manor of West Whetenham in Essex, worth around 6 marks a

---

[50] *WC*, 186–7.

[51] Virgoe, 'The Crown and Local Government', in Du Boulay and Barron, eds, *The Reign of Richard II*, 218–41.

[52] For Aubrey as commissioner of the peace, see Mitchell, 'Knightly Household', 164.

[53] *WC*, 190–1.

year, to William de Dannebury for life on 1 September 1383.⁵⁴ The grant of a manor, even a small one, was significant, and one might expect Dannebury to be a senior retainer or official, but it is entirely unclear what connection de Vere had with him.⁵⁵ William Bennington, esquire, was appointed an attorney to take custody of John of Blois in 1386, served as de Vere's ambassador regarding the ransom negotiations in Calais in 1387 and a few of de Vere's household goods in Essex ended up in his hands in 1388, so a household role might be presumed for him, but precisely what position he held is not known.⁵⁶ Another of the attorneys for Blois was Sir Thomas Nutbeam, probably related to William Nutbeam of Thanington, Kent, who had been the receiver of the seventh earl of Oxford.⁵⁷ Henry Morecroft could claim long service to the king and to the duke of Ireland in 1399, and receive a reward from the former. No other information has come to light as to what capacity he served the duke in.⁵⁸ Robert de Eure served de Vere in Ireland, and was described as de Vere's esquire, suggesting perhaps service in the duke's household or as a senior member of the affinity. Eure received a wardship in Ireland from de Vere's administration, albeit for the payment of £20; such patronage would indicate good service.⁵⁹ Richard FitzNicol was another described as an esquire of the duke of Ireland in 1386, when he testified that a protection for one Richard Pecock for service in Ireland had been obtained by fraud. He also acted as de Vere's attorney at the exchequer in October and November that year in connection with payments to the duke for the wages of his retinue mustered against the French.⁶⁰ He may well have been among the 180 men-at-arms in that retinue. One of the few men who can be identified as serving both de Vere and his mother was William Toppesfield, who, like FitzNicol, acted as de Vere's attorney at the exchequer to collect wages, though this time for the

---

54 E136/77/3; *CPR, 1396–9*, 149. It is not known how de Vere acquired the manor: Morant, *Essex*, i, 349 does not have a manorial history earlier than the 1480s.

55 *CPR, 1396–9*, 149. Dannebury appears occasionally in the chancery rolls: *CCR, 1369–74*, 600–2; *CIPM*, xvii, no. 554; CP 25/1/288/49, no. 739, calendared at www.medievalgenealogy.org.uk/fines/abstracts/CP_25_1_288_49.shtml.

56 TNA, X-Box 4278; *Preuves*, ed. Morice, 529; E357/10, rot. 20.

57 TNA, X-Box 4278; for William's role as receiver, see Bodleian, MS Rawl B 319, passim, and for the family, *HoC*, iii, 857–8.

58 SC8/184/9153.

59 *CPR, 1385–9*, 240; *RPC*, 138; https://chancery.tcd.ie/document/Patent/11-richard-ii/1. He had already served with the previous lieutenant of Ireland, Philip Courtenay: *CPR, 1385–9*, 27, 443.

60 *CPR, 1385–9*, 211; E403/515, m. 7, 12. It is not clear how closely related he was – if at all – to Sir Thomas FitzNicol, a prominent Gloucestershire knight, who served with the earl of Arundel at Radcot Bridge: *HoC*, iii, 80–2.

Scottish expedition of summer 1385. He also farmed the manor of Hedingham Vaux for Countess Maud from at least 1383 until 1388.[61]

Despite the almost complete loss of administrative and financial records for de Vere, a few individuals can be identified as playing important roles in his administration, though they are obscure men. The most significant was the clerk John Fitzmartin, who held the grand title of chancellor of the duke of Ireland in the autumn of 1387. He had been connected to Sir John Lancaster, the duke's chamberlain, since at least 1385, and it may have been this connection that brought him his entrée into the duke's service.[62] It is only a passing reference in connection to paying for expenses of the ducal household that Fitzmartin's service is known, so it is unclear how long he had occupied the office. Fitzmartin was granted the parish church of Athboy in Meath by the king on 13 May 1387; while the warrant makes no mention of de Vere, the latter had been with the king a few days earlier (on charter witness evidence) and he may have sought a reward for his servant.[63] Fitzmartin's position in de Vere's service ensured that he suffered forfeiture in the Merciless Parliament of 1388, and was not pardoned and restored until 1390.[64] Several historians describe Fitzmartin as a chancery clerk, and he may well have been so, but it is hard to find definitive evidence of this.[65] If he was, De Vere was not alone in seeking service from men who had experience in the chancery administration and appointing them to high office. John of Gaunt appointed two successive clerks of chancery to be chancellors of the palatinate of Lancaster in the 1380s, Thomas Stanley and John Scarle. The latter had connections with Gaunt

---

[61] E403/508, m. 19; BL, Harleian Roll N3, m.2. Toppesfield was an Essex man; his son or brother, Thomas, was escheator of Essex in 1397, and William and Thomas, along with Alice, wife of John Gestyngthorpe, borrowed 500 marks from the wealthy Essex lawyer, Clement Spice, in 1389: *CCR, 1389–92*, 68.

[62] SC6/773/3, m.1d; *CPR, 1381–5*, 554. Previous commentators had assumed a more general connection with de Vere (and John de Lancaster) that had brought about his exclusion from the general pardon in 1388: Leland, 'Unpardonable Sinners', 188; D. Biggs, 'The Appellant and the Clerk: the Assault on Richard II's Friends in Government, 1387–9', in G. Dodd, ed., *The Reign of Richard II* (Stroud, 2000), 65.

[63] C81/496, no. 4235; C53/161, m. 2. This may have been a confirmation as de Vere had the right of presentation to Irish benefices.

[64] *PROME*, vii, 73; *CFR, 1383–91*, 284; *CCR, 1388–92*, 192.

[65] Biggs, 'Appellant and the Clerk', 65; Dodd, 'Thomas Favent', 402; Given-Wilson, *Royal Household*, 178. A number of documents, including the parliament roll, described him generically as a 'clerk' (see preceding note) but not as a chancery clerk, and there are no entries for him in the chancery clerks card index in the Map Room at the National Archives.

pre-dating his entry into chancery service in 1375 but the point remains that experience of central government was valuable for magnate administrators.[66]

John Humbelby, described as a clerk of the duke's household in the autumn of 1387, was granted the manor of Beaumont in Essex, worth £4 p.a., in 1383, and it is presumably this holding that was referred to in the royal council where it was noted he was to be paid a pension of £4 by the grant of the duke of Ireland in a confirmation of the farm of the estates to Maud de Vere in 1388.[67] Two regional receivers can also be identified by 1387. One was William Grilleston. His role is testified by several records, although only in the context of the Audley lands.[68] He is there described as receiver-general, but he was a Devonian and clearly a regional receiver rather than the central figure in de Vere's administration.[69] This is confirmed by the fact that one Richard Roos occupied the office of general receiver of the duke of Ireland in Lonsdale and Kendal in 1387–8. Clearly such widely scattered lands as Devon and Westmorland required local receivers.[70] There would, presumably, have been at least one other receiver or receiver-general responsible for the estates of the old heartland of the earldom in Essex, Suffolk and Cambridgeshire.

Beyond East Anglia, there were a number of scattered outlying estates. Oakham in Rutland was a self-contained lordship and accounted directly to a local official. William Flores, the receiver of Oakham, was in post before, during and after de Vere's occupation of the lordship and provided continuity. How isolated estates were managed is not clear – Kensington in Middlesex, Fleet in Kent, and from 1386 Kennington in Surrey were not too far from either Castle Hedingham or London and manorial officials may have accounted

---

[66] Biggs, 'The Appellant and the Clerk', 58, 67. For the growth of use of chancery clerks in senior roles in private administrations and as councillors in the late fourteenth century, see C.W. Smith, 'A Conflict of Interest? Chancery Clerks in Private Service', in J. Rosenthal and C. Richmond, eds, *People, Politics and Community in the Later Middle Ages* (Gloucester, 1987), 176–91, and more generally on royal clerks, see A.K. McHardy, 'King's Clerks: the Essential Tools of Government', in Ambühl, Bothwell and Tompkins, eds, *Ruling Fourteenth-Century England*, 59–76. For Scarle, see McHardy, 'John Scarle', in Clark, Jurkowski and Richmond, eds, *Image, Text and Church*, 68–93.

[67] E357/10, rot. 19d; SC6/773/3, m.1d.; BL, Cotton Vespasian F XIII, no. 27 (*PPC*, i, 89); *CPR, 1385–9*, 556; *CIM, 1387–93*, 14, 92. Countess Maud brought a case in the Exchequer of Pleas against Humbelby as late as Trinity 1403: E13/119, rot. 25.

[68] SC6/826/13; SC6/971/27; *CIM, 1387–93*, 3, 89, 90.

[69] *CIPM*, xxi, no. 902; CP 25/1/45/69, no. 185; *CPR, 1385–9*, 555.

[70] *CIM, 1387–93*, 11; *CCR, 1381–5*, 290; *1385–9*, 119. It is not clear if Richard Roos was connected to the baronial family of Roos of Helmsley – the head of the family was de Vere's ward from July 1384 – though it is by no means impossible: *CP*, xi, 99–103; Dugdale, *Baronage*, i, 550–2; Ross, 'Yorkshire Baronage', 100–39.

directly with the receiver-general given they were the only manors de Vere held in those counties. In keeping with standard accounting procedures amongst the aristocracy at this time, de Vere employed at least one auditor to keep a close eye on his accounts. John Bole is clearly identified as an auditor of the duke of Ireland, both in Essex and again in the context of the administration of the Audley lands, so clearly had a role across all de Vere's estates.[71] There are a number of possible identifications for Bole; the most likely is either that he was a Londoner or of Wetherden in Essex; the latter was exempted for life from service on assizes, juries and the like on 10 May 1387, and de Vere can be placed with the king two days before this grant.[72] Bole seems to have transferred his service to Countess Maud after de Vere's fall; he was involved in her estate administration by 1388–9.[73]

It is possible to say a little about three clerics closely associated with de Vere. The first known connection with John Ripon was when he took out letters of protection to serve de Vere in the Scottish campaign of 1385.[74] However, he was by that date rector of Kedington, just a few miles from Castle Hedingham, at the centre of de Vere territorial influence, and may have come to the attention of de Vere in that context.[75] De Vere was behind Ripon's promotion to archdeacon of Wells on 1 December 1386 as the royal privy seal warrant notes that it was at the duke's supplication.[76] The grant states that the office was in the king's gift by reason of a recent vacancy in the bishopric, though by the date of the grant the temporalities had been in the hands of the incoming bishop for a month. The new bishop was Walter Skirlawe, promoted despite the king's secretary, Richard Medford, being pushed for the vacancy by the king.[77] Skirlawe had been keeper of the privy seal until just before the promotion, having resigned the office in October 1386. While the chancellor and treasurer had been dismissed in the autumn parliament of that year, Skirlawe left office without

---

[71] *CIM, 1387–93*, 3, 91–2.

[72] *CCR, 1381–5*, 119; *1385–9*, 295; *CPR, 1385–9*, 303, 400; C81/496, no. 4319. For various other Bole families, see *HoC*, ii, 273–4.

[73] BL, Harleian Roll N3, m.4.

[74] Ripon seems not to have served in Scotland as his letters of protection for half a year, granted 13 June, were revoked on 31 November; *CPR, 1385–9*, 51.

[75] *CCR, 1385–9*, 85. For a brief summary of his career, see R.A. Halliday, 'A Little Known Royal Functionary: the Brief Career of John Ripon, Rector of Kedington, 1385–8', *Suffolk Review*, 40 (2003), 19–22. He was named in the settlement of a property dispute by the bishop of London as Master John Ripon, clerk, in 1372: *Registrum Simonis de Sudbiria*, ed. Fowler, i, 200.

[76] C81/494, no. 4149.

[77] For Richard's advocacy of Medford as bishop, see Edinburgh UL, MS 183, fol. 99v.

being made to do so by parliament, and he then moved into the camp of the critics of the king, being promoted to bishop of Durham under the Appellant regime in April 1388. He has generally been seen as not 'an active partisan, but rather an acceptable and respected administrator'.[78] Yet, he did undertake a fairly dramatic political volte-face, both generally and more specifically in regard to de Vere as Skirlawe had been a feoffee for de Vere alongside Ripon in 1385. Was the grant of the archdeaconry to Ripon, a month after Skirlawe became bishop, a deliberate riposte or insult by erstwhile allies?

There seems to have been something going on behind the scenes in respect to the archdeaconry as well. The warrant notes that the archdeaconry was vacant because of 'the resignation and deprivation' of the previous incumbent, Andrew Baret, 'in the court of Rome and also by the resignation... made by the same Andrew in our realm of England'.[79] That proceedings were undertaken in Rome is perhaps surprising, although Baret was later a papal chaplain and auditor, and may have been the former by the date in question.[80] Also telling is the fact that after Ripon forfeited his offices by the judgement of the Merciless Parliament, Andrew Baret was reinstated to the archdeaconry in July 1388 notwithstanding any grant to Ripon.[81] Was some skulduggery behind Baret's replacement? Had Ripon gone to the Curia to procure Baret's deprivation and his own appointment late in 1386? The question is pertinent as it was Ripon who facilitated de Vere's divorce at the papal curia at some point before the summer of 1387.[82] Nor was this Ripon's only partisan action. Richard II's questions to the judges were witnessed by Ripon on 25 August 1387 at Nottingham, alongside de Vere and others. Ripon was also implicated, according to the indictments in the Merciless Parliament, of passing on letters from the king to the mayor of London to arrest Gloucester and try him through false indictments in November 1387.[83] Ripon was condemned in

---

[78] M.G Snape, 'Walter Skirlawe [Skirlaw], c. 1330–1406', *ODNB*. Very similar sentiments are expressed by Davies in 'Episcopate and the Political Crisis', 686–7.

[79] C81/494, no. 4149. Baret had only been appointed in the previous July: *CPR, 1385–9*, 201.

[80] *Calendar of Papal Letters, 1362–1404*, xv (auditor before 29 November 1390), 335, 363, 364.

[81] *CPR, 1385–9*, 480. Baret is in fact named as archdeacon on 26 March 1388 in the Wells records: *Calendar of the Manuscripts of the Dean and Chapter of Wells: Volume 1* (London, 1907), 299. Two further appointments to the archdeaconry were made to John Beer on 13 September 1388 and Thomas Tuttebury in 1391, but then Ripon's appointment there was ratified 26 July 1391, well before his release from prison: *CPR, 1385–9*, 508; *CPR, 1388–92*, 428, 472.

[82] *WC*, 188.

[83] *PROME*, vii, 93–4. See above, p. 107.

parliament after de Vere's fall and was caught, arrested and imprisoned in the Tower in June 1388 where he remained until 1393.[84]

The sources suggest that de Vere used successively two brothers, Richard Roughton and Thomas Roughton, as his confessors. Both were of the order of Friars Minor, and both were ordered to abjure the court in 1388.[85] Thomas was his confessor first, and was additionally described as the king's orator, in a pardon granted at Thomas's supplication in November 1384. A year later it was Richard Roughton who was described as the confessor of the king's kinsman, the earl of Oxford, in a pardon granted at his supplication and in a royal wardrobe account in February and December 1386.[86] The continuation of the *Eulogium* noted that de Vere escaped Radcot Bridge with 'his confessor, a minorite and a master in theology' but does not name him, while Knighton claimed, inaccurately, that the duke's unnamed confessor, a Franciscan friar, drowned in the marsh by the battlefield.[87] Both Roughtons survived to be criticised in the Merciless Parliament.[88] Two Friars Minor in succession would suggest de Vere's specific interest in the order, though more generally friars were very popular as confessors amongst the English nobility at this date. It is also interesting that, given the fact that both men had sufficient influence at court to intercede with the king, perhaps simply being close to de Vere ensured a certain level of influence with Richard.[89]

One other figure with de Vere connections is worth discussing briefly. Sir Edward Dallingridge had had a long and successful career as a soldier, having served under successive earls of Arundel, with John of Gaunt, and on the 1380 expedition to Brittany under Thomas of Woodstock, where he would have met Robert de Vere, if he had not before. He had, however, fallen out with John of

---

[84] *WC*, 300, 344 and n., 402 and n.

[85] *WC*, 302; *PROME*, vii, 73, 76.

[86] *CPR, 1381–5*, 483; *1385–9*, 65 (C66/320, m. 9); E101/401/16, mm. 18, 23. Thomas can be identified as a member of the order as early as 1362: *Registrum Simonis de Sudbiria*, ed. Fowler, ii, 11. He was also granted robes at Christmas 1386, where he is described as of the Norwich convent: E101/401/16, m.23. Given-Wilson, *Royal Household*, 178, refers to Richard as the queen's confessor, but his source (E101/401/16, m. 18) only refers to him as de Vere's confessor, though he may also have served the queen in that capacity.

[87] *Continuation Eulogii*, ed. Given-Wilson, 62–3; *KC*, 422–3.

[88] The goods of an unnamed friar, confessor of Duke Robert, and valued at 54s 4d were noted in the receipt rolls of the exchequer in September 1388: E401/571, *sub* 11 September.

[89] The king's own confessors – three during the reign – were all Dominican friars: Given-Wilson, 'The King's Confessors', 5.

Gaunt, at whose suit he was arrested in 1384, and then fined just over £1,000. The earl of Arundel interceded for him in the summer of that year when the king stayed at Arundel Castle, but he was rearrested in October under Gaunt's influence. It was not until January 1385 he was released and afterwards shown some marks of favour: a licence to crenellate at Bodiam in Sussex was issued that autumn.[90] While he remained in the circle of the earl of Arundel, was later thought of as 'an adherent of Thomas duke of Gloucester in the tenth year' and was elected to the Merciless Parliament in February 1388, he had a direct connection to the de Vere family, albeit with Countess Maud, rather than de Vere directly.[91] He was the farmer of her Sussex manor of Laughton between Easter 1386 and Easter 1388 and may have occupied the role for longer as the extant account covers only this period.[92] The manor was a wealthy one, being farmed at £60 p.a., but knights like Dallingridge were often too senior to occupy such a role, even if exercised through a deputy. His appointment as farmer of Laughton might have been only to bring an influential local landowner on side as far as Maud was concerned, rather than being a move with national political motivations. Nonetheless, it is also worth considering that as someone who could only have been clearly anti-Gaunt, and with the Laughton connection, he may have been sympathetic to de Vere in the critical parliaments of 1385 and 1386.[93]

De Vere seems to have had one or two followers, but no more, in most of the parliaments during his majority, as far as can be ascertained on the limited evidence. Henry English was elected in October 1383 and November 1384, Richard Roos was twice returned as knight of shire for Westmorland during de Vere's ascendancy (March 1383 and 1385), albeit this assumes that his employment with de Vere predates the only known reference to it. Dallingridge, as noted, was present in the parliaments of 1385 and 1386. If de Vere was still on good terms with his father's close associate, Sir William Wingfield, then he had connections with another MP in both parliaments of 1383 and in 1386.[94] However, de Vere seems to have made no effort to secure elections of his men, particularly in Essex.[95] This may reflect his lack of influence there, but it may also reflect the

---

[90] For the problems between Gaunt and Dallingridge, see Walker, *Lancastrian Affinity*, 127–40; idem, 'Lancaster v. Dallingridge: a Franchisal Dispute in 14th-century Sussex', *Sussex Archaeological Collections*, 121 (1983), 87–94; *HoC*, ii, 738–42.

[91] *CPR, 1396–9*, 341, dating from May 1398.

[92] BL, Harleian Roll N3, m. 4.

[93] J.L. Leland, 'Knights of the Shire in the Parliament of 1386: a Preliminary Study of Factional Affiliations', *Medieval Prosopography*, 9 (1988), 93–5; *HoC*, ii, 738–42.

[94] See above, p. 58.

[95] *HoC*, i, 392–4.

normal practice of magnates, who did not seek to pressure the electorate except at periods of political crisis. The large numbers of followers of the Appellants elected to the parliament of 1388 was exceptional.[96]

While Ralph Basset's comment that he was unwilling to risk his head for the duke of Ireland is oft-quoted, there were at least two people who shared de Vere's exile, and who, while they it is possible that they may have found their fortunes too intertwined with de Vere to escape his fate, may also have stayed with him out of loyalty or devotion. Sir John Lancaster has already been mentioned, only returning to England after de Vere's death. John Newton, esquire, had letters of protection for service in Ireland issued in February 1387, though whether he went is unclear.[97] He was, like Lancaster, an attorney at Calais for John of Blois's ransom, and indeed was described as an ambassador of the duke of Ireland in November 1387.[98] Newton was probably in Calais at the time of Radcot Bridge; he was certainly in Paris in the summer of 1388 when he was described as de Vere's servant when collecting a further instalment of John of Blois's ransom.[99] Perhaps because he was abroad, or perhaps because he was not sufficiently significant, he was not sanctioned by the Merciless Parliament, and by 1393 he was called the king's esquire.[100] De Vere, at an unknown date before his fall, granted Newton the reversion of the manor of Easton Hall for life, after the death of Elizabeth Pichard, a grant that was worth around £5 per annum to the holder.[101]

The largest annuity granted by de Vere was on 11 October 1387 and was a yearly rent of £100 to John, Lord Beauchamp. This was perhaps less to do

---

[96] For the composition of this parliament, see *HoC*, I, appendix C2 (pp. 185–91). More generally, L. Clark, 'Magnates and their Affinities in the Parliaments of 1386–1421', in Britnell and Pollard, *McFarlane Legacy*, 127–53.

[97] *CPR, 1385–9*, 278.

[98] C76/72, m. 17; *Preuves*, ed. Morice, ii, 529.

[99] See above, pp. 191, 192. There was a Kentish landowner of this name appointed to a commission to resist the French in 1386 and who was constable of Rochester Castle between at least 1384 and 1388, but since he was still in post in early 1388 and indeed was responsible for the custody of at least one of the Appellants' victims, Nicholas Dagworth, he is unlikely to be de Vere's servant: *CPR, 1385–9*, 79, 176; *CCR, 1381–5*, 482; *CCR, 1385–9*, 394–5. Nor is he the MP of the same name who sat for Stafford in the Merciless Parliament: *HoC*, iii, 834. He may be related to Thomas Newenton (Newton), esquire, who held the manor of Sandon in Essex until c. 1393, and who was a companion of Sir John Hawkwood: Starr, 'Essex Gentry', 313, 316.

[100] *WC*, 228–31; *CPR, 1391–6*, 264.

[101] *CPR, 1391–6*, 264. For Pichard, see above, p. 74.

with his ducal status or even an attempt to tie Beauchamp into the court circle – he was fully entrenched there as steward of the household – but was in recompense for Beauchamp's surrender the previous day of the office of Justice of North Wales, which the king had then granted to de Vere, alongside that of Chester.[102] Beauchamp's fee for the post had been 100 marks, so he was fully compensated and more.[103] While the two men probably knew each other very well, given their roles in the household and their likely presence at court for considerable amounts of time over the previous year or two, this was the only business connection between the two that is known.

Chris Woolgar has provided examples of the sizes of lordly households in the 1380s, when the earl of Devon, with an income of £1,000, had a household of about fifty, though a livery roll of one hundred and forty, and the bishop of Ely, Thomas Arundel, with an income of £2,500 per year, had around eighty men.[104] A generation later a not conspicuously wealthy duke, Edward of York, had a household of ninety. De Vere's household by 1387 is likely to have been of this order, a little under a hundred; not only were his financial resources bolstered by his wife's estates and royal patronage but his ducal status probably meant a commensurate requirement for an appropriate increase in the numbers of his servants. He might have had a household much closer in size to the earl of Devon's a few years earlier. Yet, without records of household expenditure, diet or wages, certainty eludes the historian and very little is known of its composition and membership. Two separate inventories of de Vere's goods at Chester after his fall contained six liveries for valets, four for minstrels and six for grooms, and four liveries for esquires, two for damsels, two for valets, two for grooms and six yards of red cloth for grooms, respectively.[105] However, given these were what was left behind at Chester, these numbers reflected a small proportion of his household, and might even denote the staff permanently resident at Chester rather than his household as such.

---

[102] *CCR, 1385–9*, 444; *CPR, 1385–9*, 357, 364. For Beauchamp, the first baron by patent created in England, and who was executed by the Appellants in 1388, see Saul, *Richard II*, 194, 341; idem, 'The Worldly Wealth of John Beauchamp of Holt', in M. Aston and R. Horrox, eds, *Much Heaving and Shoving: Late-Medieval Gentry and their Concerns. Essays for Colin Richmond* (Lavenham, 2005), 5–16; Goodman, *Loyal Conspiracy*, 23, 140; Given-Wilson, 'Richard II and the higher nobility', 118.

[103] A point made by Saul, 'Worldly Wealth', 9.

[104] C.M. Woolgar, *The Great Household in Late Medieval England* (London, 1999), 11–15. K. Mertes, *The English Noble Household 1250–1600* (Oxford, 1988), 218–19, posits much larger households on the basis of the same records.

[105] E36/66, p. 20; E101/631/13.

Robert de Vere's military following is as obscure as his household. He was certainly capable of raising substantial forces when required; his retinue for the Scottish campaign of 1385 at two knights, 118 men-at-arms and 200 archers was the largest bar the king's uncles, and he was leading almost 600 men (two bannerets, sixteen knights, 180 esquires and 400 archers) in the summer of 1386 while simultaneously 766 men were assembling in his name for service for Ireland.[106] His following in England that summer was greater than any other with the exception of Henry Bolingbroke. However, there is no extant muster roll for his 1380 service in France, the 1385 expedition to Scotland, the 1386 retinues or, of course, the Radcot Bridge campaign, so it is extremely difficult to analyse who comprised his military following or how it was recruited. Occasionally individuals can be identified through letters of protection or of attorney – though such grants are proof only of intention to serve. It is telling that in the *Soldier in Later Medieval England* database, there are only fourteen entries between 1380 and 1388 that specifically name de Vere as the captain under whom individuals were to serve, though there are a little over one hundred grants of protection or of attorney in 1386–7 for service in Ireland that can be said to be under his more general aegis.[107] One of the fourteen was for service in France in 1380 (Richard Wolmare) and five for Scotland in 1385 (John Lancaster and John Ripon are known from other connections; the remaining three were John May, clerk, Walter Helyon, a baker, and Richard de Chonal of Cheshire). Eight were to serve in Ireland, though of course they did not end up working directly with him, even if he was named as the captain. These eight were Robert Crull, treasurer of Ireland, Sir Robert de Hereford, Thomas de Ickworth, Philip Maghery, John Newton, Sir Peter de Veel, and two tradesmen, Richard de la Ryvere, a taverner and John Swon, a drover. Newton was otherwise connected with de Vere, as discussed above, but several of the others already had Irish interests and this is their only known connection with de Vere.[108]

---

[106] See above, pp. 104, 138, 139.

[107] www.medievalsoldier.org/dbsearch/. There are seventeen results, but three duplicate entries for particular individuals.

[108] For Crull and Hereford, see above, pp. 145–6; Ickworth had served in Ireland in 1380 under the earl of March, but was a Suffolk man, of Bury St Edmunds; whether he came to de Vere's attention because of this regional connection is not known: *CPR, 1377–81*, 409; *CCR, 1381–5*, 631; *CCR, 1386–9*, 19, 54, 106, 107. Maghery appears to have been from Ireland, as his name suggests (it was a contemporary term for the inner parts of the four shires obedient to Dublin), and received an office there early in Henry IV's reign: https://chancery.tcd.ie/roll/3-Henry-IV/patent. Veel, an annuitant of the Black Prince, had landed interests in the West

The military retinues in 1385 and 1386 are more sizeable than his territorial base might normally have allowed, and all the more surprising as he did not have a strong Essex and East Anglian affinity to draw upon. While acknowledging the lack of evidence, it is possible to make a number of speculative points about these two retinues. One possibility is that de Vere had been spending heavily on recruiting men into his retinue. His contemporary (and rival) Thomas, earl of Nottingham, was spending nearly 40 per cent of his annual income in the late 1390s on grants of land, cash and office to followers.[109] It is simply not possible to prove whether de Vere was doing something similar. The lack of demonstrable connections with senior East Anglian gentry would suggest not – or certainly that he was not spending on East Anglians – yet the very substantial military retinues would perhaps point the other way. Equally, it is possible that de Vere's obvious royal favour drew some men to seek out his service who had no previous connections to him or had estates in geographical proximity to his. He would have looked – and was – a man with the ear of the king and a peer on the rise, and thus an appealing prospect to offer service to.

In 1386, two further factors must have helped. He had already been raising troops and recruiting for Ireland, and it had been intended he was to lead a force of 1,500 into Ireland in the summer of 1386. Although the force for Ireland was reduced to 800 by March of that year, de Vere may have been sounding out captains before then. While many of the men who did serve in Ireland had Irish interests – notably the earl of Ormond who supplied 106 men, the bishop of Ossory who brought thirty-two and the treasurer of Ireland had thirty – it might be that among the 600 men serving with de Vere in England in the summer of 1386 were Englishmen who had initially intended to serve him in Ireland. The other point in 1386 is that it was a national emergency and de Vere may well have been able to draw substantial numbers of men from coastal counties – particularly Essex, Suffolk and Kent where he had land – where

---

Country, and had military experience in Brittany in 1381: *CPR, 1377–81*, 192; *CCR, 1377–81*, 443. No specific connection can be found between him and de Vere.

[109] R.E. Archer, 'The Mowbrays, Earls of Nottingham and Dukes of Norfolk to 1432' (unpublished DPhil., University of Oxford, 1984), 307–11. Both Given-Wilson and Carpenter suggest that spending on retinues increased in the later years of the fourteenth century: Given-Wilson, *English Nobility*, 156; C. Carpenter, 'Bastard Feudalism in England in the Fourteenth Century', in S. Boardman and J. Goodare, eds, *Kings, Lords and Men in Scotland and Britain, 1300–1625. Essays in Honour of Jenny Wormald* (Edinburgh, 2014), 72. Certainly, de Vere had given two small manors (one in reversion) to servants for life, plus the grant of the bigger manor of Cockfield to Sir John de Routh, so there is evidence of some outlay in return for service.

the threat of an invading force was very real. These men may have had little connection in some cases with de Vere. While other lords could also utilise the national emergency to recruit men, de Vere had more land in Essex in particular than Gloucester and this, combined with the other factors above, seems to have allowed him to amass substantial manpower.

It is not possible to dig deeper into the records of those serving in Ireland to see if de Vere was trying to offer opportunities for members of the de Vere affinity to benefit from his elevation to the effective rule of Ireland, or that those already connected to him saw and took opportunities. It is possible that men who took out grants of protection for service in Ireland were occupying roles in his estate administration or were otherwise connected but we lack extant records. The closest we can come is to suggest that one John Cook, described as of Horndon in Essex, who took out a protection for Irish service in May 1386 might be the same man named as the farmer of Aldham, Suffolk, in Countess Maud's receiver-general account.[110] Otherwise grants of protection are often the first or only known connection between de Vere and the man in question.

However, and acknowledging the issues around missing source material, it appears clear that de Vere lacked a broad-based affinity in Essex and Suffolk and that he had a paucity of influence in the area traditionally associated with his family. This may have been due to a lack of understanding on the part of King Richard of the real roots of magnate power and good lordship. These were estates concentrated in a region, local presence and residency, and the concomitant understanding of local issues and quarrels, which allowed the lord to support his following. Gundy has made a similar point regarding Richard's promotion of Thomas Holland, duke of Surrey, in the West Midlands after 1397.[111] To put it simply, anyone could raise a royalist stronghold like Cheshire for the king, but only de Vere could have hoped to raise Essex against the Appellants. Royal patronage had diverted and dispersed de Vere's energies and good lordship away from Essex to the court, Cheshire, Ireland and perhaps the West Country, rather than bolstering his established local roots.[112] Certainly, he seems to have spent most of his time away from his familial estates in his last two years in England. This had a detrimental effect on his ability to maintain any significant following in his family's traditional heartland but did not hamper military recruitment for national campaigns in 1385 and 1386.[113] Perhaps also a lack of a substantial local

---

[110] *CPR, 1385–9*, 156; BL, Harleian Roll N3, m. 1.

[111] Gundy, *Richard II and the Rebel Earl*, 208.

[112] See Map 2, above, p. xvii.

[113] For discussion of the separation of military and non-military service, see for example Carpenter, 'Bastard Feudalism', 60–1, 73–5; M.A. Hicks, *Bastard Feudalism* (Harlow, 1995), 185–94.

following diminished his stature as a great magnate and may have weakened him politically. Part of the reason for the prominence of men like Warwick and Arundel in the 1380s were their strong, cohesive affinities. To offer such lordship and receive such service was part of an idealised magnate identity, and lordship, in its broadest definition, was over men as much if not more than it was over land.[114] De Vere could not match these retinues and it meant in his hour of need he had few resources of his own to fall back upon. The Cestrians in his army in 1387 did not know him and nor he them, and no longstanding bonds of lordship and loyalty bound them together.

Lifestyle

There is a considerable amount of material extant amongst the records of the crown concerning the forfeited estates and goods of Robert de Vere, Alexander Neville, Michael de la Pole, John Beauchamp of Holt, Robert Tresilian, Nicholas Brembre, Simon de Burley, John Salisbury and one or two others, all of whom suffered imprisonment, exile or death as a result of the judgements of the Merciless Parliament. These have not escaped attention from historians, and those of Burley and Beauchamp have had discussion by Maud Clarke and Nigel Saul respectively, while Clarke made more general comments on the goods of the disgraced lords.[115] The single most important source is the 'Book of Forfeitures', a title taken from the opening two words of the original heading: *Liber Forisfacturarum ducis Hibernie et diversarum personarum*.[116] This details the goods of de Vere, amongst others, but only those of his found in Chester and delivered in three parcels to London – these were the responsibility of John Wodehouse, chamberlain of Chester, in whose name two accounts were made.[117] Clarke noted that these totalled £435 6s 2d and opined that this

---

[114] Davies, *Lords and Lordship*, 159–60.

[115] M.V. Clarke, 'Forfeitures and Treason in 1388', *TRHS*, 4th series, 14 (1931), 65–94; Saul, 'Worldly Wealth of John Beauchamp of Holt', 5–16.

[116] E36/66. The list is duplicated, mainly without valuations, in E364/24, rot. 7.

[117] E364/24, rot. 7 is the enrolled account of his transfer of the goods from Chester to London. There are four sections relating to de Vere in the book of forfeitures in E36/66, the first (pp. 5–8) relating to a transfer by Wodehouse in April 1388, the second (pp. 20–1) largely repeating the previous list, though without valuations, the third (p. 25), handed over in June 1388 (the original indenture for this is E101/334/23) and the fourth (p. 26) relating to a transfer in December 1388. For expenses in moving goods from Chester, see SC6/773/2. These goods, with the exception of the December transfer, are probably the ones noted in the Receipt Rolls in September 1388 as being transferred by John Wodehouse, but which were then sold to recipients including Gloucester, Derby and the bishop of Durham, which

showed 'beyond all doubt that [de Vere] had made Chester the headquarters of his splendid housekeeping'. She goes on to note that 'he may have moved his household to Chester as a preliminary to crossing to Ireland, but it seems more probably that he took up residence there in order to organise the army which he afterwards led to Radcot Bridge'.[118] As discussed above, there is no evidence that he spent any time in Chester before the summer of 1387 and he was in Bristol rather than Chester to supervise aspects of the Irish operations in July 1386. He was in Chester for two to three weeks before Radcot Bridge.

The bulk of the goods confiscated in Chester were tableware, chapel vestments, beds and bedding and clothing. One of the most expensive items amongst those valued was a bed and hangings, worth £66 13s 4d and described as of 'blue camoca, embroidered with owls and fleur de lys'. De Vere's chapel vestments were valued at a little over £100.[119] Clarke states that two of de Vere's beds and one set of his chapel furnishings can be found amongst the duke of Gloucester's goods compiled after his death in 1397 but does not note which ones, and it cannot now be easily established which she meant.[120] Clarke's case that Chester was de Vere's headquarters would have been stronger had she been aware of two further lists of de Vere's goods in Chester not recorded in the Book of Forfeitures. Three leading Cheshiremen – Peter Legh, Hugh Mascy and John de Sherd, the first two of whom were very much royalists – were indicted in the Cheshire county court in September 1388. They were accused of entering the castle of Chester on 12 January that year and breaking open doors, chests and locks of the duke of Ireland, and taking away goods including cloth of gold, silks, 'pierels' (presumably pearls) and jewels, which required three packhorses and two carriages to take away, the total value of which the presenting jury declared themselves ignorant.[121] These intriguing items contained significant wealth in the forms of jewels or other valuables, and one wonders if they also took correspondence or other records of

---

    totalled a little under £300. A further entry notes the handing over by the bishop of Ely of goods of the duke, as well as goods of others who forfeited in the Merciless Parliament worth £104: E401/571, *sub* 11 September. Possibly goods had been handed over to Ely, the chancellor, to deliver to the exchequer. The total of de Vere's goods on the Receipt Roll is almost exactly £400.

[118] Clarke, 'Forfeitures and Treason', 68.

[119] E36/66, p. 6 (two beds, worth £66 12s 4d and £50) and 6–8 (vestments – five sets worth £80, £13 6s 8d, £6, £5 and 66s 8d respectively).

[120] Clarke, 'Forfeiture and Treason', 69; Viscount Dillon and W.H. St John Hope, 'Inventory of the Goods and Chattels Belonging to Thomas Duke of Gloucester and Seized in His Castle at Pleshy, co. Essex, 21 Richard II (1397) With Their Values, as Shown in the Escheator's Accounts', *The Archaeological Journal*, 54 (1897), 275–308.

[121] CHES25/8, rot. 25.

little monetary but some political value. They were not included in the valuations recorded of de Vere's goods received in the exchequer. The legal action brought against them may well have been designed to force the goods to be handed over rather than ensure a conviction, as the same three Cheshiremen also had custody of, and accounted in the exchequer for, a further cache of de Vere's goods. There survives a particular of account by Legh, Mascy and Sherd of goods of the duke's which were left in the castle at Chester on 17 November 1387, which goods they had received and which were still in their hands at some point after early February 1388, but the document is itself undated. The date of 17 November was the date de Vere and his fellow Appellees were taken as forfeiting for treason, being the day they were first appealed of treason by the Appellants to the King in London.[122] This is an entirely separate list from any of the others. It has no valuations, and contains a miscellaneous list of clothes, banners, bedding, furnishings, a few items of jewellery, and other items belonging to de Vere, his lady (presumably Agnes but not named) and livery and robes for a dozen or so servants. Among other items it contained a 'chaplet', a chaplet, circlet or coronet, 'of great value'.[123] This was not the same item as the 'chappeletti' taken from his goods after Radcot Bridge.[124] An account of the chamberlain of Chester also notes that various vessels and other goods, of gold, silver and gilt, worth a total of £60 7s 1d belonging to de Vere were used to pay royal creditors in Chester, authorised by letter patent on 11 June.[125] It is not clear whether these are in addition to, or part of, one of these other collections of goods as insufficient detail survives.

While de Vere did perhaps spend time in Cheshire before December 1387 – a week in October 1387 is possible though doubtful – Clarke is almost certainly correct that some of what was there was as a result of his residence while raising an army before Radcot Bridge.[126] However, despite the three lists of

---

[122] See above, p. 169. The heading also notes the judgement in parliament against them as the morrow of the Purification of the Virgin Mary.

[123] E101/631/13. For the political alignment of Legh and Mascy, see Bennett, *Community, Class and Careerism*, 208. Jenny Stratford notes the difficulty of distinguishing quite what a chaplet might actually denote – a coronet is perhaps the best translation here: *Richard II and the English Royal Treasure* (Woodbridge, 2002), 16, 272, 276.

[124] One or other of the coronets might have been the gold one which King Richard placed on his head at his creation as marquess in 1385: *PROME*, vii, 1385 item 17. For the use of coronets, see J.E. Powell and K. Wallis, *The House of Lords in the Middle Ages* (London, 1968), 396–7.

[125] SC6/773/2, m. 1d; SC6/773/3, m.5d.

[126] As justice of Chester, he is said to have heard pleas at Basford, Middlewich, Tarporley, and Nantwich between 14 and 19 October according to the Cheshire plea roll,

goods, one of which was worth £435, it is not clear at all that Chester was his headquarters, however. Solely in terms of monetary value, other evidence shows de Vere had goods at least as valuable as those inventoried at Chester in London (and what is known is only what was seized by the Appellants rather than a full inventory of his residence) and we lack any full valuation of de Vere's goods at Castle Hedingham or Kennington, granted to him earlier that year.[127] A small amount of goods were seized in Essex, worth 40s.[128] De Vere's goods at Berkhamsted were valued at £11 3s 4d.[129]

The evidence for the fact that the Chester material was only a fraction of de Vere's goods comes from a variety of sources. The Chronicle of Henry Knighton records that a horse belonging to the duke was taken at Radcot Bridge carrying £4,000 in gold. Such a valuation may be doubted (could a horse have carried the weight?) and it may just have been Knighton's way of saying a lot of money. Clearly though de Vere would have needed cash to pay expenses for himself and his troops, even if their wages were to come from the exchequer after he was victorious. Knighton added that the victorious Appellants took a 'baggage cart heavily laden with gold and silver plate, clothing, bedding, tableware and other utensils, and other supplies, all of which our lords kept for themselves and their men', while they kept the £4,000 in gold for the expenses of their followers.[130] It is clear from evidence in the exchequer that the Appellants did indeed seize household goods from de Vere, perhaps at Radcot Bridge and certainly in London afterwards, and that they sold them and kept the proceeds. Five entries found in exchequer documents record that some of de Vere's goods were in the custody of John Sewale, mercer of London, and were seized by Gloucester,

---

but it should be treated with caution, as other evidence suggests he was accompanying the king towards London: CHES17/6, rots 3–6, and see Appendix, below, pp. 246–7.

[127] For Kennington, which he used at least once; see above, p. 153.

[128] E357/10, rot. 20. The account of the Escheator is confusing and appears to contain significant errors in its arithmetic. The opening line states the figure of £99 7s 11d as being taken of the goods and chattels of Robert de Vere, but the section in the account also covers possessions belonging to Michael de la Pole (£66 13s 4d) and Sir James Berners (£25 19s 2d). The account specifies only two sets of goods as belonging to de Vere at 13s 4d and 26s 8d. These, when added to the goods of de la Pole and Berners, total just over £94, rather than £99 7s 11d. What cannot be established is why the clerk then put a total at the end of the section of £126 13s 9d. No more detailed particulars of account from the escheator survive for this year in E136/77. The goods valued at 13s 4d are also noticed in *CPR, 1391–6*, 323.

[129] E357/10, rot. 20.

[130] *KC*, 423.

Derby and Nottingham. Three other entries, recording goods taken by two men of lesser status, Sir Thomas Mortimer, known to have been at Radcot Bridge, and Janico Dartasso, who may well have been,[131] do not mention how they acquired the items and these may have been spoils from the battle. Gloucester's haul comprised cloth of gold and of silk worth £148, linen de 'Lanny' worth £20 and the impressive item of a chaplet or a coronet, containing ninety pearls, five sapphires and five rubies, worth £300. Nottingham had seized pieces of velvet and of linen 'of Reynes' worth £44 13s 4d, while Derby had a piece of satin and linen 'of Reynes' worth £18 6s 8d. From their unspecified source of acquisition, Dartasso had blue and black silk called 'atteby' and a piece of satin worth £9, while Mortimer had taken cloth of gold worth £6 13s 4d and a piece of red satin and two pieces of linen cloth worth the same again. Together, all of these seized goods totalled £543, while one of the exchequer sources adds another 250 marks worth of unspecified goods was sold by Gloucester.[132]

The items seized in both Chester and in London after Radcot Bridge suggest something of the magnificence that de Vere displayed. Equally telling is the fact that in 1397 Richard II ordered repayment to the London merchant Richard Whittington of £1,093 16s 5d for mercery bought by Robert de Vere, then in the king's hands because of his forfeiture nine years earlier.[133] However, caution must be exercised as is it not clear if this represented only the most recent purchases before de Vere's fall or was a running total built up over several years. A sum of over £1,000 in a year on mercery alone would have been huge, though not disproportionately beyond other peers, whereas a few hundred pounds a year over a few years, while substantial, would not have been outrageous. An interesting comparison is the £740 spent by Henry Bolingbroke in 1391–2 on drapery, mercery, embroidery, furs and jewels.[134] This sum was matched by the earl of Warwick who spent £787 in 1420–1 to pay his tailors (and probably those of his wife), while in 1517–18 the duke of Buckingham, the richest peer of his day, spent £577 on cloth and textiles.[135] John of Gaunt

---

[131] Walker, *Political Culture*, ed. Braddick (Manchester, 2006), 118.

[132] E401/570, *sub* 2 March; E403/518, m.23, also *sub* 2 March. The sums are identical except for one entry on the latter, noting the additional 250m of goods sold by Gloucester. There is also a brief note on these goods in E364/23, rot. 6d.

[133] E403/555, m. 25; C. Barron, 'Richard Whittington: the Man behind the Myth', in idem, *Medieval London. Collected Papers of Caroline M. Barron*, ed. M. Carlin and J.T. Rosenthal (Kalamazoo, MI, 2017), 269, 316 (though the sum given there, £1,903, is a typographical error for £1,093).

[134] C. Given-Wilson, *Henry IV* (London, 2016), 71, citing DL28/1/3.

[135] C.D. Ross, 'The Household Accounts of Elizabeth Berkeley, Countess of Warwick, 1420–1', *Transactions of the Bristol and Gloucestershire Archaeological Society*, 70

allowed 2,000 marks for his great wardrobe expenses and a further 1,000 for those of his duchess.[136] However, if de Vere's £1,093 was generated by more than one year's purchases it is interesting that de Vere had bought on credit and not paid for them by the time of the downfall. Either Whittington allowed him very generous credit in the interests of not alienating an excellent customer or de Vere had defaulted on payments which would suggest spending beyond his means. Whether there were further debts to other mercers, drapers, goldsmiths and other tradesmen or artisans is impossible to determine.

Conspicuous display by the upper members of the nobility was expected, and many spent considerable sums to appear magnificent. Edward, duke of Buckingham, was said to have worn a gown worth £1,500 in 1501 at the marriage of Prince Arthur with Katherine of Aragon.[137] Piers Gaveston at the time of his capture had a 'great ruby set in gold' worth £1,000.[138] Beating all of these was the collar studded with precious stones called the 'white rose' owned by Richard, duke of York, whose value was estimated at £2,666.[139] De Vere's bed, worth £66, is put into context by that of John of Gaunt, burnt at the Savoy Palace by the rebels of 1381, which the Anonimalle Chronicle estimated to be worth 1,000 marks.[140] While de Vere's chaplet was undeniably an expensive item, it is worth noting that two other chaplets amongst Richard II's treasure in 1399 were likely to have been seized from the duke of Gloucester and the earl of Arundel, and were valued respectively at £304 6s 8d and £218, so de Vere's was not noticeably richer or more ostentatious than these.[141]

It is possible from de Vere's goods to say a little about how he dressed, though nothing, of course, of his good looks or lack thereof. Seven gowns are recorded in the various documents, varying in length, colour (mainly green and red) and fabric, though one or two were furred with miniver, and one embroidered with gold foil ('folii auri'), and a range of mantles and doublets.[142] He would thus have probably cut a fine figure, augmented by his two coronets or chaplets, and he also owned an ivory comb to keep his hair in order. Yet, again none of

---

(1951), 105; Staffordshire Record Office, D641/3/9.

[136] McFarlane, *Nobility of Later Medieval England*, 98–9.

[137] *The Great Chronicle of London*, ed. A.H. Thomas and I.D. Thornley (London, 1938), 311–13. One would be tempted to dismiss this as exaggeration except for the fact that the king loaned Buckingham £1,000 a few weeks earlier: E101/415/3, fol. 70r.

[138] From the inventory of goods transcribed in Hamilton, *Piers Gaveston*, 122.

[139] McFarlane, *Nobility*, 98.

[140] *Anonimalle Chronicle*, ed. Galbraith, 150.

[141] Stratford, *Richard II and the English Royal Treasure*, 153, 276.

[142] E101/631/13; E36/66, p. 5.

this was more ostentatious than his contemporaries: for example, the duke of Gloucester had twenty-one gowns at the time of his forfeiture a decade later, eight of which were furred.[143] Perhaps the only surviving depiction of de Vere made during his lifetime comes from the tentative identification of one of the heads carved as corbels in the nave of the church at Hatfield Broadoak in Essex, the priory of which was in the patronage of the de Vere family, and whose partial rebuilding has been dated to c. 1386. It is interesting that this carving depicts a figure wearing a coronet, rather different in style to the dukes of Gloucester and York, also possibly identified amongst the nine carvings.[144] The figure is also bearded and with long hair. Nonetheless it cannot be taken as an accurate portrayal even if the identification is correct.

Other areas of de Vere's lifestyle remain entirely opaque. What he read or owned in terms of books is unknown. Philippa did own a *Vies de saintes Pères* which was sold after her death by her executors to the abbess of Barking, and was later acquired by the duke of Orléans, from where it made its way into the Bibliothèque Nationale in Paris. However, it is, of course, unknown whether she acquired it after de Vere's abandonment of her, and even, if not, whether he read such a work amongst his wife's books.[145]

In terms of display, material culture could make an important impact. Yet visual display was not just about the money spent. What was being displayed was just as important. Anthony Tuck's memorable phrase that the grant of Ireland was designed to give de Vere 'the shadows and trappings of power without its substance' can be questioned as to the substance.[146] Tuck was however correct that it did give the marquess extra trappings. By a grant on 3 January 1386 he had licence to use the arms of Ireland, *azure* with three crowns *or* and a border *argent*, alongside his own family arms on shields, standards and the like.[147] The ducal arms of Vere quartered with Ireland appear on floor tiles discovered at the parish church at his manor of Sible Hedingham and can therefore be dated to

---

[143] Dillon and Hope, 'Inventory of... Thomas Duke of Gloucester', 303–4.

[144] F.W. Galpin, 'The History of the Church of Hatfield Regis or Broad Oak, with some account of the Priory Buildings', *EAH*, 2nd series, 6 (1898), 332–3. The nine heads, including that of the possible Robert de Vere, are illustrated in a plate following p. 332. King Richard, John of Gaunt, Eleanor de Bohun and Robert Braybrooke are among the others.

[145] A.I. Doyle, 'Books Connected with the Vere Family and Barking Abbey', *EAH*, 2nd series, 25 (1955–60), 241; *Cabinet des manuscrits de la Bibliothèque Impériale*, ed. L. Deslisle, i (Paris, 1868), 110.

[146] Tuck, *Richard II*, 82

[147] *CPR, 1385–9*, 78.

1386–7.[148] Even a century later, when Robert de Vere's legacy was by no means straightforward, the thirteenth earl of Oxford included Robert's ducal arms on the new church porch of Lavenham, Suffolk, which he partly paid for, and alongside shields of his great grandfather, grandfather, father and his own.[149]

Robert de Vere's increased prestige and pride in his new titles was evident in his own lifetime. He dated his own documents in reference to his new titles both in Ireland and in an English context. In a letter appointing William Flores of Oakham as undersheriff of Rutland he used Richard II's regnal year and 'de n[o]tre duchee primer'.[150] Yet, he had not entirely forgotten his familial origins either. Though the various lists of his goods are sparing in the detail, one worsted 'aula', a hanging, had the arms of Oxford on it, while at Chester he had two banners and three other cloths with the arms of Chester and Oxford quartered and a surcoat of the same, but also two banners just with the arms of Oxford.[151] Two years earlier, in 1385, he signed a petition that the king granted with the abbreviated form of his comital title, 'Oxen', but added a five-pointed star, the molet, from his family arms.[152]

Nor does the evidence of the material culture simply suggest conspicuous consumption and ostentatious display. De Vere's extensive and expensive chapel goods cannot be taken as evidence of religious devotion in its own right – extravagance and display might extend to the noble chapel as well as the hunt, the tournament and the feast – though it might easily denote piety as well. Nonetheless, de Vere's chapel personnel probably numbered fourteen clerks in 1388, a high number not generally matched by his peers amongst the higher nobility.[153] Other evidence could support the idea of a certain level

---

[148] D.D. Andrews, 'Sible Hedingham, St Peter. The Vestry and the Medieval Floor Tiles Discovered in It', *EAH*, 3rd series, 36 (2005), 210.

[149] The thirteenth earl on at least one occasion used the title of marquess of Dublin. The reversal of de Vere's forfeiture of 1388 (reversed in 1397, reimposed in 1399) in 1464 and his own in 1485 theoretically entitled him to use the title of duke of Ireland (but not marquess of Dublin as that grant was revoked on the grant of the dukedom): Ross, *John de Vere*, 53, 135.

[150] E368/159, rot. present. 2.

[151] E364/24, rot. 7 for the hanging (detail of arms not noted in E36/66, p. 6); E101/631/13 for the banners and 'pannus', a cloth bearing a coat of arms.

[152] SC8/224/11160.

[153] E36/66, p. 7 has fourteen surplices for chaplains amongst his household goods. For comparative figures to this one and for the relative infrequency that large chapel establishments can be seen amongst the higher nobility, see A. Wathey, *Music in the Royal and Noble Households in Late Medieval England. Studies of Sources and Patronage* (London, 1989), 52–3.

Plate 1   Arms of de Vere, Ireland and de Coucy, Porch of Lavenham Church, Suffolk, late fifteenth century. Photograph author's own. The arms in quarters 2 & 4 are those of Ingelram VII de Coucy (d. 1397), father of Philippa, with de Coucy quartered with the arms of Austria, denoting his mother, Catherine of Austria – they are not those of Leuven, depicting Agnes Lancecrone, as suggested by Greatorex, *Robert de Vere*, 48. It is odd, however, that the arms of Coucy are not quartered with those of England, to reflect Philippa's descent via her mother, Princess Isabella, from Edward III.

of religious devotion. A grant of 10s annually to a hermit, John Newton, at the hermitage of St Anne's Colchester, could be evidence of no more than a conventional piety, but could also suggest something a little deeper.[154] One

[154] *CPR, 1385–9*, 405. For an excellent discussion of religion and the nobility in this period, see J. Catto, 'Religion and the English Nobility in the Later Fourteenth Century', in H. Lloyd-Jones, V. Pearl and B. Worden, eds, *History and Imagination. Essays in Honour of H.R. Trevor-Roper* (London, 1981), 43–55. For the following point regarding funerals both rejecting ostentatious display and embracing it, see examples in ibid., 50–1.

of the sets of his goods contained thirty rosaries of great pearls, though it is possible these were intended for gifts.[155] Much more would be known of his religious interests, particular churches, houses and orders he patronised, whether he intended to embrace or reject worldly pomp at his funeral, and how much he thought he needed prayers for his soul, had his will survived. He had spent his early years in a familial environment at least conventionally religious. His father, Earl Thomas, had owned several reliquaries, including a fragment of the True Cross, which would have been Robert de Vere's eventually, after the death of Countess Maud to whom Earl Thomas bequeathed it.[156] However, the idea of de Vere's piety must not be taken too far. Simon Walker, in a study of political saints in late medieval England, referenced the fact that a book of hours dating from 1420 to 1430, now in the Fitzwilliam Museum in Cambridge, contains prayers to Robert, earl of Oxford, and noted that 'even Richard II's favourite, Robert de Vere, earl of Oxford, was thought a worthy object of devotion'.[157] While the manuscript itself is ambiguous, simply mentioning a Robert, earl of Oxford, who led an exemplary life as a Christian knight, giving charity towards the poor and undertaking penitentiary acts,[158] the Robert, earl of Oxford, mentioned is likely not to have been the duke of Ireland (almost always referred to as such rather than as earl of Oxford) but instead the sixth earl of Oxford who died in 1331.[159]

Another possible connection with literary culture in its broadest sense comes from the links extrapolated between the great late fourteenth-century

---

[155] E101/631/13.

[156] *Registrum Simonis de Sudbiria*, ed. Fowler, i, 4.

[157] Walker, *Political Culture*, ed. Braddick, 200. The same connection to the ninth earl was made by Doyle, 'Books Connected with the Vere Family and Barking Abbey', 236.

[158] Fitzwilliam Museum, Cambridge, MS 49, fol. 8r; M.R. James, *A Descriptive Catalogue of the Manuscripts in the Fitzwilliam Museum* (Cambridge, 1895), 121.

[159] A French life of 'Robert Earl of Oxford… with diverse and many great miracles' commissioned by the thirteenth earl of Oxford to be printed by Caxton was almost certainly about the sixth earl: G.D. Painter, *William Caxton. A Quincentenary Biography of England's First Printer* (London, 1976), 164–5; for discussion, Ross, *John de Vere*, 208–9. Weever's funeral monuments noted that the sixth earl was 'so prudent, his hospitalitie and other workes of charitie so wisely abundant; and his temperance with a religious zeale so admirablie conioyned, that he was surnamed the good Earle of Oxford; and the vulgar esteemed him a saint': J. Weever, *Ancient Funeral Monuments within the United Monarchy…* (London, 1631), 616. William Jenyns's ordinary, compiled c. 1380 and thus almost certainly pre-dating the duke of Ireland's career, makes reference to the arms of 'Seinte Robert, Counte de Oxenfforde': *Medieval Ordinary* (4 vols, London, 1992), iv, ed. T. Woodcock and S. Flower, 327.

poem *Sir Gawain and the Green Knight* and de Vere. Firmly associated on grounds of dialect with the north-west region and particularly Cheshire, and plausibly datable to the later 1380s (although the later 1390s are also possible), several aspects of the work and its composition have been highlighted to suggest that de Vere was the allegorical subject or, at least, obliquely referred to. Sir John Stanley, de Vere's lieutenant in Ireland, has been suggested as either the patron or, more recently, the likely author of the poem.[160] The latter possibility, though there is little to disprove it and the themes of the poems do plausibly fit with the interests of a local aristocrat, is inevitably partially speculative but certainly feasible. It has been suggested that as the poet refers to Gawain being made a duke and the use of 'ver' (or spring) referring to beautiful clothing, and that this was a dig at the expense of de Vere, 'famous for flamboyant dress', the date of composition must be therefore between de Vere's creation as a duke (13 October 1386) and Radcot Bridge (20 December 1387).[161] How famous de Vere was in his own lifetime for his dress is not clear, and the references to de Vere, if that is what they are, are sufficiently coded as not to delimit the date of composition to the height of his power. There has also been an extended case put forward that the poem was political allegory, that Richard equates to King Arthur, the Green Knight was the earl of Arundel and Gawain was Robert de Vere. This is based on heraldic arguments – notably that Gawain's device of a pentangle is

---

[160] That he was the patron: Mathew, *Court of Richard II*, 166; E. Wilson, 'Sir Gawain and the Green Knight and the Stanley Family of Stanley, Storeton and Hooton', *Review of English Studies*, new series, 30 (1979), 308–16. That he was the author: A. Breeze, 'Sir John Stanley (c. 1350–1414) and the "Gawain"-Poet', *Arthuriana*, 14 (2004), 15–30; idem, 'Did Sir John Stanley write Sir Gawain and the Green Knight?', *SELIM. Journal of the Spanish Society for Medieval English Language and Literature*, 27 (2022), 81–113, and in more detail, idem, *The Historical Arthur and the 'Gawain' Poet. Studies on Arthurian and Other Traditions* (Lanham, MD, 2023). I am grateful to Dr Breeze for alerting me to his latest work and correspondence on the matter. The sober assessment of the historical context in M.J. Bennett, 'The Historical Background', in D. Brewer and J. Gibson, eds, *A Companion to the Gawain-Poet* (Cambridge, 1997), 71–90 is excellent. For a broader discussion of Richard II and literary culture, see M.J. Bennett, 'The Court of Richard II and the Promotion of Literature', in B.A. Hanawalt, ed., *Chaucer's England. Literature in Historical Context* (Minneapolis, MN, 1992), 3–20.

[161] The literary analysis comes from A.W. Astill, *Political Allegory in Late Medieval England* (Ithaca, NY, 1999), 124–6, 129, 137. Astill reflected that this meant it was written between 1397 and 1400. The attribution to 1386-7, drawing on Astill's analysis but re-dating it, is from Breeze, 'Did Sir John Stanley Write Sir Gawain', 109 and see other works by the author in the note above.

similar to the five pointed de Vere molet – as well as the play on 'ver'/Vere.[162] Meanwhile, it has also been suggested that Gawain's dalliance with the Lady of Bertilak in the poem may also be, in reverse, a comment on de Vere's abduction/seduction of Agnes Lancecrone, and more generally a reflection of the sexual disorder of Richard's court.[163] There are some obvious notes of dissonance if identifying any of the characters in the poem too closely with actual historical figures, and much of this is inevitably very speculative. If a contrary argument is to be constructed, de Vere's extremely short association with Cheshire directly – September to December 1387 – needs to be taken into account, given the clear link with the county in dialect and subject, albeit there were slightly longer associations between de Vere and the Stanley family (March 1386–December 1387). Was he really a figure who would be identified by the reader as the allegorical subject before 1387 or much after 1388? At best the case for any kind of link concerning the composition or the subject of the poem with de Vere cannot be proven.

[162] Astill, *Political Allegory*, ch. 5 contains the full case, and 123–30 for Robert de Vere.
[163] A. Thomas, *The Court of Richard II and Bohemian Culture* (Cambridge, 2020), 113–15.

Conclusion

> This duke of Ireland doth with the king and the realm as he pleases.
>
> (Words placed in the mouths of 'many nobles' in 1387 by Froissart.)[1]

History has not been kind to Robert de Vere. Critical comments by contemporaries have become common currency amongst many later writers, whether or not they were accurate, and one of the aims of this study has been to seek to construct a more balanced and nuanced portrayal. For example, the label that Richard II's favourites were knights of Venus rather than Bellona, applied by the poisonous pen of Thomas Walsingham, has by and large stuck. Yet it is unfair in de Vere's case. By 1385 and the age of twenty-three de Vere had campaigned in France and Scotland; while neither campaign had been militarily successful, that was not his fault as he had not led either expedition. There are hints even in hostile chronicle accounts that suggest a more balanced view should be sought. De Vere may not have been a great commander but Knighton's positive description of his leadership from the front at Radcot Bridge and then his daring escape have already been noted. Froissart mentions the report at the French court of de Vere as a gallant knight as well as his distinguished tournament performance.[2] Criticism of the courtiers as unmartial was, of course, part of the similar depiction of the king that has been rightly challenged by Chris Fletcher among others.[3] Likewise, the idea that the political nation was united against de Vere and his fellow favourites in 1387–8 has been part of the dominant narrative of Richard II's reign almost since the Appellants wrote that narrative during the Merciless Parliament. Yet, as several historians have pointed out, this does not tell the whole picture. Davies has argued that the episcopate was not partisanly against Richard in 1386–7, as almost no one except Bishop Arundel of Ely acted with the Appellants, and the clergy withdrew from the Merciless Parliament of 1388 on canonical grounds.[4] Given-Wilson has noted that most of the baronage were trying to

---

[1] Froissart, ed. Johnes, ii, 263.

[2] Froissart, ed. Johnes, ii, 331, 404.

[3] Fletcher, *Richard II*, esp. chs 6 and 7.

[4] Davies, 'Episcopate', 669–71.

avoid trouble in 1387–8 rather than taking a political stand.[5] Opinion was split in London as Dodd has shown.[6]

While his legacy to his successors in the earldom was damaging, there were some later efforts to redeem his memory. An obit was endowed for de Vere at St George's Chapel, Windsor, fourteen years after his death. If seemingly an odd choice of location for an obit, it reflected his status as a knight of the Garter and was one of the very few obits for first and second-generation Garter knights outside the immediate royal family.[7] The first celebration was 20 November 1406 (the obit date was two days before the generally recognised date of his death on 22 November).[8] The obit was almost certainly paid for by his mother, as the accounts of the canons of St George's record expenses for four separate meetings with the countess between December 1405 and March 1406.[9] It remains a striking remembrance, however, given its timing during the reign of one of the victors of Radcot Bridge, Henry Bolingbroke, and de Vere's status as a proven traitor after the reimposition of his forfeiture in 1399. The thirteenth earl of Oxford reversed Robert de Vere's forfeiture in parliament in 1464, at his first available opportunity, at least in part for the sake of family honour, rather than simply for possible material gain. At some point between 1485 and 1513, a family cartulary was made, and into it was copied most of the proceedings against Robert de Vere made in the 1388 parliament as well as his patents of creation as marquess of Dublin and duke of Ireland.[10] However, family efforts at rehabilitation did not do not seem to have influenced a wider audience.

It is possible to go as far as painting de Vere as primarily the victim of political circumstances. The contradictions inherent in the polity of England in the 1380s were stark. The political nation acquiesced in Richard II taking the reins of power into his hands from 1381 onwards, and then sought to restrict the unfettered powers of the monarchy thereafter, indeed going further than almost any precedent since the 1260s in doing so with the commission of 1386. Even

---

[5] Given-Wilson, 'Richard II and the Higher Nobility', 116.

[6] Dodd, 'Thomas Favent', 411–12.

[7] A.K.B. Roberts, 'The Central and Local Financial Organisation and Administrative Machinery of the Royal Free Chapel of St George within the Castle of Windsor from its Foundation (1348) to the Treasurership of William Gillot (1415–16)' (unpublished PhD, University of London, 1942), 104.

[8] St George's Chapel, Windsor, XV.34.24, m. 3.

[9] St George's Chapel, Windsor, XV.34.23, m. 3. The obit continued to be celebrated throughout the fifteenth century. The cost of endowing an obit was approximately £200 in cash or with land and rents: Roberts, 'Central and Local', 104–5.

[10] Ross, *John de Vere*, 53–4; Bodleian, Rawl. B 248, fol. 7r–14v.

one of Richard's harshest critics hints at this. Thomas Walsingham described Thomas of Woodstock bursting into the king's chamber in 1384 and swearing that he would attack anyone, even the king, who intended to accuse John of Gaunt of treason. The chronicler added 'these words would have been a capital offence, if the king had been in proper control of the reins of government'.[11] He may have meant it as a criticism of Richard, but it could equally be used to point to the difficulties Richard faced. Richard himself angrily told critics in the parliament of 1384 that if he was not allowed all the power, he could not be blamed for all that was going wrong. Nor, therefore, should his advisors, ministers and closest supporters but they were the ones who paid the price in 1388 for Richard's attempt to exercise royal power.[12] Three died in exile while several others were beheaded as a result of the decisions and actions of the Appellants. If the king was asserting royal authority and obedience to the crown as the hallmark of his policy, after fifteen years of monarchical decline during Edward III's last years and Richard's own minority, this was hardly a surprise nor objectionable as an end.[13] In one reading, de Vere was doing little more than supporting his king against his critics in political and economic conditions during the early to mid-1380s that made the exercise of effective kingship and the successful execution of policy highly difficult.

Such a reading takes matters too far. De Vere was not an innocent victim, acting solely for an ideological cause. There were several actions that broke the contemporary political code, offended the moral and ethical standards of the day and laid him wide open to criticism. De Vere may well have been one of the ringleaders behind the attempts to arrest and perhaps dispose of Gaunt in 1385, though such actions were only made possible by the tension between the king and Gaunt. His divorce of Philippa de Coucy was thought deeply reprehensible on the personal level at the time and was highly unwise in political terms, though contemporary depictions, such as that by Lydgate that opened this book, which placed the divorce as the main cause of hostility towards him, are probably wide of the mark. Between them, Richard II and Robert de Vere did not get the balance of patronage to de Vere right. Even discounting the life grant of royal interests in Ireland, there were too many acts of patronage at a time when the available pool was limited; their financial

---

[11] *SAC*, i, 726–7.

[12] *WC*, 68–9; Dodd, 'Knighton', 257. For a fairly sympathetic take on Richard and a fairly critical one on the Appellants, see R.H. Jones, *The Royal Policy of Richard II* (Oxford, 1968), chs 3 and 4.

[13] Saul highlights the likely role of Simon Burley and Michael de la Pole in this policy: *Richard II*, 119–20.

value was less than is normally thought but the way they appeared to the political community may have hidden that. The promotion of de Vere from marquess to duke is a good example of an act of favour that was not valuable in financial terms but was objectionable in political ones. The appearance of one group, and one man in particular within that group, being overly favoured with royal grants was hugely damaging in the difficult military, fiscal and economic circumstances of the 1380s, even if the reality was less than the appearance. Perhaps also de Vere could be unlikeable in person: perhaps the account of the sulky silence when presented with unarguable achievements by his enemies was accurate and perhaps the chroniclers' depiction of him as a snide whisperer in the king's ear reflected reality. Overall, though, this is not a long charge-sheet against de Vere compared to the exaggerated, overblown articles of the Merciless Parliament.

Placing de Vere within the context of the late medieval peerage gives us some understanding of his career. It certainly makes his position at court far more understandable. As the representative of the oldest of the comital dynasties there was nothing illegitimate in his presence at court; he was a rightful counsellor of the king, rather than some upstart interloper. He was wealthier through inherited lands than has been previously realised. Had he outlived his mother he would have had an income of around £1,700 from his parents' lands and Philippa's estates, richer indeed than many of his peers. His military leadership of royal forces in December 1387, if ultimately unsuccessful, becomes more intelligible as a member of an elite warrior caste rather than a foppish courtier. Yet he was not a typical nobleman, seeking to exercise influence within a region, primarily resident there, keeping an eye on his interests and those of his followers, and very different to, say, Gundy's characterisation of the Appellant earl of Warwick. As discussed, his local influence in his family heartland of Essex and southern Suffolk was conspicuous by its absence by 1387. His prominence at court, in the household and with the king was unusual for a member of the old nobility – though not unique – and that ultimately defined his political career.

Yet he cannot be classed simply as a courtier noble. Richard did not see him that way, and nor, surely, did de Vere define himself as such. There were other paths that his career could have gone down that were not taken or were indeed blocked off. The most obvious is his duchy of Ireland. This was a serious plan, and its architects had every intention of carrying it through. Had he been allowed to go across the Irish Sea for an extended period, then the perception of de Vere as a mere favourite would have to be different, and historians would need to discuss him as a failed or successful governor of Ireland, a statesman not just a courtier. De Vere's career from his formal majority to his exile lasted less than five years. He did not really have the chance to prove his abilities or his lack thereof.

De Vere was a royal favourite only in the most literal sense, that he enjoyed the high favour of the king. It is not otherwise particularly accurate to term him a favourite in the wider sense, with all the baggage that comes with it. He does not fulfil many of the criteria identified in the first chapter as hallmarks of the favourite. He was clearly close to the king, but not to the exclusion of all others; Richard had other friends and other senior advisors. Such a relationship as postulated in this study – of close friendship – need not, of course, preclude a homosexual relationship between the two. It is simply that there is no reliable evidence that there was one. He was responsible for scandal (and sexual disorder) at court, but in his heterosexual relationships with Philippa and Agnes. De Vere's position at court did not depend on royal favour, unlike Gaveston, Despenser or Alice Perrers. He was one of the tiny band of hereditary members of the upper nobility through ancestral birth right, though subsequently promoted. He was not given the office of great chamberlain but inherited it. His marital link to the royal family was not patronage by Richard II but through Edward III's control of his wardship. In short, he was not Richard II's creation as a peer, nor as a great landowner, though the king certainly enhanced his power and status.

There is not the evidence to say that he seriously enriched himself during his short career. Doubtless the king's favour helped his finances, but if it is accepted that Ireland – and the connected grants of the ransom of Blois and the Audley lands – were a serious policy initiative, then the landed patronage to de Vere can probably be reckoned in the hundreds rather than the thousands of pounds annually. He certainly spent substantially on his clothes, accoutrements, and other symbols of his status but no more so than others in an age when conspicuous expenditure was expected. He may have taken bribes for favours or the use of his influence with, or access to, the king but there is not a single piece of evidence to show that he did so.

While his hereditary position as great chamberlain ensured his place in the process of royal patronage, there is very little evidence that he exploited this for himself, his associates and dependants. Six pardons at his supplication and six bills signed in half a decade was hardly excessive. Unlike the Despensers and perhaps the duke of Suffolk, de Vere was no serious manipulator of the common law, barely ever appearing in the legal records. Of the two cases where a verdict can be traced, he won one (Sibille) and lost one (over one of the Audley estates). This was hardly the record of a man exploiting his favour with the king to enhance his local status, bully opponents or enrich himself. Tellingly, all the available evidence suggests that while de Vere was regularly with the king, he was not constantly in attendance on him. Little flurries of grants at his supplication and the signed bills being in two groups in early 1385, let alone the charter witness evidence, is suggestive that he was not constantly haunting the royal footsteps. This is unsurprising for a peer with his own estates and the government of Ireland, albeit at a distance, to attend to. Of course, to the opponents of the court and king, de Vere was the most high profile of a group of men who they appealed of treason, and even if he was not permanently at court, one or more of the king's circle was. However, it is important to look at de Vere in isolation as well as in terms of a faction, since he was, more than any other except the king, the target of the political actions of late 1387.

De Vere was not responsible for the direction of royal policy, as, even as a teenager, Richard II made it clear who was running the country, or at least whom he thought should be running it. Richard was to prove an overly domineering king, rather than a weak-willed one such as Edward II, or a king lacking much will at all, such as Henry VI, in whose reigns it was rather easier to enrich oneself at the expense of the crown and control royal policy. There is no sense, in contrast with Edward II, that Richard was dominated by one man alone, as Edward II seems to have been by Gaveston and Despenser successively. Poorer than Despenser, granted less patronage than Gaveston, with less control over the king and royal policy than the duke of Suffolk, de Vere seems to have acquired the odium of being a medieval favourite, without truly fitting the definition of one.

Appendix

Known Locations of Robert de Vere, 1385–7

The absence of almost any private documents, such as deeds, household or estate accounts, makes the construction of a full itinerary an impossible task. Instead, known locations have been plotted below. Since many come from royal documents, there is an inherent predilection towards Robert de Vere's time at court, so the location of the king has been noted where that is known, using the royal itinerary in Saul, *Richard II*, 468–74.

NB 1: The place and date of royal charters witnessed by de Vere have been included below (C53 references) but these should be treated with some caution. See above, pp. 114–15.

NB 2: Judicial hearings at Chester recorded in the heading as being in the presence of ('coram') Robert de Vere as justice as Chester have also been included below (CHES references) but must also be treated with some caution. Those below are in the main possible but not altogether likely, though a couple in December 1387 are highly plausible, but CHES 29/91, rot. 6 has him hearing cases at Chester on 7 January 1388 when he was two weeks into his exile.

Date	Location of King	Major Events	Source
1385			
20 July – York	[with K]	Scottish expedition	*WC*, 124
July, end – Berwick	[with K]	(to end of August)	*WC*, 124
6 Aug. – Hoselaw in Teviotdale	[with K]		C53/161, m. 15
6–c. 20 Aug.– Scotland	[with K]		*WC*, 126-30
20 Aug. – Newcastle	[with K]		C53/161, m. 15
30 Sept. – Westminster	[Windsor]		C53/161, m. 14
		Parliament, 20 Oct.–6 Dec.	
2 Nov. – Westminster	[with K?]		C53/161, m. 14
1 Dec. – Westminster	[with K]	Creation as marquess of Dublin	*WC*, 144; C53/161, m. 12
6 Dec. – Westminster	[Sheen]		C53/161, m. 14
1386			
20 Mar. – London	[Westminster]		C47/10/24/8
?23 Apr. – Windsor	[unknown]	Chapter of the Garter	Beltz, *Memorials*, 248, 300*
8 June – Kennington	[Surrey]		*RPC*, 131, no.31; https://chancery.tcd.ie/document/patent/10-richard-ii/34
30 June – Kennington	[Marlborough]		X-box 4278
7 July – Westminster	[Devizes]		C53/161, m. 6
22 July – Bristol	[with K]		C53/161, m. 5
7 Aug. – Osney, Oxon.	[Oxford]		C53/161, m. 6
12 Aug. – Oxford	[with K]		*RPC*, 130, no. 9
16 Aug. – Bath	[Woodstock]		C53/161, m. 2, 5
		Parliament 1 Oct.–30 Nov.	

KNOWN LOCATIONS OF ROBERT DE VERE, 1385–7   245

Date	Location of King	Major Events	Source
13 Oct. – Westminster	[with K]	Creation as duke of Ireland	*KC*, 352
16 Oct. – Westminster	[with K]		C53/161, m. 5
20–21 Oct. – Kennington	[uncertain, ?Eltham]		E368/159, rot present. 2
?26 Dec. – Berkhamsted	[Windsor]		SC1/43/80†
1387			
1 Mar. – Westminster	[?Nottingham]		C53/161, m.1‡
8 May – Reading	[with K]		C53/161, m. 2
29 June – Lichfield	[with K]		Staff. Archives, LD30/2/2/1, fol. 15
[1–5] Aug. – Shrewsbury	[with K]	Council	*KC*, 392
25 Aug. – Nottingham castle	[with K]	Questions to the judges	*KC*, 394
[15 Sept. – Nottingham	[Leicester]		CHES 29/91, m.1**]
[15 Sept. – Leicester Abbey	[with K]		*KC*, 400]
11 Oct. – Woodstock	[with K]		C66/324, m.11
?14 Oct. – Basford, Ches.	[Woodstock]		CHES 17/6, rot. 3
?16 Oct. – Tarporley, Ches.			CHES 17/6, rot. 4
?17 Oct. – Middlewich, Ches.			CHES 17/6, rot. 5
?19 Oct. – Nantwich, Ches.			CHES 17/6, rot. 6
10–11 Nov. – London	[with K]		*KC*, 400, 402; *WC*, 206
17, 18 or 19 Nov. – left London for Chester	[London]		*WC*, 214; *KC*, 416–19
3 Dec. – Chester	[London]		CHES 29/91, rot. 2

246   Known Locations of Robert de Vere, 1385–7

Date	Location of King	Major Events	Source
10 Dec. – Chester	[London]		CHES 29/91, rot. 3
20 Dec. – Radcot Bridge	[London]††		Various Chronicles
20–1 Dec. London or Windsor	[with K]		WC, 222
Late Dec. – Queenborough, Kent	[London]		WC, 224

* It might be presumed that he would have been present at his inauguration into the order, and robes were provided for him, but this is not certain.

† Letter sent by Sir John Lancaster from Berkhamsted on Boxing Day, year likely to be 1386 and assuming Lancaster, his chamberlain, was with him. See above, p. 205, n. 16.

‡ *CChR*, v, 307 has this as 1 March 1386, but that would be the wrong regnal year for the roll, and de Vere is noted as duke of Ireland in the witness list, a title he did not receive until October 1386: C53/161, m. 1.

** The Chester plea roll reciting de Vere's letter patent is clearly dated 'quinzisme', fifteenth, at Nottingham. It is odd given the attestation of de Vere at Leicester with the king on 15 September by Knighton and cannot be easily resolved.

†† See above, p. 178 for the question of whether the king was at Windsor rather than in London.

Bibliography

Unprinted Primary Sources

UK

Bodleian Library, Oxford
Rawlinson B248 (de Vere cartulary, c. 1485–1513)

Borthwick Institute, York
Register 12 – Register of Archbishop Neville (1374–1388)

British Library, London
Additional Manuscripts
Additional Charters
Cotton MS
Harleian MS
Lansdowne MS
Royal MS
Stowe MS

Cambridgeshire Archives, Ely
K604 – Deeds of Dullingham, Stetchworth, Wicken, etc.

Canterbury Cathedral Archives
CCA-DCc-ChAnt/I/246 – Inspeximus of case in Wexford Quarter Sessions

College of Arms, London
B20 bis
M16 bis
PH 15172
Vincent 65
Vincent 86

Edinburgh University Library, Edinburgh
MS 183 (Royal Letter Book, Edward III–Henry V)

Essex Record Office, Chelmsford
D/DPr (De Vere/Bayning Papers)

Fitzwilliam Museum, Cambridge
MS 49 (Book of Hours)

Lambeth Palace Library, London
Register Arundel
Register Courtenay I–II
Register Islip

London Metropolitan Archives, London
MS 9531/5 – Register of Robert Braybrooke (1382–1404)

National Archives, London
C44 (Court of Chancery: Common Law Pleadings, Tower Series)
C47 (Chancery Miscellanea)
C49 (Chancery and Exchequer: King's Remembrancer: Parliamentary and Council Proceedings)
C53 (Chancery: Charter Rolls)
C54 (Chancery: Close Rolls)
C66 (Chancery: Patent Rolls)
C71 (Chancery: Scotch Rolls)
C76 (Chancery: Treaty Rolls)
C81 (Chancery: Warrants for the Great Seal, Series I)
C135 (Chancery: Inquisitions Post Mortem, Series I, Edward III)
C136 (Chancery: Inquisitions Post Mortem, Series I, Richard II)
C139 (Chancery: Inquisitions Post Mortem, Series I, Henry VI)
C143 (Chancery: Inquisitions Ad Quod Damnum, Henry III to Richard III)
CHES 2 (Palatinate of Chester: Exchequer of Chester: Enrolments)
CHES 17 (Palatinate of Chester: Eyre Rolls)
CHES 25 (Palatinate of Chester: Chester County Court, Flint Justice's Sessions, and Macclesfield Eyres: Indictment Rolls and Files)
CHES 29 (Palatinate of Chester: Chester County Court and Court of Great Sessions of Chester: Plea Rolls)
CP25/1 (Court of Common Pleas, General Eyres and Court of King's Bench: Feet of Fines Files, Richard I–Henry VII)
CP40 (Court of Common Pleas: Plea Rolls)
DL37 (Duchy of Lancaster and Palatinate of Lancaster: Chanceries: Enrolments)
E13 (Exchequer of Pleas: Plea Rolls)
E28 (Exchequer: Treasury of the Receipt: Council and Privy Seal Records)

E36 (Exchequer: Treasury of the Receipt: Miscellaneous Books)
E101 (Exchequer: King's Remembrancer: Accounts Various)
E143 (Exchequer: King's Remembrancer: Extents and Inquisitions)
E152 (Exchequer: King's Remembrancer: Enrolments of Escheators' Inquisitions, Henry III to Henry VIII)
E159 (Exchequer: King's Remembrancer: Memoranda rolls and Enrolment Books)
E163 (Exchequer: King's Remembrancer: Miscellanea of the Exchequer)
E199 (Exchequer: King's Remembrancer and Lord Treasurer's Remembrancer: Sheriffs' Accounts, Petitions, etc.)
E357 (Exchequer: Pipe Office: Escheators' Accounts Rolls)
E364 (Exchequer: Pipe Office: Foreign Accounts Rolls)
E368 (Exchequer: Lord Treasurer's Remembrancer: Memoranda Rolls)
E401 (Exchequer of Receipt: Receipt Rolls and Registers)
E403 (Exchequer of Receipt: Issue Rolls and Registers)
E404 (Exchequer of Receipt: Warrants for Issue)
JUST 1 (Justices in Eyre, of Assize, of Oyer and Terminer, and of the Peace, etc.: Rolls and Files)
JUST 3 (Justices of Gaol Delivery: Gaol Delivery Rolls and Files)
KB27 (Court of King's Bench: Plea and Crown Sides: Coram Rege Rolls)
KB145 (Court of King's Bench: Crown and Plea Sides: Recorda and Precepta Recordorum Files)
SC1 (Special Collections: Ancient Correspondence of the Chancery and the Exchequer)
SC6 (Special Collections: Ministers' and Receivers' Accounts)
SC8 (Special Collections: Ancient Petitions)

Northamptonshire Archives, Northampton

FH/426/7, Inquisition in Rutland after the duke of Ireland's forfeiture

Nottingham University Library, Nottingham

Mi 6/170/87, minister's account of Market Overton, 1410–11

Somerset Archives, Taunton

DD/L/P/31/2, accounts of the bailiff of Carhampton hundred, 1381, 1383–99

Staffordshire Record Office, Stafford

D641 (The Stafford Family Collection)
LD30/2/2/1 (Lichfield Dean and Chapter Act Book 1)

St George's Chapel Archives, Windsor Castle, Berkshire

XV.34, Canon Treasurer Accounts

Belgium

Algemeen Rijksarchief, Brussels (National Archives of Belgium)
Charters from Brabant, between 1388 and 1392
Accounts rolls of the bailiff of Leuven between 1388 and 1392

Rijksarchief Leuven (State Archive, Leuven)
Archive of Saint Peter's Chapel, Leuven, 1273/834

Stadsarchief Leuven (City Archive, Leuven)
SAL, 5002-5 – Financial accounts ('stadsrekeningen'), 1388–1392
SAL, 7302, 7707 – Registers of the Court of Aldermen ('schepenbankregisters'), 1390–1393

Republic of Ireland

National Archives of Ireland, Dublin
EX 2/4/1/16, accessed via https://virtualtreasury.ie/item?isadgReferenceCode=NAI%20EX%202%2F4%2F1%2F16

Printed Primary Sources

31st Report of the Deputy Keeper of the Public Records (London, 1870).
36th Report of the Deputy Keeper of the Public Records (London, 1875).
Abstracts of Feet of Fine for Sussex, vol. iii (Sussex Record Society, 23, 1916).
Anglo-Norman Letters and Petitions from All Souls MS. 182, ed. M.D. Legge (Oxford, 1941).
'Annales Ricardi Secundi et Henrici Quarti', in *Chronica monasterii S. Albani: Johannis de Trokelowe et Henrici de Blaneforde*, ed. H.T. Riley (RS, 28:3, 1866).
Anon., 'Inventory of the Goods of Alexander Neville, Archbishop of York, 1388', *Yorkshire Archaeological Journal*, 15 (1900), 476–85.
The Anonimalle Chronicle, 1307 to 1334, eds W.R. Childs and J. Taylor (Leeds, 1991).
The Anonimalle Chronicle, 1333–81, ed. V.H. Galbraith (Manchester, 1927).
The Antient Kalendars and Inventories of the Treasury of His Majesty's Exchequer, ed. F. Palgrave (3 vols, London, 1836).
The Antiquarian Repertory, ed. F. Grose (4 vols, London, 1807–9).
T. Brinton, *The Sermons of Thomas Brinton, Bishop of Rochester (1373–89)*, ed. M.A. Devlin (2 vols, Camden Society, third series, 85–6, 1954).
The Brut or the Chronicles of England, ed. F.W.D. Brie (2 vols, EETS, Original Series, 131, 136, 1906–8).
Calendar of Inquisitions Miscellaneous (8 vols, London/Woodbridge, 1916–2003).

Calendar of Inquisitions Post Mortem (26 vols, London/Woodbridge, 1904–2009).
Calendar of Ormond Deeds, 1172–1603, ed. E. Curtis (Dublin, 1932–43).
Calendar of Papal Letters, vol. 4: 1362–1404, eds W.H. Bliss and J.A. Twemlow (London, 1902).
Calendar of Petitions to the Pope, I: 1342–1419, ed. W.H. Bliss (London, 1896).
Calendar of the Charter Rolls (6 vols, London, 1916–27).
Calendar of the Close Rolls (45 vols, London, 1892–1954).
Calendar of the Fine Rolls (22 vols, London, 1911–62).
Calendar of the Letter Books of the City of London: H (1375–1399), ed. R.R. Sharpe (London, 1907).
Calendar of the Manuscripts of the Dean and Chapter of Wells (2 vols, London, 1907–14).
Calendar of the Patent Rolls (52 vols, London, 1891–1916).
Calendar of Select Pleas and Memoranda of the City of London, 1381–1412, ed. A.H. Thomas (Cambridge, 1932).
Calendarium Inquisitionem Post Mortem Sive Escaetarum, eds J. Caley and J. Bayley (4 vols, London, 1806–28).
Catalouge des rolles gascon, norman et francois conserves dans le archives de la tour de Londres, ed. T. Carte (2 vols, London, 1743).
A Catalogue of the Manuscripts preserved in the Library of the University of Cambridge, vol. I (Cambridge, 1855)
Chambre des comptes de Flandre et de Brabant: Inventoire des comptes en rouleaux, ed. H. Nelis (Brussels, 1982).
Chambre des Comptes de Lille. Catalogue des chartes du sceau de l'Audience, ed. H. Nelis, vol. I (Brussels, 1915).
Chartularies of St Mary's Abbey, Dublin, ed. J.T. Gilbert (2 vols, RS, 80, 1884–6).
Collectanea Topographica et Genealogica, v (London, 1838).
Continuatio Eulogii. The Continuation of the Eulogium Historiarum, 1364–1413, ed. C. Given-Wilson (Oxford, 2019).
The Chronica Maiora of Thomas Walsingham, 1376–1422, trans. D. Preest and ed. J.G. Clark (Woodbridge, 2005).
The Chronicle of Adam Usk, 1377–1421, ed. C. Given-Wilson (Oxford, 1997).
'Chronicle of Dieulacres Abbey, 1381–1403', in M.V. Clarke and V.H. Galbraith, 'The Deposition of Richard II', *BJRL*, 14 (1930), 125–81.
The Chronicle of England by John Capgrave, ed. F.C. Hingeston (RS, 1, 1858).
The Chronicle of Louth Park Abbey, ed. E. Venables (Lincoln Record Society, 1, 1889).
Chronicon Angliae ab Anno Domini 1328 usque ad Annum 1388, ed. E.M. Thompson (RS, 64, 1874).
Chronicon Galfridi le Baker de Swynebroke, ed. E.M. Thompson (Oxford, 1881).
Chronique de la Traison et Mort de Richart Deux Roy Dengleterre, ed. B. Williams (RS, 1846).

Chronique du Religieux de Saint-Denys, ed. M.L. Bellaguet, vol. I (Paris, 1839).
Diplomatic Correspondence of Richard II, ed. E. Perroy (Camden Society, 3rd series, 48, 1933).
Dudley, Edmund, *The Tree of Commonwealth*, ed. D.M. Brodie (Cambridge, 1948).
Ecclesiastical Cause Papers at York: the Court of York 1301–1399, ed. D.M. Smith (Borthwick Texts and Calendars, 14, 1988).
An English Chronicle, 1377–1461, ed. W. Marx (Woodbridge, 2003).
Favent, Thomas, *Historia Mirabilis Parliamenti*, ed. M. McKisack, in *Camden Miscellany XIV* (Camden Society, 3rd series, 37, 1926).
——, 'History or Narration Concerning the Manner and Form of the Miraculous Parliament at Westminster in the Year 1386, in the Tenth Year of the Reign of King Richard the Second after the Conquest, Declared by Thomas Favent, Clerk', trans. Andrew Galloway, in *The Letter of the Law: Legal Practice and Literary Production in Medieval England*, eds E. Steiner and C. Barrington (Ithaca, NY, 2002), 231–52.
Feet of Fine for Essex, eds P.H. Reaney and M. Fitch (4 vols, Colchester, 1899–1964).
Foedera, Conventiones, Literae…, ed. T. Rymer (20 vols, 2nd ed., London, 1728).
Froissart J., *Chronicles of England, France, Spain and the Adjoining Countries*, ed. T. Johnes (2 vols, London, 1839).
——, *Oeuvres*, ed. K. de Lettenhove (Brussels, 26 vols, 1867–77).
Gesta abbatum monasterii Sancti Albani, a Thoma Walsingham, ed. H.T. Riley (3 vols, RS, 28:4, 1867–9).
Gower, John, *The Major Latin Works of John Gower. The Voice of One Crying and the Tripartite Chronicle*, ed. E.W. Stockton (Seattle, WA, 1962).
——, *Poems on Contemporary Events*, ed. D. Carlson and trans. A.G. Rigg (Toronto, 2011).
The Great Chronicle of London, ed. A.H. Thomas and I.D. Thornley (London, 1938).
'Henry of Marleborough's Chronicle', ed. J. Ware, in *Ancient Irish Histories* (2 vols, Reissued Dublin, 1809), vol. II.
Het Leenhof van Dendermonde tijdens de vijftiende eeuw. Nadere toegang op het archief van de Rekenkamers, ed. W. Stevens (Brussels, 2013).
Historia Anglicana, ed. H.T. Riley (2 vols, RS, 28:1, 1863–4).
Historia Vitae et Regni Ricardi Secundi, ed. G.B. Stow (Philadelphia, PA, 1977).
The Historians of the Church of York and its Archbishops, ed. J. Raine (3 vols, RS, 71, 1879–94).
The Historical Collections of a London Citizen, ed. J. Gairdner (Camden Society, new series, 17, 1876).
The Household of Edward IV: The Black Book and the Ordinances of 1478, A.R. Myers (Manchester, 1959).

Inventaire des archives des Chambres des Comptes, précédé d'une notice historique sur ces anciennes institutions, eds L.P. Gachard et al. (6 vols, Brussels, 1837–1996).
Inventaire des chartes et cartulaires des Duchés de Brabant et de Limbourg et des Pays d'Outre-Meuse, ed. A. Verkooren, vol. I (Brussels, 1910).
Inventaire ou table alphabétique et analytique des noms de personnes contenus dans les registres aux gages et pensions des Chambres des Comptes, ed. J. Proost (Brussels, 1890).
'Inventory of the Goods and Chattels Belonging to Thomas Duke of Gloucester and Seized in His Castle at Pleshy, co. Essex, 21 Richard II (1397) With Their Values, as Shown in the Escheator's Accounts', eds Viscount Dillon and W.H. St John Hope, *The Archaeological Journal*, 54 (1897), 275–308.
Irish Exchequer Payments, 1270–1446, ed. P. Connolly (Dublin, 1998).
John Benet's Chronicle, 1399–1462: an English Translation with New Introduction, ed. A. Hanham (Basingstoke, 2015).
John Leland's Itinerary. Travels in Tudor England, ed. J. Chandler (Stroud, 1993).
'Judgement against the Younger Despenser', ed. G.A. Holmes, *EHR*, 70 (1955), 261–7.
The Kirkstall Abbey Chronicles, ed. J. Taylor (Thoresby Society, 42, 1952).
Knighton's Chronicle, 1337–96, ed. G.H. Martin (Oxford, 1995).
Letters and Papers, Foreign and Domestic of the Reign of Henry VIII, eds J.S. Brewer, R.H. Brodie and J. Gairdner (23 vols in 38, London, 1862–1932).
Lydgate, John, *The Minor Poems of John Lydgate. II: Secular Poems*, ed. H.M. McCracken (EETS, Original Series, 192, 1934).
Maidstone, Richard, *Concordia (The Reconciliation of Richard II with London)*, trans. A.G. Rigg and ed. D.R. Carlson (Kalamazoo, MI, 2003).
Medieval Ordinary, eds T. Woodcock and S. Flower (4 vols, London, 1992).
Mémoires pour servir de preuves à l'Histoire ecclésiastique et civile de Bretagne, ed. P.H. Morice (2 vols, Paris, 1742–6).
'A Metrical History of the Deposition of Richard II, attributed to Jean Creton', ed. J. Webb, *Archaeologia*, 20 (1814), 1–423.
More, Thomas, *The Complete Works of St. Thomas More. II: The History of King Richard III*, ed. R.S. Sylvester (London, 1963).
Otterbourne, T., 'Chronicon Rerum Angliae', in T. Hearne, ed., *Duo Rerum Anglicarum Scriptores Veteres* (Oxford, 1732).
Parliament Rolls of Medieval England, eds C. Given-Wilson, P. Brand, S. Phillips, W.M. Ormrod, G. Martin, A. Curry and R. Horrox (17 vols, Woodbridge, 2005).
The Paston Letters, ed. J. Gairdner (6 vols, London, 1904).
Paston Letters and Papers of the Fifteenth Century, ed. N. Davis (3 vols, EETS, Supplementary Series, 20–22, 2004–5).
Pedes Finium, ed. W. Rye (Cambridge Antiquarian Society Publications, 1891).

'Petition of the Lady Isabella, Countess of Bedford', ed. J. Bain, *The Archaeological Journal*, 36 (1879), 174–6.
'The Petition of Edmund Dudley', ed. C.J. Harrison, *EHR*, 87 (1972), 82–99.
Plantagenet, Henry, duke of Lancaster, *Le Livre des seyntz medicines / The Book of Holy Medicines*, ed. C. Batt (Medieval and Renaissance Texts and Studies, 419, 2015).
Political Poems and Songs, ed. T. Wright (2 vols, RS, 14, London, 1859).
The Political Songs of England from the Reign of John to that of Edward II, ed. T. Wright (Camden Society, 1st series, 6, 1839).
Polychronicon Ranulphi Higden, ed. J.R. Lumby, vol. 9 (RS, 41, 1866).
Preaching in the Age of Chaucer. Selected Sermons in Translation, ed. S. Wenzel (Washington, DC, 2008).
'Private Indentures for Life Service in Peace and War 1278–1476', eds M. Jones and S. Walker, in *Camden Miscellany XXXII* (Camden Society, fifth series, 3, 1994), 1–190.
Proceedings and Ordinances of the Privy Council, ed. N.H. Nicolas (7 vols, London, 1834–7).
The Register of Simon Sudbury, Archbishop of Canterbury, 1375–1381, ed. F.D. Logan (Canterbury and York Society, 110, 2020).
Registrum Simonis de Sudbiria, eds R.C. Fowler and C. Jenkins (2 vols, Canterbury and York Society, 34, 38, 1927–38).
The Reign of Richard II, ed. A.K. McHardy (Manchester, 2012).
Report from the Lords Committees Touching the Dignity of a Peer of the Realm (5 vols, London, 1829).
A Roll of the Proceedings of the King's Council in Ireland for a portion of the Sixteenth Year of the Reign of Richard II, A.D. 1392–3, ed. J. Graves (RS, 69, 1877).
Rotulorum Patentium et Clausorum Cancellarie Hibernie Calendarium, ed. E. Tresham (Dublin, 1828).
The Royal Charter Witness Lists 1426–1516, ed. J. Ross (List and Index Society, 316, 2012).
The Royal Charter Witness Lists of Edward II (1307–1326), ed. J.S. Hamilton (List and Index Society, 288, 2001).
The St. Albans Chronicle. The Chronica Maiora of Thomas Walsingham, eds J. Taylor, W.R. Childs and L. Watkiss (2 vols, Oxford, 2003–11).
Sir Gawain and the Green Knight, eds J.R.R. Tolkein and E.V. Gordon, 2nd edn, rev. N. Davis (Oxford, 1967).
The Soldier in Later Medieval England Online Database, www.medievalsoldier.org.
'Some Notes from the Register of Henry de Wakefield, Bishop of Worcester on the Political Crisis of 1386–8', ed. R.G. Davies, *EHR*, 86 (1971), 547–58.
Somers Tracts. A Collection of Scarce and Valuable Tracts…, ed. Sir. W. Scott (13 vols, 2nd edn, London, 1809–15).

Statutes and Ordinances and Acts of the Parliament of Ireland from the Reign of King John to that of Henry V, ed. H.F. Berry (Dublin, 1907).
Statutes of the Realm (11 vols, London, 1810–28).
Testamenta Vetusta, ed. N.H. Nicolas (2 vols, London, 1826).
'Two Entries from the Register of John de Shirburn, Abbot of Selby 1369–1408', ed. G.S. Haslop, *Yorkshire Archaeological Journal*, 41 (1964), 287–97.
Vita Edward Secundi. The Life of Edward the Second, ed. W.R. Childs (Oxford, 2005).
Weever, J., *Ancient Funeral Monuments within the United Monarchy ...* (London, 1631).
The Westminster Chronicle, 1381–94, eds L.C. Hector and B.F. Harvey (Oxford, 1982).
Wykeham's Register, ed. T.F. Kirby (2 vols, Hampshire Record Society, 1896–9).
Year Books of Richard II. 8–10 Richard II, 1385–7, eds L.C. Hector and M.J. Hager (Year Books Series, 4, Ames Foundation, 1987).

Secondary Sources

Ambler, S.T., *The Song of Simon de Montfort: England's First Revolutionary and the Death of Chivalry* (London, 2019).
Ambühl, R., *Prisoners of War in the Hundred Years War. Ransom Culture in the Late Middle Ages* (Cambridge, 2013).
Andrews, D.D., 'Sible Hedingham, St Peter. The Vestry and the Medieval Floor Tiles Discovered in it', *EAH*, 3rd series, 36 (2005), 207–11.
An Inventory of the Historical Monuments in Essex, Volume 1: North West (London, 1916).
An Inventory of the Historical Monuments in Essex, Volume 3: North East (London, 1922).
Archer, R.E, 'The Estates and Finances of Margaret of Brotherton, c. 1320–1399', *Historical Research*, 60 (1987), 264–80.
——, 'Rich Old Ladies: The Problems of Late Medieval Dowagers', in A.J. Pollard, ed., *Property and Politics. Essays in Late Medieval English History* (Gloucester, 1984), 15–35.
Armstrong, C.A.J., 'Politics and the First Battle of St. Albans', in idem, ed., *England, France and Burgundy in the Fifteenth Century* (London, 1983), 1–72.
Ashe, L., *Richard II. A Brittle Glory* (London, 2016).
Astill, A.W., *Political Allegory in Late Medieval England* (Ithaca, NY, 1999).
Bagerius, H. and Ekholst, C., 'Kings and Favourites: Politics and Sexuality in Late Medieval Europe', *Journal of Medieval History*, 43 (2017), 298–319.
Bailey, M., *After the Black Death. Economy, Society and the Law in Fourteenth Century England* (Oxford, 2021).

——, *The Decline of Serfdom in Late-Medieval England: from Bondage to Freedom* (Woodbridge, 2014).
Baldwin, J.F., *The King's Council in England during the Middle Ages* (Oxford, 1913).
Barber, R., 'Joan, suo jure countess of Kent, and princess of Wales and of Aquitaine [called the Fair Maid of Kent], c. 1328–1385', *ODNB*.
Barron, C.M, 'The Deposition of Richard II', in J. Taylor and W. Childs, eds, *Politics and Crisis in Fourteenth Century England* (Gloucester, 1990), 132–49.
——, 'Froissart and the Great Revolt', in J.A. Lutkin and J.S. Hamilton, eds, *Creativity, Contradictions and Commemoration in the Reign of Richard II. Essays in Honour of Nigel Saul* (Woodbridge, 2022), 11–34.
——, *London in the Late Middle Ages. Government and People, 1200–1500* (Oxford, 2004).
——, 'The Quarrel of Richard II with London 1392–7', in F.R.H. Du Boulay and C.M. Barron, eds, *The Reign of Richard II: Essays in Honour of May McKisack* (London, 1971), 173–201.
—— 'Richard Whittington: the Man behind the Myth', in idem, *Medieval London. Collected Papers of Caroline M. Barron*, ed. M. Carlin and J.T. Rosenthal (Kalamazoo, MI, 2017), 267–334.
——, 'The Tyranny of Richard II', *BIHR*, 41 (1968), 1–18.
Beem, C., 'Woe to Thee, O Land! The Introduction', in idem, ed., *The Royal Minorities of Medieval and Early Modern England* (Basingstoke, 2008), 1–16.
Begent, P.J. and Chesshyre, H., *The Most Noble Order of the Garter. 650 Years* (London, 1999).
Bell, A.R., 'Medieval Chroniclers as War Correspondents during the Hundred Years War. The Earl of Arundel's Naval Campaign of 1387', in C. Given-Wilson, ed., *Fourteenth Century England VI* (Woodbridge, 2010), 171–84.
Bellamy, J.G., *The Law of Treason in the Later Middle Ages* (Cambridge, 1970).
Beltz, G.F., *Memorials of the Order of the Garter* (London, 1841).
Bennett, M.J., *Community, Class and Careerism. Cheshire and Lancashire Society in the Age of Sir Gawain and the Green Knight* (Cambridge, 1983).
——, 'The Court of Richard II and the Promotion of Literature', in B.A. Hanawalt, ed., *Chaucer's England. Literature in Historical Context* (Minneapolis, MN, 1992), 3–20.
——, '"Defenders of Truth": Lord Cobham, John Gower, and the Political Crisis of 1387–88', in J.A. Lutkin and J.S. Hamilton, eds, *Creativity, Contradictions and Commemoration in the Reign of Richard II. Essays in Honour of Nigel Saul* (Woodbridge, 2022), 35–52.
——, 'The Historical Background', in D. Brewer and J. Gibson, eds, *A Companion to the Gawain-Poet* (Cambridge, 1997), 71–90.
——, *Richard II and the Revolution of 1399* (Stroud, 1999).
——, 'Richard II and the Wider Realm', in A. Goodman and J.L. Gillespie, eds, *Richard II. The Art of Kingship* (Oxford, 1999), 187–204.

——, 'Richard II, Queen Anne, Bohemia: Marriage, Culture and Politics', in P. Brown and J. Čermák, eds, *England and Bohemia in the Age of Chaucer* (Cambridge, 2023), 13–38.
——, 'Stanley, Sir John (c. 1350–1414)', *ODNB*.
Benton, G.M., 'Essex Wills at Canterbury', *EAH*, 2nd series, 21 (1934), 234–69.
Benz, L., 'Conspiracy and Alienation: Queen Margaret of France and Piers Gaveston, the King's Favorite', in Z. E. Rohr and L. Benz, eds, *Queenship, Gender, and Reputation in the Medieval and Early Modern West, 1060–1600* (Cham, 2016), 119–41.
Biggs, D.L., 'The Appellant and the Clerk: the Assault on Richard II's Friends in Government, 1387–9', in G. Dodd, ed., *The Reign of Richard II* (Stroud, 2000), 57–70.
——, 'Patronage, Preference and Survival: the Life of Lady Margaret Sarnesfield, c. 1381–c. 1444', in L.E. Mitchell, K.L. French and D.L. Biggs, eds, *The Ties that Bind. Essays in Medieval British History in Honor of Barbara Hanawalt* (Farnham, 2011), 143–58.
Bird, R., *The Turbulent London of Richard II* (London, 1949).
Bird, W.H.B., 'The Peasant Rising of 1381: the King's Itinerary', *EHR*, 31 (1916), 124–6.
Bothwell, J., 'The Management of Position: Alice Perrers, Edward III and the Creation of a Landed Estate, 1362–1377', *Journal of Medieval History*, 24 (1998), 31–51.
Breeze, A., 'Did Sir John Stanley Write Sir Gawain and the Green Knight?', *SELIM. Journal of the Spanish Society for Medieval English Language and Literature*, 27 (2022), 81–113.
——, *The Historical Arthur and the 'Gawain' Poet. Studies on Arthurian and Other Traditions* (Lanham, MD, 2023).
——, 'Sir John Stanley (c. 1350–1414) and the "Gawain"-Poet', *Arthuriana*, 14 (2004), 15–30.
Brooks, N., 'The Organisation and Achievements of the Peasants of Essex and Kent in 1381', in H. Mayr-Harting and R.I. Moore, eds, *Studies in Medieval History Presented to R.H.C. Davis* (London, 1985), 247–70.
Brown, A.L., 'The Authorization of Letters Under the Great Seal', *BIHR*, 37 (1964), 125–56.
Brown, R.A., Colvin, H.M. and Taylor, A.J., *History of the King's Works. II The Middle Ages* (London, 1963).
Burgtorf, J., '"With My Life, His Joyes Began and Ended": Piers Gaveston and King Edward II of England Revisited', in N. Saul, ed., *Fourteenth Century England V* (Woodbridge, 2008), 31–51.
Butler, S.M., *Divorce in Medieval England. From One to Two Persons in Law* (Abingdon, 2013).
Campbell, B.M.S., *English Seigneurial Agriculture, 1250–1450* (Cambridge, 2000).

Carpenter, C., 'Bastard Feudalism in England in the Fourteenth Century', in S. Boardman and J. Goodare, eds, *Kings, Lords and Men in Scotland and Britain, 1300–1625. Essays in Honour of Jenny Wormald* (Edinburgh, 2014), 59–92.

——, 'Beauchamp, William, First Baron Bergavenny, c. 1343–1411', *ODNB*.

——, 'Political and Constitutional History: Before and After McFarlane', in R.H. Britnell and A.J. Pollard, eds, *The McFarlane Legacy: Studies in Late Medieval Politics and Society* (Stroud, 1995), 175–206.

Carpenter, D., *Henry III: the Rise to Power and Personal Rule, 1207–1258* (London, 2020).

Catto, J., 'Religion and the English Nobility in the Later Fourteenth Century', in H. Lloyd-Jones, V. Pearl and B. Worden, eds, *History and Imagination. Essays in Honour of H.R. Trevor-Roper* (London, 1981), 43–55.

Castor, H.R, 'The Duchy of Lancaster and the Rule of East Anglia, 1399–1440: a Prologue to the Paston Letters', in R.E. Archer, ed., *Crown, Government and People in the Fifteenth Century* (Stroud, 1995), 53–78.

——, *The King, the Crown and the Duchy of Lancaster. Public Authority and Private Power, 1399–1461* (Oxford, 2000).

Challet, V. and Forrest, I., 'The Masses', in C. Fletcher, J.P. Genet and J.L. Watts, eds, *Government and Political Life in England and France, c.1300–c.1500* (Cambridge, 2015), 279–316.

Chaplais, P., *Piers Gaveston. Edward II's Adoptive Brother* (Oxford, 1994).

Chrimes, S.B., 'Richard II's Questions to the Judges, 1387', *Law Quarterly Review*, 72 (1956), 365–90.

Clark, L., 'Magnates and their Affinities in the Parliaments of 1386–1421', in R.H. Britnell and A.J. Pollard, eds, *The McFarlane Legacy. Studies in Late Medieval Politics and Society* (Stroud, 1995), 127–53.

Clarke, M.V., 'Forfeiture and Treason in 1388', *TRHS*, 4th series, 14 (1931), 65–94.

Clarke, P.D., 'Petitioning the Pope: English Supplicants and Rome in the Fifteenth Century', in L. Clark, ed., *The Fifteenth Century XI. Concerns and Preoccupations* (Woodbridge, 2012), 41–60.

Clementi, D., 'Richard II's Ninth Question to the Judges, 1387', *EHR*, 86 (1971), 96–113.

Cohn, S.K., Jr, *Popular Protest in Late Medieval English Towns* (Cambridge, 2013).

Coleman, J., *English Literature in History, 1350–1400. Medieval Readers and their Writers* (London, 1981).

Cokayne, G.E., *The Complete Peerage*, ed. V. Gibbs et al. (13 vols, London, 1910–59).

Copsey, R., *Biographical Register of Carmelites in England and Wales 1240–1540* (Faversham, 2020).

Costain, T., *The Last Plantagenets* (New York, 1962).

Crooks, P., 'Factions, Feuds and Noble Power in the Lordship of Ireland, c. 1356–1496', *Irish Historical Studies*, 35 (2007), 425–54.
——, 'Representation and Dissent: "Parliamentarianism" and the Structure of Politics in Colonial Ireland, c. 1370–1420', *EHR*, 125 (2010), 1–34.
——, 'The "Calculus of Faction" and Richard II's Duchy of Ireland, c. 1382–9', in N. Saul, ed., *Fourteenth Century England V* (Woodbridge, 2008), 94–115.
Davies, R.G., 'Alexander Neville, Archbishop of York 1374–1388', *Yorkshire Archaeological Journal*, 47 (1975), 87–101.
——, 'The Episcopate and the Political Crisis in England of 1386–1388', *Speculum*, 51 (1976), 659–93.
Davies, R.R., *Lords and Lordship in the British Isles in the Late Middle Ages*, ed. B. Smith (Oxford, 2009).
——, 'Richard II and the Principality of Chester, 1397–9', in F.R.H. du Boulay and C.M. Barron, eds, *The Reign of Richard II. Essays in Honour of M. McKisack* (London, 1971), 256–79.
Davis, V., 'Irish Clergy in Late Medieval England', *Irish Historical Studies*, 32 (2000), 145–60.
D'Avray, D.L., 'Authentication of Marital Status: A Thirteenth-Century English Royal Annulment Process and Late Medieval Cases from the Papal Penitentiary', *EHR*, 120 (2005), 987–1013.
——, *Medieval Marriage. Symbolism and Society* (Oxford, 2005).
Deslisle, L., *Cabinet des manuscrits de la Bibliothèque Impériale*, i (Paris, 1868).
Dobson, R.B., 'The Authority of the Bishop in Late Medieval England: the Case of Archbishop Alexander Neville of York, 1374–1388', in B. Vogler, ed., *Miscellanea Historiae Ecclesiasticae*, 8 (Louvain, 1987), 181–91.
——, 'Neville, Alexander', *ODNB*.
Dodd, G. and Petit-Renaud, S., 'Grace and Favour: the Petition and its Mechanisms', in C. Fletcher, J.P. Genet and J.L. Watts, eds, *Government and Political Life in England and France, c.1300–c.1500* (Cambridge, 2015), 240–78.
Dodd, G., 'Henry Knighton, the Commons and the Crisis of Governance in the 1380s', *Historical Research*, 94 (2021), 235–66.
——, *Justice and Grace. Private Petitioning and the English Parliament in the Late Middle Ages* (Oxford, 2007).
——, 'Patronage, Petitions and Grace: the "Chamberlains' Bills" of Henry IV's Reign', in G. Dodd and D. Biggs, eds, *The Reign of Henry IV. Rebellion and Survival, 1403–1413* (York, 2008), 105–35.
——, 'Richard II and the Fiction of Majority Rule', in C. Beem, ed., *The Royal Minorities of Medieval and Early Modern England* (Basingstoke, 2008), 103–59.
——, 'Was Thomas Favent a Political Pamphleteer? Faction and Politics in Later Fourteenth-Century London', *Journal of Medieval History*, 37 (2011), 397–418.

Doyle, A.I., 'Books Connected with the Vere Family and Barking Abbey', *EAH*, 2nd series, 25 (1955–60), 222–43.
Duffy, S., *Ireland in the Middle Ages* (Basingstoke, 1997).
Dugdale, W., *The Baronage of England* (2 vols, London, 1675–6).
Duls, L.D., *Richard II in the Early Chronicles* (The Hague, 1975).
Dunn, A., *The Peasants' Revolt. England's Failed Revolution of 1381* (2nd edn, Stroud, 2004).
——, *The Politics of Magnate Power in England and Wales 1389–1413* (Oxford, 2003).
——, 'Richard II and the Mortimer Inheritance', in C. Given-Wilson, ed., *Fourteenth Century England II* (Woodbridge, 2002), 159–70.
Dunn, C., *Stolen Women in Medieval England. Rape, Abduction, and Adultery, 1100–1500* (Cambridge, 2013).
Eiden, H., 'Joint Action against "Bad" Lordship: The Peasants' Revolt in Essex and Norfolk', *History*, 83 (1998), 5–30.
Egan, S., 'Richard II and the Wider Gaelic World: A Reassessment', *Journal of British Studies*, 57 (2018), 221–52.
Elliot, J.H. and Brockliss, L.W.B, eds, *The World of the Favourite* (New Haven, CT, 1999).
Fairweather, F.H., 'Colne Priory, Essex, and the Burials of the Earls of Oxford', *Archaeologia*, 87 (1937), 275–95.
Federico, S., 'Queer Times: Richard II in the Poems and Chronicles of Late Fourteenth-Century England', *Medium Aevum*, 79 (2010), 25–46.
Fletcher, C., 'Corruption at Court? Crisis and the Theme of *luxuria* in England and France, c. 1340–1422', in S.J. Gunn and A. Janse, eds, *The Court as a Stage. England and the Low Countries in the Later Middle Ages* (Woodbridge, 2006), 28–38.
——, *Richard II. Manhood, Youth and Politics, 1377–99* (Oxford, 2008).
Ford, A., 'The Essex Sessions of the Peace and the "Peasants' Revolt" of 1381', *EAH*, 4th series, 10 (2019), 142–8.
Frame, R., *English Lordship in Ireland, 1318–1361* (Oxford, 1982).
——, 'Two Kings in Leinster: The Crown and the Mic Mhurchadha in the Fourteenth Century', in T.B. Barry, R. Frame and K. Simms, eds, *Colony and Frontier in Medieval Ireland. Essays Presented to J.F. Lydon* (London, 1995), 155–75.
Fryde, N., *The Tyranny and Fall of Edward II, 1321–6* (Cambridge, 1979).
Galpin, F.W., 'The History of the Church of Hatfield Regis or Broad Oak, with Some Account of the Priory Buildings', *EAH*, 2nd series, 6 (1898), 327–41.
Geaman, K.L., *Anne of Bohemia* (Basingstoke, 2022).
——, 'Anne of Bohemia and her Struggle to Conceive', *Social History of Medicine*, 29 (2016), 224–44.

———, 'A Personal Letter Written by Anne of Bohemia', *EHR*, 128 (2013), 1086–94.
Gilbert, J.T., *History of the Viceroys of Ireland* (Dublin, 1865).
Gillespie, J.L., 'Isabella, Countess of Bedford (1332–1379)', *ODNB*.
———, 'Richard II: King of Battles?', in idem, ed., *The Age of Richard II* (Stroud, 1997), 139–64.
———, 'Thomas Mortimer and Thomas Molineux: Radcot Bridge and the Appeal of 1387', *Albion*, 7 (1975), 161–73.
Given-Wilson, C., *Chronicles. The Writing of History in Medieval England* (London, 2004).
———, 'The Earl of Arundel, the War with France and the Anger of King Richard II', in R.F. Yeager, T. Takamiya, and T. Jones, eds, *The Medieval Python: the Purposive and Provocative Work of Terry Jones* (Basingstoke, 2012), 27–38.
———, *The English Nobility in the Late Middle Ages. The Fourteenth Century Political Community* (London, 1987).
———, *Henry IV* (London, 2016).
———, 'The King's Confessors and the Royal Conscience in Late Medieval England', in J. Bothwell and J.S. Hamilton, eds, *Fourteenth Century England XII* (Woodbridge, 2022), 1–28.
———, 'Perrers [*other married name* Windsor], Alice (*d.* 1401/02)', *ODNB*.
———, 'Rank and Status among the English Nobility, c. 1300–1500', in T. Huthwelker, J. Peltzer and M. Wemhöner, eds, *Princely Rank in Late Medieval Europe: Trodden Paths and Promising Avenues* (Ostfildern, 2011), 97–117.
———, 'Richard II and his Grandfather's Will', *EHR*, 93 (1978), 320–37.
———, 'Richard II and the Higher Nobility', in A. Goodman and J.L. Gillespie, eds, *Richard II. The Art of Kingship* (Oxford, 1999), 107–28.
———, 'Richard II, Edward II and the Lancastrian Inheritance', *EHR*, 109 (1994), 553–71.
———, 'Royal Charter Witness Lists, 1327–1399', *Medieval Prosopography*, 12 (1991), 35–93.
———, *The Royal Household and the King's Affinity* (New Haven, CT and London, 1986).
Goodman, A., *The Loyal Conspiracy. The Lords Appellant under Richard II* (London, 1971).
———, *John of Gaunt. The Exercise of Princely Power in Fourteenth Century Europe* (London, 1992).
Gransden, A., *Historical Writing in England, c.1307–early Sixteenth Century* (London, 1982).
Gray, H.L., 'Incomes from Land in 1436', *EHR*, 49 (1934), 607–39.
Greatorex, J., *Robert de Vere, 1362–ca. 1392, 9th earl Oxenforde, & King Richard II* (Lavenham, 2018).
Green, D., *The Black Prince* (Stroud, 2001).

——, 'Edward the Black Prince and East Anglia: An Unlikely Association', in W.M. Ormrod, ed., *Fourteenth Century England III* (Woodbridge, 2004), 83–98.

——, *Edward the Black Prince. Power in Medieval Europe* (Harlow, 2007).

——, 'The Household of Edward the Black Prince: Complement and Characteristics', in C. Woolgar, ed., *The Elite Household in England, 1100–1550* (Donington, 2018), 355–71.

——, 'The Later Retinue of Edward the Black Prince', *Nottingham Medieval Studies*, 44 (2000), 141–51.

Green, M.A.E., *Lives of the Princesses of England* (6 vols, London, 1849–55).

Griffiths, R.A., *The Reign of King Henry VI* (London, 1981).

Gundy, A.K., *Richard II and the Rebel Earl* (Cambridge, 2013).

Gunn, S.J., 'The Accession of Henry VIII', *Historical Research*, 64 (1991), 278–88.

Halliday, R.A., 'A Little Known Royal Functionary: the Brief Career of John Ripon, Rector of Kedington, 1385–8', *Suffolk Review*, 40 (2003), 19–22.

——, 'Robert de Vere, Ninth Earl of Oxford', *Medieval History*, 3 (1993), 71–85.

Halsted, E., *A Historical and Topographical Survey of the County of Kent* (12 vols, Canterbury, 1797–1801).

Hamilton, J.S., 'Gaveston, Piers, earl of Cornwall', *ODNB*.

——, *Piers Gaveston, Earl of Cornwall, 1307–1312* (Detroit, MI, 1988).

——, 'Tout and the Royal Favourites of Edward II', in C.M. Barron and J.T. Rosenthal, eds, *Thomas Frederick Tout (1855–1929): Refashioning History for the Twentieth Century* (London, 2019), 123–36.

Hanrahan, M., 'Defamation as Political Contest During the Reign of Richard II', *Medium Aevum*, 72 (2003), 259–76.

Harvey, A.S., *The De La Pole Family of Kingston Upon Hull* (East Yorkshire Local History Society, 1957).

Harvey, I.M.W., 'Was there Popular Politics in Fifteenth-Century England?', in R.H. Britnell and A.J. Pollard, eds, *The McFarlane Legacy. Studies in Late Medieval Politics and Society* (Stroud, 1995), 155–74.

Harriss, G.L., 'The Dimensions of Politics', in R.H. Britnell and A.J. Pollard, eds, *The McFarlane Legacy. Studies in Late Medieval Politics and Society* (Stroud, 1995), 1–20.

——, *King, Parliament and Public Finance in Medieval England to 1369* (Oxford, 1975).

Hartland, B., 'Policies, Priorities and Principles: the King, the Anglo-Irish and English Justiciars in the Fourteenth Century', in B. Smith, ed., *Ireland and the English World in the Late Middles Ages: Essays in Honour of Robin Frame* (Basingstoke, 2009), 130–40.

Hefferan, M., 'Household Knights, Chamber Knights and King's Knights: the Development of the Royal Knight in Fourteenth-Century England', *Journal of Medieval History*, 45 (2019), 80–99.

——, *The Household Knights of Edward III: Warfare, Politics and Kingship in Fourteenth-Century England* (Woodbridge, 2021).
Helmholz, R.H., *Marriage Litigation in Medieval England* (Cambridge, 1974).
Hibbard, L.A., 'The Books of Sir Simon Burley, 1387', *Modern Language Notes*, 30 (1915), 169–71.
Hicks, M.A., *Bastard Feudalism* (Harlow, 1995).
——, *The Wars of the Roses* (New Haven, CT and London, 2010).
Holmes, G.A., *The Estates of the Higher Nobility in Fourteenth Century England* (Cambridge, 1957).
——, *The Good Parliament* (Oxford, 1975).
Horrox, R., 'Caterpillars of the Commonwealth? Courtiers in Late Medieval England', in R.E. Archer and S. Walker, eds, *Rulers and Ruled in Late Medieval England. Essays Presented to Gerald Harriss* (London, 1995), 1–16.
——, 'Hastings, William, first Baron Hastings, (c. 1430–1483)', *ODNB*.
——, 'Shore [née Lambert], Elizabeth [Jane] (d. 1526/7?)', *ODNB*.
Hulbert, J.R., 'Chaucer and the Earl of Oxford', *Modern Philology*, 10 (1913), 433–7.
Jack, R.I., 'Entail and Descent: the Hastings Inheritance 1370–1436', *BIHR*, 38 (1965), 1–19.
James, M.R., *A Descriptive Catalogue of the Manuscripts in the Fitzwilliam Museum* (Cambridge, 1895).
Johnson, P.A., *Duke Richard of York, 1411–1460* (Oxford, 1988).
Johnston, D., 'Chief Governors and Treasurers of Ireland in the Reign of Richard II', in T.B. Barry, R. Frame and K. Simms, eds, *Colony and Frontier in Medieval Ireland. Essays Presented to J.F. Lydon* (London, 1995), 97–115.
Jones, M., 'The Fortunes of War: the Military Career of John, Second Lord Bourchier (d.1400)', *EAH*, 3rd series, 26 (1995), 145–61.
——, 'The Ransom of Jean de Bretagne, Count of Penthèivre: an Aspect of English Foreign Policy, 1386–8', *BIHR*, 45 (1972), 7–26.
Jones, R.H., *The Royal Policy of Richard II* (Oxford, 1968).
Jones, W.R., 'Political Uses of Sorcery in Medieval Europe', *The Historian*, 34 (1971–2), 670–87.
Justice, S., *Writing and Rebellion. England in 1381* (Berkeley, CA, 1994).
Kaeuper, R.W., 'Law and Order in Fourteenth-Century England: the Evidence of Special Commissions of Oyer and Terminer', *Speculum*, 54 (1979), 734–84.
Keen, M.H., 'Coucy, Enguerrand [Ingelram] de, earl of Bedford (c. 1340–1397)', *ODNB*.
King, A., '"War,", "Rebellion" or "Perilous Times"? Political Taxonomy and the Conflict in England, 1321–2', in R. Ambühl, J. Bothwell and L. Tompkins, eds, *Ruling Fourteenth-Century England. Essays in Honour of Christopher Given-Wilson* (Woodbridge, 2019), 113–32.
Kirby, J.L., *Henry IV of England* (London, 1970).

——, 'The Issues of the Lancastrian Exchequer and Lord Cromwell's Estimates of 1433', *BIHR*, 24 (1951), 121–51.
Lacey, H., *The Royal Pardon: Access to Mercy in Fourteenth-Century England* (York, 2009).
Lawrence, M., 'Edward II and the Earldom of Winchester', *Historical Research*, 81 (2008), 732–40.
——, 'Rise of a Royal Favourite: the Early Career of Hugh Despenser the Elder', in G. Dodd and A. Musson, eds, *The Reign of Edward II: New Perspectives* (York, 2006), 205–19.
Lecuppre, G., 'Faveur et trahison a la cour d'Angleterre', in M. Billore and M. Doria, eds, *La trahison au Moyen Age. De la monstruosite au crime politique, Ve–XVe siècle* (Rennes, 2009), 197–214.
Leland, J.L., 'Burley, Sir Simon (1336? –1388)', *ODNB*.
——, 'Knights of the Shire in the Parliament of 1386: a Preliminary Study of Factional Affiliations', *Medieval Prosopography*, 9 (1988), 89–103.
——, 'Unpardonable Sinners? Exclusions from the General Pardon of 1388', *Medieval Prosopography*, 17:2 (1996), 181–95.
Lewis, K.J., *Kingship and Masculinity in Late Medieval England* (Abingdon, 2013).
Lewis, N.B., 'The "Continual Council" in the Early Years of Richard II, 1377–80', *EHR*, 41 (1926), 246–51.
——, 'The Last Medieval Summons of the English Feudal Levy', *EHR*, 73 (1958), 1–26.
Lewis, N.B and Palmer, J.J.N., 'The Feudal Summons of 1385', *EHR*, 100 (1985), 729–46.
Liddell, W.H. and Wood, R.G.C., eds, *Essex and the Great Revolt of 1381* (Chelmsford, 1982).
Liddy, C.D. and Haemers, J., 'Popular Politics in the Late Medieval City: York and Bruges', *EHR*, 128 (2013), 771–805.
Lutkin, J., 'Isabella de Coucy, Daughter of Edward III: the Exception who Proves the Rule', in C. Given-Wilson, ed., *Fourteenth Century England VI* (Woodbridge, 2010), 131–48.
Lydon, J.F., 'Ireland and the English Crown, 1171–1534', *Irish Historical Studies*, 29 (1995), 281–94.
——, *The Lordship of Ireland in the Middle Ages* (Dublin, 1972).
MacCulloch, D., *Thomas Cromwell: A Life* (London, 2019).
MacKinnon, A.D., 'The Arrangements of Monuments and Seating at St. Andrew's Church, Earls Colne, During the 17th and Early 18th Centuries', *EAH*, 3rd series, 28 (1997), 165–80.
Majendie, L.A., 'Notes on Hedingham Castle, and the Family of De Vere, Earls of Oxford', *EAH*, 1st series, 1 (1858), 75–82.
Mathew, G., *The Court of Richard II* (London, 1968).

Maurer, H., *Margaret of Anjou. Queenship and Power in Late Medieval England* (Woodbridge, 2003).
Maxwell-Lyte, H.C., *Historical Notes on the Use of the Great Seal of England* (London, 1926).
——, *A History of Dunster and the Families of Mohun and Lutterell* (2 vols, London, 1909).
McDonald, A.J., *Border Bloodshed. Scotland, England and France at War, 1369–1403* (East Linton, 2000).
McFarlane, K.B., *Lancastrian Kings and Lollard Knights* (Oxford, 1972).
——, *The Nobility of Later Medieval England* (Oxford, 1973).
McHardy, A.K., 'John Scarle: Ambition and Politics in the Late Medieval Church', in L. Clark, M. Jurkowski and C. Richmond, eds, *Image, Text and Church, 1380–1600: Essays for Margaret Aston* (Toronto, 2009), 68–93.
——, 'King's Clerks: the Essential Tolls of Government', in R. Ambühl, J. Bothwell and L. Tompkins, eds, *Ruling Fourteenth-Century England. Essays in Honour of Christopher Given-Wilson* (Woodbridge, 2019), 59–76.
Mertes, K., *The English Noble Household 1250–1600* (Oxford, 1988).
Milner, J.D., 'Sir Simon Felbrigg, K.G.: the Lancastrian Revolution and Personal Fortune', *Norfolk Archaeology*, 37 (1978), 84–91.
Mitchell, S., 'The Knightly Household of Richard II and the Peace Commissions', in M.A. Hicks, ed., *The Fifteenth Century II: Revolution and Consumption in Late Medieval England* (Woodbridge, 2001), 45–54.
——, 'Richard II: Kingship and the Cult of Saints', in D. Gordon, L. Monnas and C. Elam, eds, *The Regal Image of Richard II and the Wilton Diptych* (London, 1997), 115–24.
Morant, P., *The History and Antiquities of Essex* (2 vols, London, 1768).
Morgan, P., 'Historical Writing in the North-West Midlands and the Chester Annals of 1385–88', in G. Dodd, ed., *Fourteenth Century England IX* (Woodbridge, 2016), 109–29.
——, *War and Society in Medieval Cheshire 1277–1403* (Chetham Society, 3rd series, 34, 1987).
Mortimer, I., 'Sermons of Sodomy: A Reconsideration of Edward II's Sodomitical Reputation', in G. Dodd and A. Musson, eds, *The Reign of Edward II: New Perspectives* (York, 2006), 48–60.
Müller, W.P., *Marriage Litigation in the Western Church* (Cambridge, 2021).
Musson, A. and Ormrod, W.M., *The Evolution of English Justice. Law, Politics and Society in the Fourteenth Century* (Basingstoke, 1999).
Myers, J.N.L., 'The Campaign of Radcot Bridge in December 1387', *EHR*, 42 (1927), 20–33.
Nicholas, N.H., 'An Account of the Army with which King Richard II Invaded Scotland in the Ninth Year of his Reign, A.D. 1385', *Archaeologia*, 22 (1829), 13–19.

O'Byrne, E., 'O'Brien (Ó Briain), Brian Sreamach', *Dictionary of Irish Biography*, https://www.dib.ie/.
——, *War, Politics and the Irish of Leinster, 1156–1606* (Dublin, 2003).
Oliver, C., *Parliament and Political Pamphleteering in Fourteenth-Century England* (York, 2010).
Ormrod, W.M., 'Coming to Kingship: Boy Kings and the Passage to Power in Fourteenth-Century England', in N.F. McDonald and W.M. Ormrod, eds, *Rites of Passage. Cultures of Transition in the Fourteenth Century* (York, 2004), 31–49.
——, *Edward III* (New Haven, CT and London, 2011).
——, 'Government by Commission: the Continual Council of 1386 and English Royal Administration', *Peritia*, 10 (1996), 303–21.
——, 'Knights of Venus', *Medium Aevum*, 73 (2004), 290–305.
——, 'Monarchy, Martyrdom and Masculinity: England in the Later Middle Ages', in R.H. Cullum and K.J. Lewis, eds, *Holiness and Masculinity in the Middle Ages* (Cardiff, 2004), 174–91.
——, 'Montagu, William [William de Montacute], first earl of Salisbury (1301–1344)', *ODNB*.
——, 'The Peasants' Revolt and the Government of England', *Journal of British Studies*, 29 (1990), 1–30.
——, 'The Sexualities of Edward II', in G. Dodd and A. Musson, eds, *The Reign of Edward II: New Perspectives* (York, 2006), 22–47.
Oschema, K., 'The Cruel End of the Favourite. Clandestine Death and Public Retaliation at Late Medieval Courts in England and France', in K-H. Spiess and I. Warntjes, eds, *Death at Court* (Wiesbaden, 2012), 171–95.
Otway-Ruthven, A.J., *A History of Medieval Ireland* (London, 1968).
——, *The King's Secretary and the Signet Office in the Fifteenth Century* (Cambridge, 1939).
Painter, G.D., *William Caxton. A Quincentenary Biography of England's First Printer* (London, 1976).
Palmer, J.J.N., *England, France and Christendom, 1377–99* (London, 1972).
——, 'English Foreign Policy, 1388–99', in F.R.H. Du Boulay and C.M. Barron, eds, *The Reign of Richard II. Essays in Honour of May McKisack* (London, 1971), 75–107.
——, 'The Impeachment of Michael de la Pole in 1386', *BIHR*, 42 (1969), 96–101.
——, 'The Last Summons of the Feudal Army in England, 1385', *EHR*, 83 (1968), 771–5.
——, 'The Parliament of 1385 and the Constitutional Crisis of 1386', *Speculum*, 46 (1971), 477–90.
Patterson, L., 'Court Politics and the Invention of Literature: The Case of Sir John Clanvowe', in D. Aers, ed., *Culture and History 1350–1600. Essays*

on *English Communities, Identities and Writing* (Hemel Hempstead, 1992), 7–41.
Payling, S.J., 'Legal Right and Dispute Resolution in Late Medieval England: the Sale of the Lordship of Dunster', *EHR*, 126 (2011), 17–43.
——, 'The Politics of Family: Late Medieval Marriage Contracts', in R.H. Britnell and A.J. Pollard, eds, *The McFarlane Legacy. Studies in Late Medieval Politics and Society* (Stroud, 1995), 21–47.
Pedersen, F., *Marriage Disputes in Medieval England* (London, 2000).
Perroy, E., *The Hundred Years War*, trans. W.B. Wells (London, 1951).
Peverley, S.L., 'Political Consciousness and the Literary Mind in Late Medieval England: Men "Brought up of Nought" in Vale, Hardyng, Mankind and Malory', *Studies in Philology*, 105 (2008), 1–29.
Philips, J.R.S., *Edward II* (London, 2010).
Pollard, A.J., 'The People and Parliament in Fifteenth Century England', in H.W. Kleineke, ed., *The Fifteenth Century X: Parliament, Personalities and Power: Papers Presented to Linda S. Clark* (Woodbridge, 2011), 1–16.
——, 'The People, Politics and the Constitution in the Fifteenth Century', in R.W. Kaeuper, ed., *Law, Justice and Governance: New Views on Medieval Constitutionalism* (Leiden, 2013), 311–29.
Poos, L.R., *A Rural Society after the Black Death: Essex 1350–1525* (Cambridge, 1991).
Potter, D., 'The King and his Government under the Valois, 1328–1498', in idem, ed., *France in the Later Middle Ages* (Oxford, 2002), 155–82.
Powell, E., 'After "After McFarlane": The Poverty of Patronage and the Case for Constitutional History', in D.J. Clayton, R.G. Davies and P. McNiven, eds, *Trade, Devotion and Governance: Papers in Later Medieval History* (Stroud, 1994), 1–16.
Powell, J.E., 'The Riddles of Bures', *EAH*, 3rd series, 6 (1974), 90–8.
Powell, J.E. and Wallis, K., *The House of Lords in the Middle Ages* (London, 1968).
Prescott, A.J., 'Brembre, Sir Nicholas (d. 1388)', *ODNB*.
——, 'Essex Rebel Bands in London', in W.H. Liddell and R.G.C. Wood, eds, *Essex and the Great Revolt of 1381* (Chelmsford, 1982), 55–66.
Probert, G., 'The Riddle of Bures Unravelled', *EAH*, 3rd series, 16 (1984), 53–64.
Raeymakers, D. and Derks, S., eds, *The Key to Power?: the Culture of Access in Princely Courts, 1400–1750* (Leiden, 2016).
Rawcliffe, C., 'Parliament and the Settlement of Disputes by Arbitration in the Later Middle Ages', *Parliamentary History*, 9 (1990), 316–42.
Richardson, H.G. and Sayles, G.O., 'Irish Revenue 1278–1384', *Proceedings of the Royal Irish Academy*, 62 (1962), 87–100.
Richmond, C., 'After McFarlane', *History*, 68 (1983), 46–60.

Rogers, A., 'Parliamentary Appeals of Treason in the Reign of Richard II', *American Journal of Legal History*, 8 (1964), 95–124.

Rosenthal, J.T., 'The King's "Wicked Advisors" and Medieval Baronial Rebellions', *Political Science Quarterly*, 82 (1967), 595–618.

Roskell, J.S., *The Commons and their Speakers in English Parliaments, 1376–1523* (Manchester, 1965).

——, *The Impeachment of Michael de la Pole, Earl of Suffolk, in 1386 in the Context of the Reign of Richard II* (Manchester, 1984).

Roskell, J.S., Clark, L. and Rawcliffe, C., eds, *History of Parliament: The Commons 1386–1421* (4 vols, Stroud, 1992).

Ross, C.D., 'Forfeiture for Treason in the Reign of Richard II', *EHR*, 71 (1956), 560–75.

——, 'The Household Accounts of Elizabeth Berkeley, Countess of Warwick, 1420–1', *Transactions of the Bristol and Gloucestershire Archaeological Society*, 70 (1951), 81–105.

——, *Edward IV* (London, 1974).

Ross, J., *John de Vere, Thirteenth Earl of Oxford, 1442–1513. The Foremost Man of the Kingdom* (Woodbridge, 2011).

——, 'A Rich Old Lady Getting Poorer. Maud, Countess of Oxford, and the de Vere Estates, 1371–1413', in L. Clark and J. Ross, eds, *The Fifteenth Century XX: Essays Presented to Rowena Archer* (forthcoming, Woodbridge, 2024).

——, 'Seditious Activities: the Conspiracy of Maud de Vere, Countess of Oxford, 1403–4', in L. Clark, ed., *The Fifteenth Century III. Authority and Subversion* (Woodbridge, 2003), 25–42.

——, 'Vere, Richard de, Eleventh Earl of Oxford (1385–1417), Magnate and Soldier', *ODNB*.

——, 'Vere, Thomas de, Eighth Earl of Oxford (1336x8–1371), Magnate and Soldier', *ODNB*.

Round, J.H., *The King's Serjeants and Officers of State with their Coronation Services* (London, 1911).

Saul, N., 'A Farewell to Arms? Criticism of Warfare in Late Fourteenth-Century England', in C. Given-Wilson, ed., *Fourteenth Century England II* (Woodbridge, 2002), 131–45.

——, 'The Despensers and the Downfall of Edward II', *EHR*, 99 (1984), 1–33.

——, 'Magna Carta in the Late Middle Ages, c. 1320–c.1520', in L. Clark, ed., *The Fifteenth Century XIX: Enmity and Amity* (Woodbridge, 2022), 123–36.

——, *Richard II* (London, 1997).

——, 'The Worldly Wealth of John Beauchamp of Holt', in M. Aston and R. Horrox, eds, *Much Heaving and Shoving: Late-Medieval Gentry and their Concerns. Essays for Colin Richmond* (Lavenham, 2005), 5–16.

Scattergood, V.J., 'Two Medieval Book Lists', *The Library*, 5th series, 23 (1968), 236–9.

Scofield, C.L., *The Life and Reign of Edward IV* (2 vols, reissued, Stroud, 2016).

Sherborne, J., 'The Defence of the Realm and the Impeachment of Michael de la Pole in 1386', in J. Taylor and W. Childs, eds, *Politics and Crisis in Fourteenth Century England* (Gloucester, 1990), 97–116.

——, 'Indentured Retinues and English Expeditions to France, 1369–1380', *EHR*, 79 (1964), 718–46.

Simms, K., *Gaelic Ulster in the Middle Ages. History, Culture and Society* (Dublin, 2020).

——, 'The Ulster Revolt of 1404 – an Anti-Lancastrian Dimension', in B. Smith, ed., *Ireland and the English World in the Late Middle Ages: Essays in Honour of Robin Frame* (Basingstoke, 2009), 141–60.

Simpson, A., *The Connections between English and Bohemian Painting during the Second Half of the Fourteenth Century* (London, 1984).

Smith, B., *Crisis and Survival in Late Medieval Ireland. The English of Louth and their Neighbours, 1330–1450* (Oxford, 2013).

Smith, C.W., 'A Conflict of Interest? Chancery Clerks in Private Service', in J. Rosenthal and C. Richmond, eds, *People, Politics and Community in the Later Middle Ages* (Gloucester, 1987), 176–91.

Snape, M.G., 'Skirlawe [Skirlaw], Walter, c. 1330–1406', *ODNB*.

South, H.P., 'The Question of Halsam', *Proceedings of the Modern Language Association of America*, 50 (1935), 362–71.

Starkey, D. et al., *The English Court from the Wars of the Roses to the Civil War* (London, 1987).

Starkey, D., 'Henry VI's Old Blue Gown: the English Court under the Lancastrians and Yorkists', *The Court Historian*, 4 (1999), 1–28.

Steel, A., *Richard II* (Cambridge, 1941).

Storey, R.L., 'Liveries and the Commissions of the Peace, 1388–1390', in F.R.H. Du Boulay and C.M. Barron, eds, *The Reign of Richard II* (London, 1971), 131–52.

Stow, G.B., 'Chronicles Versus Records: the Character of Richard II', in J.S. Hamilton and P.J. Bradley, eds, *Documenting the Past. Essays in Medieval History Presented to George Peddy Cuttino* (Woodbridge, 1989), 155–76.

——, 'Richard II in Thomas Walsingham's Chronicles', *Speculum*, 59 (1984), 68–102.

Stratford, J., *Richard II and the English Royal Treasure* (Woodbridge, 2002).

Strohm, P., 'Northampton [Comberton], John (d. 1398)', *ODNB*.

Sumption, J., *Divided Houses. The Hundred Years War III* (London, 2009).

Swanson, R.N., 'An Ambivalent 'First Yorkist': Edmund of Langley, Duke of York (d. 1402)', in C.M. Barron and C. Steer, eds, *The Ricardian XXXIII. Yorkist People: Essays in Memory of Anne F. Sutton* (2023), 23–34.

Taylor, J., *English Historical Literature in the Fourteenth Century* (Oxford, 1987).

Thomas, A., *The Court of Richard II and Bohemian Culture* (Cambridge, 2020).

Thornton, C., Ward, J. and Wiffen, N., eds, *The Fighting Essex Soldier: Recruitment, War and Society in the Fourteenth Century* (Hatfield, 2017).

Tompkins, L., 'Alice Perrers and the Goldsmiths' Mistery: New Evidence Concerning the Identity of the Mistress of Edward III', *EHR*, 130 (2015), 1361–91.

——, '"Edward III's Gold-Digging Mistress": Alice Perrers, Gender and Financial Power at the English Royal Court, 1360–1377', in C. Sarti, ed., *Women and Economic Power in Premodern Royal Courts* (Pittsburgh, PA, 2020), 59–71.

——, '"Said the Mistress to the Bishop": Alice Perrers, William Wykeham and Court Networks in Fourteenth-Century England', in R. Ambühl, J. Bothwell and L. Tompkins, eds, *Ruling Fourteenth-Century England. Essays in Honour of Christopher Given-Wilson* (Woodbridge, 2019), 205–26.

Tout, T.F., *Chapters in the Administrative History of Medieval England* (6 vols, Manchester, 1920–33).

Tuchman, B.W., *A Distant Mirror. The Calamitous Fourteenth Century* (Basingstoke, 1979).

Tuck, A., 'Anglo-Irish Relations, 1382–93', *Proceedings of the Royal Irish Academy*, 69 (1970), 15–31.

——, 'Pole, Michael de la, First Earl of Suffolk', *ODNB*.

——, *Richard II and the English Nobility* (London, 1973).

——, 'Richard II's System of Patronage', in F.R.H. Du Boulay and C.M. Barron, eds, *The Reign of Richard II. Essays in Honour of May McKisack* (London, 1971), 1–20.

——, 'Vere, Robert de, Ninth Earl of Oxford, Marquess of Dublin, and Duke of Ireland (1362–1392)', *ODNB*.

Vale, M.A., *Charles VII* (London, 1974).

——, 'Courts', in C. Fletcher, J.P. Genet and J.L. Watts, eds, *Government and Political Life in England and France, c.1300–c.1500* (Cambridge, 2015), 24–40.

——, *The Princely Court. Medieval Courts and Culture in North-West Europe 1270–1380* (Oxford, 2001).

Valente, C., 'The Deposition and Abdication of Edward II', *EHR*, 113 (1998), 852–81.

The Victoria County History of Buckingham, ed. W. Page (5 vols, London, 1905–20).

The Victoria County History of Cambridge and the Isle of Ely, ed. L.F. Salzman et al. (10 vols, London, 1938–2002).

The Victoria County History of Essex, ed. A.H. Doubleday et al. (12 vols, 1903–).

The Victoria County History of Middlesex, ed. W. Page et al. (13 vols, London, 1911–).

The Victoria County History of Rutland, ed. W. Page (2 vols, London, 1908–36).

Virgoe, R., 'The Crown and Local Government: East Anglia under Richard II', in F.R.H. Du Boulay and C.M. Barron, eds, *The Reign of Richard II* (London, 1971), 218–41.

Walker, S.J., 'Lancaster v. Dallingridge: a Franchisal Dispute in 14th-century Sussex', *Sussex Archaeological Collections*, 121 (1983), 87–94.
——, *The Lancastrian Affinity, 1361–99* (Oxford, 1990).
——, 'Lordship and Lawlessness in the Palatinate of Lancaster, 1370–1400', *Journal of British Studies*, 28 (1989), 325–48.
——, *Political Culture in Later Medieval England*, ed. M.J. Braddick (Manchester, 2006).
——, 'Rumour, Sedition and Popular Protest in the Reign of Henry IV', *Past & Present*, 166 (2000), 31–65.
Wallon, H., *Richard II* (2 vols, Paris, 1864).
Watts, J.L., *Henry VI and the Politics of Kingship* (Cambridge, 1996).
——, 'Pole, William de la, First Duke of Suffolk', *ODNB*.
——, 'Popular Voices in England's Wars of the Roses, c. 1445–c. 1485', in J. Dumolyn et al., eds, *The Voices of the People in Late Medieval Europe: Communication and Popular Politics* (Turnhout, 2014), 107–22.
——, 'The Pressure of the Public on Later Medieval Politics', in L. Clark and C. Carpenter, eds, *The Fifteenth Century IV: Political Culture in Late Medieval Britain* (Woodbridge, 2004), 159–80.
——, 'The Problem of the Personal: Tackling Corruption in Late Medieval England, 1250–1550', in R. Kroeze, V. André and G. Geltner, eds, *Anti-Corruption in History: From Antiquity to the Modern Era* (Oxford, 2017), 91–102.
——, 'Public or Plebs: the Changing Meaning of "the Commons", 1381–1549', in H. Pryce and J.L. Watts, eds, *Power and Identity in the Middle Ages: Essays in Memory of Rees Davies* (Oxford, 2007), 242–60.
Ward, J., *The Essex Gentry and the County Community in the Fourteenth Century* (Chelmsford, 1991).
Warner, K., *Hugh Despenser the Younger and Edward II: Downfall of a King's Favourite* (Barnsley, 2018).
Wells-Furby, B., *Aristocratic Marriage, Adultery and Divorce in the Fourteenth Century* (Woodbridge, 2019).
Woolgar, C.M., *The Great Household in Late Medieval England* (London, 1999).
Wolffe, B., *The Royal Demesne in English History. The Crown Estate in the Governance of the Realm from the Conquest to 1509* (London, 1971).
Xu, M., 'Analysing the Actions of the Rebels in the English Revolt of 1381: the Case of Cambridgeshire', *Economic History Review*, 75 (2022), 881–902.

Unpublished dissertations

Archer, R.E., 'The Mowbrays, Earls of Nottingham and Dukes of Norfolk to 1432' (unpublished DPhil., University of Oxford, 1984).
Crooks, P.J., 'Factionalism and Noble Power in English Ireland, c.1361–1423' (unpublished PhD, Trinity College Dublin, 2007).

Featherstonhaugh, C.C., 'Earls and the Crown in England, 1360–1385' (unpublished PhD, University of Cambridge, 2014).

Fildes, K.E., 'The Baronage in the Reign of Richard II, 1377–1399' (unpublished PhD, University of Sheffield, 2009).

Fletcher, C.D., 'Manhood, Youth and Politics in the Reign of Richard II, 1377–99' (unpublished DPhil., University of Oxford, 2003).

Green, D.S., 'The Household and Military Retinue of the Black Prince' (2 vols, unpublished PhD, University of Nottingham, 1998).

Lawrence, M.J., 'Power, Ambition and Political Rehabilitation: the Despensers, c. 1281–1400' (unpublished DPhil., University of York, 2005).

Leland, J.L., 'Richard II and the Counter-Appellants: Royal Patronage and Royalist Politics' (unpublished PhD, Yale University, 1979).

McKenzie, C., 'Ladies and Robes of the Garter: Kingship, Patronage, and Female Political Agency in Late Medieval England, c.1348–1445' (unpublished PhD, University of Southampton, 2019).

Mitchell, S.M., 'Some Aspects of the Knightly Household of Richard II' (unpublished PhD, University of London, 1998).

Roberts, A.K.B., 'The Central and Local Financial Organisation and Administrative Machinery of the Royal Free Chapel of St. George within the Castle of Windsor from its Foundation (1348) to the Treasurership of William Gillot (1415–16)' (unpublished PhD, University of London, 1942).

Ross, C.D., 'The Yorkshire Baronage, 1399–1435' (unpublished DPhil, University of Oxford, 1950).

Ross, J., 'The de Vere Earls of Oxford, 1400–1513' (unpublished DPhil, University of Oxford, 2005).

Stansfield, M.M.N, 'The Holland Family, Dukes of Exeter, Earls of Kent and Huntingdon, 1352–1475' (unpublished DPhil., University of Oxford, 1987).

Starr, C., 'The Essex Gentry 1381–1450' (unpublished PhD, University of Leicester, 1999).

Towson, K., 'Henry Percy, First Earl of Northumberland: Ambition, Conflict and Cooperation in Late Medieval England' (unpublished PhD, University of St Andrews, 2004).

Index

Aiscough, William, bishop of
 Salisbury 41
Albert of Wittelsbach, duke of Lower
 Bavaria, count of Holland 185, 186
Aldham, Suffolk, manor of xviii, 56
 n.53, 72, 105 n.128, 224;
 advowson of 72
Amiens, France 198
Amys, Essex, manor of 69
Anne of Bohemia, Queen of
 England 33, 65, 77, 80, 114, 118, 155
 n.30, 165, 190, 218 n.86
 her attendants and servants 158–9,
 190
Anjou, France 42
Anonimalle Chronicle, the 230
Antrim, sheriff of, Robert
 FitzEustace 144
Appellant, Lords 3, 10, 14, 24, 25, 132,
 167, 178, 183, 220
 appeal of treason against de Vere and
 others, 1387 1–3, 152, 169–70, 183–5,
 227, 242
 allegations in 1388 against de Vere and
 others 6, 152
 patronage and enrichment 86, 133,
 183–4
 release of John of Blois 130, 184
 negotiations with the French 169–
 70, 183
 domination of the king 183
 Radcot Bridge 184
 allegations not found
 treasonous 183–5
 Ireland 123, 184
 propaganda 6, 169, 237
 see also Beauchamp, Thomas, earl of
 Warwick; Fitzalan, Richard, earl
 of Arundel; Henry IV; Mowbray,

 Thomas, earl Marshal; Thomas of
 Woodstock
Aquitaine, France *see also* Gascony
 grant of, to John of Gaunt 120
Archer, Robert, of Rowenhale 112 n.163
Argentein, Sir John 75
Armenia, Leo, king of 92 n.77
Arthur, Prince of Wales (d. 1502) 230
Arundel castle, Sussex 219
Arundel, earl of, *see* Fitzalan
Arundel, Thomas, bishop of Ely,
 archbishop of York, archbishop
 of Canterbury, chancellor of
 England 20, 150 n.5, 152, 153, 166,
 194, 221, 226 n.117, 237
Arundel, Sir William xv, 190
 his wife *see* Lancecrone, Agnes *under*
 remarriage
Ashton, Lancashire, manor of xviii, 88
 n.61
Aston Sandford, Buckinghamshire,
 manor of xviii, 56 n.53, 73, 74
Athboy, Meath, church of 214
Atholl, earl of, David Strathbogie 113
Audeyn, John, of Essex 112 n.163
Audley, Sir James de 131
 his estates *see* Vere, Robert de *under*
 estates and financial situation *and*
 Ireland
Audley, Nicholas 132
Axewater, Devon, maritime commission
 in 139
Aylesbury, Buckinghamshire 141

Badlesmere family 94
Badlesmere, Giles, Lord Badlesmere (d.
 1338) 45
 his wife, Elizabeth Montagu 55 n.49
Badlesmere, Kent, manor of xviii, 55, 56
 n.53, 71, 72, 94

Baillol, Catherine de   48
Balscot, Alexander de, bishop of Ossory, bishop of Meath   138, 143, 146, 147, 223
Banastre, John, of Farington   159, 160
Bar, duke of, Robert de Montbéliard   118
Baret, Andrew, archdeacon of Wells   217
Barking, abbess of (Sibyl de Felton)   231
Barnstaple, Devon   xviii, 133 n.64
Basford, Cheshire   227 n.126, 245
Basset, Ralph, Lord Basset of Drayton (d. 1390)   155 n.30, 177, 220
Bath, Somerset   244
Bath and Wells, bishop of, *see* Harewell, John; Skirlaw, Walter de
Bavaria, John of, Prince-Bishop of Liège   196
Beauchamp, John, of Holt, Lord Beauchamp of Kidderminster, keeper of the jewels   115, 124, 155 n.30, 225
  de Vere's annuity to   132, 210, 220–1
Beauchamp, Richard, earl of Warwick (d. 1439)   229
Beauchamp, Sir Roger, Baron Beauchamp of Bletso (d. 1380)   37, 50, 63
Beauchamp, Thomas, earl of Warwick (d. 1401)   43, 53, 77 n.7, 105, 167, 168, 170, 175, 191 n.201, 225, 240
  Radcot Bridge campaign   178–80, 182
Beauchamp, William, Lord Bergavenny, captain of Calais (d. 1411)   191–2
Beaufort, Edmund, duke of Somerset (d. 1455)   13, 14, 15, 17, 21, 23, 24, 30 n.68, 33
Beaufort, John, earl of Somerset, marquess of Dorset (d. 1410)   121–2
Beaufort, Margaret, countess of Richmond (d. 1509)   40, 42
Beaufort, Roger de   61–2
Beaumont, Essex
  manor of Newhall   xviii, 60, 71, 74
  manor of Bernhams   xviii, 55 n.52, 71, 75, 215

Beaumont, John, Lord Beaumont (d. 1396)   155 n.30, 185
Beaumont, Margaret (née de Vere), Lady Beaumont (d. 1398)   xv, 63, 185 n.173
Beer, John   217 n.81
Belknap, Sir Robert, chief justice of the Common Pleas   157
Bellyster, Adam, of Cheshire   172 n.113
Bennington, William, esquire   213
Berkeley, Sir Edward de   65
Berkhamsted, Hertfordshire   62, 152, 153, 161, 167, 205 n.16, 228, 245, 246
Berners, Sir James   228 n.128
Berry, Jean of, duke of (d. 1416)   192
Berwick, Northumberland   244; siege of (1320)   25
Billericay, Essex, battle at (1381)   76
Black Book of the Royal Household, The   108
Blackcastle, county Meath, Ireland   140
Blagdon, Somerset   xviii, 133 n.64
Blois, Charles de, count of Penthièvre   129
Blois, Guy de   129
Blois, John (Jean) de, of Penthièvre
  custody of   129, 213
  ransom of   112, 128–31, 152, 205, 206, 213, 220
    payments made 1387–1392   131, 170, 186, 191–3
  release of   129, 163, 170
Bockingfield, Kent, manor of   xviii, 55, 56 n.53, 57, 72, 195
Bodiam castle, Sussex   219
Bohun family, earls of Hereford and Essex   93, 202
Bohun, Eleanor de, duchess of Gloucester   93, 202, 231 n.144
Bohun, Humphrey de, earl of Hereford and Essex (d. 1373)   93, 202
  daughters of, *see* Bohun, Mary de; Bohun, Eleanor de
Bohun, Joan de, countess of Hereford   75, 93 n.86, 94 n.90, 202

Bohun, Mary de, countess of Derby   93, 94 n.90
Bole, John, auditor of de Vere and Countess Maud   155 n.32, 207, 216
Boroughbridge, battle of (1322)   181
Bourehall, Essex, manor of   xviii, 71
Bourgchier, John, Lord Bourgchier (d. 1400)   52, 53, 202
Bourton-on-the-Hill, Gloucestershire   179
Bovey Tracey, Devon   xviii, 133
Bowet, Henry, royal clerk   163
Brabant, Belgium   1, 187
  records of the duchy of Brabant   189
Brabant, Jeanne, duchess of (d.1406)   189
Bradesshagh, Henry de, of Lancashire   172 n.113
Bradwell, Essex, manor of   76–7, 204
Brantingham, Thomas, bishop of Exeter   153
Bray, Reginald, minister of Henry VII   14–15
Braybrooke, Robert, bishop of London   115, 150 n.5, 162, 168, 231 n.144
Brembre, Nicholas, mayor of London   1, 11, 79, 103, 107–8, 130, 149, 170, 225
  Radcot Bridge campaign   175, 178
Brentwood, Essex   76 n.4
Brest, Brittany   52, 169
Bridgewater, Somerset, maritime commission in   139
Brinton, Thomas, bishop of Rochester   18, 27 n.60, 61
Bristol   81, 112 n.159, 138, 139, 226, 244
Brittany   45, 52, 76, 129, 218, 223 n.108
  campaign of 1380 in   52–3, 76, 96
  civil war in   129
Brittany, duke of, *see* Montfort, John IV
Brom, Robert   207 n.30
Bruges, Belgium   193
Brussels, Belgium   189

Buckingham, earl of, *see* Thomas of Woodstock
Buckinghamshire, de Vere estates in   60
Buckton, Sir Peter   209
Bures, Alice de   47
Bures, Sir Andrew de   47

Bures Giffard, Essex, manor of   xviii, 55, 71
Burford, Oxfordshire   179
Burgh, Hubert de, chief minister of Henry III   15
Burgundy, duke of, *see* Philip, duke of Burgundy
Burley, Sir John   72, 89
Burley, Sir Simon   11, 62, 64, 70, 81 n.33, 84, 95, 118, 167, 204 n.12
  advice and policy   4, 5, 115, 155, 239 n.13
  and Dover and his role in Kent   86–7, 176
  and Lyonshall   72, 89, 183
  contemporary defamation of   18–19, 79
  chamberlain   36, 63, 70, 108, 111
  feoffee to Robert de Vere   105, 209, 210
  goods   225
Burton, Cheshire   138
Bury St. Edmunds, Suffolk, liberty and town of   60, 209, 222 n.108
Butler, Eleanor, née Darcy, countess of Ormond   146
Butler, James, earl of Ormond (d. 1382)   55 n.49, 126
Butler, James, earl of Ormond (d. 1405)   119, 125, 138, 141, 142, 143–4, 147, 223
Bygayn alias Cornewaill, Peter, of Cheshire   172 n.113

Calais   45, 46, 52, 65, 131, 169, 186, 191–2, 213, 220
  attempts to raise troops from   176
  pale   169
Calais, captains of, *see* Beauchamp, William; Devereux, Sir John

Calf, Richard, sheriff of Crosslands of Ulster 144
Calverton, Buckinghamshire, manor 60, 65, 74, 105 n.128
Camber, William la 55 n.52
Cambridge, earl of, *see* Edmund of Langley
Cambridgeshire
   commissions in 76
   gentry in 211
Canterbury Cathedral Priory, Irish lands of 143
Canterbury, archbishop of, *see* Arundel, Thomas; Courtenay, William; Stratford, John; Sudbury, Simon
Capgrave, John, his *Chronicle* 193
Carloll, John 142
Carnforth, Lancashire, manor of xviii, 88 n.61
Carrickfergus, Ireland, castle of 119
Casterton, Westmorland, manor of xviii, 88 n.61
Castile, Spain, *see under* Hundred Years War
Castle Camps, Cambridgeshire, manor of xviii, 71
   legal case relating to 204
Castle Hedingham, Essex xviii, 46, 71, 74, 81, 105, 215, 228
   nunnery 211
   priory 56, 72
   residence 59–60, 69
Caxton, William, printer 234 n.159
chamber, royal
   and control over access to the king 35–8, 108–11
   knights of the 36, 176
chamberlain, great, of England, office of 35–8, 51 and *see* Vere, Robert de, *under* great chamberlain
chamberlain of the royal household 35–8, 63–4, 108–10
   and *see also* Burley, Simon; Vere, Aubrey de

chancellors of England *see* Arundel, Thomas; Pole, Michael de la; Scrope, Richard; Sudbury, Simon
Charing Mews, London 168, 170
Charles I, king of England 151
Charles V, king of France 52
Charles VI, king of France 36, 169, 186–7, 188, 189
Charles VII, king of France 36
Charles, duke of Orléans (d. 1465) 43
Charlton, Kent, manor of xviii, 55, 72
charters, royal, witnesses to 114–15, 122, 150, 214
Chaucer, Geoffrey 111
Chaundler, Henry 93 n.86
Cheddworth, Robert 55 n.52
Chepstow, Monmouthshire, maritime commission in 139
Cherbourg, France 145, 169
Chesham, Buckinghamshire, manor of xviii, 55 n.52, 56 n.53, 57, 72
Cheshire, maritime commission in 139; dialect of 235
Chester, city and palatinate of 160, 166, 174, 189, 245, 246
   and John of Gaunt 172
   and Robert de Vere 166–7, 171–4, 183–4, 226–8, 236
   bastion of royal power 124
   castle, constable of, Sir Thomas Molyneux 173
   Cestrian loyalty to the Black Prince and Richard II 171, 172
   chamberlain of Chester *see* Wodehouse, John
   exchequer, accounts, revenues, seal 61, 138 n.83, 184
   military supplies 174
   vice-justice of, Sir Thomas Molyneux 173
chivalry, court of, case in 82, 110
Chonal, Richard de, of Cheshire 222
Cirencester, Gloucestershire 178
Clifford, Lewis 62
Clifford, Richard, royal clerk 163, 210
Clifton, Sir Robert 140, 172

Clipstone, Nottinghamshire   184
Clisson, Oliver de, constable of
    France   187
  secretary of   192
Cobham, John, Lord Cobham (d.
    1408)   208
Cockfield, Suffolk, manor of   xviii, 71,
    204, 206
Coggeshall, Sir Henry   207
Coggeshall, John   204
Coggeshall, Thomas   208
Coggeshall, Sir William   47 n.8, 101–3,
    207–8
Coghill, Yorkshire, manor of   xviii, 88
    n.61
Colchester, Essex
  castle and fee farm, grant to de
    Vere   xviii, 88, 90–1, 93, 94, 95, 167,
    207
  fee farm of   60, 90–1, 93
Combe Martin, Devon, manor of   xviii,
    133 n.64
commission of 1386   26, 124, 129–30, 134,
    152–4, 166, 210, 238
confessor, royal   41, 218 n.89
Connacht, Ireland, county of   144
Continuatio Eulogii, The   19, 150, 218
Conway (Conwy), Wales   138
Cook, John, of Horndon, Essex   224
Copeland, Cumberland, maritime
    commission in   139
Corbyn, Ralph, of Chester   112 n.163
Cork, city of   142 n.102
Cornwall
  de Vere estates in   131–3
  earldom of   42
  stannary of   61, 66, 67
Coucy, Ingelram de, earl of Bedford   xv,
    47, 84, 89, 90, 190, 198, 233
  career of   48, 88–9
  hatred of de Vere   187, 188
  mother of, Catherine of Austria   233
  wife of, *see* Isabella of Woodstock
Coucy, Mary de, daughter of
    Ingelram   48, 90, 118

  husband of, Montbéliard, Edward
    de   118
Coucy, Philippa de, countess of Oxford,
    duchess of Ireland (d. 1411)   xv, 49,
    198, 207, 233, 241
  book of   231
  divorce   6, 34, 158–66, 239
  dower   198
  financial arrangements during
    minority   50
  financial settlement on after
    1387   164–5, 198
  lands of, *see* Vere, Robert de, *under*
    estates and financial situation
  marriage and relationship with Robert
    de Vere   47, 48, 150, 159, 164, 199
  relationship with Countess
    Maud   165, 212
  royal maintenance for her   88, 90,
    95, 198
Coupland, John de and Joan his
    wife   88–9
Courtenay, Edward de, earl of Devon (d.
    1419)   52, 150 n.5, 194, 202, 221
Courtenay, Elizabeth (d. 1395), wife of
    John de Vere; wife of Sir Andrew
    Lutterel   xv, 57, 58, 60, 65 n.101, 71,
    73, 74, 105 n.128
Courtenay, Sir Philip   119, 143–4, 154
Courtenay, William, bishop of London,
    archbishop of Canterbury,
    chancellor   50, 150 n.5, 153, 158, 162,
    194, 199
courtiers, royal, criticism of   3, 7, 38, 237
Cowley, Buckinghamshire   55 n.50, 72
Crécy, battle of   45, 80
Crepping, Essex, manor of   xviii, 55,
    60, 74
Cromwell, Thomas, minister of Henry
    VIII   14, 15, 17
Croucheman, William   55 n.52
Crull, Robert, treasurer of Ireland   138,
    147, 222
  accounts of, 1386–1388   134, 140, 142–3
  choice of, as treasurer of
    Ireland   145–6

early career 145
military service in Ireland 137, 146, 223
Cruswiche, Essex, manor of xviii, 73
Cumberland
    de Vere manors in 88
    Scottish raids in 106
Cumberland, earl of, *see* Neville, John
Curtis, William 179

Dagworth, Nicholas 220 n.99
Dalkey, county Dublin, Ireland 144
Dallingridge, Sir Edward 218–9
Dannebury, William de 213
Darcy, John, constable of Rathmore castle 142
Dartasso, Janico 191, 229
Dartington, Devon xviii, 133
Dautre, John 197 n.222
Davenant, Nicholas 76 n.3
Derby, Derbyshire 178
Derby, earl of, *see* Henry IV
Desmond, earl of, *see* FitzGerald, Gerald
Despenser, Henry, bishop of Norwich, and expedition of 1383 96–7
Despenser, Hugh, Lord Despenser (d. 1349) 55 n.49
Despenser, Hugh, the older, earl of Winchester 17, 23, 39, 40, 42
Despenser, Hugh, the younger 15, 17, 39, 40, 115
    alleged homosexual relationship with Edward II 31–2, 33, 80
    as royal favourite 4, 12, 13, 14, 23, 241, 242
    chamberlain and control of access to king 37, 38
    trial and death of 25, 27, 42
Despenser, Thomas, Lord Despenser, earl of Gloucester (d. 1400) 177
Devereux, Sir John xv, 62–3, 65, 70
Devon, de Vere estates in 131–3
Devon, earl of, *see* Courtenay, Edward de
Devizes, Wiltshire 244
Dieulacres chronicle 7, 160, 161
Doddinghurst, Essex, manor of xviii, 71

Doket, Roger 110
Dongan, John, bishop of Sodor and Man 145
Dordrecht, The Netherlands 185
Doreward, John 111 n.158, 208–9
Dover, Kent
    castle at 86, 87, 176
    troops from 176
Down, bishop of, Ross, John 141
Downham, Essex, manor of xviii, 55 n.52, 71
Drury, Sir Roger 209
Dublin, Ireland
    archbishop of, *see* Waldeby, Robert; Wikeford, Robert
    castle of 123, 142, 144
    cathedral, prebendary of 145
    sheriff of 137, 144
    taxation in county of 144
Dudley, Edmund, minister of Henry VII 10, 31
Duffield, Richard 112 n.163
Dugdale, William 105
Dullingham, Cambridgeshire, manors ('Beauchamps', Poyneshall, 'Chalers') 68–9
Dunster Castle, Somerset 131
Durham, city of 107
Durham, bishop of, *see* Fordham John; Skirlawe, Walter

Earls Colne, Essex
    de Vere residence at 47, 59, 204, 211, 212
    manor of xviii, 56 n.53, 72, 105 n.128, 211
    priory of 47, 56, 59 n.66, 72, 196, 198–200, 211
Easthampstead, Berkshire 160 n.60
Easton Hall, Essex, manor of xviii, 55, 74, 220
Eastwood, Essex, manor of 66
Edinburgh, Scotland 106
Edmund, earl of Kent (d. 1330) 42

Edmund of Langley, earl of Cambridge, duke of York (d. 1402)   65, 96, 105, 113 n.163, 117, 125, 194, 231
  charter witness   122, 150
  justice of Chester   124, 171, 184
Edmund, St, king of East Anglia   149 n.3
Edward I, king of England   123
Edward II, king of England   120–1, 181, 242
  and favourites   13, 17, 22, 23, 25, 26, 33–4, 38
  alleged homosexual relationships   31–2, 33, 80
  death of   27
  deposition of   22, 25, 26
Edward III, king of England   7, 22, 23, 35, 36–7, 48, 50, 92, 129, 233, 239
  daughter of, *see* Isabella, countess of Bedford
  grants by   45, 47, 49, 57 n.63, 84, 88, 132
  his circle in the 1370s   3, 18, 19, 20, 21, 24
  mistress of, *see* Perrers, Alice
  will of   92–3, 132, 183
Edward IV, king of England   20, 22, 32, 34
  mistress of, Shore, Elizabeth (Jane)   20, 35
  queen of, Woodville, Elizabeth   22, 32
Edward, earl of Rutland, duke of Aumale, duke of York (d. 1415)   34, 177, 194, 221
Edward of Lancaster, Prince of Wales (d. 1471)   33
Edward of Woodstock, the Black Prince (d. 1376)   46, 50, 61, 70, 80–1, 153, 171, 184 n.166
  secretary of, Fordham, John   62; *see also* Vere, Aubrey de
  servants and retainers of   58 n.62, 61, 62, 80–1, 145, 222 n.108; and *see also* Vere, Aubrey de
Edward the Confessor, king and saint   149
Elmham, William de   65

Eltham, Kent, royal palace at   81, 111, 150, 166, 245
Empson, Richard, minister of Henry VII   30
English Chronicle, The   20
English, Henry de   105, 112, 207, 210, 211, 219
  Margaret, wife of, widow of Sir John Waweton   207
Ermyn, William de   65
Essex
  commissions in   76, 136
  de Vere estates in   56 n.54, 60, 94–5, 204, 212, 224
  gentry of   201–2, 211
  stewardship of the forest of   55, 60, 212
Eues, Thomas del, of Lancashire   172 n.113
Eure, Robert de, esquire   140, 213
Eure, Walter   142
Everdon, Thomas, lieutenant of the treasurer of Ireland   143
Evesham, Monk of, chronicle of   98, 100
exchequer, royal
  accounts of de Vere's goods   226 n.17, 227–9
  funding for de Vere in Ireland, *see* Vere, Robert de, *under* Ireland
  funding for military expeditions   96, 106, 120, 134, 136
Exeter, bishop of, *see* Brantingham, Thomas
Exning, Suffolk   102, 208
Exton, Sir Nicholas, mayor of London   114, 175

Falmouth, Cornwall   53 n.41
Favent, Thomas, writer, and his *Historia*   7, 19, 79, 149
  on Radcot Bridge   173, 174, 175, 181
favourites, royal; and *see also* Vere, Robert de
  accusations against   12, 26–7, 30–43
  age of   17, 19
  alienation of royal resources   41–2

as chief ministers and
ministers 15–19
constitutional action against 24–7
control over access to king 30, 35–8, 108
deaths of 27
definition of 13–15
deposition of kings 23
excessive affection between kings and favourites 33–4
female 19–21
financial enrichment and patronage 28, 35, 38–42
foreign war 16, 21, 30, 41
homosexuality between favourites and kings 30, 31–2, 33
king's friends 21–2
language used by chroniclers 18–19
manipulation of the law 30, 39–40
nobility, and 27–8
promotion of 30
public/popular opinion, and 29–30
sexual misbehaviour 17, 34–5
sorcery 17, 32
treason 1–3, 18, 30, 31, 42–3
unmanliness 155–6
violent action against 24–5, 27
Felbrigg, Norfolk, church of 158 n.51
Felbrigg, George, esquire 91 n.72
Felbrigg, Sir Simon 158
his wife, Margaret, daughter of the duke of Teschen 158
Feriby, Agnes 209 n.39
Feriby, Robert 209
Feriby, Thomas, clerk 209
Ferrers, Sir Henry 185
Fethard, county Tipperary, Ireland, church of 140
Fingal, Ireland, county of 144
Fingrith, Essex, manor of xviii, 71
Firth of Forth, Scotland 106
Fitzalan, Elizabeth, countess of Nottingham, duchess of Norfolk, daughter of Richard 136

Fitzalan, Richard, earl of Arundel (d. 1397) 43, 105, 125, 136, 167, 170, 190, 194, 219, 225, 235
castle at Reigate 168
charter witness to de Vere's promotions 122, 150
coronet of 124 n.28, 230
in government 63, 82, 114, 153
naval action off Margate 155–6, 209
opposition to Richard II 153, 168
Peasants' Revolt 53
Radcot Bridge campaign 126, 178–80, 182, 213 n.60
FitzEustace, Adam 144
FitzEustace, Robert, sheriff of Ulster 144
FitzGerald, Gerald, earl of Desmond (d. 1398) 141, 142, 143–4
FitzGerald, Maurice, earl of Kildare (d. 1390) 141, 142, 143–4
Fitzmartin, John, chancellor to Robert de Vere 155 n.32, 185, 214
FitzNicol, Richard, esquire 213
FitzNicol, Sir Thomas 213 n.60
Fitzpain, Robert xv, 54
Fitzwalter, Walter, Lord Fitzwalter (d. 1386) 52, 53, 67–8, 69, 76, 201–2, 208
daughter of, Alice de Vere 67–8, 105
wife of, Percy, Eleanor 67
Flanders 128
English campaigns in, *see under* Hundred Years War
Flanders, count of, *see* Mâle, Louis de; Philip, duke of Burgundy
Fleet, Kent, manor of xviii, 56 n.53, 57, 72, 215
Flint Castle, Wales 166, 174
Flintshire, Wales
justice of, Sir Thomas Molyneux 173
undersheriff of, *see* Ithel, Hywel ap Tudor ap
Flores, William, receiver of Oakham 215, 232
Fordham, John, bishop of Durham, treasurer of England, keeper of the privy seal 62, 150 n.5, 151

Index

Framlingham, Suffolk 203
France
  de Vere's exile in, *see* Vere, Robert de, *under* exile
  importance of chamberlains in 36, 37
  war with England *see* Hundred Years War
Frating, Essex xviii, 55, 57, 73
Fremington, Devon, manor and hundred xviii, 133 n.64
friars
  and John of Gaunt 99
  as confessors 218
Frodesham, Thomas, chaplain 146
Frodesham, William, admiral of Ireland 139, 141, 146
Froissart, Jean, chronicler 16, 46, 52, 80, 106, 175 n.128
  on de Vere in exile 8, 185–9, 193, 194, 196
  on relationship between de Vere and Richard II 4, 80, 88, 193, 237
  on Robert de Vere's divorce 158, 159, 161, 165
Furness, Lancashire, maritime commission in 139

Gambon, William 132
Garter, Order of the 122, 238
Gascony 45, 61, 62, 145
Gaveston, Piers, earl of Cornwall (d. 1312) 22, 32, 33–4, 43, 44, 115, 230
  alleged homosexual relationship with Edward II 31–2, 80
  as royal favourite 4, 12, 13, 14, 17, 241, 242
  chamberlain 37–8
  downfall and death of 2, 23, 25, 27, 42
  lieutenancy in Ireland 120–1
  promotion and enrichment of 38–9, 40, 42
Gestyngthorpe, Alice, wife of John 214
Ghent, Flanders, Belgium 128
Gilbert, John, bishop of Bangor, treasurer of England 152

Gloucester, duke of, *see* Thomas of Woodstock
Gower, John, poet, his works 19, 167 n.87, 196
Great Abington, Cambridgeshire, manor of xviii, 56 n.53, 72, 105 n.128
Great Bentley, Essex, manor of xviii, 72, 105 n.128
  church 59 n.66
  residence at 46, 59, 212
Great Canfield, Essex, manor of xviii, 71, 207
great councils
  1383, September 97
  1387, at Shrewsbury and Nottingham 155, 156–8, 217
  1394, February 194–5, 197
Great Hormead, Hertfordshire, manor of xviii, 56 n.53, 72
Great Radwinter, Essex, manor of 58 n.64
Gregory XI, Pope 61
Grey, Reginald, Lord Grey of Ruthin (d. 1388) 36
Grey, Thomas, marquess of Dorset (d. 1501) 35
Grilleston, William, de Vere's receiver 215

Hadleigh Castle, Essex, and park 66, 76 n.4, 212
Hales, Sir Robert, treasurer of England 63
Hall, Walter atte, of Knipton, Leicestershire 112 n.163
Halsall, Sir Gilbert 172
Halsham, John 112 n.163, 113
  wife of, Philippa Strathbogie 113
Halstead, Essex 202
Harewell, John, bishop of Bath and Wells 63, 115 n.177
Haringey, Middlesex 168, 212
Hastings, John, earl of Pembroke (d. 1375) 36–7
Hastings, Laurence, earl of Pembroke (d. 1348) 46

Hastings, William, Lord Hastings, chamberlain of the household (d. 1483) 22, 35
Hatfield Broad Oak Priory, Essex 211
  depiction of Robert de Vere at 231
Haukeston, Sir John 171 n.107
Haverfordwest, lordship of 40
Haversham, Henry de 55 n.50
Hawkwood, Sir John 46, 208, 209 n.99
Hedingham Vaux, Essex, manor of xviii, 55 n.52, 56 n.53, 57, 73
Helions Bumpstead, Essex, manor of xviii, 71, 207
Hellond, Suffolk xviii, 72 see also Aldham
Helyon, Walter, baker 195 n.214, 222
Henhowe, Suffolk 102, 103
Henmale, Robert 58 n.64
Henley-on-the-Heath, Surrey 160
Henry I, king of England 36, 45, 82
Henry III, king of England 13, 15, 21, 25, 26, 123, 150, 164
Henry IV, of Bolingbroke, king of England, earl of Derby 66, 70, 77 n.7, 93, 194, 209, 229
  as king 20, 109, 121–2, 145, 198 n.230, 238
  early life at court 49, 50, 51, 53, 80
  military retinues 105, 136
  opposition to Richard II and Radcot Bridge campaign 167, 168, 178–80, 182
  relations with Richard II 83, 114
  seizure of de Vere's goods 225 n.117, 228, 229
Henry V, king of England 43, 145
Henry VI, king of England 23, 24, 26, 27, 33, 109, 114, 242
  confessors of 41
  ministers/favourites of 13, 15, 16, 17, 21, 24
  queen of, Margaret of Anjou 20, 33
  son of, Edward of Lancaster 33
Henry VII, king of England 14–15, 23, 30, 230 n.137

Henry VIII, king of England 15, 17, 51 n.33
Henry, earl of Lancaster (d. 1345) 35
Henry of Grosmont, duke of Lancaster (d. 1361) 10
Hereford, Sir Robert 137, 146, 222
  wife of, Elizabeth Butler, countess of Ormond 146
Holland, count of, Albert of Wittelsbach, duke of Lower Bavaria 185, 186
Holland, John, earl of Huntingdon, duke of Exeter (d. 1400) 98, 132, 133, 183
Holland, Thomas, earl of Kent (d. 1360) 35
Holland, Thomas, earl of Kent (d. 1397) 53, 77 n.7, 115, 145
Holland, Thomas, earl of Kent, duke of Surrey (d. 1400) 123, 134, 224
Holme, Westmorland, manor of xviii, 88 n.61
Holne, Devon, manor of xviii, 133 n.64
Holsworthy, Devon, manor of xviii, 133 n.64
Horsham, Sir John de 46
Hoselaw in Teviotdale, Scotland 244
household, royal
  chamberlain of, see Burley, John; Latimer, William
  steward of, see Beauchamp, Roger; Montagu, John; Neville, John; Pole, William de la
Hul, Ralph of the 112 n.163
Hulle, John del, of Lancashire 172 n.113
Humbelby, John, clerk of de Vere's household 71, 215
Humphrey, duke of Gloucester (d. 1447) 38
Hundred Years War
  course of the war in the early 1380s 10, 44, 52–3, 96–7
  diplomatic negotiations 62, 103–4, 129, 169
  English campaigns in Flanders 45, 96–7

English expeditions to Castile and
    Portugal   61, 96, 128, 139, 163, 201
  loss of Normandy, 1450   43
  projected French invasion of England
    in 1386   136–7
  Scotland, French troops in (1384)   104
Huntingdon, Huntingdonshire   178, 194
Huntingdonshire, commissions in   76
Hurdicott, Wiltshire, manor of   55, 56
  n.53

Ickworth, Thomas de   222
Ilchester, Somerset, fee farm of   112
Inchiquin, Ireland   55, 126
Ipswich, Suffolk   102
Ireland
  appeal of Anglo-Irish to Richard II
    (1385)   119
  English lordship in, fourteenth
    century   10, 119–20
  grant to, and administration of,
    Robert de Vere *see* Vere, Robert de,
    under Ireland
  inalienable possession of the
    crown   122–3
  other grants of, and lieutenancies
    in   120–7, 134
  records of   9
Isabeau of Bavaria, queen of France   32,
  188
Isabella of France, Queen of
  England   32–3, 35
Isabella of Woodstock, countess of
  Bedford, daughter of Edward
  III   xv, 47–9, 50, 70, 83, 88–90, 203,
  233
  estates and finances   49, 84
Italy   46 n.8, 208
Ithel, Hywel ap Tudor ap   172

Jacquetta of Luxembourg, duchess of
  Bedford (d. 1472)   32
James, John   47, 48, 201
Jean, duke of Berry (d. 1416)   192
Jeanne, duchess of Brabant (d.
  1406)   189

Jenyn, William, his Ordinary   234 n.159
Joan of Kent, Princess of Wales   35, 62,
  75, 99
Joan of Navarre, Queen of England   198
John (Jean) II, king of France   48, 88,
  103
John, king of England   125
John of Gaunt, duke of Lancaster   7,
  81, 114, 117, 120, 194, 201, 209, 211,
  229–30, 231 n.144
  affinity in Lancashire and Cheshire,
    and resentment of in political
    communities   172–4
  and foreign policy   96, 100–1, 103–4
  and London   62, 103, 107
  and Scottish expedition in 1385   105–
    106, 182
  and Walter Sibille case   101–3
  appointment of chancery clerks in his
    administration   214
  expedition to Castile 1386 *see under*
    Hundred Years War
  his wife, Constance of Castile   96
  his palace at the Savoy   230
  plots against:
    Carmelite Friar in 1384   98–9,
      100–1, 210, 239
    in 1385   4, 6, 99–101, 116, 239
  relations with Aubrey de Vere   62–3,
    65–6, 197
  relations with Sir Edward
    Dallingridge   218–9
  relations with Richard II   66, 83, 97,
    98–9, 101, 116, 239
  relations with Robert de Vere   122,
    124–5 and *see also* plots (above)
  St. Malo expedition, 1378   51, 62

Katherine of Aragon, Princess of Wales,
  Queen of England   230
Kedington, Suffolk   216
Kemp, John, of Finchingfield   68
Kendal, Westmorland, lordship of   xviii,
  88 n.61, 89, 215

Kennington, Surrey, manor and palace   xviii, 153, 167, 215, 228, 244, 245
Kensington, Middlesex, manor of   xviii, 71, 215
Kent   136
  de Vere interests in   60, 94, 223
  rebels in   53, 76
Kent, earl of, *see* Holland
Kildare, earl of, *see* FitzGerald, Maurice
King, Daniel   200
King's Bench, court of, case concerning de Vere and Walter Sibille   102–3
Kingsdown, Kent   xviii, 55, 72
Kings Langley, Hertfordshire, royal palace at   81
Kneeton, Yorkshire, manor of   xviii, 88 n.61
Knighton, Henry, chronicler, and his *Chronicle*   6, 18, 79, 121, 123 n.26, 150, 154, 158, 168, 170
  on the Radcot Bridge campaign   174, 177, 179, 181, 218, 228
Knolles, Sir Robert, campaign in 1372   145

Lancashire
  John of Gaunt's affinity   172
  manors in   88
  maritime commission in   139
Lancaster, duke of, *see* Henry of Grosmont; John of Gaunt
Lancaster, Joan   205, 206 n.19
Lancaster, Sir John de   112 n.158, 138, 146, 170, 185, 205–6, 214, 222, 246
  exile   192, 196–7, 205–6, 220
  feoffee for de Vere   105, 205, 210, 211
Lancaster, palatinate of   120, 172 n.110
Lancecrone, Agnes, duchess of Ireland   xv, 34, 78, 79, 80, 233, 241
  abduction of   159–61, 236
  during de Vere's exile   189–90
  goods of   160, 227
  marriage to de Vere   161–3, 164, 165
  remarriage, probable   190
  social background   158–9

  tomb, probable   190 n.197
Landwade, Cambridgeshire   102
Langacre, Devon, manor of   xviii, 133 n.64
Langdon, Essex, manor of   69
Langham, Rutland, manor of   93 n.86
Langley and Bradley, Berkshire, manor of   xviii, 46, 56 n.53, 73
Langport, Kent   xviii, 72
Latimer, John, Carmelite friar   98–9, 101 n.112, 210
Latimer, William, Lord Latimer (d. 1381)   14, 19, 36–7
Laughton, Sussex, manor of   xviii, 55, 56, 57, 72, 219
Lavenham, Suffolk
  advowson of   72
  church   232, 233
  manors in   xviii, 56 n.53, 60, 72, 105 n.128, 209
Lee, Walter atte   93 n.86, 115 n.177
Legh, John   171 n.107
Legh, Peter   171 n.107, 226, 227
Leicester, Leicestershire   155, 178
  abbey   168, 245, 246
Leicestershire, manors in   91
Leuven, Brabant, Belgium   189, 190, 193
  Augustinian Friars   196–7
  St Peter's Church   196–7
Lichfield, Staffordshire   154, 155, 245
Lincolnshire, manors in   91
Lionel of Antwerp, duke of Clarence (d. 1368)   119, 120, 127, 134
Liston, Essex, manor of   66 n.107
Little Yeldham, Essex, manor of   xviii, 71
Liverpool, Lancashire   138
London   244, 245, 246
  and John of Gaunt   62, 103
  Guildhall   107
  royal entry into, 1387   168
  support for Richard in 1387   168, 175–6, 177, 238
  Tower of London   53
London, bishop of *see* Braybrooke, Robert; Courtenay, William; Sudbury, Simon

customs official in *see* Chaucer, Geoffrey
mayor of *see* Brembre, Nicholas;
  Exton, Nicholas; Northampton,
  John of; Walworth, William
Louis X, king of France 37
Louis, duke of Orléans (d. 1407) 231
Louth, Ireland 119
Louth Park Abbey, Lincolnshire,
  chronicle composed there 7
Louvain, Sir Nicholas de 65 n.101
Lutterel, Sir Andrew xv, 57 n.63
Lydgate, John, 'Of the Sudden Fall of
  Princes' 1, 239
Lyhert, Walter, bishop of Norwich 41
Lylle, William, of Sussex 112, 206
Lyneside, Cumberland, manor of xviii,
  88 n.61
Lynhales, William de, of
  Lancashire 172 n.113
Lyonshall, Herefordshire, castle and
  manor of xviii, 54, 56 n.53, 71, 72,
  89, 183

MacMurrough, Art, king of
  Leinster 142–3
Maghery, Philip 222
Magna Carta 26
Maidstone, Richard, his *Concordia* 176
  n.133
Maine, France 42
Mâle, Louis de, count of Flanders (d.
  1384) 96, 103
Malweden, John, of Walden, Essex 113
March, earl of, *see* Mortimer
Marcoll, John 197 n.222
Margaret of Anjou, queen of
  England 20, 33
Margaret of Brotherton, countess and
  duchess of Norfolk 203
Margaret of France, queen of
  England 42
Margate, Kent, naval action off 155
Marigny, Enguerrand de, chief
  chamberlain of France 37
Market Overton, Rutland, manor
  of xviii, 46, 55, 56, 57, 58 n.62, 73, 94

Marlborough, Wiltshire 36, 244
Marleborough, Henry of,
  chronicler 147, 174
Mascy, Hugh 226, 227
Massy, Richard, of Rixton 172
Maud, Empress of the Holy Roman
  Empire, queen of England 45, 90
May, John, clerk 222
Meath, Ireland, county of 145
Meath, Ireland
  bishop of, *see* Balscot, Alexander de
  sheriff of 137, 145
Medford, Richard, secretary to Richard
  II 105, 115, 210, 216
Medritz, Martin 112
Mendham, Suffolk, manor of xviii, 55
  n.52, 73, 74
Meryet, John de 68
Middleton Tyas, Yorkshire, manor
  of xviii, 88 n.61
Middlewich, Cheshire 227 n.126, 245
Mile End, Essex 53
Milton and Paston, Northamptonshire,
  manor of xviii, 46, 55, 56 n.53, 73
Minehead, Somerset 131
Mohun, Joan, Lady Mohun
  (d. 1404) 21, 65 n.101, 131
Mohun, John de, Lord Mohun
  (d. 1375) 131 n.56
Moleyns, Margery, Lady 21
Molyneux, Richard 173
Molyneux, Sir Thomas 171, 172–4, 179,
  180
Montbéliard, Edward de, marquis of
  Pont-à-Mousson 118
Montbéliard, Robert de, duke of
  Bar 118
Montagu, John, earl of Salisbury
  (d. 1400) 177
Montagu, John, Lord Montagu (d. 1389),
  steward of the household 122 n.21,
  150 n.5
Montagu, William, earl of Salisbury
  (d. 1344) 21–2, 35

Montagu, William, earl of Salisbury
 (d. 1397)   53, 77 n.7, 82, 99–100, 105,
 122, 150 n.5, 177
Montfort, John IV, duke of Brittany
 (d. 1399)   52, 129–30
Montfort, Simon de, earl of Leicester
 (d. 1265)   25
Moor End, Northamptonshire   198
More, Sir Thomas   20, 22
Morecroft, Henry   213
Moreton-in-Marsh,
 Gloucestershire   179
Mortimer family, estates of   87, 119, 134,
 144
Mortimer, Edmund, earl of March, earl
 of Ulster, lord of Connacht
 (d. 1381)   46, 87, 119, 134, 222 n.108
Mortimer, Roger, earl of March
 (d. 1330)   33, 35
Mortimer, Roger, earl of March
 (d. 1398)   119, 126, 144
Mortimer, Sir Thomas   126, 179, 229
Mowbray, Thomas, earl Marshal, earl of
 Nottingham, duke of Norfolk
 (d. 1399)   51, 105, 111, 167, 194, 211, 223
 estates   70, 203
 plot against John of Gaunt in
  1385   99–101
 Radcot Bridge campaign   178–80, 182
 relations with Richard II   80, 81, 83,
  84, 110, 136, 155
 relations with Robert de Vere   83, 84,
  113, 122, 150, 156
 seizure of de Vere's goods   229
 wife of, Elizabeth Fitzalan   136
Munster, Ireland, military expenses
 in   142

Nájera, Spain, battle of   61
Nantes, Brittany   52
Nantwich, Cheshire   227 n.126, 245
Naylinghurst, Robert de   68
Neve, William le   105
Neville, Alexander, archbishop of
 York   11, 149, 150 n.5, 153, 155 n.30,
 157, 162, 168, 170, 225

 appealed of treason in 1388   1, 86, 130,
  185
 flight of, before Radcot Bridge   169
 his residence at York Place   170
 in exile with de Vere   186, 188, 189,
  193, 194
Neville, John, Lord Neville (d. 1388)   14,
 19, 36, 118
Neville, Richard, earl of Salisbury
 (d. 1460)   24
Neville, Richard, earl of Warwick
 (d. 1471), the 'Kingmaker'   24, 34
Newcastle upon Tyne ,
 Northumberland   92 n.81, 104, 244
Newport, Essex   61, 67
Newton, John, esquire, attorney and
 servant of de Vere   137, 191, 192,
 220, 222
Newton, John, hermit   186, 233
Newton, Sir John   53, 220
Newenton (Newton), Thomas   220 n.99
nobility, the
 and 'aristocratic constitutionalism'   28
 and confessors   218
 and foreign war   21, 28, 85
 and parliament   29, 230
 and patronage   28, 86
 and Richard II   10, 12, 84–5, 97, 237–8
 and royal favourites see under
  favourites, royal
 at court   11, 27, 108
 conspicuous display   230
 counsel to the king   35, 37
 household chaplains   232
 reaction to promotions in the
  peerage   121–2, 125, 149–50
Norfolk, gentry in   211
Norleigh, Devon, manor of   xviii, 133
 n.64
Normandy, France   42, 43
Northampton, Northamptonshire   61,
 178
Northampton, John of, mayor of
 London   103, 107–8
Northumberland, earl of, see Percy, Henry

Norwich, bishop of, *see* Despenser, Henry
Norwich, Norfolk, fee farm of   91 n.72
Nottingham, Nottinghamshire   155, 245
  great council at, *see under* great councils
Nottingham, earl of, *see* Mowbray, Thomas
Nutbeam, Sir Thomas   213
Nutbeam, William, of Thanington, Kent   213
Nymet Tracy, Devon, manor of   xviii, 133 n.64

Oakham, Rutland, lordship of   xviii, 86, 93, 94, 95, 112 n.163, 167, 183, 215
  annuities assigned on   93
  receiver of, William Flores   215
O'Brien, Brian, of Thomond   119
O'Byrne, Gerald   142–3
Old Romney, Kent, manor of   xviii, 55, 56 n.53, 57, 72
Olney, John   191 n.201
O'Neill family   119
O'Neill, Niall, king of Tyrone   119
Ongre, Walter, of Linton   204
Ordainers, Lords (1310)   25
Orléans, dukes of *see* Charles, duke of Orléans; Louis, duke of Orléans
Ormond, earl of, *see* Butler, James
Osney, Oxfordshire   244
Ossory, bishop of, *see* Balscot, Alexander de
Otterbourne, Thomas, chronicler   195
Oundle, Henry, attorney of de Vere   204
Oxford, Oxfordshire   140, 244
  provisions of (1258)   26

Palmer, Richard   69
pardons, royal   113–14
Paris, France   186, 187–8
parliament   26, 29
  1308   25, 30
  1310   25
  1311   26, 30
  1321   23, 37
  1327   25, 26, 30
  1376 ('Good Parliament')   1, 18, 21, 29, 36, 87
  1378   63
  1380   63
  1381   101
  1383 (October)   97, 103
  1384 (April) at Salisbury   81, 98, 101, 210, 239
  1384 (November)   101–2, 101
  1385   117, 118, 127–8
  1386 ('Wonderful Parliament')   16, 31, 130, 134, 137, 139, 142, 144, 148, 149, 150–2, 156, 157, 166
  1388 ('Merciless Parliament')   1, 7, 10, 30, 44, 69, 130, 141, 142, 157, 165, 169, 171, 176, 177, 179 n.148, 186, 197, 214, 217, 218, 219, 220, 225, 237
    for appeal of treason against de Vere *see* Appellant, Lords *under* allegations
  1390 (November)   101
  1391   101
  1394   101
  1406   198 n.230
  1450   25, 30, 31
  1459 ('Parliament of Devils')   25
  1461   26
Passenham, Northamptonshire   65–6
Paston family   22, 40
Paston, Margaret   40
patronage, royal, *see* favourites, royal *under* financial enrichment *and* Vere, Robert de *under* royal patronage
Peasants' Revolt of 1381   10, 29, 30, 44, 49, 53–4, 70, 77, 82, 97, 103, 230
  and de Vere estates   75–6
  Essex in   75
Pecock, Richard   213
Pelham, Sir John de   46, 57
Pembroke, earl of, *see* Hastings
Pembroke, earldom of   40
Percy family   105
Percy, Eleanor, Lady Fitzwalter   67

Percy, Henry, earl of Northumberland (d. 1408) 65, 113, 114, 150 n.5, 168, 177
  brother of, *see* Percy, Sir Thomas; son of, *see* Percy, Sir Ralph
Percy, Sir Ralph 113
  wife of, Philippa Strathbogie 113
Percy, Sir Thomas 64, 76
Perers, Sir Edward, lieutenant of the treasurer of Ireland 143, 146
Perrers, Alice, mistress of Edward III 4, 19–20, 21, 24, 32, 37, 39, 40, 89, 241
petitions to the king 63–4, 81–2, 109–10
Philip IV, king of France 37
Philip, duke of Burgundy (d. 1404) 103, 169, 192, 197
Pichard family 74
Pichard, Edward 74
Pichard, Elizabeth 55 n.52, 74, 220
Pichard, Nicholas 55 n.52, 74
Pilkington, Robert, of Lancashire 172 n.113
Pleshey, Essex, castle of 94, 202, 212
Poitiers, battle of 45, 81
Pole, Michael de la, earl of Suffolk, chancellor 4, 5, 11, 14, 16, 81, 94, 102, 106 n.131, 115, 122, 155, 167, 168, 210, 211, 239 n.13
  appealed of treason in 1387–8 1, 86, 130, 169, 183
  as chancellor 87, 127
  contemporary defamation of 16–17, 18–19, 75, 79
  creation as earl of Suffolk 40, 84–5, 95, 117–18, 203
  flight before Radcot Bridge 169, 176
  goods of 225, 228 n.128
  impeachment in 1386 21, 29, 40, 137, 149, 150–2, 157
  in exile with de Vere 186, 188, 192 n.204, 193
  questions to the judges, 1387 156–8
Pole, William de la, duke of Suffolk 15, 17, 21, 29, 38, 39, 40, 44, 115, 241, 242
  as favourite 12, 13, 14, 16
  death of 27

financial enrichment of 25, 40, 41
  treason, alleged 25, 41, 42–3
  son of, John de la Pole 42
Pont-à-Mousson, marquis of, Montbéliard, Edward de 118
Pope *see* Gregory XI; Urban VI
Portugal, English expeditions to, *see under* Hundred Years War
Poynings, Lady Blanche 21
Preston, Suffolk, manor of xviii, 55 n.52, 56 n.53, 57, 73
Princess of Wales *see* Joan of Kent
privy seal, keeper of, *see* Fordham, John
public/popular opinion *see under* favourites, royal
Pulford, Cheshire 174

Queenborough, Kent, castle and lordship of xviii, 91–4, 95, 132, 167, 174, 185, 246

Radcliffe, Sir Ralph 172
Radcot Bridge, battle of 1, 135, 147, 166, 246
  army movements before 175, 178
  course of battle 178–81
  participants at 126, 172–3
  troop numbers 174, 182
Ramsey, Essex, manor of xviii, 55 n.52, 56 n.53, 57, 73, 209
Rathmore castle, county Limerick, Ireland 142
Rawreth, Essex 208
Rayleigh, Essex, manor, honour and park 66
Reading, Berkshire 154, 155, 245
Rehoboam, Old Testament king 23
Reigate Castle, Surrey 168
Revell, John 71
Rheims, France, siege of 45
Richard II 34, 116, 153, 160, 216, 218, 229, 231 n.144, 235, 242
  1377–82 10, 12, 44, 98, 210, 238
  continual councils 63–4
  criticism of minority government 77, 87

early promise and political restrictions on his power   77, 238–9
Peasants' Revolt   53–4
use of his signet seal in government   82, 87, 210
1383–87
    campaign of 1385 to Scotland   106–7
    criticism of advice to   97, 239
    and John of Gaunt   66, 83, 97, 98–9, 101, 116, 239
    views on nobility and court   12, 84–5, 97, 117–18, 224
    views on war and peace with France   53, 96–7, 129, 131
    female company   20–1
    parliamentary pressure on government   117, 150–2
    commission of 1386   152–4, 238
    his 'gyrations'   154–5, 168, 171
    questions to the judges   156–8, 168
    and the Pope in 1386–7   162–3
    attitude to de Vere's divorce   165–6
    building support for confrontation   166–7, 171, 176
    appellant opposition to, autumn 1387   168–9, 237
    chamber and household knights of   176
    Radcot Bridge campaign   175–6, 177–8
    patronage of, *see* Vere, Robert de, *under* royal patronage
Ireland, and *see also* Vere, Robert de, *under* Ireland
    inalienable possession of the crown   122–3
    expeditions to   120, 127, 143 n.105
    interest in   119, 120–1, 125, 134
    creating favourites king of Ireland   123–4, 184
    bastion of royal power   124–5
action against Appellants in 1397   25, 177
and de Vere in exile, attempt to reverse his banishment   185, 186, 188, 190, 194–5
and Edward II   121
at de Vere's funeral   198–9
confessors of   41
coronation of   51, 62, 110
deposition
    (?1387)   1, 3, 24, 26
    (1399)   4, 26–7
death of   27
loyalty to, as Black Prince's son   69, 171
personal relationships
    childlessness   79–80
    friends amongst the nobility   22, 82–4
    influenced by women   20–1
    marriage of   33, 65, 77, 79–80
    possible homosexual relationships   31–2, 77–80, 241
    with Robert de Vere, *see* Vere, Robert de, *under* personal relationships
Richard III, king of England   22, 35
Richard, duke of York (d. 1460)   23, 24, 26, 230
Richelieu, Cardinal (Armand Jean du Plessis)   15
Ridgate, John del, of Lancashire   172 n.113
Ringwold, Kent, manor of   xviii, 55, 56 n.53, 72
Ripon, John, archdeacon of Wells   105, 157, 170, 185, 210, 216–18, 222
    appointment as archdeacon   112, 216–17
    his journey to Rome   161, 163
Robinson, Walter, of Lancashire   172 n.113
Roche-Derrien, La, battle of   129
Roches, Peter des, chief minister of Henry III   15
Rochester, bishop of, *see* Brinton, Thomas
Rochester, Kent
    castle   220 n.99
    cathedral   190

Rochford, Essex, hundred of 67
Roos, John, Lord Roos of Helmsley (d. 1393) 91, 215 n.70
Roos, Richard, de Vere's receiver 215, 219
Roos, Thomas, Lord Roos of Helmsley (d. 1384) 91
  wife of, Beatrice Stafford 91
Roos, William, Lord Roos of Helmsley (d. 1414) 91 n.74
Ross, John, bishop of Down 141
Roughton, Richard, friar minor, de Vere's confessor 185, 218
Roughton, Thomas, friar minor, de Vere's confessor 218
Rouhale, Dr Richard 163
Rous, Sir Robert 63, 64
Routh, Sir John de 112, 206, 223 n.109
Rushook, Thomas, bishop of Chichester, king's confessor 41, 155 n.30, 157
Rutland
  de Vere manors in 94
  forest of 93
  sheriff of 93
  undersheriff of, William Flores 232
Ryalle Book 109
Ryvere, Richard de la, taverner 222

St Albans
  abbey of 51
  first battle of (1455) 24, 30 n.68
St Anne's hermitage, Colchester 186, 233
St Denys, Paris, monk of 186, 188
St George's Chapel, Windsor 238
St John's Abbey, Colchester, Essex 211
St Malo, France 51, 62
St Mary Graces, abbey of, London 132
St Paul's, London, annalist of 34
St Valery, honour of 61
Salisbury, Wiltshire, parliament at 98
Salisbury, earl of, *see* Montagu
Salisbury, Sir John 169, 225
Salisbury, Paul 64
Sandon, Essex, manor of 220 n.99

Sarnesfield, Sir Nicholas, and his wife Margaret 159 n.51
Savage, Edmund, steward of the liberty of Ulster 144
Saville, Thomas, serjeant at arms 138
Saxton, Cambridgeshire, manor of xviii, 60, 74, 105 n.128
Scarle, John, chancellor of the duchy of Lancaster 179 n.148, 214
Scotforth, Lancashire, manor of xviii, 88 n.61
Scotland, and *see also* Hundred Years War
  campaign of 1385 in 92 n.81, 104–5, 106–7, 182, 244
  war with 42, 45, 104, 128
Scott, Sir Walter, his *Somers Tracts* 150–2
Scrope, Richard, bishop of Coventry and Lichfield 154
Scrope, Richard, Lord Scrope, chancellor (d. 1403) 87, 153
Scrope, William, earl of Wiltshire (d. 1399) 177
Segrave, Hugh de, treasurer of England 65, 66, 67, 115 n.177, 122 n.21
Selby, Robert, treasurer of Calais 192 n.204
Sewale, John, mercer of London 228
Seys, Degory 174, 185
Sheen, Surrey, royal palace at 81 n.33, 111, 244
Sheperd, John, of Lancashire 172 n.113
Sheppey, Isle of, Kent 92, 185 n.174
  chace and warren on 92
Sherd, John de 226, 227
Shiplake, Sussex, hundred of 55, 72
Shirburn, John de, abbot of Selby 188
Shore, Elizabeth (Jane) 20, 35
Shrewsbury, Shropshire, great council at 154, 156, 158, 245
Shriggley, Sir John 146
Sibille, Walter, merchant of London 101–3, 208, 241
Sible Hedingham, Essex
  manor of xviii, 46, 71, 75

parish church   231 n.144
Sir Gawain and the Green Knight   235–6
Skirlawe, Walter, bishop of Bath and Wells, Coventry and Lichfield and Durham, keeper of the privy seal   105, 115 n.177, 122 n.21, 210, 216–17, 225 n.117
Slake, Nicholas, royal clerk   99, 105, 210
Sluys, Flanders   136
Smithfield, London   53
Sodor and Man, bishop of, John Dongan   145
Somerset, de Vere estates in   131–3
Somerset, duke of, *see* Beaufort, Edmund
Sotherton, John, of Lancashire   172 n.113
South Molton, Devon, manor and hundred   xviii, 133 n.64
Sparke, Henry   68
Spice, Clement   68, 214
Stafford, Beatrice, Lady Roos of Helmsley   91
Stafford, Edward, duke of Buckingham (d. 1521)   229, 230
Stafford, Hugh, earl of Stafford (d. 1386)   82, 105, 122, 132, 209, 210, 211
Stafford, Sir Ralph   83–4, 132, 211
Stafford, Staffordshire   220 n.99
Stanbury, John, bishop of Bangor   41
Stanley, Sir John, deputy to de Vere in Ireland   135, 136, 137–8, 139, 146, 147, 159, 172
  and *Sir Gawain and the Green Knight*   235–6
  early career and connections with de Vere   145
  military activity in Ireland, 1386   144–5
  role in government of Ireland   140–1, 144
Stanley, Thomas, chancellor of palatinate of Lancaster   214
Stanley, William, of the Wirral   159, 160
Stansted Mountfitchet, Essex, manor of   xviii, 71, 75, 207

Staunton, Somerset, manor of   xviii, 132, 133 n.64
Steeple Bumpstead, Essex, manor of   xviii, 55 n.52, 71, 75, 207
Stepney, Middlesex, rector of church, Robert Crull   145, 146
Stony Stratford, Buckinghamshire   65–6
Storey, Geoffrey, abbot of St John's Colchester   211
Stow-on-the-Wold, Gloucestershire   178, 179
Stratford, John, archbishop of Canterbury, chancellor of England   23
Strathbogie, David, earl of Atholl   113
Strathbogie, Lady Philippa   113
Stury, Sir Richard   93 n.86, 155
Stuteville, William, clerk   68–9
Sudbury, John de   68
Sudbury, Simon, bishop of London, archbishop of Canterbury, chancellor of England   46, 47, 49, 53, 64, 70
Suffolk
  de Vere estates in   60, 212
  gentry of   201, 203, 211
Suffolk
  duke of, *see* Pole, William de la
  earl of, *see* Pole; Ufford
Sussex
  de Vere estates in   60
  support for Appellants   182
Swaffham, Cambridgeshire, manor of   xviii, 73
Sweetman, Master Maurice   140
Swon, John, drover   222
Swords, Dublin, prebendary of, Robert Crull   145

Tackbeare, Cornwall   xviii, 133 n.64
Tailboys, William, esquire   39
Talbot, Sir Richard, sheriff of Dublin   144
Tarporley, Cheshire   227 n.126, 245

Tendring, Essex, hundred of   90, 93 n.86, 207
Thames, River   107, 178, 180, 185
Thomas, earl of Lancaster (d. 1322)   29 n.63, 42
Thomas of Woodstock, earl of Buckingham, duke of Gloucester (d. 1397)   46, 50, 51, 93, 105, 110, 113 n.163, 137 n.76, 153, 194, 201, 205, 219, 239
  advice to the king   97, 101
  and Ireland   125, 126, 134
  and Peasants' Revolt   53, 76, 77 n.7
  chancellor of, Thomas Feriby   209
  charter witness to de Vere's promotion   150
  goods   230, 231
  interests and associates in Essex   12, 53, 94–5, 100, 202, 208, 209, 224
  lands and finances   82, 84, 94, 95
  military expedition to Brittany, 1380–1   50, 52, 76, 96, 218
  murder plot against, 1387   4, 167–8, 170, 217
  opposition to Richard II   97, 166, 168, 169
  promotion to dukedom   84, 117
  Radcot Bridge campaign   178–80, 181, 182, 212
  seizure of de Vere's goods   225 n.117, 228, 229
  wife of, see Bohun, Eleanor de
Thornton in Lonsdale, Yorkshire, manor of   xviii, 88 n.61, 215
Thremhall Priory, Essex   211
Thundersley, Essex, manor and park   66
Tickford, Buckinghamshire, alien priory of   146
Tilbury-iuxta-Clare, Essex, manor of   xviii, 55 n.52, 71
Tintern, abbot of (perhaps John Wysbeche)   143
Toppesfield, Thomas   214 n.61
Toppesfield, William   213–4
Tristernagh, county Westmeath, Ireland   144
treason

  appeal of (1388)   1–3, 152, 169, 183–5, 227, 242
  defeat in foreign war   21, 42–3
  use of royal banners   181
  See also favourites, royal *under* treason
  Statute of (1352)   2
treasurers of England see Fordham, John de; Gilbert, John; Hales, Sir Robert; Segrave, Hugh; Wakefield, Henry
Tresilian, Robert, chief justice of King's Bench   1, 79, 105, 130, 149, 157, 210, 225
Trier, Germany   186, 190, 191
Trivet, Sir Thomas   145, 170
Tuttebury, Thomas   217 n.81
Twyford, Sir Nicholas   101–3
Tyler, Wat   53
Tyrell, Sir Thomas   47, 48, 201

Ufford, Ralph de, chief justice of Ireland   47
Ufford, Robert de, earl of Suffolk (d. 1369)   47
Ufford, William de, earl of Suffolk (d. 1382)   49, 53, 63, 70, 77 n.7, 203
Ulster, county and liberty of   144, 145
Ulster, earl of, see Mortimer
  sheriff of Crosslands of Ulster, Richard Calf   144
Urban VI, Pope
  grant and revocation of Robert and Philippa's divorce   162
  papal curia, records, appeals to, and litigation in   157, 161, 217
  Richard II's diplomatic correspondence   157, 162, 163
Usk, Adam of, chronicler   31, 123
Utrecht, The Netherlands   186

Vale Royal, abbot of   140
Veel, Sir Peter de   222
Vere, de, family   35, 45, 54, 198, 202, 211, 231
  estates of   6, 11, 58 n.64, 70, 94, 207
  residences of, see Castle Hedingham; Earls Colne; Great Bentley

Vere, Alice de (née Fitzwalter), countess of Oxford (d. 1401)   xv, 67–8, 105
Vere, Aubrey de, first earl of Oxford (d. 1194)   45, 90
Vere, Aubrey de, tenth earl of Oxford (d. 1400)   xv, 47, 53, 76, 105, 115, 131 n.56, 145, 194, 198, 204 n.12, 205, 207
   auditor of, Davenant, Nicholas   76 n.3
   councillor, 1388–92   194, 197
   early career of   60–3
   estates of   58, 60, 66–7, 71, 73, 74
   purchases of   68–9
   expelled from court in 1388   66, 69, 70, 185, 197
   influence in Essex   67, 70, 94, 212
   marriage of   67–8
   military service   51, 62–3
   restoration of title and estates of earl of Oxford, 1393   6, 195–8
   relations with John of Gaunt   62–3, 65–6, 197
   relationship with Robert de Vere   65, 69–70
   role in government during Richard II's minority   50, 63–4, 70
   service to Black Prince   61–2, 63, 69, 70, 80, 197
   service in 1385 expedition   69, 104–5
   wife of, *see* Vere, Alice de
Vere, John de (d. 1350)   xv, 57, 60
   wife of, *see* Courtenay, Elizabeth
Vere, John de, seventh earl of Oxford (d. 1360)   xv, 45, 57, 60, 63, 74, 185 n.173, 213
   estates and finances of   54–6
   military service   45–6
   service to Black Prince   46, 80
Vere, John de, twelfth earl of Oxford (d. 1462)   198
Vere, John de, thirteenth earl of Oxford (d. 1513)   6, 51 n.33, 91 n.72, 232, 234 n.159, 238
   use of title marquess of Dublin   232 n.149
Vere, Maud de, daughter of John, seventh earl of Oxford   56

Vere, Maud de (née Badlesmere), countess of Oxford (d. 1366)   xv, 45, 54–6, 60, 74
Vere, Maud de (née Ufford), countess of Oxford (d. 1413)   xv, 46, 47, 56, 195, 199, 207, 234, 238
   administrative records of   9, 56 n.53
   dower and jointure settlements of   57–9, 70, 71, 72–3, 88, 94, 194
   finances   73
   farm of de Vere's estates from 1388   197, 206, 215
   influence in Essex   212
   servants and officials of   74, 201, 209, 214, 216, 219, 224
   steward of her household, Robert Feriby   209
   support for Philippa de Coucy   165, 212
   visit to de Vere in exile   193–4
Vere, Richard de, earl of Oxford, eleventh earl (d. 1417)   xv, 56 n.53, 105, 198
Vere, Robert de, sixth earl of Oxford (d. 1331)   209, 234
Vere, Robert de, ninth earl of Oxford, marquess of Dublin, duke of Ireland (d. 1392)
   AFFINITY, HOUSEHOLD AND ADMINISTRATION OF
   and Essex gentry   201–3, 205, 207–9, 219–20
   Earl Thomas's connections   201
   estate administrators   201, 214–16
   feoffees in 1385   205, 207, 209–11
   followers in exile   220
   followers in parliament   219–20
   household servants   213, 215, 221
   household size   221
   key followers/retainers *see* English, Henry; Lancaster, Sir John; Newton, John; Routh, Sir John
   lack of affinity & influence in Essex and Suffolk   12, 211–2, 223, 224–5, 240
   lack of time spent in East Anglia   203–5, 224

religious houses in Essex 211
royal grants to servants at de Vere's
 supplication 111–13
CAREER
1377–82, minority
 commissions to 53, 76–7, 204, 205
 control of his estates 47, 52
 custody/wardship of 47, 49
 financial arrangements 50
 military service 50, 51–2, 222
 Peasants' Revolt 53–4, 70, 75–6
 role at court 50
1383–5, and *see also* Vere, Robert de,
 under royal patronage
 advice to the king 97–8, 106–7
 defamation suit against Walter
  Sibille 101–3, 208, 241
 engagement in council and
  administration 107–8
 possible involvement in plots
  against John of Gaunt 4,
  98–101, 116, 239
 royal charter witness 114–15
 service against Scotland in
  1385 104–7, 244
 warrants at information of 115
1385–7
 1385, promotion to marquess of
  Dublin 44, 85, 118, 121–2, 227,
  238, 240
 1386, promotion to duke of
  Ireland 44, 149–50, 238, 240
 admission to the Order of the
  Garter 122, 238
 and Sir Philip Courtenay 154
 appointment as justice of
  Chester 124, 160, 163, 166–7,
  183–4, 221
 appointment as justiciar of North
  Wales 166–7, 221
 grants to (1387) 152–3
 in company with the king on his
  'gyrations' 154–5
 military role under Richard
  II 166–7, 171

possible plot against Thomas, duke
 of Gloucester 4, 167–8, 170
questions to the judges 156–8
relations with John of
 Gaunt 124–5
royal charter witness 115
scandal of his adultery and
 divorce 161, 167, 239
target of 1386 parliament 150–2
threatened invasion of 1386 136–7
Ireland (1385–7) 3, 86, 117, 240–1
 crossing to Ireland 130, 135–7
 de Vere's administration in 137–8,
  140–3, 147, 154
 de Vere's personal role in
  government 137–8, 140–2, 147
 exchequer 138, 142 and *see also*
  Crull, Robert
 finances
  Audley estates 133, 183, 241
  exchequer grants for 134, 135,
   138–9, 140
  financial resources 127, 134, 147
  lack of parliamentary
   taxation 127–8
  ransom of John of Blois 112, 128,
   131, 134, 152, 186, 191–3, 241
  revenues in Ireland 128, 134
 government personnel and military
  forces in
  Cestrians serving in Ireland 172
  choice of senior officials 145–7
  deputy in, *see* Stanley, Sir John
  former lieutenant in, *see* Courtenay, Sir Philip
  protections for service in 137,
   139–40, 213, 220, 222
  shipping to 139, 146
  size of army, musters and
   service 127, 128, 135, 138–40,
   205, 209, 223
 powers granted 120, 122, 123
 rumours of being made king of
  Ireland 123
 seals 140 n.91, 141, 147

serious nature of the grant 125–7, 135
1387, Radcot Bridge Campaign
　army movements 175, 178–9
　course of events at the battle 179–82
　escape from 180–1
　recruitment of forces 171–4
　troop numbers 171, 174, 182
　use of royal banner 171, 177, 181
1388–92, exile
　appealed of treason in 1387–8 1–3, 152, 169, 183–5, 227, 242
　finances 191–4
　flight from England and immediate places of refuge 185–6
　in France 186–9
　in Leuven/Brabant 187, 189, 190, 193
　possible reversal of banishment 194–5
1392, death 195
　burial in Leuven and dispute over 196–7
　reburial at Earls Colne 198–9
　tomb 199–200
ESTATES AND FINANCIAL SITUATION 57–9, 71–4, 95, 240
　administration 215–16
　Audley estates 86, 131–3, 183, 215, 216
　de Coucy estates 88–90, 95, 159, 183, 206, 215
　effect of dowager holdings 57–9, 70, 88
　enfeoffment of estates 1385 205, 207, 209–11
　financial value of royal patronage 93–4
　Queenborough, Kent, grant of 91–3
　Roos estates, grant to 91
GREAT CHAMBERLAIN OF ENGLAND 11, 51, 145, 205 n.16
　confirmation of office 45, 82, 110
　endorsing royal petitions as 63–4, 81–2, 109–11

　influence exercised through office 108–11, 241
　personal exercise of office 108, 110
　role in controlling access to the king 35–6
MATERIAL GOODS
　at Chester 166, 221, 225–8
　bedding 226, 227, 228, 230
　books 231
　chapel goods 226, 232–4
　clothing 228, 230–1
　coronets, chaplets 201, 227, 229, 231
　mercery and other purchases 226, 229–30
　plate and cash at Radcot Bridge 227, 228–9
MILITARY RETINUES
　in Ireland *see* Vere, Robert de, *under* Ireland
　invasion threat of 1386 136–7, 139, 222–4
　Scotland 1385 104–5, 205, 213, 214, 222–3
PERSONAL RELATIONSHIPS
　childlessness 79–80
　divorce of Philippa, and its timing, its grounds 34, 158–66, 239
　friendship 50, 70, 80–4, 241
　marriage and relationship with Philippa de Coucy 47, 48, 150, 159, 164, 199
　pardons at de Vere's supplication 112–14, 241
　possible homosexual relations 78–80, 241
　relationship with Agnes Lancecrone 34, 80, 158–63, 164, 165
　relationship with Aubrey de Vere 65, 69–70
　relationship with Richard II 240–1
　Richard's support for his divorce 165–6
　sorcery 32, 78
　support for the king

at coronation   51, 80, 82
in 1381   53–4, 70, 80, 82
against his enemies, 1385–7   83, 170–1, 239
time in his company   51, 59–60, 81–2, 83, 110–1, 136, 241–2
PERSONALITY   51
  courtly skills   80, 188–9, 237
  depiction as sullen/sulky   156, 240
  piety and religious patronage   218, 232–4
  pride in titles   140 n.91, 232
ROYAL PATRONAGE TO   239–41
  1383–5   86, 87–95, 107
  1386–7   152, 153
  Ireland *see* Vere, Robert de, *under* Ireland
SOURCE MATERIAL FOR HIS LIFE AND CAREER CHRONICLES   4, 6–8
  loss of his own administrative documents   9
  private sources, lack of   9–10
  royal administrative documents   8–9
  sources for his material goods   225–8

arms used (Vere, Ireland, Chester)   167 n.87, 231–3
as great nobleman and earl   11, 114, 240
as royal favourite   116, 239–42
birth   47
Chester as his headquarters   166, 226–8
confessors of, *see* Roughton, Richard; Roughton, Thomas
contemporary defamation of   18, 19 , 44, 46, 237
depiction of, at Hatfield Broadoak   231
historians' views on   4–5
legal cases   9, 203–4, 241
military service of   85, 116, 126, 237
subject of *Sir Gawain and the Green Knight*   234–6

tomb, commemoration and obits for   198–9, 234, 238
will of, possible   105, 234
Vere, Thomas de, eighth earl of Oxford (d. 1371)   xv, 45, 59 n.66, 60, 81, 234
  death of   46
  estates and wealth of   54–8, 126
  household of   201
  military service of   45–6
Vernon, Nicholas   138 n.81
Vernon, Sir Ralph   171 n.107
Villiers, George, duke of Buckingham   151
Vita Edwardi Secundi   34, 38

Wakefield, Henry de, bishop of Worcester, treasurer of England   105, 209, 210–11
  his register   174, 179, 180
Waldeby, Robert, archbishop of Dublin and York   194
Wales
  justice of North Wales   166–7
  maritime commission in North Wales   139
  North Wales as bastion of royal power   124
Wallingford, Oxfordshire, castle and honour   61, 67
Walscroft, Richard, of Lancashire   172 n.113
Walsingham, Thomas, monk of St. Albans, and his chronicles   6, 7–8, 13, 16–17, 18, 32, 62, 76, 87, 99, 100, 106, 121, 123, 130, 149, 158, 161, 167–8, 170, 193, 239
  allegations against Robert de Vere and Richard II   4, 78–9, 150
  character portrayals of de Vere   4, 50–1, 155–6, 175
  Cronica Maiora   78
  dating and editions of his work   7–8
  depiction of Richard II at de Vere's funeral   8, 199
  on Radcot Bridge campaign   174, 181–2
Walton, Sir William de   69 n.121

Walworth, William, mayor of London 53
Warbeck, Perkin 14, 23
Warton, Lancashire, manor of xviii, 88
Warwick, earl of, *see* Beauchamp; Neville
Waterton, Hugh 66
Waweton, Sir John 207
Weever, John, his *Funeral Monuments* 200, 234 n.159
Welbury, Hertfordshire, manor of xviii, 55, 57, 72
Wells, Somerset, archdeaconry of 216–17; and *see also* Ripon, John
West Dean, Sussex, manor of xviii, 55, 56 n.53, 57, 72
West Lydford, Somerset, manor of xviii, 133 n.64
Westminster
　Abbey 168
　　coronations at 62
　Hall 169 n.94
　royal palace at 81, 111, 244, 245
　tournament at, 1385 99
Westminster Chronicle 6, 7, 8, 18, 21, 81, 83, 92, 97, 106, 108, 117, 121, 123 n.26, 133, 166, 167–8, 185, 212
　on plots against Gaunt 98, 99, 100
　on Radcot Bridge campaign, 173, 174, 175, 178, 179, 180, 181
　on Robert de Vere's divorce 161, 162–3, 165
Westmorland, manors in 88; MP for 219
West Whetenham, Essex, manor of xviii, 71, 212
Westwick, Hertfordshire, manor of xviii, 55 n.52, 56 n.53, 57, 73
Wexford, Ireland, quarter sessions at 143
Whitchurch, Buckinghamshire, manor of xviii, 56 n.53, 73, 74
White, Richard, prior of St John Jerusalem at Kilmainham, justiciar of Ireland 141
Whitheved, William, esquire 139

Whitstable, Kent, manor of xviii, 55, 56 n.53, 57, 72
Whittington, Lancashire, manor of xviii, 88 n.61
Whittington, Richard, merchant of London 229–30
Wigpet in Arkesden, Essex, manor of 69 n.121
Wigston Magna, Leicestershire, manor of xviii, 56 n.53, 57, 73
Wikeford, Robert, archbishop of Dublin 142, 146, 150 n.5, 155 n.30
Wiltshire, sheriff of, *see* Lancaster, Sir John
Winchester castle, Hampshire 160
Winchester, bishop of, *see* Wykeham, William of
Windrush, River 179
Windsor Castle, Berkshire 154, 167, 178, 185, 244, 246
　St George's chapel in 238
Windsor, William, Lord Windsor (d. 1384) 40, 120
Wingfield, Lady Joan 56, 58 n.62
Wingfield, Sir William 46, 47, 58, 71, 73, 81, 219
Woburn Abbey, Bedfordshire 112
Wodehouse, John, chamberlain of Chester and North Wales 138 n.81, 171, 225, 227
Wodyngfield, Thomas, esquire 112 n.163
Wolmare, Richard 222
Wolsey, Thomas, Cardinal, chief minister of Henry VIII 15–16, 17
Woodham Walter, Essex 68, 201
Woodstock, Oxfordshire 244, 245
Woodville, Elizabeth, queen of England 22, 32
Worcester, bishop of, *see* Wakefield, Henry de
Wrabness, Essex, manor of xviii, 47, 73, 75, 209
Writtle, Essex, hospital at 82
Wyresdale, Lancashire, manor of xviii, 88 n.61

Wykeham, William of, bishop of Winchester, minister of Edward III   15, 63, 105, 115 n.177, 150 n.5, 153, 162, 209, 210

York, Yorkshire   244
York
   archbishop of, *see* Arundel, Thomas; Neville, Alexander; Waldeby, Robert
   duke of, *see* Edmund of Langley; Richard, duke of York
Yorkshire, manors in   88, 91
Youghal, Ireland   55, 126

Zouche, William, Lord Zouche (d. 1396)   98, 155 n.30

Printed in the United States
by Baker & Taylor Publisher Services